"Talent develops in quiet places, character in the full current / human character."

— Johann von Goethe —

"We're all leading lives that are d't and yet the same."

— Anne Frank —

"Should I, after tea + cakes + ices have the strength to force the moment to its crisis?"

— T.S. Eliot —

The literature on egalitarianism is a crowded one but, in her ambitious and engaging book, Christine Sypnowich is able to carve out a distinctive position that takes human flourishing to be central. She defends her novel 'egalitarian perfectionism' by careful engagement with topical issues such as racial justice, gender equality, multiculturalism and liberal neutrality about the good. *Equality Renewed* is at once an original contribution to egalitarianism and a splendid analysis of the central debates of political philosophy.

Kok-Chor Tan, *University of Pennsylvania, USA*

Consequences have no pity.
Our deeds carry the consequences.
They are hardly ever confined
to ourselves.

DUTIES HAVE NO FEELINGS. — paraphrase of Geo. Eliot

"The best liar is he who makes the smallest amount / lying go the longest way."

— Samuel Butler —

# Equality Renewed

How should we approach the task of renewing the ideal of equality?

In this book, Christine Sypnowich proposes a theory of equality centred on human flourishing or wellbeing. She argues that egalitarianism should be understood as aspiring to make people more equal in the constituents of a good life. Inequality is a social ill because of the damage it does to human flourishing: unequal distribution of wealth can have the effect that some people are poorly housed, badly nourished, ill-educated, unhappy or uncultured, among other things. When we seek to make people more equal our concern is not just resources or property, but how people fare under one distribution or another. Ultimately, the best answer to the question 'equality of what?' is some conception of flourishing, since whatever policies or principles we adopt, it is flourishing that we hope will be more equal as a result of our endeavours.

Sypnowich calls for both retrieval and innovation. What is to be retrieved is the ideal of equality itself, which is often assumed as a background condition of theories of justice, yet at the same time, dismissed as too homogenising, abstract and rigid a criterion for political argument. We must retrieve the ideal of equality as a central political principle. As for innovation, her approach calls for a new direction that, instead of focussing on cultural difference, or the idea of political neutrality, proposes an egalitarian political philosophy that conceives of the state as enabling the betterment of its citizens.

**Christine Sypnowich** is Professor of Philosophy and Queen's National Scholar at Queen's University at Kingston, Canada. She is the author of *The Concept of Socialist Law* (Oxford, 1990), and editor (with David Bakhurst) of *The Social Self* (Sage, 1995), and *The Egalitarian Conscience: Essays in Honour of G.A. Cohen* (Oxford, 2006). Her work has appeared in such journals as *Political Theory*, *Oxford Journal of Legal Studies*, *New Left Review* and *Politics and Society*.

# Routledge Innovations in Political Theory

# Equality Renewed

Justice, Flourishing and the Egalitarian Ideal

## Christine Sypnowich

"It is folly to expect men to do all that they may reasonably be expected to do"
— Richard Whately

Routledge
Taylor & Francis Group

NEW YORK AND LONDON

First published 2017
by Routledge
711 Third Avenue, New York, NY 10017

and by Routledge
2 Park Square, Milton Park, Abingdon, Oxon, OX14 4RN

First issued in paperback 2018

*Routledge is an imprint of the Taylor & Francis Group, an informa business*

*Library of Congress Cataloging in Publication Data*
Names: Sypnowich, Christine, author.
Title: Equality renewed : justice, flourishing and the egalitarian
ideal / Christine Sypnowich.
Description: New York : Routledge, 2017. | Series: Routledge
innovations in political theory | Includes bibliographical references
and index.
Identifiers: LCCN 2016032658 | ISBN 9781138208810 (hbk)
Subjects: LCSH: Equality. | Social justice.
Classification: LCC JC575 .S96 2017 | DDC 320.01/1–dc23
LC record available at https://lccn.loc.gov/2016032658

ISBN 13: 978–0–367–00032–5 (pbk)
ISBN 13: 978–1–138–20881–0 (hbk)

Typeset in Bembo
by Wearset Ltd, Boldon, Tyne and Wear

For David, Rosemary and Hugh

# Contents

# Preface

This book is about the significance of human flourishing, or what's often called 'the good life,' for the idea of equality. The project has been a long time in the making. A number of people, many of them good friends, provided invaluable advice and support along the way, and the book's history reminds me of how, as Aristotle says, philosophy and friendship are constituents of a life well lived.

I am particularly grateful to colleagues at my home institution, Queen's University, at the Philosophy Colloquium, the Political Studies Department, the Saturday Club, the Political Philosophy Reading Group, and 'The Justice League,' my graduate student research group. Our graduate students are tremendous, and I have been very lucky to have their stimulating influence, invaluable feedback, and friendship as I've thought about the issues of this book; I mention many of them by name below. I am also indebted to my department's wonderful administrative staff, Marilyn Lavoie, Judy Vanhooser and Susanne Cliff-Jungling, all three models of cheerful efficiency and generous assistance. In addition, I very much appreciate the excellent advice provided by the two anonymous referees. Many thanks also to the terrific team at Routledge, Natalja Mortensen, Lillian Rand and Amy Thomas, as well as Matt Deacon at Wearset, for being so patient, supportive and helpful in the preparation of the manuscript for publication.

For their helpful contributions, academic and otherwise, I am grateful to David Dyzenhaus, Cheryl Misak, Harry Brighouse, Adam Swift, Gillian Brock, David Miller, Meira Levinson, Daniel Weinstock, Stephen Macedo, Antony Duff, Sandra Marshall, Diana Coole, John Tasioulas, Lucia Zedner, Tim Lankester, John Broome, Robin Archer, Andrew Glyn, Jonathan Dancy, Sarah Dancy, Hanjo Glock, Lois McNay, Murray Hunt, Annis-May Timpson, Claire Chambers, Leslie Green, Joseph Fishkin, Andrée-Anne Cormier, Patti Lenard, Kok Chor Tan, Arash Abizadeh, Joseph Heath, Colin Macleod, Christoph Henning, Erik Olin Wright, Robin Blackburn, Brad Hooker, G.M. Tamas, David Wiggins, Felix Mikhailov, Vladislav Lektorsky, Will Kymlicka, Rahul Kumar, Kerah Gordon-Solmon, Henry Laycock, Sergio Sismondo, Jackie Duffin, Nancy Salay, Stephen and Deborah Leighton, Alistair and Ruth Macleod, Jon Miller, Paul Fairfield, Sue Donaldson, Deborah Knight, Josh Mozersky, Udo Schüklenk, Jackie Davies, Al Fell, Lorne Maclachlan, France

Pellicano, Carlos Prado, Christine Overall, Margaret Moore, Andrew Lister, Colin Farrelly, Sandra den Otter, Mick Smith, Eleanor MacDonald, Bob Wolfe, Keith Banting, John McGarry, Mark Walters, Grégoire Webber, Chris Essert, Jean Thomas, Anya Hageman, Bev Lapham, William Brooke, Christopher Lowry, Jeremy Butler, Omar Bachour, Kyle Johannsen, Joanna Tinus, Brennen Harwood, Ryan McSheffrey, Miriam Sabzevari, Christina Malezis, Erik Zhang, Kijin Sung, Aidan Wakely-Mulroney, Aidan Hayes, Greg Affleck, Tristan Rogers, Adam Reid, Sue Rosenberg, John Lazar, Paul and Karen Rennie, Wendy Webster, Jane Blumberg, Kelly Morris, Ina Matthews, Haynes Hubbard, Mary Running and Marjorie Keates.

I have benefitted from the comments and criticisms of audiences at Balliol College, Nuffield College and Corpus Christi College in Oxford; Keele University; the University College London Institute of Education; Queen Mary University; Stirling University; the University of Edinburgh; the University of St. Andrew's; the University of Reading; the University of California, San Diego; the University of Toronto; McGill University; and Waterloo University; and at a number of conferences and symposia: the Philosophy of Education Society of Great Britain annual conference at New College, Oxford; the William Morris Society in Toronto; the Symposium on Compatriot Preference at the University of Western Ontario; the Equal Opportunity Workshop of the European Consortium for Political Research Conference in Granada; the Political Neutrality Conference at the Centre de Recherche en Ethique de l'Université de Montréal; the Canadian Philosophy Association annual meeting at Laval University; the Marx and Philosophy Conference at the University of London; the Centenary William Morris Conference at Exeter College, Oxford; the Explorations in Difference, Law and Literary Studies Conference, University of Alberta; the Legal and Social Philosophy Association annual conference, University of Bristol; and the Canadian Political Science Association annual meeting, University of Victoria.

In 2001–2, I was privileged to hold a Visiting Fellowship at Corpus Christi College, Oxford. There I found a congenial community who welcomed me as one of their own and enabled me to think, both theoretically and personally, about the nature of flourishing. I thank members of the Corpus Senior Common Room for their generosity. I would also like to express my appreciation to the Social Sciences and Humanities Research Council of Canada for funding my research, and to Queen's University for additional funding and for granting me sabbatical leave.

I thank my parents, Marcia and Peter Sypnowich, who lovingly taught me much, by instruction and example, about clear writing, critical thinking and living well. I give thanks also, for their love, friendship and stimulating conversation, to all my siblings and siblings-in-law who epitomise flourishing in many ways: Paula, Catherine Mary and John; Martin, Claudio and Laure.

This book took longer than expected to produce because of my involvement in community issues, defending local heritage and attempting to save the oldest high school in Ontario from closure, experiences that offered real-world examples of the nature, and fragility, of sources of flourishing. If Oscar

Wilde thought socialism took too many evenings, who knows what he would have made of local politics in Kingston. I am grateful to comrades in a number of campaigns: all my neighbours in Barriefield Village, and particularly Craig Sims, Janice Couch, George Lovell, Maureen Garvie, Barb Carr, David Craig, Betsy Donald, Doug Morrow, Stephen Burnett, Bob Cardwell, Claudia and Michael Rosebery, Maureen Eagan, Bob Hotrum, Heidi and Ted Bergeron, Hélène Lavoie, Joan Axelrad, Cheang-Ghee Khoo, Barry and Alicia Gordon, Bonnie Thompson, Sean Conboy, Megan Willoughby, Chris Macrae, Susan Palosci, Lynda Wilde, Neil Dukas, Joe and Shirley Stertz, Karen and Nadia Patience, Marc Claege, Dennis La Rocque, Kathy Burke, Erik and Kim Lockhart, Veronica Desjardins, Ben Darrah, Margaret Bissell, John Fisher, Eva Toth, Maureen and Fraser Saunders, Helga and Klaus Stegemann, Pierre and Julia Du Prey, Sylvain Gagnon, Eric Walton, Jennifer Henstock, Liz Westgarth, Steve and Joanne Page, Gord and Heather Manning, Ann-Marie Smith, Graham Mutch, Fran O'Heare, Michael and Bobbi Shaw; as well as Arthur Cockfield, Lindsay Davidson, David Gordon, Carl Bray, Lea Westlake, Katherine Rudder, Mariah Rowe, Sarah and James Gibson-Bray, Ken Ohtake, Rob Baker, Leslie Galbraith, Jay and Toby Abramsky, Valerie Hamilton, Joanne and Deanna Choi, Arunima Khanna, Amanda Black, Sue Streight, Terri Hodges, Don Taylor, Vicki Schmolka, John Grenville, Helen Finley, Kathleen O'Hara, Mary Farrar, Pat Hodge, Karen Pagratis, Gord Dalton, Graham Lodge, Sammi King, Gisèle Pharand, Anne Lougheed, Peter Burpee, Paul Christianson, Bill Patterson, Brian Osborne, Rob Fonger, Alan Gummo, Tim Soper and David McCallum.

In the course of working on this project I lost a dear friend and the philosophical world lost one of its best. I owe a special thank you to Jerry Cohen, whose model of philosophical acumen and creativity, fellowship and good fun, remains unparalleled years after his death, and whose work on equality and socialism has been a formative influence on my work.

Finally, besides friendship and philosophy, there is a third 'f' that is constitutive of flourishing, for me at least, and that's family. My work, often done very early in the morning before others have stirred, was much enhanced, over the years, by the company of four feline companions: Koshka, Kolya, Luna and Felix. But most important, this book is dedicated to my husband, daughter and son, without whom flourishing, both personally and philosophically, would be unthinkable. I met my husband, David Bakhurst, when we were both graduate students in Oxford, many years ago, and I feel extraordinarily lucky to have found a kindred spirit, my intellectual comrade and life partner, who has been by my side every since. David generously read the whole manuscript and provided invaluable advice on revisions in short order, a supererogatory kindness if ever there was one. I thank him from the bottom of my heart for everything. Our children, Rosemary and Hugh, grew up whilst this book took shape, and patiently put up with 'Mum's working on her book' but also, as they emerged from the delightful years when they were small to become such fine young people, have exemplified human wellbeing in many ways. I am so grateful to have all these Bakhursts in my life.

# Acknowledgements

Parts of the book are revised versions of portions of published essays. I am grateful for permission to draw on the following:

'Justice, Community and the Antinomies of Feminist Theory,' *Political Theory*, 21, 3, 1993. Reproduced with permission by Sage Journals.

'Some Disquiet About Difference,' *Praxis International*, 13, 2, 1993. Reproduced with permission by John Wiley and Sons.

'Equality and Nationality,' *Politics and Society*, 24, 2, 1996. Reproduced with permission by Sage Journals.

'Impartiality After Difference,' *Review of Constitutional Studies*, 3, 2, 1996. Reproduced with permission by the Review of Constitutional Studies and the Centre for Constitutional Studies.

'Race, Culture and the Egalitarian Conscience,' *Canadian Journal of Philosophy*, 29, 2, 1999. Reproduced with permission by Routledge, an imprint of Taylor & Francis Group.

'How to Live the Good Life: William Morris's Aesthetic Conception of Equality,' *Queen's Quarterly*, 107, 3, 2000. Reproduced with permission by Queen's Quarterly.

'The Culture of Citizenship,' *Politics and Society* 28, 4, 2000. Reproduced with permission by Sage Journals.

'Egalitarianism Renewed,' in R. Beiner and W. Norman, eds, *Canadian Political Philosophy: Contemporary Reflections*, Oxford: Oxford University Press, 2001. Reproduced with permission by Oxford University Press.

'Cosmopolitans, Cosmopolitanism and Human Flourishing,' in G. Brock and H. Brighouse, eds, *The Political Philosophy of Cosmopolitanism*, Cambridge: Cambridge University Press, 2005. Reproduced with permission by Cambridge University Press.

'A New Approach to Equality,' in R. Merrill and D. Weinstock, eds, *Political Neutrality: A Re-evaluation*, London: Palgrave Macmillan, 2014. Reproduced with permission by Palgrave Macmillan.

'Conservatism, Perfectionism and Equality,' in D. Bakhurst and P. Fairfield, eds, *Education and Conversation: Exploring Oakeshott's Legacy*, London: Bloomsbury, 2016. Reproduced with permission by Bloomsbury Academic, an imprint of Bloomsbury Publishing PLC.

I am also grateful for permission to quote the following song lyrics:

Janis Joplin, Michael McClure, Bob Neuwirth, 'Mercedes Benz.' Reproduced with permission by Strong Arm Music (ASCAP), c/o Wixen Music Publishing, Inc.

Stompin' Tom Connors, 'Sudbury Saturday Night.' Reproduced with permission by Crown-Vetch Music.

# Introduction

## Human Flourishing and the Century of Equality

In the spring of 1991, just a few months before the attempted coup on Gorbachev and the subsequent fall of communism, I made a trip to Moscow. I had last been there in the mid-1980s, in the heyday of glasnost and perestroika, when Western Leftists could nurture the hope that a democratic socialism was in the making. On this trip however, I confronted the unravelling of this possibility, with the hitherto unthinkable social chaos that had begun to pervade the city. In the old days Moscow had been almost pathologically well ordered and law-abiding: theft, vandalism, even graffiti were unheard of. If one made the mistake of dropping a sweet wrapper on the pavement, scolding from fellow citizens (particularly the *babushkas* or grandmas) was the inevitable result. Now crime was an issue, and in gargantuan proportions. As soon as our friends met us in the airport, they warned us of baggage handlers who stole the contents of suitcases and taxi drivers who robbed and murdered their Western passengers. We ourselves observed en route to our hotel the total disregard of motorists for the directions of traffic policemen or the most obvious rules of the road. Once settled in, we learned that the age-old system of bribes to obtain restaurant tables and services was now undertaken exclusively in the hitherto banned foreign currency of American dollars; travelling in the city we saw that one could purchase from street vendors, not just overpriced cosmetics and trinkets from Asia, but also poor facsimiles of Western pornography. At one market, even weapons were for sale. In the academy, young scholars at the Institute of Philosophy, in their abhorrence of things socialist, were absorbed in a curious blend of philosophising drawn from Derrida and Foucault, New Age trends and Slavophile romanticism about Mother Earth.

Shaken by all this, I sought refuge in the Tretiakov Gallery and its special exhibition of Bolshevik art. Here I found sustenance for my flagging socialist spirit. One of the works was a poster depicting a Russian woman, with arms outstretched, welcoming a woman from one of the Islamic republics, who was represented with the veil or hijab coming away as she stepped forward into her Soviet sister's embrace. The poster was emblazoned with a slogan that said something like: 'welcome, sisters from the republics!' The picture was both moving and disconcerting. Moving, because its appeal to the ideal of universal comradeship, a belief in the fundamental equality of human beings and the possibility of liberation from repressive custom and tradition. Disconcerting, because the picture was of an ideal now lost, but also because the ideal itself was ambiguous. The universal community of equality was after all premissed on the abandonment, if not the forcible removal, of particular cultural identities. The price for stepping into modernity and equal citizenship was the loss of one's place and sense of self in a traditional heritage. And in the symbolic order of socialist realism there was no concession that this was a loss to regret. Now, as I wandered the streets of Moscow, the socialist ideal of equality was, in turn, being abandoned where it once had seemed so entrenched.

## What's Wrong with Equality?

Is equality an ideal of the past? The twentieth century might be dubbed the century where the ideal of equality had the greatest practical and philosophical influence. The idea that all human beings should be treated as equals shaped political movements, public policy and philosophical debate. Equality motivated revolutions and wars, movements and struggles. Problems of equality were central to the development of societies as diverse as the Soviet Union and the United States, Canada and Cuba, South Africa and Britain. The ideal of equality underlay the suffrage movements that extended the vote to propertyless men and women. Equality animated the civil rights movements in the United States and the anti-apartheid movement in South Africa to give all members of a society the same rights and freedoms. In the postwar era, equality seemed impregnable in both West and East, for all the ideological confrontation of the Cold War. In the capitalist democracies, the welfare state was being forged, with entitlements to health care, unemployment insurance, public education, and welfare. In the countries of the Soviet empire, central planning provided the economic system with which to realise, however ineptly, Marx's slogan of 'from each according to his abilities and to each according to his needs.'[1]

How things have changed. Today it is not the behemoth of Soviet socialism but its collapse that provides the context for reflection on equality. Moreover, not only has the egalitarian ideology of Soviet communism been swept aside and replaced by a harsh creed of survival of the fittest, but also capitalist democracies in the West have come to challenge egalitarian principles. Thus we have witnessed the decline of the postwar welfare state, sometimes at the hands of putatively progressive governments, responding to diminished confidence in the ideal of equality wrought by 'New Right' parties, or the imperative to commit to a programme of austerity. The dynamics are complex, but perhaps the beleaguering of equality is the result, in part, of its success. This is not to say that people are more equal: the gap between people from rich and poor countries has grown, and within affluent countries there is a widening gap between the haves and have-nots.[2] As Piketty documents in his influential work, there has been a 'spectacular increase in inequality,' such that 'inequalities of wealth that had supposedly disappeared are close to regaining or even surpassing their historical highs.'[3] However, if we measure what people consume, standards of living in the West have improved over the past thirty years, even in societies like the United States where inequality has grown the most. There is more ownership of consumer durables, size of living space has increased, and people's life expectancy has improved. As the 2011 London riots demonstrated, where political action was coordinated via texting on cell phones, even those of bleak prospects and modest means possess sophisticated personal communication devices. Yet, although there has been an expansion in low-earning jobs, the end of the twentieth century saw an even greater expansion in higher earning jobs.[4] Disadvantage has not been eliminated because it has been mitigated in certain significant ways.

Equality's fortunes in the realm of political theory have been similar. Equality figured as both an undisputed framework and a subject of controversy in most political theories written in the last century. Its power was such that rival concepts took on an egalitarian cast. Thus liberty was couched as an ideal to which all are equally entitled; community is a characteristic of the truly egalitarian society; and democracy was the political system that holds government accountable to all its citizens equally. The currency of equality was such that philosophies across the spectrum all claimed to be egalitarian, insisting on individuals' equal rights to liberty and property or the importance of the redistribution of wealth to further equal wellbeing. Critics of equality increasingly made their case in purportedly egalitarian terms. Consider, in the history of equality's struggles, how a sexual division of labour often relied on chivalrous concepts of women's special virtues that were portrayed as unlike but no less worthy than male attributes. In the domain of race, the 'separate but equal' doctrine paradoxically used the idea of equality to ward off the egalitarian cause, in a way that would ultimately undermine the case for racial segregation.

As for resistance to social welfare, libertarians pride themselves on rejecting the redistribution of wealth by appeal to an argument based on equality, that is, that an equal entitlement to liberty would be infringed by the taxation required to remedy economic disadvantage. Thus, insofar as conservative critics have found success, as the egalitarian project suffered a backlash on several fronts, it was in large part because of their capacity to frame their opposition in terms of equality, in rhetoric if not substance. It would be archaic today to propose that human beings are rightly born to a hierarchy of status or station, or that there is a class of superior persons who should rule the inferior. Some conservatives might still think such things, but they don't dare say them. We are all egalitarians now, it might be said, in the triumphalist spirit that characterised the millennium and the dawn of the twenty-first century.

However, millennial triumphalism about equality would be misplaced. Equality is not an ideal that has enjoyed some kind of undisputed, hegemonic influence in the domain of theory any more than the realm of practice. Equality has been a target in both senses of the word: it has been a goal to which philosophers have aspired, but also an object of criticism and challenge.

This is a book about equality and how the ideal should be renewed in political philosophy. My aim is to rejuvenate the ideal by critically assessing contemporary challenges in political theory and reformulating the ideal's philosophical underpinnings. To this end, I deploy a new approach based on the idea of human flourishing, which demonstrates the relevance and power of a reinvigorated egalitarianism. I call for both retrieval and innovation. What is to be retrieved is the ideal of equality itself, which we have on the one hand unreflectively assumed, and on the other carelessly rejected, allowing it to be tainted by its connection with failed historic experiments and impugned by new progressive claims. We must retrieve the ideal of equality as a central political principle.[5] As for innovation, my approach calls for a new direction. I reject the concept of the neutral state – an idea that dominates contemporary political philosophy – for a view of the state as enabling the betterment of its citizens. I argue that if we understand equality as centred on a concept of human flourishing, we can illuminate several debates in contemporary political philosophy and thereby affirm the egalitarian ideal.

It is hardly surprising that an idea so central to political debate over the last century should find criticism and attack. More surprising is that the ideal of equality has been rocked from within. There are two kinds of challenge at issue here. First, the most successful challenges to equality in the twentieth century had egalitarian roots: challenges posed by nationalism, multiculturalism, and the broad, cultural Left that emerged from debates within feminism and postmodernism. The second challenge is that egalitarian thought of the past generation has abandoned its original commitment to human wellbeing, a commitment that makes sense of equality, and, as I will argue, resolves a variety of egalitarian conundrums, including the problems of cultural difference. Indeed, these two challenges, the problem of difference, and the neutralism of liberal political thought, are connected.

Liberals have long been exercised by the problem of whether equality occludes diversity. This concern has been prominent in recent debates, but the problem of difference dogged equality a long time before that. Nationalist movements in particular contended that states that purported to treat their members equally were, in their disrespect for national differences, in fact unequal. Some of these movements, of course, responded to inegalitarian policies ranging from the denial of equality of opportunity to ethnic cleansing, but they also expressed dissatisfaction with the ideal of equality itself. Equality as a cardinal Enlightenment ideal had a homogenising aspect, an urge to understand all human beings by a common criterion, be it humanity, social class, or citizenship. Can one have equality without universality, that is, the idea of human beings as members of a universal moral order? If the answer to this is no, then many were prepared to say: So much for equality.

The idea of difference came to the fore in the 1990s and is now so much part of the political wallpaper that it is easy to forget how significant were its interventions. But in order to appreciate the contemporary shape of egalitarian debate, we need to understand the impact of the view that equality is tainted by a disregard for diversity. The difference critiques were, in a sense, the perspectives of the 'freedom fighter,' taking aim at oppression, and in that way building on the egalitarian project in their very rejection of it. They were not, on the face of it, hostile to furthering the equal wellbeing of individuals, yet they took issue with the idea of a common humanity that justified equal entitlement to respect and resources. They sought the special recognition of ethnic groups, secession for national minorities, separate arrangements for distinctive cultures, scope for the ethic of particular groups. They thus moulded a number of debates in political philosophy, about multiculturalism, distributive justice, and the nature of democracy.

The difference critiques initiated a fruitful process of self-reflection and revision on the part of egalitarians. But these critiques also had some costs. It was unclear whether equality was being served or rejected, and those who had no desire to promote equality could interpret these debates as a licence to dump the constraints of egalitarianism from their political agendas. This was particularly easy to do in light of the claim by advocates of difference that politics could not be understood in terms of discharging a responsibility to members of a common project, but rather merely reflected the assertion of particular and incommensurable interests. It has been said that the previous century, although it appeared to be characterised by a conflict between capitalism and communism, was in fact dominated by conflicts between nationality and ethnicity.[6] Such conflicts, bringing with them calls for secession, forced emigration and war, invited philosophical resolution that seemed unconnected to, if not in tension with, the ideal of equality. The result has been a sense of pessimism and loss among the Left about equality's prospects. My book seeks to remedy this.

Along with the challenge of difference came a second challenge, the philosophical preoccupation with neutrality. Here it appears that equality's greatest problem is, to put it baldly, what egalitarian philosophers have done to it. It is often remarked that political philosophy was in the doldrums for most of this century. Rebirth came in 1971, with the publication of Rawls's *A Theory of Justice*.[7] Before Rawls, Anglo-American political philosophy lived in the shadow of positivist views that had dominated philosophy in the early part of this century. The strict delineation of conceptual from empirical enquiry, and of matters of fact from matters of value, so characteristic of logical positivism, lingered in the ordinary language philosophy that succeeded it. But whereas ethics could turn itself into a meta-discipline concerned with the scope and limits of taken-for-granted moral concepts, the intrinsically controversial nature of political prescriptions meant that such a metamorphosis was not available for political theory. As a branch of philosophy that sought to direct rather than merely describe human practices, political theory was therefore cast as a non-subject, its place taken by the paltry exercises of ordinary language that interrogated the senses in which speakers use political vocabulary. This was a long way from the Ancient Greeks' original idea of political philosophy as reasoned inquiry into how we ought to live in common. The diminished role of political philosophy as a normative exercise doubtless reflected, not just an empiricist outlook in philosophy, but also a smug acceptance of the empirically given; i.e. the liberal institutions of capitalist democracies in the postwar period. The dogmatism about politics that came with the Cold War helps explain why political philosophy was in a state of stagnation. Such complacency was jolted, however, by conservative attacks on the welfare state, attacks that prompted the considered response of Rawls.

Rawls's thesis is that inequalities are justified only if they are to the advantage of the worst-off in society. According to Rawls's thought experiment, if individuals deliberate about principles of justice without knowing who they are to be in the society they are designing, they would opt for basic liberties along with a redistributive scheme; moreover, they would be concerned that society not use political means to endorse one way of living over another. Rawls thus rejuvenates the social contract tradition, founding political prescriptions on claims of a quasi-empirical kind about human reasoning and motivation. In later work, Rawls developed this theme of neutrality into the idea of 'political liberalism,' in which the state is liberal in a narrowly political sense. The state must eschew any commitment on what Rawls calls 'comprehensive doctrines,' i.e. substantive philosophical or moral views. Citizens must be reasonable and not ask their fellow citizens to live by others' creeds. They should thus subscribe to the value of neutrality, a value that, nonetheless, emerges from practices current in contemporary liberal societies.[8]

Something like Rawlsian neutrality came to be the position of most liberal egalitarians. Indeed, even liberal defenders of multicultural citizenship, who one would expect to offer some argument about value, have put their case in neutral terms. My colleague, Will Kymlicka, is the most prominent advocate of this idea, in his argument that protection of minority cultures is derived from the neutral liberal's commitment to choice. But it is unclear whether the case for equality can proceed without making some kind of commitment on questions of value, of how we should live, in particular the value of autonomy and our need for the resources to lead autonomous lives. Resolute in its avoidance of questions of the good, egalitarian debate ends up operating with a model of the person that is so uninspired it looks, as one commentator put it, 'suspiciously like the modern office worker.'[9] Rawls resuscitated political philosophy, but perhaps he did so by keeping it semi-conscious, for in banning controversy about value from the domain of public debate, political philosophy became curiously apolitical.

Connected to the focus on neutrality are a number of other implausible commitments. There is the hyper-individualistic premiss that one is entitled to the remedy of disadvantage no matter what, manifest in the 'welfare for surfers' credo of Van Parijs,[10] or arguments that to equalise citizens' welfare requires us to sate the expensive tastes of the few. These moves are understandable; they were premissed on the idea that equality requires satisfaction of needs and should therefore not be tied to individuals' ability to contribute to need satisfaction, nor, given the diversity of needs and interests, subject to some crude common denominator. But the result has hardly attracted adherents to the egalitarian cause. As Anderson has put it, 'if much recent academic work defending equality had been secretly penned by conservatives, could the results be any more embarrassing for egalitarians?'[11] All this has highlighted vulnerabilities in philosophical egalitarianism in a way that makes the call for attention to the inequalities of race, sex and ethnicity particularly compelling.

## A New Approach

How should we approach the daunting task of renewing the ideal of equality? I propose a theory of equality centred on human flourishing or wellbeing. Distribution of resources, goods or income is, after all, merely instrumental to the fundamental goal of living well. There is a certain sterility in zeroing in on money or goods as a matter of social justice. The mere fact that there are disparities of wealth is undeniably the preoccupation of both influential scholarly works such as *Capital in the Twenty-First Century*, and the political activism exemplified by the Occupy Wall Street movement, and it certainly signals injustice. However, its significance for egalitarians should lie in the consequences of disparities for how people live, how inequality of income affects people's quality of life. Relational egalitarians have responded by focussing only on our relative status or standing vis-a-vis each other, that is, on relations of respect and democratic citizenship,[12] but this threatens to excise economic issues altogether. I am interested in wellbeing more broadly, in people's ability to live well, which is clearly determined to a significant extent by their access to material goods. Here I will note a few features of my approach that I develop in the chapters that follow.

Human flourishing requires a 'culture of citizenship,' which provides the sense of membership and reciprocity necessary for equalisation, but which also figures as a means of access for political participation and the pursuit of autonomy essential for flourishing. Accordingly, it is the task of the egalitarian state to enable citizens to live worthwhile lives. This involves an emphasis on culture as a source of the individual's development. Minority cultures do this, but so of course does the majority one. Living well requires possibilities provided by culture, in the widest sense of the word. They include such things as literature, art galleries, music, education, physical activity, enjoyment of nature, sporting spectacles, traditional crafts, or historic architecture. There is no single way of living well; the human flourishing approach must be resolutely pluralist.

An important feature of a well-lived life is autonomy. A vital autonomy-enabling social condition is freedom from interference, and it cannot be stressed too much that my call for an interest in the kinds of choices people make retains the traditional liberal antipathy to coercion. But non-interference is insufficient. A second set of social conditions that enable autonomy are institutions that assure some minimum level of material wellbeing, since autonomy is undermined by hunger and homelessness. Autonomy refers to self-determination, and this means individuals should live under conditions where they are authors of their lives and masters of their fate. I propose that in addition to autonomy, human wellbeing involves objectively valuable pursuits and contentment, which in turn require arrangements that attend to material wellbeing and that make available activities and practices that facilitate living well.

In the course of developing this view I will consider how it might be characterised. It has been dubbed 'perfectionist,' but it is important that our understanding of cultural enrichment eschew the idea of perfection per se. Human fulfilment is an open-ended task that can be achieved in a variety of worthwhile ways. Cultural diversity provides possibilities that benefit not just the adherents of particular cultures, but us all. The society seeking equality of flourishing thus needs to be a supportive environment for a wide range of cultural practices that promote wellbeing. Indeed, for all the talk in philosophy of a neutral liberal state, the liberal state in practice is in fact perfectionist to some degree, deploying subsidies or grants to support valuable cultural possibilities.

The difficulty in attending to the reality of politics was brought home to me some time ago when I was on a radio programme as a member of a lively three-philosopher panel on 'The Public Good.' Reflecting on it afterwards I was struck by how we philosophers were incapable, in some fundamental sense, of seriously addressing our subject matter: the idea of the public good. Schooled in the neutralist liberalism that dominates political philosophy, we took for granted that seeking a consensus on value was symptomatic of a dangerous, moralising conservatism. We thus sidestepped the issue of the public good per se by considering the means by which individuals might pursue their private goods and discussing what means, be they healthcare, education or social welfare, the public was obligated to provide. However, our host assumed the cogency of the idea of the public good, and took it as the first premiss of a discussion of politics. For most citizens and political leaders, too, the phrase 'public good' is no embarrassment, but inherent in the task of governance, which includes supporting institutions of culture, enabling a degree of civility in citizens' dealings with each other, and providing conditions of self-development and improvement that enriches individual and community: in short, to enable human flourishing.

This book tackles a range of topics in making the case for a flourishing approach to equality. In the first part, Challenges to Equality, I consider the debates in political philosophy that emerged in the last generation about sex, race and cultural difference. I argue that these debates, for all their influence on today's cultural-political landscape, have been unable to capture what is at stake in remedying injustice, that is, human wellbeing. My human flourishing approach, I contend, serves as an important corrective to the weaknesses of the preoccupation with 'difference' and provides a case for renewing the ideal of equality.

Chapter 1, Beyond Difference, describes how the idea of difference emerged to present one of the most exciting and formidable challenges to liberal conceptions of justice, a challenge that continues to prompt invaluable soul-searching about egalitarian commitments and goals. I assess the debates about human diversity and contend that the idea of equality must remain our compass; difference itself is an inadequate normative framework. Instead of identity as such, we should focus on the interests that accrue from different identities and the extent to which they reflect inequalities that require political redress. In so doing, we cannot help but refer to a common measure of wellbeing.

Chapter 2, Race, Culture and the Egalitarian Conscience, takes up the difference that has been the source of the most challenging of intractable injustices: race. Here I consider the twin approaches of 'colour blindness,' whereby the appropriate response to racism is to treat race as irrelevant both philosophically and politically, and 'colour consciousness,' whereby race is the basis of policies of affirmative action, reparations, and a cultural identity. I recommend that whilst we should not deny the reality of race, we should not make too much of racial difference. To attend to racial injustice requires a conception of our common humanity and our common interest in living flourishing lives.

The deep-seated conviction that the universal is never truly so, that it always excludes the other, the alien and different, emerged philosophically in feminist debate. Chapter 3, Androgyny and Girl Power: Sex, Equality and Human Goods, focuses on the feminist challenge to the egalitarian ideal, which shifted from insisting on equal treatment under the rules, to a questioning of the partiality of the rules themselves. The idea that women's interests were best served by being treated the same as men was inevitably refined in light of women's biological distinctiveness; but it also came to be revised because of claims about cultural and moral differences between men and women. I argue that instead of fixating on the nature of gender and gender identity, we should focus on the sources of human wellbeing, for women and men, and on how to organise a society that enables equal human flourishing, in all its diverse forms, regardless of sex or gender.

The second part of the book, Liberal Revisionism, focusses on two prominent political philosophers in the liberal tradition. In Chapter 4, Impartiality, Difference and Wellbeing, I consider Rawls's political liberalism. I argue that the answer to the difference challenge is not to retreat, as Rawls does, behind the vulnerable fortress of neutrality. Rawls's ideas of reason, impartiality and cooperation are, on the one hand, indispensable for social life; without them, the claims of difference threaten to destroy the possibility of social justice of any kind. However, these resources must be justified, ultimately, by reference to a substantive conception of the good, one that is in fact implied by Rawls's own argument. Chapter 5, Equality and the Antinomies of Multicultural Liberalism, considers Kymlicka's highly influential argument for multicultural citizenship. I maintain that the argument for 'group-differentiated citizenship' deploys criteria of autonomy and equality that bear a problematic relationship to the idea of cultural rights. I conclude that a focus on culture's relation to human wellbeing requires a much more radical revision of liberal political philosophy that focusses on equal human flourishing.

The third part of the book, Equality and Living Well, elaborates my flourishing account of equality. Chapter 6, What Equality Is and Is Not, initiates the flourishing approach with a look at three conceptual challenges to egalitarianism. The first is that egalitarianism is mired in a commitment to 'levelling down,' where equality of resources is to be preferred over any other distribution, even if equality reduces the resources available to the better off at no benefit to the worse off. The second problem is that of talent and its recognition; here it is charged that egalitarian distribution implies effacing or ignoring talent. The third problem is that of the relation between equality and partiality, in which the promotion of equality is taken to involve the elimination of any special regard one has for one's own interests or the interests of particular others. These three problems demonstrate that: first, equality is important because of its effect on wellbeing, rather than having some kind of intrinsic value independent of human beings' welfare or interests; and second, the egalitarian ideal is best served by aiming for equality in flourishing rather than in the distribution of goods, resources, or even welfare.

Chapter 7, Human Flourishing and the Use and Abuse of Equality, sets out the philosophical context of an egalitarianism centred on the idea of flourishing that seeks to improve and equalise human wellbeing. First, I show how my flourishing approach has historical antecedents in socialist writings from Morris to Marx to Beveridge, but that it also draws on the ideas of contemporary egalitarians such as Sen and Nussbaum. I explain how flourishing consists in autonomy, objectively worthwhile pursuits, and satisfaction, and how public policy might remedy shortfalls in wellbeing. The argument endorses perfectionism, but in a version equipped to ward off the charge of paternalism often brought against perfectionism. I argue that a flourishing approach to equality promises a robust political philosophy that can withstand common objections made to theories of equality, on the one hand, and theories of the good life, on the other.

Chapter 8, Autonomy and Living Well, takes up this question: Can a theory of equality focussed on human flourishing respect individuals' freedom to choose how to live? The view that we should hold people responsible for their choices, discussed in the previous chapter, follows from another liberal principle, that is, that we should respect people's capacity to make choices. But the emphasis on choice sits awkwardly with perfectionism, since people can make choices detrimental to their flourishing. Here we have the crux of a fundamental controversy in the idea of egalitarian perfectionism. On the one hand, its focus on flourishing suggests people need direction as to how to live, and on the other, because choice is a constituent of flourishing, flourishing seems undermined by such direction. Perfectionism continues to be dogged by the problem of paternalism. I argue that a proper appreciation of the nature of agency and choice renders my flourishing approach consistent with, and moreover, conducive to, the liberal commitment to individual autonomy.

My human flourishing account of equality can be deployed to consider those most vexing matters of inequality, that is disparities between the haves and have-nots in the global context. This is the subject of Chapters 9 and 10. Debates about equality tend to take as their premise the relations among citizens in a single society. However, problems of inequality obviously go beyond a particular territory or country; indeed, disparities in flourishing are most egregious from an international perspective. And yet we lack the capacity to redress global injustice: institutional resources, human motivation and the concepts of political philosophy all presume the predominance of the nation-state paradigm and its corollary of obligations among citizens.

In Chapter 9, Equality and the Public Good: Local and Global, I point out that the idea that society should promote a culture favourable to human flourishing raises the thorny problem of 'the public good,' the idea with which I began this book. If, as I argue, we should seek to make people's shared environment conducive to choices that enable human flourishing, then it seems inevitable that we would seek to further the public good. I address the complaint that the idea of the public good evokes a supra-individual entity or a conservative affection for tradition, arguing that the concept can specify substantive goods yet remain inclusive and universal enough to apply to the problems of global inequality. Chapter 10, Cosmopolitans, Cosmopolitanism and Human Flourishing, further subjects my flourishing approach to perhaps the toughest test of an egalitarian theory, what it can contribute to the promotion of equality, not among citizens, but around the globe. Few egalitarians would dispute that richer peoples have duties of redistribution to poorer peoples. The question is how extensive these duties of global justice are, particularly in comparison to the duties of domestic justice. I argue that focusing on rendering human flourishing more equal enables us to find a middle course, which affirms our cosmopolitan duties whilst recognising the critical role of a culture of self-determining citizenship. If we are to attempt to remedy global inequality, then we must consider how cultural practices affect human flourishing.

In the Conclusion, I wrap up the book's argument and consider some of its implications for larger issues in political theory such as utopianism and democracy. I note the importance of a political philosophy that is alive to utopian aspirations, that doesn't flinch from ambitious political ideals, yet is moderated by a sense of our human limitations.

As we make our way through the twenty-first century, equality is both taken for granted and dismissed, a victim of its practical successes, however chequered, and its philosophical confusions. What is needed is a new, vigorous understanding of equality founded on the principle of human well-being. Greater equality should mean greater access to a plurality of worthwhile ways of living. In the argument that follows, I set out the limitations of current theories of justice, as well as the features of an alternative egalitarian position. I hope that equality is thereby renewed.

## Notes

1 K. Marx, 'Critique of the Gotha Programme,' 531.
2 This is the case in affluent societies such as Canada, the U.S. and the U.K., as well as globally. According to the Broadbent Institute's reports, Canadians 'underestimate

the breadth and depth of wealth inequality' which has worsened in the period 1998–2012, with the top 20 per cent owning 67.4 per cent of the country's wealth and the bottom 30 per cent owning less than 1 per cent of the wealth. See the Broadbent Institute, 'The Wealth Gap: Perceptions and Misconceptions in Canada,' and 'Haves and Have-Nots: Deep and Persistent Wealth Inequality in Canada.' Income inequality is particularly severe in the U.S., which is the 43rd most unequal country in the world, and is confronting rates of inequality not seen since the Great Depression, with the top 1 per cent taking home more than 20 per cent of all personal income, largely due to the high rise in pay for company executives, giving rise to protest movements such as Occupy Wall Street. See CIA, *World Fact Book*, 2011. In the U.K., where the poorest tenth of people receive only 1 per cent of total income, whilst the richest tenth take home 31 per cent: 'it is predicted that, on current trends, the U.K. will rapidly return to levels of inequality not seen since Victorian times,' M. Haddad, *The Perfect Storm: Economic stagnation, the rising cost of living, spending cuts, and the impact on UK poverty*. According to the World Bank, although the growing prosperity of countries such as China has meant that the disparity between rich and poor globally has lowered slightly, income inequality within countries is worse than ever; moreover, the poorest 24 countries have only 1 per cent of total world income. Conference Board of Canada, 'World Income Inequality: Is the world becoming more unequal?'

3  T. Pinketty, *Capital in the Twenty-First Century*, 24, 471.
4  E.O. Wright and H. Brighouse, 'On Alex Callinicos's *Equality*,' 193–222. See A. Callinicos, *Equality*, ch. 1.
5  'Retrieval' comes from C.B. Macpherson, *Democratic Theory: Essays in Retrieval*. Macpherson sought to retrieve the liberal tradition's political commitment to autonomy that, he claimed, was undermined by some liberals' economic allegiance to private enterprise.
6  This is a theme in E. Hobsbawm, *Age of Extremes*.
7  J. Rawls, *A Theory of Justice*.
8  J. Rawls, *Political Liberalism*.
9  J. Wolff, 'Fairness, Respect and the Egalitarian Ethos Revisited,' 339.
10  P. Van Parijs, 'Why Surfers Should be Fed: The Liberal Case for an Unconditional Basic Income.'
11  E. Anderson, 'What Is the Point of Equality?,' 287.
12  Also a point stressed by Pinketty, who worries about inequality as a 'source of powerful political tensions,' but who is otherwise surprisingly unrevealing about what is bad about inequality per se, *Capital in the Twenty-First Century*, 570.

# Part I

# Challenges to Equality

# 1   Beyond Difference

That human beings and human cultures are heterogeneous is not a novel thought. But in the last twenty-five years the idea of difference has emerged, in the academy and in popular culture, as a profound challenge to the assumptions and practices of politics, particularly politics grounded in the idea of equality. To take two striking historical cases from the end of the last century, the former Soviet Union, bound together by a seemingly impregnable authoritarian system, and Canada, united around what seemed a harmonious social-democratic consensus, found themselves in the throes of fragmentation. In these cases, the claims of various ethnic and regional identities put into question the modern idea of citizenship as membership in a collective, universal entity that subsumes diversity and particularity in order to treat its members as equals. These political developments were mirrored in philosophical theory by the rise to prominence of the concept of difference. Difference was invoked to challenge both liberal and socialist forms of modern polities as sources of a false universalism. Feminist and postmodern critics both sought to expose a myth of commonality in political thought since the Enlightenment. Instead of 'the citizen,' 'the self,' or even 'the proletariat' or 'Party,' these critics posited political subjects bearing diverse and incommensurable identities that cannot be subsumed within the confines of a single discourse.

As is often the case with intellectual innovation, an idea that began as a radical intervention is now almost a commonplace. Today it is widely acknowledged that we must heed the significance of cultural identity and seek to recognise its importance in people's lives. Thus it might seem that the concept of difference is now so firmly engrained that it is beyond criticism. And this, it might be argued, is something we owe to those who brought the concept to prominence a generation ago. However, the concept of difference manifests itself in a variety of ways in political theory, from radical poststructuralist identity politics, which seeks thoroughly to transcend the categories of modern political thought to establish a new 'imaginary,' to forms of multiculturalism that are a variation, albeit an important one, on traditional liberal themes.

In this chapter, my target will be any form of difference politics, radical or otherwise, that extols the virtue of cultural identity over identification with

transcultural political values. I believe that although many advocates of difference were motivated by concerns about equality – that some cultures are
more equal than others, as it were – there is often a profound tension
between the recognition of difference, on the one hand, and the political
ideal of equality, on the other. I propose to explore this tension. After exam-
ining the complex roles of difference and universality in the liberal and
Marxist traditions, I proceed to argue that, whilst an emphasis on difference
can be a useful antidote to abstract universalism and a welcome invitation to
value the diversity of human experience, social justice is not best pursued by
the politics of difference or identity. Rather, what is required is a form of
egalitarianism that focuses on human flourishing beyond the confines of cultural identity, and that combines a pluralistic vision of the good with a universalist commitment to equality. This conception of egalitarianism will be
developed in subsequent chapters.

## The Metaphysics of Sameness: From the Enlightenment to Marx

Whilst the idea of difference is often presented as an attack on the conceptions of the Enlightenment, it may be argued that it was the Enlightenment
that unleashed the idea of difference. After all, both in its epistemic project
of grounding rational understanding in the deductions or observations of
the individual subject, and in its political project of assuring the agent some
measure of liberty, the Enlightenment's starting point was the distinctness
of individuals and the distinctiveness of their particular viewpoints. In Descartes's epistemic individualism and Hobbes's founding of political obligation on self-interest, we see the idea of the uniqueness of individual
perspectives that cannot be subordinated to the authority of the community.
Difference is inherent in the atomistic subject who doubts the authenticity
of others' very existence, on Descartes's view, or who is at odds with other
self-interested subjects in Hobbes's war of all against all.[1] Difference persists
in contemporary liberalism insofar as it embraces a pluralism about values,
where political questions are divorced from the natural sympathies or personal choices of disparate selves. The market economy fits easily into this
picture as the context within which such selves can pursue their diverse
material interests.

However, notwithstanding its scope for diversity, the Enlightenment
project has obvious homogenising aspects. First, it assumes the individual has
certain immutable and universal characteristics, such as rationality, autonomy
and self-interest. Indeed, the Cartesian subject is so abstractly drawn that it is
difficult to see as a particular person of any kind.[2] Individuals are thus easily
aggregated, however isolated they may be from each other. Second, the individual is assumed to have a set of trans-historical concerns; individuals might
put their liberty or property to different purposes, but all individuals are said
to value liberty and property. Classical liberalism was thus charged with generalising from a model of the person specific to market societies – the 'possessive

individual' in Macpherson's phrase – to the nature of all human beings.[3] Liberal theories of rights, accordingly, were criticised for presupposing a false universalism; Marx in particular argued that the supposed 'natural rights' proclaimed by the American and French revolutionaries were in fact the rights of 'man as a bourgeois not man as a citizen who is considered to be the *true* and *authentic* man,'[4] and that the image of market and state as shaped by the free choices of individuals was an ideological illusion, masking the actual conflicting interests and struggles between classes.[5]

In light of this, one might expect that Marxism itself would not fall prey to a false universalism. For Marxists, true diversity was only possible in a society without the division of labour, private property and class divisions, where individuals might take on a variety of tasks and form a variety of attachments. Thus the famous description of communist society where one can 'hunt in the morning, fish in the afternoon, rear cattle in the evening, criticise after dinner ... without ever becoming hunter, fisherman, shepherd or critic.'[6] Nevertheless, Marxism, too, could be said to be imprisoned in a metaphysic of sameness. First, in its preoccupation with the material, Marxism excludes other kinds of oppression from its analysis, or simply deduces them from the logic of capitalist exploitation; thus Engels explains the subordination of women in terms of relations of private property.[7] Second, this 'economism' prompts Marxism to designate one agent, the working class, with the task of human emancipation. Third, Marxism plays down difference in the depiction of communism itself, a univocal, harmonious community, marking the '*genuine* resolution of the conflict between man and nature and between man and man.'[8] We thus have the paradox in Marxist theory that the elimination of the division of labour not only makes it possible for the individual to enjoy a life of diversity, but also ensures that a certain unanimity characterises social relations as a whole.

## 'Vive la Difference'

These images of universal emancipation, be they liberal or Marxist, have prompted many objections. Feminists in particular took issue with the Enlightenment model of the person. On the face of it, Descartes's rationalism and Hobbes's contractualism look hospitable to a gender-neutral epistemology or politics. But feminists argued that persons are not self-contained atoms, but embodied, intersubjective beings. Feminists here appealed not to abstract reason or the deliverances of hypothetical states of nature, but to (among other things) empirical studies of early child development, where relations of attachment with caring others, and to one's own gendered body, bring diverse selves into existence.[9] Poststructuralist feminists took the embodiedness of the subject further, arguing that the female body is the source of an alternative episteme,[10] suggesting that the Cartesian or Hobbesian self refers not to an abstract human nature, but to a historically contingent, male nature. In this, feminists joined Marxists in suggesting that the idea of a universal human essence is an ideological construct that camouflages unequal relations of power. At the same time feminists took issue with Marxism for ignoring the specificities of sex and thereby placing women at the rear of the proletariat's march through history. The bleak prospects for a partnership between these two emancipatory agendas caused some feminists to decry the union of Marxism and feminism as an 'unhappy marriage.'[11]

However, having liberated itself from the universalism of liberal and Marxist theory, feminist theory was then itself accused of offering a homogenising account of oppression. Issues of race, ethnicity and culture prompted soul-searching among feminists about the extent to which the category 'woman,' introduced as an antidote to the false universal 'man,' abstracts from important distinctions emerging out of diverse identities, and therefore fails to 'appreciate difference.'[12] Feminism had been accused of elitism since the suffrage movement, when the vote for women was often pursued at the expense of alliances with workers for material equality or, in the United States, the abolitionist cause. Increasingly, however, feminism had to negotiate its place within a wider disenchantment with the 'grand narratives' of traditional emancipatory politics, now contested by a plethora of social movements spanning issues of personal and global politics.

Postmodern advocates of difference targeted modernity's confidence in the ideals of rationality, unity, certainty and progress. Thus a foundation for knowledge, a unitary self, a transparent linguistic medium between world and person, an emancipatory political agent, humanist ideals of freedom or fraternity, the objectivity of moral and aesthetic judgement: all were deconstructed with the ideas that the individual subject is imprisoned within language or discourse, and that there is no reliable vantage point from which to perceive, let alone evaluate, the world. Whether or not the postmodern perspective was compatible with the liberatory projects of the 'rainbow coalition,' so-called given the diversity of its members in search of greater equality, was the subject of considerable debate.[13] But there was reason to be guarded on this score. Postmodernism's 'breakdown of the grand narrative,' Heller and Feher noted, can take forms as diverse as 'relativistic indifference of respective cultures to one another,' or 'the thoroughly inauthentic "third worldism" of first-world intellectuals.'[14] In fact, quietism sometimes seemed the most likely prospect. Lyotard's 'polytheism of values,' meant that political judgement can only be local and internal to the values themselves, suggesting an almost Burkean reverence for the traditional deliverances of the community. Rorty's critique of foundationalism generated a self-conscious 'bourgeois liberalism' that could muster not much more than the injunction not to be cruel.[15] Feminist postmodernism seemed more likely to yield strategies for realising equality, but its mode of critique was often so thoroughgoing as to suggest a rejection of politics per se in favour of more amorphous modes of liberation, through poetic expression, dance, or styles of self.[16]

Foucault's preoccupation with power offered the most hope for the insurgent postmodern voice, in an effort to rouse 'docile bodies' to challenge the oppression with which they have hitherto colluded. But Foucault suggests that discourses so determine the ground rules of their own unmasking that all emancipation can only be partial and qualified. At times Foucault goes so far as to reduce all struggles for equality to 'the form that made an essentially normalizing power acceptable,'[17] threatening a paralysis that stymies social change altogether. Thus postmodernism 'decay[s] into the radiant emanations of cynicism.'[18]

For all this, it cannot be denied that the idea of difference was advanced in order to further the interests of disadvantaged people and thus an egalitarian ideal of some kind seemed to persist. This was apparent in two examples of difference arguments: the critique of liberalism developed by the feminist social theorist Iris Marion Young; and the critique of socialism made by Ernesto Laclau and Chantal Mouffe, once prominent post-structuralist Marxists in France and Britain.

Young contended attention to difference should 'broaden and deepen' traditional commitments to equality. She proposed a new approach to social justice that eschews liberal ideals of neutrality and enlarges the focus of distributive justice to take account of the diverse perspectives of people disadvantaged on the basis of race, sexuality and culture. For Young, the solution was not a communitarian ideal of unmediated community united by a common conception of the good, since that too, threatens to occlude diversity. Rather, she proposed participatory democracy, affirmative action, group representation in political bodies and, in order to eliminate the prejudices of universalist thinking, a cultural revolution involving the 'politicization' of 'habits, feelings and expressions of fantasy and desire,' 'a kind of social therapy.'[19]

In contrast to Young's engagement with liberal political philosophy, Laclau and Mouffe situated their arguments in a 'postMarxist' terrain. Their ideas are strikingly similar to Young's, however, in their critique of a universal emancipatory subject, which they rejected as both implausible and oppressive. They nonetheless recommended certain Marxist tools, such as Althusser's idea of overdetermination, and Gramsci's concept of hegemony. Overdetermination revises economic determinism, since it allows that not just material forces, but a variety of other factors shape culture and politics;[20] and hegemony reveals how wielding political power requires cultural dominance, the control of intellectual life, everyday norms, and the 'common sense' of society.

Laclau and Mouffe thus sought to overhaul historical materialism to produce a politics of diversity and openness that disrupts the 'logic of equivalence' of traditional egalitarian thought. They urged 'articulatory practices' whereby diverse 'subject positions' of class, race, occupation or sexuality can find expression in 'floating signifiers' that do not predetermine or foreclose the political form, but rather crystallise into 'nodal points' of common resistance. Social antagonisms can thus give rise to coalitions where the socialist struggle to abolish capitalism is complemented by other struggles in a 'proliferation of radically new and different spaces.'[21]

These visions of an open, democratic politics that includes and empowers the disenfranchised and downtrodden on their own terms are compelling. Yet how these different identities are to come together in the interests of equality remains a thorny question.

## Difference's Discontents

I have suggested that some of the interest in difference was inspired, at least implicitly, by egalitarian sentiments, but that it is hard to see how the ideals of difference and equality can be rendered consistent in a way that might form the basis of an egalitarian politics. This was a concern for a number of critics of difference, including some, such as Laclau and Rorty, who were originally among the idea's first exponents, but who had grown sceptical.[22] Rorty, for example, urged the Left in America to overcome its quarrels over difference and form a united front to reinvigorate movements for social justice. Laclau eventually conceded that, 'if universalism does not necessarily lead in a democratic direction, particularism does not do so either,' and argued that demands for change cannot help but 'be made in terms, not of difference, but of some universal principle that the ethnic minority shares with the rest of the community.'[23]

In my view, there are grounds to think that the politics of difference is a poor foundation for the promotion of equality. These grounds can be distilled into four general claims. The first is that difference discussions often focus on *sham inequality* in the sense that the difference in question does not amount to inequality of a morally or politically problematic kind. The second contention is that difference politics, with its focus on cultural parity, sometimes advocates *sham equality*, whilst leaving real inequalities intact. This is related to a third point, that indiscriminately respecting cultural difference can reinforce *real inequality* internal to cultures and shift attention away from economic inequality. Fourth, advocacy of difference serves to undermine the relation between *commonality and equality*, and thereby weakens the pursuit of equality of any kind. I shall consider each in turn.

### Sham Inequality

It might be thought that difference politics must be consistent with the value of equality because one significant motive for focussing on difference is precisely the thought that some people are worse off than others. Members of marginalised cultures are unfairly disadvantaged because their identities are undermined by the dominant culture or cultures. However, some reply that difference politics is prone to finding inequality where there is none, or none that matters. This claim involves a number of considerations. In a famously inconoclastic argument, Barry takes aim at the idea of difference from the perspective of a liberal commitment to impartiality, individual freedom and distributive justice. He argues that, contra defences of multiculturalism, the varying strengths of cultures, per se, are not evidence of inequality. Individuals have complex relations to their identities, which can be multi-layered, shifting, overlapping, and therefore in tension with individuals' interests or desires. Given this dynamism, we cannot appeal to people's identities to deliver reliable judgements about justice or political strategy.[24] As Appiah warns, a focus on identity risks a 'Medusa Syndrome,' where society ossifies people's identities.[25]

Further, in the vagaries of cultural representation what is at issue is not the robustness of a culture as such, but, as Freeman puts it, 'whether some important right or other requirement of justice is violated.'[26] For example, under-representation of members of an ethnic group in a particular profession or office may constitute evidence of an unjust inequality, but it is also possible, according to Barry, that under conditions of equality of opportunity, individuals will make choices, doubtless shaped by their cultural forms, which will lead to a diverse distribution of outcomes. The resulting distribution is not necessarily inequality in any relevant political sense.[27] According to Appiah, 'people are wronged when they are decisively excluded from the exercise of power,' and thus matters of culture should not be assumed to have political relevance.[28]

One issue here is the role of assimilation. The assimilation that occurs when members of a minority group appropriate the norms and practices of the dominant group might be a function of the inevitable advantage enjoyed by majorities, whose pursuits will tend to have greater currency than those of minorities.[29] Assimilation may be a rational move for those aiming to better their life prospects. This is particularly so if the minority culture is itself hierarchical, and thereby limits opportunity to some of its members, as we will discuss further below. We must distinguish between forced and voluntary inclusion of minorities within majority societies. Such distinctions get lost, Levy contends, if we focus on culture per se, rather than the individuals who inhabit cultures.

> Saying that diversity is valuable ... is overinclusive. It doesn't distinguish between a language dying off because the state kills all its speakers and a language dying off because its speakers voluntarily abandon it for a language that has wider use.[30]

It is incontrovertible, however, that minority cultural identities can unjustly disadvantage persons and that the solution involves the recognition of those identities rather than their transcendence.[31] Forcing a group to adopt the practices of the majority, as was done to Aboriginal people in Canada whose children were taken and put into residential schools, is an example. Such a policy was justified by reference to a mistaken conception of equality wherein Aboriginal children should be rid of the burden of their minority culture, but the psychological damage done to them and their parents in fact rendered Aboriginal people profoundly unequal members of Canadian societies. The state was guilty of abominable injustice in these cases. It is important to distinguish such clear cases of domination from the majoritarianism of cultural supply and demand, which, though we might critically interrogate the oppressive practices at work, is not necessarily unjust, and does not necessarily produce unequal wellbeing. In sum, it is not that inequality never arises from cultural difference; it can. But the politics of difference is too quick to find inequality where there is none, or at least no unjust inequality.

### Sham Equality

If the inequalities we decry are in fact sham inequalities, we risk endorsing a vision of equality that is no more than sham equality. Egalitarianism is a sham if our efforts to produce equality have no such effect, or worse, make us less equal. Should we value all cultures equally in recognition of the significance of culture to individual identity? There is a potential paradox here, for any argument about the relevance of culture to identity cannot at the same time hold that one's own culture has no particular priority in one's affections or concerns. If culture is in essence an object of special attachment for its members, then cross-cultural equality, where people across cultures equally value all cultures, is misconceived. Moreover, as Waldron argues, we do not truly appreciate a culture's value if we insist it get automatic respect on the basis of its identity-conferring properties. On the contrary, it shows a 'vain and self-preoccupied contempt' for culture, if it is affirmed simply because it is an aspect of a person's identity. Indeed, this model of cultural recognition seems to presuppose that members of the minority culture seek approbation from a point of view external to them, the point of view of outsiders who are not expected to actually understand or engage with the culture.[32] But this is a poor conception of cultural recognition.

The idea that all cultures should receive equal affirmation suggests our goal is equal self-esteem. But self-esteem involves a host of factors about people's psychological dispositions that are often irrelevant to political equality.[33] Equality is a value that should be rendered objectively in some sense, measured by reference to a criterion that lies outside of the particular claims of any interested party. As Levy puts it, 'an identity-claim is no substitute for an argument' because such claims do not come to terms with 'the fact of our cohabitation and coexistence.'[34] The principle of equality cannot be taken to require that one value other cultures as much as one's own, or that one's opinion of other cultures never causes offence, a view that is, as Appiah puts it, 'intolerant of intolerance of intolerance'.[35] The majority culture, too, cannot simply impose itself without opening it up to question and debate. Equality will be a sham if it relies on some idea of immunity to dispute or reckoning from others. Such immunity would violate the principles of free debate and open discussion necessary for equal citizenship.

A second consideration is that where differences are born of oppression it is not clear that 'recognising' them will be in any way emancipatory. It has been said that brands of feminism that celebrate a feminine ethic end up reproducing stereotypes that are obstacles to the equality of men and women. A similar criticism can be applied to other group identities, where attending to difference can make a virtue of prejudice. The issue is complicated by the different ontological status of different differences, as it were. Some seem a social construction, as is argued of race, whereas others have significant physical aspects, as in the case of disability,[36] and others are complex combinations of various factors.

This point does not go unrecognised by Young, who notes the multifarious ways material practices of oppression can construct the identity of the oppressed. Her focus on 'cultural imperialism,' however, prompts her to advocate the inclusion of unmediated 'heterogeneous and partial discourses' to combat racism, sexism, and all the other 'isms' that are exclusionary, without considering the ways in which some discourses are more liberating than others. Inclusive democracy may not suppress legitimate grievances based on structural disparities, but nor does it offer any standard for distinguishing legitimate from illegitimate claims. No egalitarian would want to 'shut down dialogue' about policy. But mere dialogue, particularly in a context where group membership itself is assumed to supply relevant authority, is no guarantee that egalitarian policy will emerge in the absence of a normative framework of one kind or another (particularly if, as I pursue below, the groups in question are hierarchical either institutionally or culturally).

Laclau and Mouffe are more cognizant of the dangers of taking identities as the basis for democratic politics. They chart a 'progression of articulation' from domination, where the dominated are unaware of their status, through subordination, where the subordinate are aware of their subordination, to oppression, which forms the basis of insurgency. However, the process of articulation is itself not much 'articulated' in their theory; articulation ends up looking like little more than a promissory note that justice will win out. Moreover, this distinction between levels of consciousness is rather difficult to square with Laclau and Mouffe's understandable suspicion of Marxist ideas of false consciousness and their insistence that radical democracy consists simply in a 'polyphony of voices,' each of which constructs its own irreducible discursive identity.

A third problem arises from the nature of diversity itself. The politics of difference risks being stymied in differences that are ultimately irreconcilable. For example, the demands of gay and lesbian groups are not obviously compatible with those of cultural groups that seek the preservation of traditions. The economically disadvantaged who benefit from national social welfare programmes may be at odds with those who advocate regional autonomy, or religions that adhere to a doctrine of self-help. What is the likely outcome of such impasses?

It may be countered that the risks are worth taking. After all, the critique of universalism suggested by the idea of difference underscores the extent to which the universal is in fact the particular – the propertied, men or Caucasians, to take some classic examples – camouflaged as the general. Xenophobia is rampant, as 'the other' is excluded from and oppressed by the pseudo-universalist ontology, metaphysics and justice.

Nonetheless, in refusing to assess the demands of any group by appeal to criteria that lie beyond it, politics is reduced to little more than a brokerage function, as was advocated by liberal pluralist theories in the 1960s.[37] At best, the result is a politics of compromise rather than one of principle; at worst, parochialism runs rampant or, as critics of interest-group theory have long argued, the most powerful (best financed) voices will tend to hold sway. With loss of confidence in a common criterion of justice, 'exclusionary discourses' can develop which lead to intransigency and new forms of xenophobia. Not justice or democracy, but paralysis, crisis or balkanisation may thus be consequences of the idea of difference, so long as transcultural standards with which to assess the claims of difference are ruled out.

### Real Inequality

The focus on cultural equality has often been criticised for neglecting 'real inequality'. The criticism has two aspects: one motivated by a concern for inequalities that are non-cultural in kind, and thus fall outside the multiculturalist framework; the other focussed on inequalities within cultures that the multiculturalist framework finds hard to get into focus.

Gitlin laments how the 'cant of identity' has sidelined addressing deep-seated economic inequality:

> The politics of identity is silent on the deepest sources of social misery: the devastation of cities, the draining of resources away from the public and into the private hands of the few. It does not organize to reduce the sickening inequality between rich and poor.

Difference politics disregards the social and economic inequalities of property and class. For Gitlin, difference politics merely 'retints the class gulf without changing its depth,' so that the feminist insight that the personal is political, is transformed into the dogma that 'only the personal is political.'[38] Fraser similarly argues for a typology of recognition *and* distribution, in order to affirm the ongoing importance of distributive justice, the prospects for which she fears recede whilst identity-based claims predominate.[39] For his part, Barry begins and ends his polemic with a grim summary of persisting economic inequality within liberal democracies. Multiculturalism may find fault with egalitarian policies focussed solely on material disadvantage, but the pursuit of cultural recognition is no substitute for those policies.

This brings us to the second aspect of the real inequality theme: the problem of inequality within cultures. There is a strange inconsistency about protecting minority cultures in order to render their members the equal of members of majority cultures, whilst doing nothing to address inequalities within cultures.[40] Moreover, the inequalities within cultures might be worsened by a policy of cultural protection. Appiah has excellent political intelligence here:

> every 'culture' represents not only difference but the elimination of difference: the group represents a clump of relative homogeneity, and that homogeneity is perpetuated and enforced by regulative mechanisms designed to marginalize and silence dissent.[41]

Thus the critique launched by difference politics can be made on behalf of beleaguered groups within cultures, such as women or sexual minorities. Okin has argued that 'multiculturalism is bad for women' because policies that protect cultures entrench the disparity of power between dominant and subordinate groups within a culture.[42] Levy dubs this problem that of 'internal cruelty,' and notes its complexity, since victims of such cruelty might nonetheless wish to have their cultures protected in some qualified way. The task is to avoid what Green dubs a 'mosaic of tyrannies' where exit from one's culture is the only option for oppressed minorities within minorities.[43]

The problem of the oppression of vulnerable members of minority groups invites a range of responses.[44] Chambers contends it is incumbent on egalitarians to intervene in minority cultures to secure their weaker members autonomy and opportunity.[45] Certainly if the protection of culture means isolation from external influences so that hierarchical practices persist, then recognising cultures and ensuring their members are equal look like contradictory goals. Sometimes multiculturalists are so concerned to promote a nuanced, porous understanding of culture that they lose sight of the character and motivations of traditional and illiberal cultures.[46] Kernohan thus argues that a consistent egalitarian liberalism must permit state advocacy to eliminate cultural practices that are oppressive.[47]

Finally, the preoccupation with culture can lead it to misdiagnose inequalities that have other origins. In such cases, cultural remedies to inequality will be ineffectual or deleterious. American commentators advanced this argument in debates on race, contending that to focus on recognising African-American identity was an 'escape from the hard and expensive challenges' of combatting racism, and in some variants it could 'doom' black Americans to 'second class citizenship.'[48] At root the impulse to affirm difference is driven by a conviction that one's identity should not disadvantage one in social life. Giving identities a voice may be one way of accomplishing this, but if the identities themselves are the products of oppression, and if the power to overcome oppression lies elsewhere, then justice may require mitigating difference, or at least the difference that difference makes.

### Commonality and Equality

The final concern is that the politics of difference threatens to undermine the idea of membership in a common project, an idea adherence to which is a precondition of any effort to remedy inequality among persons. Postmodern scepticism attends any effort to articulate a theory of social change whereby diverse social groups coalesce around common goals. On the postmodern view of difference, political projects can only aspire to the cohabitation of plural identities. Difference is thus bound to defeat the political theories that seek to transcend it. Thus Barry likens contemporary exponents of difference to the reactionaries of the Counter-Enlightenment, concerned with essential differences between peoples and suspicious of universal humanist goals.[49]

From a philosophical point of view, it is not clear that universalism of some kind is avoidable. After all, the fate that met feminists, who rejected the false universalism of androcentric discourse only to find themselves accused of false universalism in the face of racial, sexual and cultural diversity, is a fate that awaits anyone who attacks universalism by affirming an identity. Tully lambastes the 'billiard-ball conception of culture' that depicts cultures as 'separate, bounded and internally uniform';[50] Benhabib complains of the 'reductionist sociology of culture' that reifies cultures as distinct, separate and monolithic.[51] Difference unleashes an endless cycle of accusations and inclusions. Eager to accommodate the grievances of all, sympathetic egalitarians are pushed to recite ever-longer moralising inventories of identities in a futile attempt to dam up the floods of interminable difference. But the accusation of false universalism is never far away.

Ultimately there are as many differences as selves, and thus our invocations of difference always risk essentialism, wherein we reify a certain identity without attention to differences within the identity itself, or the damage done to the new 'other' the reclaimed identity leaves in its wake. Doing justice to the differences that characterise human beings looks futile because the effort to 'do justice' to different identities seems to work to mute their salience. The preoccupation with particular local identities emerges as a kind of 'neo-foundationalism' to ward off the vertigo that besets radical thinkers who have been persuaded by the postmodern critique of foundations but who yearn for the security of the old forms of collectivism the postmodern critique destroyed. We are better off keeping faith with a universalist conception of equality, however much we may harbour suspicions about it.

There is an important distinction to be drawn between a universalism that fails to fulfil its promise and a particularism that repudiates the universal. That we do not always live up to the ideal of universality does not mean that the ideal is of no value. Subjecting the claims of a purportedly inclusive social order to immanent critique to render it truly inclusive is thus important as both strategy and ideal. The critique of difference should make us alert to the ways in which supposedly egalitarian practices were in fact untrue to the principle of equality, but this does not mean rejecting the principle as a mere ruse behind which always hide inegalitarian postures and policies. There are many modern institutional forms that have the character of an aspiration to commonality, from the global justice aims of the United Nations, to the more modest example of the contemporary nation-state which, for all its history of bigotry and partiality, has within it the kernel of an emancipatory promise, the aspiration to unity in diversity, in its civic conception of membership.

The achievement of this promise would doubtless require far-reaching social change, but the commitment to equal membership is a valuable ideal to guide such change. In multicultural Canada, the idea of common citizenship underlay calls for the protection of national welfare programmes in the face of efforts by right-wing politicians, regional and national, to curtail them. It made possible the movement for desegregation in the United States. That members of diverse groups might embrace a more general identity is all the more important in our times, when conflict between particular identities threatens to undermine equality in societies as diverse as the former Soviet republics, post-apartheid South Africa, Western European nations, and countries in the Middle East.

Commonality is inherent in the ideal of citizenship, which requires justifying one's demands to others. Thus multiculturalism can enhance citizenship if it is inclusive, exhibiting the virtues of compromise, commitment to good government, openness and reflection. This variant is one of 'pluralistic integration,'[52] and seeks not recognition for recognition's sake, or exemption from public rules, but accommodation so that members of minority groups can be full participants. Thus this qualified multiculturalism underscores the idea of membership in an entity that commands us to justify our claims to all members, rather than simply express them and demand recognition.

The idea of justification according to a common standard, Waldron suggests, plays a role akin to the way money and prices sort the competing values people put on their desires and possessions.[53] 'Impersonal mediating institutions,' according to Levy, order and reckon local demands.[54] Commonality is thus important in the minimal sense of a common currency that enables one's interests to be reconciled with those of others. More ambitiously, the common also provides a motive for attending to others. A sense that you and I, for all our differences, are both human beings with needs and interests, who aspire to live lives of dignity, will make it more likely that we will be prepared to contribute to measures that promote the wellbeing of both of us.

It is useful to recall that the liberal tradition, concerned with social conflict since Hobbes, takes as its task the mediation of differences among persons. There are some standard liberal resources for mitigating difference. Rights, for example, are employed to defend and resolve individual differences. Whilst rights emerged in the classical liberal tradition as rights to property, the content of rights has shifted over time, permitting new entitlements to political participation and social welfare, thus debunking the Marxist view of rights as inherently bourgeois. Phillips argues that multiculturalism is best understood in terms of individual rights, not group rights, and as such should be viewed as the elaboration 'of standard citizenship rights that ought to be enjoyed by all.'[55]

Some exponents of difference have also adduced a role for rights. Young suggests that 'the specificity of each group requires a specific set of rights for each, and for some a more comprehensive system than for others.'[56] Laclau and Mouffe emphasise that the liberal discourse of individual rights 'permits different forms of articulation and redefinition which accentuate the democratic movement.'[57] The discourse of rights, however, cannot map on to difference in any direct way. Rights cannot take the brute datum of diverse identities at face value; indeed, 'reified notions of culture' where individuals' cultural identity is assumed to define their interests end up denying their agency as rights bearers.[58] Interests must be capable of being formulated in general enough terms to count as rights, which are, after all, accorded on the basis of a common entitlement we are all owed. Otherwise, rights will not be recognised by others as worthy of commanding duties. Questions of human needs, the constituents of human dignity, the prerequisites of self-respect, the sources of human flourishing, these are universal ideals to which rights refer and which rights seek to equalise. Whilst rights discourse can be useful to specify and meet particular needs – parents' rights to childcare, or Aboriginal peoples' rights to land – it does so by reference to a common ideal about a fulfilling or empowered life that should be available to all.

The idea of the common not only justifies rights, it is also consolidated by rights discourse. Rights can produce a sense of shared commitment; though conflict is the occasion for rights, a spirit of community results from the institutionalisation of rights. This is a longstanding feature of American patriotism, which identifies the Bill of Rights as the repository of national ideals.[59] In Canada, the more recent Charter of Rights has had some success in fostering national unity, and calls for more extensive rights such a right to healthcare and proposals for a social charter have been made in the spirit of common values.[60]

## Equality's Prospects

The moral here is that it is important to attend to difference so that no one is excluded from political recognition and participation, so that are all equally part of a 'we' that is the source of social unity. A notion of commonality is implicit in the work of at least some advocates of difference – for example, Young, Laclau and Mouffe – for all their apparent disenchantment with the idea.[61] Nonetheless, it may be suspected that such a claim is at root the nostalgic lamentation of a has-been Marxist (I refuse the term post-Marxist!), who cannot relinquish the ideal of fraternity essential to the socialist project, an ideal that is no more than an impossible 'Rousseauist dream' of a 'unity of subjects with one another' or the utopia of a transparent society embodied in the 'Ideal City.'[62]

Of course, there is no going back. There is no doubt that classical Marxism was shown to be inadequate in light of the diversity of social injustices and the ways with which to counter them, and the importance of a provisional and open approach to theory. The fate of the Bolshevik project confirms the impossibility of simply incanting old orthodoxies, be they about class or revolution, in the context of a new political order.[63] We should heed Marx's advice that historical conditions must inform theory, and theory must develop as those conditions change. It was also no bad thing that liberal politics, which threatened to assume a post-Cold War triumphalism, was chastened by the challenge of difference. Its traditional emphasis on the liberty-possessing individual proved inadequate in the face of ethnic or national strife, strife in which liberal politicians had colluded, sometimes knowingly, in their haste to dismantle the old Communist order. Thus by the late 1990s even stalwart defenders of difference-blind liberal egalitarianism were proclaiming that 'we are all multiculturalists now.'[64]

I continue to think, however, that the salutary insights of difference theory must be reconciled with a form of egalitarianism that operates with a universal conception of equality. How, then, to proceed? As we saw above, there is a significant problem with establishing the appropriate egalitarian measure. On the one hand, we aspire to transcend subjectivity in order to remedy real injustices as opposed to merely perceived ones. Assuring all a high level of self-esteem is clearly a poor criterion of equality (as is taking the existence of high self-esteem as evidence that equality has been reached). On the other hand, when we equalise we seek to improve the lot of real existing persons, who presumably are expected to experience that improvement. Equality must involve some reckoning of the impact of a policy on a person's capacity to live well. Sen's focus on the effect of distributive schemes on individuals' lots in life is instructive. Once we recognise that real inequality 'cannot be readily deduced from the magnitude of inequality of incomes, since what we can or cannot do, can or cannot achieve, do not depend just on our incomes,' then we need to invoke a broader conception of equality focussed on the notion of living well.[65]

The idea of living well, however, does not figure very clearly in the literature critical of difference. This is in part because the framework of neutral liberalism adopted by many of the critics forswears questions of the good. Barry exemplifies this: 'Principles of justice designed for the basic structure of a society ... cannot be deployed directly to address other moral questions.'[66] Yet in his argument about culture, Barry draws on the notion of valuable ways of living. For example, he expresses scepticism about special exemptions from a state curriculum, contending that education provides individuals with the 'opportunity to live better lives' or to 'live well.'[67] It might be argued that children are a special case, not yet capable of making autonomous decisions, and thus exceptions that prove the liberal neutralist rule. However, the interests of children are not easily severed from those of their adult selves. We say that children need to be loved, to develop their talents, to become autonomous, in order to prepare them for adult lives that we suppose ought to take a certain form, working with a conception of a flourishing adult life for which children are being prepared.

In my view, we must look to a conception of human flourishing to reconcile the demands for cultural recognition with the goals of distributive justice. The flourishing conception has classical philosophical antecedents. For Aristotle, happiness or eudaimonia refers to the idea of fulfilling our capacities: activity, informed by reason, in the pursuit of excellence. The ancient Greek conception of 'the good life' is clearly a long way from hedonistic conceptions of happiness, but Aristotle certainly believed contentment was an element of eudaimonia, if not its primary nature: the happy person 'needs the goods of the body and external goods.'[68] Marx's conception of species-being wherein individuals self-actualise through labour as free, creative activity is similar in its emphasis on the development of human potential, and also the wellbeing that follows.[69] Wellbeing involves more than the satisfaction of biological needs. A society which treats its members justly, and thus seeks to render them materially equal, should therefore focus on human flourishing and look to a variety of social forms as vehicles for egalitarian policy.

We cannot determine genuine from sham inequality or equality without considering how people are doing under one distributive scheme as opposed to another. And once we ask how people are doing, we cannot help but enter the terrain of cultural resources. Cultural resources are varied, but they involve goods that enable individuals to live well. The answer to the difference challenge, then, is to consider how equality consists of access to cultural resources that a society might identify and foster. An idea of the common is essential here. The liberal tradition tends to eschew ideas of the common good for a neutral system of resource distribution and individual rights. Universal values are absent from such accounts, and thus it is hardly surprising that advocates of difference insist on the protection of micro-systems of value.

Classical Marxism offered us the commonality of social class, but this is a rather restricted communitarianism since class assumes there will be insiders and outsiders even if, for Marx, the working class is the vast majority of humankind, whose interests are universal, and whose goal is the elimination of class. Here some heresy in socialist doctrine is required, so that social unity is not just the outcome of establishing equality, but its means. That is, in order to address inequality in current, class-divided, ethnically diverse, capitalist societies, we need to forge a society-wide sense of the common now, rather than deferring such a project for the spoils of class struggle. This requires social unity in the form of a commitment to the idea of equality and a conception of the cultural resources necessary for living well. Cohen's ideal of community, where justice requires individuals being prepared to contribute for the sake of the satisfaction of needs other than their own, is one way of motivating the egalitarian ideal.[70]

We are thus led back to the problem of difference. For a common conception of wellbeing confronts the variety of people's capacities to achieve it. Sen holds that human diversity affects the extent to which a person has an adequate level of functioning, which can be impeded by certain kinds of difference: intellectual and physical differences among persons, climatic and epidemiological differences among peoples. From the point of view of a political order, these are not differences to be affirmed or celebrated, but rather to be mitigated by means of the appropriate, nuanced, distribution of resources and opportunities. The idea of mitigating is useful when we consider how cultural difference can inflict costs on members of minority cultures who seek to live a fully human life. It is not the culture that is to be mitigated, of course, but the costs of practicing it, which will require cultural adjustment on the part of the majority or the minority, depending on the case. In some cases, a minority culture is salutary for the wellbeing of us all – for example, Aboriginal peoples' relationship to the land not only demands that the settler majority forge a more just political order, but also, that this relationship be allowed to inform an environmental consciousness premised on a richer connection to nature that is conducive to greater human flourishing for us all. As Kymlicka admits, making use of 'the special ecological wisdom held by indigenous peoples' thus involves going beyond the terms of liberal distributive justice.[71]

Sometimes the recognition of particular differences is a way of furthering unity. An example is religious dress that conflicts with the dress codes of workplaces or schools, or the uniforms of public service, thus posing a choice between cultural observance and equal opportunity. It makes sense to adjust standards of dress to enable participation by religious minorities. However, if safety or security are at issue, then accommodation may be required on the part of the religious observer, not the workplace or school. As Parekh puts it, a distinction should be made between those 'cultural inabilities that can be overcome with relative ease by suitably reinterpreting the relevant cultural norm or practice,' and those that are so fundamental to an individual's sense of identity that they 'cannot be overcome without a deep sense of moral loss.'[72] The purpose of cultural accommodation is to enable the full participation and flourishing of all citizens, a universal ideal if ever there was one. Difference enters the egalitarian domain not as something to be affirmed for its own sake, but something that must be addressed, recognised, accommodated or mitigated – to enable equal human flourishing.

## Conclusion

In *Not for Profit*, Nussbaum asks what it is about human life that makes it

> so easy to lapse into hierarchies of various types – or even worse, projects of violent group animosity? What makes powerful groups seek control and domination? What makes majorities try, so ubiquitously, to denigrate or stigmatize minorities?'[73]

There is no doubt that the politics of difference has provided a salutary challenge to mainstream thinking by forcing us to recognise that egalitarian emancipation is not a likely prospect unless those questions can be addressed in a way that recognises the importance to individuals of cultural identity.

However, a second challenge has been harmful, and that is the way difference has dislodged the idea of equality itself. If individuals bear identities that are incommensurable and require special recognition, then inequalities that attend some identities, or inequalities that lie outside questions of identity, move off the political radar. I have argued that equality must remain our compass: the idea of difference, on its own, is an inadequate normative framework. This is something Nussbaum herself recognises in her affirmation of 'democratic institutions based on equal respect and the equal protection of laws,'[74] and the creation of a 'social culture' that strengthens 'the tendencies that militate against stigmatization and domination' and cultivates 'the tendency to see others as distinct individuals.'[75] So instead of identity as such, we should focus on the interests that accrue from different identities and the extent to which they point to inequalities that require political redress. Do our policies enable individuals to have a better life, a life that individuals themselves experience as better? Our egalitarian goals must centre on wellbeing, a concept neither wholly objective nor wholly subjective, which must have recourse to a common measure. We need to reinvigorate the idea of commonality in the face of a politics of fragmentation in order to focus on the idea of human flourishing. It remains to be seen how this idea should be developed to yield a satisfying egalitarian theory; that is the subject of future chapters. The immediate task is to consider in more depth two particular kinds of difference that challenge the commonality inherent in equality: race and sex.

## Notes

1  R. Descartes, *The Meditations* and T. Hobbes, *Leviathan.*
2  It may be that each distinct individual must justify her beliefs for herself, and must do so precisely because her point of view is unique, but there is nothing about the method Descartes prescribes for her to do so that is distinctive to her situation. In that sense, as epistemic subjects we are all alike.
3  C.B. Macpherson, *Possessive Individualism.*
4  K. Marx, 'On the Jewish Question,' 43.
5  K. Marx and F. Engels, 'German Ideology,' 160–1.
6  Ibid., 160.
7  F. Engels, 'The Origin of the Family, Private Property and the State.'
8  K. Marx, 'Economic and Philosophical Manuscripts,' 84.
9  N. Chodorow, *The Reproduction of Mothering,* and C. Gilligan, *A Different Voice.*
10 L. Irigaray, *This Sex Which Is Not One,* and I. de Courtivron, ed. and introd., *New French Feminisms,* and J. Butler, *Gender Trouble.*
11 H. Hartmann, 'The Unhappy Marriage of Marxism and Feminism: Toward a More Progressive Union.'
12 b. hooks, 'Sisterhood: Political Solidarity between Women,' and M. Lugones and E. Spelman, 'Have We Got a Theory for You! Feminist Theory, Cultural Imperialism and the Demand for "The Woman's Voice."'
13 See J. Habermas, 'Modernity versus Postmodernity,' C. Taylor, 'Foucault on Freedom and Truth,' G. Horowitz, 'The Foucauldian Impasse: No Sex, No Self, No Revolution,' L. Nicholson, ed., *Feminism/Postmodernism,* D. Haraway, *Symians, Cyborgs and Women.*
14 A. Heller and F. Feher, *The Postmodern Political Condition,* 5.
15 J.-F. Lyotard, *The Postmodern Condition,* R. Rorty, 'Postmodern Bourgeois Liberalism,' and *Contingency, Irony and Solidarity.*
16 See selections by J. Kristeva and L. Irigaray in de Courtivron, ed., *New French Feminisms,* and G. Spivak, 'French Feminism in an International Frame.'
17 M. Foucault, *The History of Sexuality, Vol. 1: An Introduction,* 144, and *Power/Knowledge.*
18 D. Haraway, *Symians, Cyborgs and Women,* 184.
19 I.M. Young, *Justice and the Politics of Difference,* 153. See also I.M. Young, *Intersecting Voices: Dilemmas of Gender, Political Philosophy and Policy,* 157.
20 However, as Kolakowski complains, this 'obvious truth' is not particularly Marxist, nor is it very helpful in accounting for, or predicting, historical change; see L. Kolakowski, *Main Currents of Marxism, Vol. 3 The Breakdown,* 485.
21 E. Laclau and C. Mouffe, *Hegemony and Socialist Strategy: Towards a Radical Democratic Politics,* 176–81.
22 Of course, much of the literature critical of difference started not from a concern for equality, but from a right-wing suspicion of multiculturalism, identity politics and 'political correctness' more generally. Perhaps the most prominent American reaction was D. D'Souza, *Illiberal Education: The Politics of Race and Sex on Campus.* See also popular Canadian writings such as N. Bissoondath, *Selling Illusions: The*

*Cult of Multiculturalism in Canada*, and R. Gwyn, *Nationalism without Walls: The Unbearable Lightness of Being Canadian.*

23 R. Rorty, *Achieving Our Country*, and E. Laclau, 'God Only Knows,' *Marxism Today*, December, 1991, 57, and 'Universalism, Particularism and the Question of Identity,' 51. (Intriguingly, neither Rorty nor Laclau acknowledge their roles as exponents of the positions whose implications they here abhor.)

24 B. Barry, *Culture and Equality*, 75–6. See also T. Gitlin, *The Twilight of Common Dreams*, 206–10.

25 K.A. Appiah, *The Ethics of Identity*, 110.

26 S. Freeman, 'Liberalism and the Accommodation of Group Claims,' 25.

27 *Culture and Equality*, 108. J. Levy, *The Multiculturalism of Fear*, 136.

28 Appiah, *The Ethics of Identity*, 136–7.

29 Barry, *Culture and Equality*, 75–6.

30 Levy, *Multiculturalism of Fear*, 108.

31 As Barry's critics have argued; see J. Tully, 'The Illiberal Liberal: Brian Barry's Polemical Attack on Multiculturalism,' J. Squires, 'Culture, Equality and Diversity,' B. Parekh, 'Barry and the Dangers of Liberalism.'

32 J. Waldron, 'Cultural Identity and Civic Representation,' 170.

33 This problem persists in contemporary 'social equality' arguments for deploying criteria of esteem and respect. See C. Fourie, 'To Praise and To Scorn.'

34 Levy, *Multiculturalism of Fear*, 49.

35 Appiah, *The Ethics of Identity*, 154.

36 Though of course whether some physical feature constitutes a disability often depends on context. Deafness, for example, is not a disability in a culture where sign language is the dominant form of expression. See C. Padden and T. Humphries, *Inside Deaf Culture*, ch. 7.

37 See R. Dahl, *Who Governs? Democracy and Power in an American City*, and the compelling critique, S. Lukes, *Power: A Radical View.*

38 Gitlin, *Twilight of Common Dreams*, 236, 225, 152.

39 N. Fraser, 'From Redistribution to Recognition?,' 69–70.

40 J. Carens, *Culture, Citizenship and Community: A Contextual Exploration of Justice as Evenhandedness*, 27.

41 Appiah, *The Ethics of Identity*, 152.

42 S.M. Okin, *Is Multiculturalism Bad for Women?*; see also M. Nussbaum, *Sex and Social Justice*, ch. 1 and 4. S. Benhabib criticises Okin for falling into the 'outsider trap,' to be corrected by a 'complex cultural dialogue,' in *The Claims of Culture: Equality and Diversity in the Global Era*, 103.

43 L. Green, 'Internal Minorities and their Rights.' A. Phillips also warns against the 'almost-exclusive reliance on exit' in *Multiculturalism without Culture*, 134, 157.

44 See A. Eisenberg and J. Spinner-Halev, eds, *Minorities within Minorities: Equality, Rights and Diversity*, and Levy, *Multiculturalism of Fear*, 51–62.

45 C. Chambers, 'All Must Have Prizes,' 168.

46 As P. Kelly observes, 'Introduction: Between Culture and Equality,' in P. Kelly, ed., *Multiculturalism Reconsidered: 'Culture and Equality,'* 16.

47 A. Kernohan, *Liberalism, Equality and Cultural Oppression.*

48 A. Schlesinger, *The Disuniting of America*. See also Barry, *Culture and Equality*, ch. 6.

49 Barry, *Culture and Equality*, 9.

50 J. Tully, *Strange Multiplicities*, 10.

51 Benhabib, *The Claims of Culture*, 4, 103. See also U. Narayan, 'Undoing the "Package Picture" of Cultures,' 1083.

52 J. Spinner-Halev, 'Cultural Pluralism and Partial Citizenship,' in C. Joppke and S. Lukes, eds, *Multicultural Questions*. See also J. Spinner-Halev, *The Boundaries of Citizenship*, 76.

53 J. Waldron, 'Money and Complex Equality.'

54  *Multiculturalism of Fear*, 50.
55  Phillips, *Multiculturalism without Culture*, 164. See also B. Parekh, *Rethinking Multi-culturalism: Cultural Diversity and Political Theory*, 134.
56  Young, *Justice and the Politics of Difference*, 183.
57  Laclau and Mouffe, *Hegemony and Socialist Strategy*, 176.
58  Phillips, *Multiculturalism without Culture*, 8–9.
59  Thus it might be said that what Americans have in common, paradoxically, is that they have rights against the community.
60  I develop some of these ideas in 'Rights, Community and the Charter.'
61  Young underscores the extent to which 'inclusion' is the motivation for her difference theory, appealing to 'global democracy,' in *Inclusion and Democracy*, ch. 7.
62  Young, *Justice and the Politics of Difference*, 229–32, and Laclau and Mouffe, *Hegemony and Socialist Strategy*, 176–93.
63  See E.M. Wood, *The Retreat from Class*, and A. Callinicos, *Equality*. See my 'The Future of Socialist Legality,' 193.
64  N. Glazer, *We Are All Multiculturalists Now*.
65  A. Sen, *Inequality Reexamined*, 28.
66  B. Barry, *Justice as Impartiality*, 216.
67  Barry, *Culture and Equality*, 212, 221, 224.
68  And: 'Those who say that the victim on the rack or the man who falls into great misfortune is happy if he is good are ... talking nonsense,' Aristotle, *Nichomachean Ethics*, 1153b16–1154a6.
69  K. Marx, 'Economic and Philosophical Manuscripts,' 75–8.
70  G.A. Cohen, *Rescuing Justice and Equality*, ch. 1.
71  W. Kymlicka, *Politics in the Vernacular: Nationalism, Multiculturalism and Citizenship*, 151.
72  Parekh, *Rethinking Multiculturalism*, 241.
73  M. Nussbaum, *Not For Profit: Why Democracy Needs the Humanities*, 28.
74  Ibid.
75  Ibid., 44.

# 2 Race, Culture and the Egalitarian Conscience

Does recognising difference contribute to our pursuit of equality or hamper it? We have seen that egalitarians are a muddle on this question, and understandably so. It is now almost a truism to say that the pursuit of equality may require treating different individuals differently. As Dworkin puts it, 'sometimes treating people equally is the only way to treat them as equals; but sometimes not.'[1] When considering how to distribute resources to people in different circumstances, with different needs or capacities, the principled egalitarian will call for an unequal distribution of resources. After all, giving a strapping lad the same-size meal as his bird-like great-aunt treats them both the same, but it will result in unequal levels of wellbeing. It is for the sake of equality that we treat them differently in the matter of the size of their respective suppers.

Marx was the first to put the case for treating people differently on egalitarian grounds. Indeed, he was critical of concepts of justice that relied on the idea of treating everyone the same. That will only aggravate their inequality, Marx argued, so that 'one will in fact receive more than another, one will be richer than another, and so on. To avoid all these defects, right instead of being equal would have to be unequal.' The famous principle of communism, 'from each according to his abilities, to each according to his needs,' is premissed on the idea that equality involves the recognition of difference, in our capacity to contribute, and in our requirements for distributive shares.[2] Yet Marx justified differentiated treatment with an ideal of commonality. Under communism, much that divides us is abolished, be it hierarchical arrangements of production, access to leisure and culture, or double standards in sex and love. Thus whilst Marx insisted on the importance of taking individual differences into account to further equality, this was justified with a view of difference as arbitrary and inessential in matters of justice.

The muddle emerges, however, once we invoke the idea of difference. As we saw in the previous chapter, this idea came to prominence in the 1990s to accommodate human diversity in public institutions and in the distribution of rewards and opportunities. Such invocations of difference were a response to inequality. However, they sometimes suggested policies that were not just short-term strategies for egalitarian ends, but constituted a wholesale revision of equality that forsakes the idea of universality, even as a goal. Difference heralds a world divided into different 'identities': e.g. blacks, whites, Hispanics, Asians; female, male, transgendered; gay, straight, queer, bisexual; and, as they say in Quebec, francophones, anglophones and 'allophones.'[3] Such an emphasis on difference is potentially inegalitarian. Once we see difference as non-arbitrary and essential, we do not just undermine our sense of commonality; we can enthrone inequality itself, the very thing that prompted us to attend to difference in the first place. After all, a canonical version of respect for difference is found in Aristotle, who held that what is just is equal, but that not everyone was to be counted as an equal; the propertyless, women and slaves, for example, were not the equals of the propertied male citizen: 'if they are not equal, they will not have what is equal ... this is the origin of quarrels and complaints – when either equals have and are awarded unequal shares, or unequals equal shares.'[4]

The spectre of Aristotle continues to haunt our thoughts on equality. Aristotle's idea of essential differences has its analogue in the modern era in Huxley's satire of a brave new world where hierarchy is constructed and indoctrinated.[5] Adherents to the idea of difference may abhor such a world, but they deploy typologies and distinctions based on culture, race, gender, or language that suggest essentialism about difference. This essentialism takes different forms. For some, what is essential is that human beings are defined by their respective identities, even if those identities themselves are not essential in the sense of immutable and unchangeable. A person's identity may be contingent, a fluid construct amenable to transformation, but what is not mutable is that she is constituted by that identity. For others, individuals have their particular identities essentially: they cannot be changed. Both positions can be invoked to progressive ends. For example, some have argued that since sexual identity is dynamic people should be entitled to create whatever sexual identity they see fit; others have argued that since sexual identity is a fact of biological nature, those born into the 'wrong bodies' should have the opportunity to have their gender reassigned. It is race, however, that is perhaps the most essentialised difference, and this has rarely led to progressive outcomes. Only consider that era in the history of the United States when the segregation of black and white people was preserved under the banner of 'separate but equal,' prompting many to insist that a genuine egalitarian posture must be 'colour-blind.'

Race is the quintessentially American issue of difference and equality and it is a difference that has had a particularly noxious history. For all the talk of our 'post-racialist' times, and the milestone of Barack Obama's election as president of the United States, racism is frustratingly persistent in the face of varying strategies for (and varying commitments to) its eradication.[6] With race, egalitarians must grapple with a nest of complex issues: slavery, segregation and poverty, biology, class and culture. Despite its American-ness, the issue of race extends beyond borders and territory, throwing into relief the difficulties of difference.

In this chapter I examine two challenging positions on the issue of race that emerged in the context of the difference debates, those of Appiah and

Gutmann respectively. Though they call for us to be 'colour conscious,' both agree that colour blindness remains an ideal. Appiah makes the radical argument that we ought to forsake the concepts of race and racial identity altogether in our efforts to combat racism. Gutmann, in contrast, argues that we must attend to colour in order to achieve the ideal of a society where the colour of one's skin has no bearing on one's prospects. I consider both positions and argue that the idea of colour consciousness loses sight of the egalitarian ideal, and of the egalitarian imperative that motivated it. Human flourishing, I conclude, is a useful compass with which to move beyond race to a society of true equality.

## Race and Colour

Appiah rejects the very idea that humanity consists of different races. His argument is rooted in the philosophy of language. His method is to analyse what the word 'race' means to see whether anything actually answers to our concept, and he contrasts two philosophical accounts of meaning. On the first, the ideational view, the meaning of a word is given by specifying the criteria for its use. Someone knows the meaning of the word if they have mastered these criteria. In the case of 'race' two crucial factors comprise the criteria for its deployment, skin colour and ancestry. We typically declare that someone is of some race in virtue of the fulfilment of one or both these criteria. Appiah notes, however, that neither criterion is conclusive. Skin colour (or any other physiological characteristic) is neither necessary nor sufficient to put someone in a racial category. Consider, for example, the variety of skin colours within the population called 'Hispanic.' And we find many cases where the ancestry criterion is inconclusive, particularly in cases of mixed parentage. And of course the two criteria are sometimes in tension; it is well known that brothers and sisters can have different skin colours – and hence be of different races by the skin colour criterion – but have the same parents, thus being of the same race by the ancestry criterion.[7] So neither criterion suffices to give 'race' a clear meaning.

Appiah notes a subtler view of the relation between meaning and criteria, derived from Wittgenstein. This is the idea that there can be a number of loosely related (and rather messy) criteria associated with the use of a term so that it is correctly deployed when some or other subset of those criteria is fulfilled. Appiah argues that even on such a 'family resemblance' account the concept of race is in bad shape. For if we actually look at 'the sorts of things people believe about what they call "races" and see what races would have to be like for these things to be true of them' we must conclude that there is nothing in the world which fits those beliefs.[8]

Appiah proceeds to consider a second view of meaning, the referential theory. This approach is typically invoked to account for the meaning of 'natural kind terms' (like 'water,' 'iron'). Here the meaning of such a term is given by its relation to the substance (whatever it is) to which the term refers; causal relations link the substance itself to utterances of the term that refers to it. The meaning of the term 'water' is thus the substance $H_2O$, which is causally correlated with our utterances of the term. On such an account, the meaning of a term may be something that transcends the understanding of competent speakers of the language (who may know nothing about the nature of the substance that gives the term its meaning). Appiah considers whether there are any phenomena, any facts of the matter (presumably facts about genetics or biology), which might be correlated causally with our use of the term 'race.' He concludes there are not.[9] There are black, brown, yellow and white people, with some loose set of physical features that correspond to these different skin colours, but these characteristics have the same status as eye or hair colour: there is a huge variety of physical attributes amongst humankind, but no racial essence underlies the diversity. 'Race,' like 'sorcery,' is not a natural kind term; there is no deep phenomenon of nature, biology or genetics, which might give it meaning.

Of course, this does not mean that there are no phenomena charted by the word 'race.' Consider the concept's history, from, say, Jefferson to Victorian natural history and Arnold's idea of Celtic literature. Jefferson the abolitionist was alas also a racialist, convinced of inherent differences between blacks and whites that necessitated segregation. He thought the body was a sign of difference, rather than a cause, but with Darwin and the advent of race science in the late nineteenth century, biology was deemed the determining factor. Against this background Arnold developed the idea that different literatures were correlated with different peoples, not just because of differences in customs and traditions, but also because of biological differences that, he claimed, were the ultimate origin of cultural differences. But the fact is that what our 'race talk' really amounts to is a jumbled mess of notions, derived from a time when we thought that talk of races reflected essential biological characteristics of people, and which is now overladen with social, cultural, political and other significances. Race talk is simply incoherent.

The results of this analysis are, of course, limited. Appiah's findings are useful against those who suppose that the concept of race has (or could be given) scientific respectability. It refutes racists who invoke speculative biology to argue that each human individual carries a certain racial essence. Nonetheless, as Appiah astutely observes, whilst bigots might profess an 'extrinsic racism' based on a hierarchical view of racial characteristics, this may just be a cover for their 'intrinsic racism,' a mere preference for people 'of their own kind,' which is immune to argument.[10]

In any case, it is not clear that Appiah's account discredits the deployment of the concept of race per se. First, that the criteria that govern its use are vague is hardly surprising. The same would go for many central concepts in political philosophy such as nationhood or equality. Like race, the criteria for these terms seem to work well in central cases, but they do not deliver clear answers in hard cases. (One might also wonder whether the inability of theories of meaning to cope with these concepts tells us more about the inadequacy of the theories rather than the concepts.) Second, as Appiah admits, the concept of race is a political reality regardless of whether we can define it

to the philosopher's satisfaction. As Mills puts it, the conventional assumptions of liberal philosophy that society can be modelled on a 'raceless social
contract' belie the reality of race; racism is, after all, 'predicated on a politics
of the body.'[11] We should 'unlearn racial seeing,'[12] but this is in light of a
history where race, a constituent of what Hacking calls 'making up people,'[13]
shapes the identification of others and ourselves. Although Appiah insists on
race's groundlessness, he is no less insistent on the reality of its consequences.
The erroneous signifier nonetheless produces a signified.

## Seeing Through Colour

Gutmann is also critical of the idea of race, and proposes we forsake talk of
race for talk of colour. As she puts it, race consciousness 'assumes that racial
identity is a scientifically based fact of differentiation among individuals that
has morally relevant implications for public policy.' A policy of 'colour consciousness,' however, demonstrates 'the ways in which skin colour and other
superficial features of individuals adversely and unfairly affect their life
chances.'[14] We attend to colour because 'we do not yet live in a land of fair
equality of opportunity for all.'[15] The idea that we should distinguish between
an inegalitarian concept of difference between blacks and whites that goes by
the term 'race,' and an egalitarian concept that goes by the name 'colour,' is
arguably a combination of overly subtle conceptualisation and naïve political
strategy. Gutmann tests her counsel in the thorny questions of preferential
hiring and admissions policies in universities, and her answers, I will argue,
demonstrate the difficulty of pursuing equality by means of consciousness
about difference.

Colour consciousness, Gutmann maintains, dictates preferential treatment for
black Americans in order to break down racial stereotypes and provide role
models for black children and 'diversity models' for all citizens.[16] Her main
example involves a school board, facing austerity measures, which laid off a
white teacher instead of an equally qualified black teacher in an otherwise white
department at Piscataway High School in Iowa. Whilst the case exercised American public opinion, it is hard to see what all the fuss was about. First, it was a
tie-breaking policy, not an outright quota rule. Second, although racially motivated tie-breaking rules are sometimes argued to be problematic when it comes
to hiring – on the grounds that it is hard to be confident that we have ascer-
tained a genuine tie between potential employees – this was a matter of an inevitable layoff. Both teachers had the imprimatur of employment, and one had to
be let go, a tie had to be broken.

Gutmann's strategy, though, is to go further and argue against claims on
behalf of the white teacher, maintaining that no one is owed a particular job
on grounds of justice, and moreover, that colour can be an appropriate qualification for a job. However, in my view, although it may be true that the
laid-off white teacher did not have a right to the particular teaching position
she lost, removing her from her position was certainly a harm and, like all

budget-induced layoffs, arbitrary and to that extent unjust, even if it was, all-things-considered, the least unjust course. Moreover, though no one can claim a right to a particular job, we expect government to scrutinise how people are hired and fired.[17] Society rightly takes an interest in how such decisions are made – that is why we have human rights codes which proscribe discrimination, and why Gutmann, after all, recommends strategies of discrimination of a colour-conscious kind. We obviously do not approve of racists taking skin colour as a disqualification for hiring. The experiences of well-qualified black candidates finding themselves out of the running as soon as they make their appearance at the interview is an injustice that is rightly the object of political remedy. This is not because anyone has an a priori claim to a particular job but, contra Gutmann, because one's skin colour is irrelevant in the assessment of one's qualifications for any job.

These points arise in Gutmann's more difficult example, the AT&T 'Model Plan,' which involved fifty thousand cases of preferential hiring over six years in the United States. According to Gutmann, the plan transformed the work force, breaking down racial and gender divisions of employment throughout the company. It was achieved, however, by passing over 'white men who (everybody conceded) had better qualifications and (in many cases) greater seniority.'[18] Moreover, those passed over could not be described as 'the advantaged' more generally; in effect, it was the marginally more advantaged who were sacrificed. Gutmann quotes Walzer's remark that preferential hiring 'won't fulfil the Biblical prophecy that the last shall be first; it will guarantee, at most, that the last shall be next to last.'[19] Preferential hiring in this case looks more like a matter of jostling for last place. Gutmann admits that a 'massive reparations policy' for black Americans coupled with far-reaching social welfare policies would do more to overcome racial injustice than preferential hiring. She claims, however, that we need first to establish preferential hiring, which is 'fairer and faster than color blind alternatives which burden the weakest group to avoid burdening the next-weakest.'[20] But if doing justice to some involves doing injustice to others, the fact that it does justice (and injustice) faster may be little consolation.

That justice needs to be done is clear. Black people in the United States are constantly denied the dignity of personhood. African-Americans face discrimination whilst grocery shopping, job hunting, apartment seeking – in short, they face discrimination in a myriad of encounters with fellow Americans. Moreover, African-Americans are often excluded from positions of power, and shut out of the educational opportunities that might lead to such positions. They are disproportionately represented amongst the poor, the undereducated, the ill, the drug-addicted, the beaten, the imprisoned, the homeless and the fatherless. Indeed, Sen points out that mortality rates for black men and women in America fall behind that of poor people in developing countries, such as Indians in the state of Kerela.[21] Small wonder then, that there is a crisis in self-respect amongst African-Americans, or what West calls a 'pervasive spiritual impoverishment.'[22]

Does the awful fact of racism justify preferential hiring? There is an inter-generational clumsiness to the approach as a means of reparation for past wrongs. Suppose we want to rectify the unfairness suffered by a distant generation, call it G1, where betas were discriminated against in favour of alphas. Today's generation, G5, thus decides to give preference to betas over alphas. But this does not redress the discrimination suffered by G1: it is not the G5 beta, after all, who was unfairly deprived, nor is it the G5 alpha in particular who benefitted. Moreover, if the preferred G5 beta happens to be advantaged compared to the G5 alpha, then the policy simply compounds inequality. It may be that the G5 beta is nonetheless the victim of unfair discrimination, if not to the degree of G1 betas. African-Americans today still bear the scars of slavery, however distant the institution. McGary suggests that what is at issue is not just retribution for a past wrongdoing, but recognition of the persisting effect of slavery on the self-respect of black people.[23] The flip side of this, of course, is the unearned benefits of whiteness, both in terms of historically inherited privilege and continued preferential treatment.[24] Critical Race Theorists thus emphasise that racism, both past and present, advances the interests of white people.[25]

Affirmative action, however, is a blunt instrument to respond to past wrongs. This is captured in Boxill's remark, 'Insofar as beneficiaries have been denied equal opportunities, they deserve compensation; but it is not clear what compensation they deserve.'[26] The inter-generational reparations problem thus gives some basis for the term 'reverse discrimination.' And such discrimination can burden the apparent beneficiary, too, who bears the stigma of an apparently arbitrary benefit, thus evoking disdain and suspicion from colleagues, and fuelling the fire of the policy's detractors.

Some have argued that the positive results of reverse discrimination compensate for such problems. Gutmann's role-models rationale is outcome-oriented in this way. Being black is understood as an asset that renders the black candidate more qualified, all things being equal, because of the good that hiring a black person can do.[27] This was Dworkin's position in the famous Bakke case.[28] Affirmative action puts black people in milieus usually thought of as white preserves, and thereby serves an important social goal. But the impact of preferential treatment might be negative, or only partially positive, precisely because it is perceived as an injustice. Gutmann argues it is unprincipled to heed the effects of backlash,[29] but once we admit outcome-oriented arguments, preferential treatment is vulnerable to such objections. Affirmative action has also been said to exacerbate the problem of poverty in black communities, by providing opportunities for largely wealthier African-Americans that removes them from the neighbourhoods for which they acted as 'social buffers.'[30]

A more promising tack, perhaps, is to defend affirmative action as a device for achieving fair procedures. Given the enormous evidence of disadvantage faced by African-Americans, America would seem to fail as a 'well-functioning meritocracy,' and thus affirmative action enables a fair evaluation of the talent and promise of black candidates. If we add to this the probability that black people sometimes do not even perceive themselves as candidates in the absence of measures like affirmative action, it would seem the policy does not compromise 'equality of opportunity,' but promotes it.[31] However, although we can easily acknowledge that American society is riddled with systemic racism that impedes the flourishing of African-Americans, we cannot say for certain, that *this* person was disadvantaged in the relevant sense and degree and is thus more meritorious (because more disadvantaged?) than this or that rival.

## Positions and Needs

What of our earlier intuition that the promotion of equality often requires unequal treatment? The idea of need was central in this: the same level of need-satisfaction sometimes requires different shares for different people, be it of income or health care, housing or education. This should be uncontroversial for egalitarians (it is doubtless controversial for non-egalitarians!). It would be churlish to complain that my friend with colitis gets more medical resources than I do; and it would be similarly graceless for my childless colleague to feel hard done by because of my maternity leaves.[32]

When it comes to positions (i.e. university places, jobs, offices), we can seek to correct disadvantages that impair individuals of certain backgrounds in the pursuit of their ambitions. And if the connection between positions and material rewards is attenuated, one's success at the former does not have consequences for the latter. There is also force in the socialist idea of abolishing or mitigating the division of labour by rotating offices and positions to enable greater equality of positional wellbeing. West argues that insofar as we seek to remedy economic disadvantage, affirmative action should be based on social class, so a race-based affirmative action strategy must be seen as a 'redistributive measure,' that will 'enhance the standard of living and quality of life for the have-nots and have-too-littles.'[33]

Unlike our medical examples, however, the desire for positions is not need-based (in the strict sense of need, at least). Thus, in contrast to extra food for big appetites or additional health resources for poor health, the desire for positions is more universally shared. They are things we all want, or at least want to have open to us to want. We might not think we all merit high positions – we do not all have the same talent, qualifications, or ambition – but we will be concerned that it is only talent, qualifications and ambition that accounts for whom amongst us is successful. So long as there is a scarcity of positions, we will be acutely conscious of the fact that other people's success in gaining them increases our chance of failure. Positions are features of a public culture: they confer status and power on their holders; they have symbolic rewards and thus have an impact on the culture of community, the institutions of democracy, and so forth. Ford complains that the 'phobia' about quotas is 'largely a conceptually driven obsession that is dramatically out of proportion to any practical risks.'[34] But it is relevant that the American policy of affirmative action, when introduced in 1965, was originally understood in the 'weak' sense of tiebreaking, promoting recruitment, and remedying material disadvantage. 'Strong' affirmative action, in the sense of an outcome-based approach, such as reverse discrimination, preferential treatment or quotas, came to overtake that original understanding of the term.[35]

West concedes that affirmative action 'imperfectly conforms' to egalitarian redistributive ideals, but takes the persistence of material inequality to make it a strategic necessity: 'progressives must secure whatever redistributive measures they can, ensure their enforcement, then extend the benefits if possible.'[36] This suggests that egalitarians should endorse any means, so long as it shifts goods from the haves in the direction of the have-nots. But such a 'Robin Hood' view of redistribution takes no interest in the important distinction between fair and unfair redistributions. Our universalist (or colourblind) ideals, whilst acknowledging the need for difference in the distribution of material goods, are in tension with difference as a strategy for distributing positions.

It is worth noting the obvious, that our efforts at the material level have been pretty paltry, and equal wellbeing in the form of health, education or standards of living is far from a reality. So we cannot conclude at this point that the distribution of positional wellbeing is unresponsive to material equality. Thus we should concentrate on remedying material inequality, both for its own sake and to effect improvements in positional wellbeing that will further racial justice. Current approaches to the problem of racism (and sexism) that aim for parity can avoid the taint of procedural injustice by a proactive policy that seeks out minority candidates, promotes their careers, and builds networks of support. Indeed, the idea of parity so construed is a better way of responding to what Medina calls 'epistemic arrogance' and 'active ignorance' where the privileged are accustomed to being 'immune to contestation,' for it will produce the kinds of minority candidates who are equipped to deal with the challenges of infiltrating a white domain.[37] A more thoroughgoing egalitarianism pursues racial parity by devoting resources to members of disadvantaged groups for education and training, and seeking to remedy differences in capacity due to social circumstance. Appiah notes we might even try to discover how to eliminate those differences in endowments that remain once differences in advantage are eliminated.[38] Actively recruiting among underrepresented minorities will thereby produce outstanding candidates from minority groups, 'epistemic heroes,' who are courageous and capable in pursuing participation, despite the dissonance of seeking positions of power from a background that assumes powerlessness.[39]

Concepts like the public good or quality of life are not often considered in egalitarian argument. But they should be. Racism means unjust treatment and a diminished quality of life for the persecuted; but it also poisons a public culture, spawning a range of social ills, be they mistrust and incivility, fatalism, violence and despair, insecurity and urban decay, a diminished quality of life for all. Moreover, such ills contribute to wider forms of inequality, as the economically disadvantaged members of all racial groups tend to live and work in less secure circumstances and bear the brunt of the culture of intolerance. Our efforts to correct racial injustice should be wary of strategies that intensify resentment among the less privileged, and instead seek measures that are in keeping with a truly egalitarian ethos.

## Counter-Cultures

Gutmann's colour-conscious perspective prompts her to support the idea of redrawing electoral districts so that black citizens are better able to elect black candidates. Proportional representation is valuable, she says,

> not because black people 'think alike, share the same interests and will prefer the same candidates at the polls' but because blacks ... are more likely (as a matter of contingent, historical fact) to place the interest of overcoming racial injustice at the top of their agenda.[40]

Gutmann contends that without racialised proportional representation, African-Americans, being a minority, are consistently unable to elect the representatives of their choice.[41] Note that colour consciousness here is of a kind different from other parity policies, which are fundamentally assimilationist in orientation, enabling in Walzer's words, 'a kind of escape from group life for people whose identity has become a trap,' giving 'opportunities to individuals, not a voice to groups.'[42] Proportional representation on the basis of race supposes the persistence of identities, and the entrenchment of group life.

On the other hand, proportional representation does not appear to exact unjust burdens, as is so often charged in the case of affirmative action. As Thernstrom puts it, 'a white denied a seat on a city council cannot claim entitlement on the ground of "merit".'[43] Qualification for office is not measured by meritocratic standards of the kind we encounter in hiring, and there are a number of grounds, based on democracy and sound public policy, to have a government that is more representative of the governed. The 'voice-of-colour thesis,' that people of oppressed races have unique perspectives that enhance the understanding of the white majority, is particularly salutary for political office.[44] It thus makes sense for political parties to adopt aggressive recruitment strategies to produce a diversity of candidates, to seek out minority candidates in particular, and for governments to seek parity in the appointment of ministers or special advisors. Racialised electoral districts, in contrast, run counter to these integrative efforts, dividing citizens into groups, with a fragmentising effect on public culture. Black representatives will be reduced to 'special interest' advocates, and worse, white representatives will thus be 'let off the hook' when it comes to considering perspectives other than their own. As Thernstrom warns, a 'heightened sense of group membership works against that of common citizenship.'[45] It seems naïve to think we can adopt colour-conscious strategies with the object of ultimately minimising the significance of colour, that we can be merely instrumentally colour-conscious.

Consider what Appiah calls the 'substitution of cultures for races,' prompted by multiculturalism in the United States.[46] This is illustrated by the rise of the term, 'African-American,' now firmly established as a successor to 'black.' To call oneself an African-American invites a parallel with the designation afforded citizens of immigrant cultures, e.g. Korean-Americans or Italian-Americans. (Appiah, incidentally, is straightforwardly an African-American, having immigrated to the United States from Ghana.) On the one hand, this may be deemed the 'gallant' response of a 'downtrodden and despised people' who seek greater self-respect.[47] The term allows us to appreciate African-Americans' complex identities, the layered and multifarious relationship that they, like their fellow citizens, have to American society. On the other hand, the move might seem to devalue the authenticity of black Americans: who better qualifies as an American, 'period,' than a black person whose ancestors were amongst the first inhabitants of the United States? It appears that the way to gain power and respect is to dilute one's claim to the common identity of being American.[48] One long-time colour-blind liberal regretfully concedes that 'multiculturalism is the price America is paying for its inability or unwillingness to incorporate' African-Americans into society.[49] Here we have perhaps the saddest indictment of the failure of colour-blind strategies to beat racism, as egalitarians opt for, in Phillips's words, 'substituting bland talk of cultural diversity for a more pointed analysis of racism.'[50]

## Recognising and Misrecognising

In his philosophy of cultural recognition Taylor argues that individual well-being requires a sense of authenticity that comes from being faithful to one's identity. The idea of being true to oneself is often couched in highly individualistic terms, but Taylor points out that authenticity involves interaction with others; it is dialogical. Authenticity thus requires recognition not only by like others who share our culture, but by unlike others, outside our culture. This is what underlies, for example, the idea that Quebec be recognised as a distinct society in Canada's constitution.[51]

It is clearly the case that African-Americans share a social identity in the United States. Appiah, however, is doubtful that they share a cultural identity, a common set of values, beliefs and practices. To assume a common culture reinstates the Arnold view of a world where different bodies have different essences, so that whites can lay claim to Shakespeare and blacks to jazz, a disservice to blacks and whites, jazz and Shakespeare.[52] Such views might serve to strengthen the subjugated culture, as Arnold sought to enhance the prestige of the Celts' minority culture in Britain. The 'black power' movement of the 1960s and 1970s seemed a clear political imperative to heighten the identity of a subjugated group in the context of ongoing racism. Though militant and separatist, black power was explicitly focussed on eliminating oppression and building equality, goals that are less apparent in calls for recognition of a distinctively African identity, which see identity as an end in itself.[53]

Cultural recognition is an odd way of couching the problem of race in America, where one insists on an African identity which marks one as distinct from white Americans, and at the same time seeks recognition from these white others. In fact, Appiah writes, African-Americans are who they are because of their membership, however distorted, in American society. This wider membership is the basis for a cross-identity appeal to justice and equality, in contrast to the relativistic assumption that no culture can be assessed by those outside of it.[54] Ford argues that common cultural norms 'emerge from the collision of a multiplicity of older traditions' and as such are less monolithic and univocal than is usually supposed. Moreover, he argues, 'institutions and societies require *some* set of shared norms: it often matters less what the norms are than that they are shared.'[55] Minority norms, in contrast, focus on what is not shared, and can bring with them the exclusionary politics of sexism or anti-gay views.

The fate of the black diaspora around the world confirms the elusiveness of a quest for true cultures. Hall has trenchantly observed of Caribbean identities that 'questions of identity are always questions about representation. They are always questions about the invention, not simply the discovery, of tradition.'[56] The great black American intellectual, Du Bois, spoke of Africa as his fatherland, but he also conceded that it was neither the land of his father nor of his father's father, and that his mother's connection was tenuous. African culture can be difficult to link to black Americans, so that to choose Africa over other sites of discrimination or colonisation, as Appiah incisively observes, ends up being a choice 'that racism imposes on us – and just the choice we must reject.'[57]

Taylor distances himself from multiculturalists who demand that all cultures are given equal value a priori; this, he says, involves a refusal genuinely to engage with a culture and is thus inimical to recognition.[58] But if this is so, we face a conundrum. On the one hand we prize our identity, as an essential aspect of ourselves; we cannot take on other identities, but we believe that their bearers, too, require cultural recognition and we thus look to the state to recognise all cultures. On the other hand, we harbour private judgements about the worth of other cultures in comparison to our own, judgements which are likely to be self-serving, and which render the possibility of cooperation across cultures fragile and insecure.

As we saw in the last chapter, there are grounds for scepticism about the 'politics of recognition.' When I say I recognise a person I am saying that I know who the person is; I cannot recognise someone I have never encountered before. It is thus odd to expect recognition of the unfamiliar, the different. Indeed, if we are asked to recognise strangers who share superficial characteristics like skin colour or an accent, then we are likely to accentuate their otherness. Recognition is a curious measure for political life. The demand for recognition is unabashedly subjective in its orientation, shaped by the perceptions of subjects who are defined as occupying perspectives we do not occupy, and with no measure but the say-so of those who seek to be recognised. If they misperceive their situation, if they are paranoid or power-mad, we have no recourse. Thus the politics of difference is self-perpetuating in a way that seems immune to any reliable measures of success or failure.

Indeed, the idea of survival implies that culture is preserved for its own sake, with no necessary relation to the interests of individuals, now or in the future. 'Survivance' in its Quebecois variant is explicitly decoupled from individuals' rights or freedoms. Taylor goes so far as argue that recognition involves collective goals such as 'making sure that there is a community of people here in the future' or that 'future generations continue to identify' with the culture in question.[59] That collective identity accompanies skin colour is hard to square with the fight against racism. Such a view, Selby contends, makes race 'a matter of ontology, sinking us right back into the quicksand of essentialism.'[60] Black solidarity should have no truck with the biological idea of race or the idea of a racial cultural identity. For Selby, 'if there were no racial stigma, this valorization of blackness would be unnecessary, even obnoxious,' yet in the real world of racism, black pride and black solidarity are crucial to overcome racial inequality.[61] Homosexuals, too, have insisted on the primacy of gay identity to provide a positive badge to counter the longstanding negative one. Such moves, however, are best regarded as strategies, not as goals in themselves. Thus 'speaking as someone who counts in America as a gay black man,'[62] Appiah makes the following moving comment:

> If I had to choose between Uncle Tom and Black Power, I would, of course, choose the latter. But I would like not to have to choose. I would like other options. The politics of recognition requires that one's skin colour, one's sexual body, should be politically acknowledged in ways that make it hard for those who want to treat their skin and their sexual body as personal dimensions of the self. And 'personal' doesn't mean 'secret' but 'not too tightly scripted' ...[63]

## Class Consciousness

One theme in the debate about affirmative action is the role of social class. Gutmann is concerned to refute a 'class not race' argument for preferential treatment that is sometimes broached in the United States. She argues that the fact that being poor is an obstacle to success in American society does not erase the obstacle of race. The appropriate response, she holds, is to use 'both class and colour' as considerations in, for example, university admissions or jobs.[64] The concept of social class, 'that most neglected of American identities,'[65] however, resists such compromises. Class is not a cultural identity per se, although progressives sometimes emphasise the value of working class culture, as was evident in claims made on behalf of threatened mining communities in the 1980s British miners strike. But social class is unique in that to do justice to it requires, not its recognition in public institutions and the allocation of rewards and opportunities, but its elimination. Marxists ask us to be class-conscious in order to devise strategies that spell the end of class, the

end of social divisions based on economic position. It is therefore disingenu-
ous, evidence of a peculiarly American myopia on the subject, to include class
in the list of identities to be recognised, or to speak of 'classism' rather than
capitalism in the call for social change. Thus even if economic reductionism
is decried as 'White Marxism,'[66] it is no solution to offer up a racial reductionism and treat class as an identity like race.

The debate about affirmative action, however, assumes the intractability of
class. If we are considering how we ought to mete out advantages, status,
income and position, then we are not remedying class, we are just rotating its
disadvantages, at best aiming for a society where some escape a bleak class
destiny, others are divested of a privileged one, but class divisions remain.
Some jump class, others slip down, like a game of snakes and ladders. The
injustice intrinsic to class persists in this framework. We are colour conscious
or class conscious in light of an egalitarian ideal where race is irrelevant and
class has disappeared. This ideal does not mean, of course, a society of sameness or homogeneity. Variety will remain due to the wide array of human
needs, and because there is 'diversity in the service of individual wellbeing.'[67]
Despite that diversity, there are ways of living, Appiah cautions, that are
unworthy of us. There are 'boundaries to Millian diversity,' and they may be
set by autonomy itself, which is undermined by some – perhaps too 'tightly
scripted' – ways of life. In thinking about combatting the inequalities of race,
we should focus on how the flourishing of human beings requires an unfettered path to a life well lived, so individuals may choose from a plethora of
valuable ways of living, shaped by a variety of cultures and interests. At issue
is a life characterised by 'ethical success,' the 'creation and experience of
significant things.'[68] Thus in combatting racism we must make it possible for
those hitherto barred from flourishing to have the opportunity to fulfil their
potential, to realise their capacities; in short, to live well.

## Conclusion

Wellbeing or flourishing is what we seek to improve when we attend to
inequality. Racism undermines human flourishing, not just for the members
of racial minorities who are the victims of appalling prejudice and discrimination, but for all members of society, who experience the public bads of injustice, mistrust, incivility, insecurity, poverty and urban blight. In order to
remedy the disadvantage of racism, we must ensure that our strategies
improve human wellbeing. Quotas or reverse discrimination are at odds with
the norms of procedural justice, and can undermine the community's values.
They thus threaten to diminish human wellbeing and are poor instruments
for racial equality. Instead, policies that tackle material inequality, and that
seek to empower racialised others, through education, job training, and
support networks, are our best course.

Whilst Gutmann's call for colour consciousness and Appiah's deconstruc-
tion of race seem at odds, they are united in their hope that the colour-blind
ideal might one day be realised. Neither is attracted to fatalistic views of

inequality which stress incommensurable cultural identities. They both aspire to a society where all individuals 'have effective access to many cultural possibilities, no single one of which comprehensively defines any person's identity and all of which are subject to change by the creative efforts of individuals.'[69] And perhaps the main reason for being hopeful that such a society is possible is the simple fact that it is the white philosopher who counsels attention to colour whilst the black philosopher makes a case against it. Their work would have a very different impact if Appiah and Gutmann had taken each other's position.[70]

We are different in our needs and desires, talents and characters, advantages and disadvantages. And the terrain of politics is where these differences come to light, produce conflict and, we continue to hope, are remedied or resolved. But these differences matter in politics because of our common humanity, our sameness as moral beings, that gives us each equal claim to consideration. The persistence of an ugly racism in the United States where blacks and whites are so cruelly unlike each other in their life prospects, health, education, income, careers, political positions, family structure and psychological wellbeing, has understandably prompted many to forsake such universal ideals. Yet, without the idea of commonality, we cannot articulate our differences or heed those of others, nor can we redress the material inequalities that beset a disproportionate number of African-Americans. In order to make people equal in their wellbeing, an idea that implies an objective, common measure, however diversely it might be realised, we should be provisionally colour conscious. We cannot deny the reality of racial difference, nor abdicate responsibility for remedying the injustice of its effects. We can, however, rein in the politics of difference. In the rich diversity of flourishing lives, and in the political domain of contest and debate, there will continue to be plenty with which to distinguish one from another. Let us turn now to consider a persisting difference that besets the politics of equality to which this book aspires: the difference of sex and gender.

## Notes

1  R. Dworkin, 'Liberalism,' 126.
2  Marx, 'Critique of the Gotha Programme,' 531.
3  'Allophone' is Quebecois slang for immigrants and their descendants.
4  Aristotle, *Nichomachean Ethics*, 1131a6–27.

5     Delta children wear khaki. Oh no, I don't want to play with Delta children. And Epsilons are still worse. They're too stupid to be able to read and write. Besides they wear black, which is such a beastly colour. I'm *so* glad I'm a Beta.... Alpha children wear grey. They work much harder than we do, because they're so frightfully clever. I'm really awfully glad I'm a Beta, because I won't work so hard. And then we are much better than the Gammas and Deltas. Gammas are stupid. They all wear green, and Delta children wear khaki. Oh no, I *don't* want to play with Delta children.

A. Huxley, *Brave New World*, 27

6  Compare O. Patterson's optimistic account, *The Ordeal of Integration: Progress and Resentment in America's 'Racial' Crisis*, ch. 1, and P. Taylor, *Race: A Philosophical*

*Introduction*, 184. Taylor counsels the need for a 'brake on the runaway hopes of post-racial exuberance' to see how race 'continues to frame our individual experiences and shared prospects.'

7  K.A. Appiah, 'Race, Culture, Identity: Misunderstood Connections,' 34–6.
8  Ibid., 37.
9  See K.A. Appiah, *In My Father's House: Africa in the Philosophy of Culture*, 34–7.
10  Ibid., 13–15.
11  C. Mills, *The Racial Contract*, 124, 53.
12  L. Alcoff, *Visible Identities: Race, Gender and the Self*, 197.
13  I. Hacking, 'Making Up People,' cited by Appiah, 'Race, Culture, Identity,' 78.
14  A. Gutmann, 'Responding to Racial Injustice,' 112.
15  Ibid., 125.
16  Ibid., 131. Gutmann, writing in the 1990s, tends to use the term 'black'; Appiah prefers 'African-American,' though not without commentary and qualification (I offer some reflections on the term later in this chapter). One disadvantage of 'African-American' is that it is restricted to the confines of the U.S. Here I use both terms.
17  Or at least egalitarians believe this. But see J.J. Thomson, 'Preferential Hiring.'
18  Gutmann, 'Responding to Racial Injustice,' 136. Parenthetical remarks are Gutmann's.
19  Ibid., 136, citing M. Walzer, *Spheres of Justice*, 154.
20  Ibid.
21  See A. Sen, *Development as Freedom*, 96.
22  C. West opens his book, *Race Matters*, with what might be called an ordinary extraordinary story about unsuccessfully hailing a taxicab in New York. Over an hour, ten cabs refuse him and he is forced to take the subway and walk to his appointment with his publishers, arriving late.
23  H. McGary, 'Forgiveness and Slavery,' 110–12. B.E. Lawson notes the need for a word like 'refugee' to designate the descendants of slaves to capture the idea that slavery has persistent and profound cultural and psychological effects; see 'Moral Discourse and Slavery.'
24  H. Winant, 'Behind Blue Eyes: Whiteness and Contemporary U.S. Racial Politics.' (Interestingly, presumably in deference to South Americans, Winant deploys the more specific term 'North American' to refer to the U.S., overlooking those of us above the 49th parallel!)
25  R. Delgado and J. Stefanic (eds), *Critical Race Theory: An Introduction*, 8.
26  B. Boxill, 'Equality, Discrimination and Preferential Treatment,' 338.
27  See Ibid., 339–41 and B. Boxill, 'The Morality of Preferential Hiring.'
28  See R. Dworkin, *A Matter of Principle*, chs. 14–16.
29  Gutmann, 'Responding to Racial Injustice,' 149.
30  W.J. Wilson, *The Truly Disadvantaged: The Inner City, the Underclass, and Public Policy*.
31  L.C. Harris and U. Narayan, 'Affirmative Action as Equalizing Opportunity: Challenging the Myth of "Preferential Treatment." '
32  But see P. Casal and A. Williams, 'Rights, Equality and Procreation.'
33  West, *Race Matters*, 63.
34  R. Ford, *Racial Culture: A Critique*, 194.
35  See L.P. Pojman, 'The Moral Status of Affirmative Action,' 240–1.
36  West, *Race Matters*, 65, 64.
37  J. Medina, *The Epistemology of Resistance*, 32.
38  Appiah, 'Race, Culture, Identity: Misunderstood Connections,' 102.
39  Ibid., 213.
40  Gutmann, 'Responding to Racial Injustice,' 154.
41  Of course, this is the fate of many a minority in a 'first past the post' system – it applies to many Tory voters in British elections that produce Labour governments, people not usually thought to be beset by bias or disadvantage.

42 M. Walzer, 'Pluralism: A Political Perspective,' 251.
43 A. Thernstrom, *Whose Votes Count? Affirmative Action and Minority Voting Rights*, 242.
44 Delgado and Stefanic (eds), *Critical Race Theory*, 10.
45 Thernstrom, *Whose Votes Count?*, 243.
46 Appiah, 'Race, Culture, Identity,' 83. The cultural turn in anti-racist thought can be found in some important recent works; see R. Gooding-Williams, *Look, a Negro! Philosophical Essays on Race, Culture and Politics* and M.K. Asante, *The Afrocentric Manifesto*.
47 West, *Race Matters*, 4, 32, 28.
48 Thus in his introduction to the Appiah and Gutmann essays, D. Wilkins laments the tenuous links between Africa and African-Americans that 'separates African-Americans from every other group of hyphenated Americans,' yet speaks hopefully of 'our rich cultural heritage' as something democratic institutions ought to foster, 'Introduction,' 15. For an interesting critique of the term 'African-American' see R.W. Grant and M. Orr, 'Language, Race and Politics: From "Black" to "African-American."'
49 N. Glazer, *We Are All Multiculturalists Now*, 146.
50 A. Phillips, *Multiculturalism without Culture*, 56.
51 C. Taylor, 'The Politics of Recognition.'
52 Appiah, 'Race, Culture, Identity,' 90.
53 Compare S. Carmichael and C.V. Hamilton, *Black Power: The Politics of Liberation in America*, and M.K. Asante, *The Afrocentric Manifesto*.
54 Ibid., 84.
55 Ford, *Racial Culture*, 153. Thus Ford rejects 'diversity' rationales for affirmative action, for a racial justice justification for requiring that 'prestigious selective universities be racially inclusive,' 57.
56 S. Hall, 'Negotiating Caribbean Identities,' 5.
57 Appiah, *In My Father's House*, 41–2.
58 Taylor, 'Politics of Recognition,' 70–1.
59 Ibid., 58–9.
60 T. Selby, *We Who Are Dark: The Philosophical Foundations of Black Solidarity*, 232.
61 Ibid., 97.
62 K.A. Appiah, 'Identity, Authenticity, Survival: Multicultural Societies and Social Reproduction,' 162–3.
63 Appiah, 'Race, Identity, Culture,' 99.
64 Gutmann, 'Responding to Racial Injustice,' 146. See R. Kahlenberg, 'Class, Not Race,' and O. Patterson, *The Ordeal of Integration: Progress and Resentment in America's 'Racial' Crisis*, 'Conclusion.'
65 Appiah, 'Race, Identity, Culture,' 80.
66 See C. Mills, *From Class to Race: Essays in White Marxism and Black Radicalism*, and *Radical Theory, Caribbean Reality: Race, Class and Social Domination*.
67 Appiah, *The Ethics of Identity*, 153.
68 Ibid., 170.
69 Gutmann, 'Responding to Racial Injustice,' 175.
70 I am indebted to an anonymous referee for the *Canadian Journal of Philosophy* for this point.

# 3 Androgyny and Girl Power: Sex, Equality and Human Goods

Of all struggles for equality, the one that has perhaps met with the most success is the struggle for equality between men and women. Of course, sexual inequality remains acute in many non-Western countries, and women and men remain unequal in the West too: women continue to earn, on average, less than men; women continue to do a disproportionate share of childcare and housework; and women are still the victims of sexual violence. But it is striking how much in a mere generation or two social attitudes have changed. Whereas my mother grew up assuming her destiny was solely to be a wife and mother, my daughter assumes that any walk of life is open to her. Of course, the dominant beliefs of a generation are not necessarily accurate guides to the reality of social forces. My mother became a high-ranking civil servant later in life and thus turned out to have more options than she once supposed, whereas my optimistic daughter will undoubtedly discover her opportunities are more constrained than she realised. Nonetheless it is now a commonplace belief that men and women are more or less equal in ability and equally entitled to pursue opportunities in the public and private domains, a belief that would have been thought radical not long ago. And this belief is expressed in real moves towards equality: women's higher participation in employment, and in high-earning and high-status positions; more gender parity in housework and childcare; and women's greater self-determination in the experience of sexual relations and in matters of reproduction.

There is, however, a paradox. If the feminist movement has made the greatest strides in the pursuit of equality, it must also be said that recent feminist theory has been suspicious of the concept's value. Feminists have argued that the ideal of equality, by occluding sexual difference, has ended up repressing femininity and disempowering women, rather than producing a society where both masculinity and femininity can flourish. In this chapter, I consider the problem of equality and wellbeing in light of the debate about sexual difference. I argue that the seemingly intractable questions of gender need not be solved in order for us to make progress on equality. If we instead focus on human flourishing, we can illuminate the obstacles to equality posed by gender and sex, thereby opening up an inclusive egalitarianism that seeks justice for all.

## Androgyny

To what extent can women and men extricate themselves from the influence of stereotypes and social roles and live as equals? Such stereotypes are many, and they sometimes find expression in social theory. There is the view of women's subjectivity as fundamentally passive, whether seen as an innate identity or the effect of repressive norms. Indeed, sometimes the very ideal of agency is rejected as a masculine preoccupation, to be countered with a feminine ideal of human bonds of nurturing and care. At the other extreme is the idea of the autonomous agent, androgynous or subversive, able to shake off any and all norms in spontaneous acts of sexual defiance. Thus for many feminists, sexual equality depends on the prior clarification of gender identity. In what follows I will explore this theme by considering two models: on the one hand, the norm of androgynous individualism, and on the other, the ethic of care.

From the outset feminists were concerned to depict women as fully functioning, capable agents, similar to men in all relevant respects. Thus in the eighteenth-century the pioneering feminist Wollstonecraft took liberal ideas about individuals as bearers of rights and applied them to women, arguing that, like men, women possessed fundamental rights to liberties and opportunities. Differences between the sexes she put down to the inferior enculturation of girls which, once brought into line with the male norm, would enable women to become self-determining, autonomous agents, just like men. Indeed, so optimistic was Wollstonecraft that she speculated that under the right social conditions physical strength would be more or less equal in men and women. Who knew what women were capable of, once they ceased to be brought up like hot house plants, deprived of exertion or stimulation?[1] Mill endorsed this view: women should be allowed the same opportunities as men and would thereby show themselves to be no less capable than their male counterparts.[2] Socialist ideas of sexual equality also presupposed the irrelevance of sexual difference. Marx and Engels insisted that women possessed an equal capacity for productive labour; and the Bolshevik Bogdanov, in a prescient anticipation of transgender politics perhaps, went so far as to propose an egalitarian utopia where it would be difficult to discern exactly who is what sex.[3]

With the reinvigoration of feminist ideas in the 1970s, there emerged the idea of gender, a social construction, to be distinguished from sex, a biological fact. And feminists articulated an egalitarian ideal of androgyny, where masculine and feminine characteristics would have no necessary connection to biological sex, as likely to devolve upon men as on women. For some feminists, the androgyny called for drastic measures; e.g. Firestone proposed that test-tube babies become the norm to eliminate biological difference in reproduction.[4]

The idea that reproduction was the chief obstacle to androgynous equality is manifest in Thomson's famous argument for abortion. Thomson used the model of the autonomous agent to argue against the idea of obligations to the foetus. The issue in the abortion debate is usually thought to turn on whether the foetus is a person. Thomson, however, produced a case for the pro-choice position with a very radical first premiss: that is, even if we suppose foetuses are persons from the moment of conception, women are free to abort them. To prove this, she produced an argument from analogy where a woman wakes up one morning to discover she has been kidnapped and a world-famous violinist with a fatal kidney ailment is plugged into her circulatory system. For his life to be saved, he must stay plugged into her for nine months. Must the woman allow her body to be used in this way?

Thomson claims that it would be an act of great charity, a supererogatory action, for the woman to sustain the violinist, but she should feel free to 'abort' him, should she wish: 'For if you do not kill the violinist unjustly, you do not violate his right to life.'[5] Just as the woman has no obligation to the violinist, person though he may be, she has no obligation to the foetus. The decision to carry a pregnancy to term is tantamount to a decision to be a Good Samaritan; women are autonomous agents, just like men, with no intrinsic duties to help others. Thus the feminist position here affirms a libertarian conception of social relations where individuals own their bodies and its powers.

This essay has had enormous influence. MacKinnon made a more radical call for liberation from what she considered the coercion of heterosexual sex and not just its consequences, but she did not take issue with the idea that the foetus is a person who can be killed because it infringes women's rights to autonomy.[6] *Roe v. Wade* found that the right to have an abortion, subject to certain conditions, followed from the American constitutional right to privacy. Canada's Supreme Court struck down legislation restricting abortion because it abridged women's right to security of person. Justice Wilson, in a minority opinion, argued further that the constitutional right to liberty required abortion on demand in the early stages of pregnancy.

Thomson's argument is obviously emancipatory for women in its insistence that women are not 'natural' mothers, always obligated to nurture others, but self-determining persons empowered to make choices. However, the argument has anti-feminist implications too. First, its libertarian logic suggests that neither men nor women have obligations to nurture others in virtue of their membership in a human community; there are no connections of care or kinship beyond those into which we contract as free agents. Yet some might argue that community is not something that one 'opts' into, like a life insurance policy. Community is inescapable. Without it, human beings could not become the autonomous individuals capable of honouring their obligations to those who nourished them. Failure to recognise the significance of attachment, and the distinctive forms of knowledge it brings, amounts to a form of what Fricker calls 'epistemic injustice' where woman is wronged 'in her capacity as knower,' an injustice that compounds the injustice of the sexist division of labour itself.[7]

Second, not only is the self-ownership model a problematic philosophical anthropology, it also begets an inegalitarian politics. The analogue of the view that the foetus has no right to occupy the woman's body is the position that the needy have no claim on the property of the well off, and thus a host of state services funded through taxes become problematic. And here women might be the losers, since they face special obstacles to self-sufficiency in a free market. Domestic labour and care for others, traditionally female pursuits, do not have market value, and community services such as shelters for battered women, or economic support for single-parent families, also do not sit well with the self-ownership ethic, with its ideology of self-sufficiency. (The vulnerable people at stake in these cases, unlike Thomson's world-famous violinist, do not even have the interests of music lovers on their side!) Why should one be obligated to part with one's rightfully acquired resources to assist another?[8] Thus women are invited to behave as possessive individuals, self-maximising market actors. Indeed, essential to Thomson's argument is her rejection of the idea that a right to life involves a right to the resources that sustain life.[9] The anti-egalitarian implications of the violinist analogy are that there are no social obligations to the needy, among whom women have historically been prominent; men and women are free to look out only for themselves.

A third problem is Thomson's understanding of women's embodiment. By rendering pregnancy analogous to giving domicile to a body-squatting male violinist, who intrudes on and immobilises the woman's person, the argument preys on legitimate female fears of violation, rape and loss of identity. The invasion is particularly stark since there is no scope here for the consensual acts that produce unwanted foetuses, or the complicating presence of third parties such as fathers and physicians. The analogy also construes the relation between mother and foetus as that between two normally autonomous individuals, both with their own claims, who are thrown together by chance, in order to ask whose claims should prevail, whose rights should trump.[10] But if the foetus has any legitimate claims they must derive not from the character the foetus has antecedent to and independent of its relationship to the mother, but from the unique character of the mother-foetus relationship. [11]

Thus the biggest weakness of Thomson's article is what seems to be its strength: its use of analogy. For what makes her argument so perverse is precisely that the relation between mother and foetus is not analogous to that between woman and dependent violinist because it is not analogous to *anything*. Being pregnant may be a bit like being forced to share your organs with a famous violinist, but only a bit. Nor does the foetus in the womb bear much resemblance to a violinist who must be sustained by another's organs. The relation between human mother and foetus is a relation like no other.[12] Indeed its uniqueness lies both in its distinctive form of burden, but also its singular form of fulfilment – as one philosopher suggests, an experience of the sublime that only women can have.[13] This is why the abortion question is so vexing.

The formulaic approach of analogies, typical of liberal analytical philosophy, neglects the particular and inhibits reflection on the ways in which women are shaped by certain special relationships. Liberal contractarianism's emphasis on the abstract bearer of rights seems inappropriate for a feminist politics concerned with the significance of being embodied as female. Thus Thomson's essay prompts a reappraisal of the androgyny ideal. Recent research on the relevance of sex for brain development, temperament and character, and moreover, greater awareness of the phenomena of transgendered persons who insist on a gender identity at odds with their bodies, have called into question the idea that gender identity is easily manipulable.[14] Moreover, if women's reproductive capacity is downplayed and androgyny is understood as masculinisation, the result is not an inclusive, humanist notion of personhood. As Fraser put it, 'far from challenging sexism,' such approaches 'actually reproduced it – by devaluing femininity.' Thus 'the way to do justice to women' may be to '*recognise*, not minimise, gender difference.'[15]

## A Female Ethic

The feminist thesis, 'the personal is political,' led Thomson to import political institutions such as rights into the personal domain to free women from obligations of care. Cultural feminists took the opposite tack and urged that uniquely female obligations should prompt political renewal; that is, that the personal be exported as a model for the political. Cultural feminism is a loose category of diverse positions, but what they share is a critique of the autonomous individual as a male construction dating from the Enlightenment and a suspicion of the liberal egalitarian politics that followed.

The earliest manifestation of cultural feminism is a French poststructuralist feminism that emerged in the 1970s. This school has been called 'new' French feminism to distinguish it from the ideas of the 'grande dame' of French feminism, de Beauvoir, whose unease with women's bodies makes her a problematic model.[16] Irigaray contended that feminist critique must go beyond political reform to indict the phallocratic system's source: language itself, or in the terminology of Lacan, the symbolic order. Because women experience sexual pleasure (jouissance) that is multiple and amorphous, they have a way of knowing that is out of keeping with – and superior to – the unitary, quantitative and literal world of the phallic signifier.[17] Kristeva found an oppositional force in a maternal and relational ethic to which women have special access.[18] On this view, feminism does not aim for parity, equal rights under the prevailing standards; rather, it starts from, and affirms, the difference between men and women.

This approach finds parallels in the psychological studies of Chodorow and Gilligan. Using psychoanalytic object-relations theory, Chodorow argued that the role of motherhood is reproduced in girls, whereas that of autonomous action in the public domain is inculcated in boys. Defining themselves by reference to their mothers, boys develop an ethic of separation that fosters ideas of impartiality and justice, whereas girls develop an ethic of attachment and care. Gilligan built on this work to refute Kohlberg's conclusions about the development of morality in children. Kohlberg argued that how children resolve moral problems correlates with their sex: whereas boys use the abstract criteria of justice, girls draw on ideas of care, seeking a resolution through dialogue and forsaking rights in order to help others. Gilligan's feminist argument affirmed this gendered understanding of morality, but in order to question its normative hierarchy. Women have a 'different voice' that, while not a substitute for, complements the typical male one.

Gilligan has been said to pull her punches, and others have argued that instead of a call for the peaceful coexistence of male and female ethical voices, her work should be read as evidence of the superiority of the female voice. A provocative example is Daly's *Gyn/Ecology*, in which a female linguistic and moral order is linked with a feminist environmentalism. In her inimitably playful prose, Daly suggested that the 'hagocracy's' transcendence of 'male-functioning' and 'stag-nation' will bring with it a greater respect for nature's elemental forces. Since Daly there have been more measured but similar calls for a feminine ethic, such as Ruddick's 'maternal thinking,' a feature of women's 'cultures, traditions and inquiries which we should insist upon bringing to the public world.'[19]

The focus on the personal domain, so often counterposed to the domain of law, also inspired ideas of a feminine jurisprudence. West urged that liberal legalism's preoccupation with procedures to protect individual freedom be revised in light of women's 'material and existential circumstance' of connection and intimacy.[20] Nedelsky argued that we 'reconceive rights as relationship' to better reflect 'the ways in which our essential humanity is neither possible nor comprehensible without the network of relationships of which it is part.'[21]

There is much to be said for these approaches. First, there is the strategic point of insisting on the value of women's perspectives. As we noted in the previous chapter, to affirm a subjugated set of values has an irreducibly egalitarian aspect, whatever the values might be. This is particularly important as a counter to conceptions of androgyny that so often portray a world without sexual differences as a world where all act like men. Second, there is the substantive value of many traditional female tasks, which reminds us that 'feminine' values are integral to any repertoire of human flourishing. Caring for others, empathy and intimacy, have intrinsic value, as is evidenced by the importance of friends, family and comrades to a life well lived.

Nonetheless, the cultural feminist approach has its costs. There is some tension between disavowing universal justice for an ethic of particular affections and insisting that the alternative ethic is universally female. Thus the emphasis on gender identity, as we saw in Chapter 1, produced worries of an unrepresentative feminism focussed on the interests of the more privileged of women, who are moneyed and leisured enough to be full-time mothers, and whose family structure conforms to the sexual division of labour dictated by the middle class white ideal. Like the liberalism it criticised, cultural feminism looked guilty of abstracting from diverse, historical reality to fashion a universal model of human agency: in this case, the privileged caring woman, rather than the self-interested individual.[22]

In McNay's incisive portrait of the dilemmas of sexual difference and agency, she notes the dominant 'negative paradigm of identity formation, of subjectification as subjection' where individuals have little capacity for agency.[23] This paradigm exaggerates obstacles to freedom, since even under the most straightened conditions women can act autonomously to some degree; moreover, men, too, are trapped by the regime of masculine privilege whereby 'the dominant is dominated by his domination,' in a process akin to the master-slave dialectic posited by Hegel.[24] By depicting women's agency as 'the inherent indeterminacy of symbolic structures rather than as the result of social practice,'[25] this model affords little prospect for human beings to act, consciously and in concert, to change their lot. This is aggravated, McNay notes, by cultural feminist accounts that decry an emphasis on agency in the first place, offering instead a conception of femininity as immanence and dependence on the model of the mother-child relationship.[26] Cultural feminism thus gave up too quickly on the ideal of androgyny. In assuming the pairing of sex and identity, the argument reproduces the traditional division of labour from which women sought liberation, and seems to exclude men from an important sphere of self-realisation, just as sexists in the past sought to exclude women. Moreover, this view prejudges women's choices about how to live and risks celebrating the effects of oppression, perpetuating the culture of the weak, romanticising women's existing duties and removing women from the struggle for power.[27]

Finally, we might cast doubt on the relevance of this ethic for politics. So-called 'maternal' moral sentiments can inform the welfare state and the administration of justice, but the special relation of mother and child is a problematic model for politics. The raison d'etre of this relation is, after all, the inability of one party to care for itself, the duty of the other party to assume this care, and the precedence that this duty takes before others. It is a relation founded on natural inequality, and it depends on a bond between mother and child that is often assumed to take priority over other commitments. It is thus in many ways a poor model for the impersonal, but equal, relations of strangers that characterises citizenship. [28]

These considerations also tell against Okin's attempt to forge a rapprochement between liberal politics and the ethic of care. Okin argues that liberals such as Rawls should consider the family a subject of justice, to correct its inequalities, and to develop in family members the moral sense necessary for justice in the public realm. Moreover, Okin contends that rather than impartiality, justice is best served by empathy, a 'preparedness to listen carefully to the very different points of view of others.'[29] Okin's call for dialogue among diverse perspectives is valuable, but her approach is at odds with Rawls's project of defending egalitarian justice without reference to contentious altruistic motives, and moreover, it reprises some of the weaknesses of cultural feminism. Even if the empathy that Okin calls for were possible (which many cultural feminists, insisting on the essential differences between female and male experience, would deny), Rawls himself would doubtless object to its inclusion. His idea of a veil of ignorance where we reason about justice deprived of information about others or ourselves seeks to do away with controversial appeals to motives such as empathy or altruism, and would not permit us to step in other people's shoes in the empathetic way that Okin commends. So long as we live in a society characterised by inequality, prejudice, and moral uncertainty, we will either fail to empathise or, if we succeed, the results may reflect the very failings that empathy is supposed to overcome. What am I supposed to do when called upon to empathise with the sexist? And what may I expect of sexists when it is their turn to empathise with me? It is part of the attraction of Rawls's theory that he drives us to consider the needs of some hypothetical, worst-off person without demanding any skills of empathy on our part.

Okin herself indicates that there may be some difficulty achieving empathy across sexual boundaries. For Okin, the empathy needed to supplement Rawls's theory can only be fostered in the elusive ideal of the justly ordered, ungendered family. She fatalistically concludes that in a gender-structured society there will be a distinct standpoint of women that 'cannot be adequately taken into account by male philosophers,' however intent on neutrality. It turns out, then, that the empathy required for gender justice can only be achieved once gender differences have been eliminated in reality.[30] Present injustice limits the extent to which empathy is possible, and yet empathy is required to combat injustice: we are left, on Okin's account, with the unhappy conclusion that the union between the care perspective and the justice perspective is both necessary and unattainable.

## Girl Power

There are, however, other more radical approaches to the task of understanding gender identity. Butler, for example, conceptualised gender as performance, thereby enabling a sense of a pre-given script, yet also scope for agency in its enactment.[31] This raises the question of how we can distinguish between the forces at work that promote subversion, and those that undermine it; subversion seems arbitrary and contingent, at the mercy of the 'instability' of power relations.[32] Feminist theory therefore began to teeter between essentialist and constructionist accounts of gender, between a conception of gender as either immutable or fluid.[33] Even those feminists who disavowed essentialism were divided on whether sexual inequality is the product of a symbolic order that dictates gender roles, or structures of material inequality that endow one sex with more power than the other. Paradoxes abound as to how sexism might be altered: on the former view, gender is more ephemeral, but less susceptible to overthrow by social practice; on the latter, sexism is institutionally entrenched but more easily targeted by egalitarian politics.[34]

Feminist theory thus found itself mired in an impasse.[35] Earlier feminists invoked gender to denote feminine and masculine characteristics that were acculturated, in contrast to the innate differences of biological sex. Today however, 'gender' applies to all matters of relations between men and women: thus gender studies; gendered and transgendered individuals; the designation of gender, not sex, on surveys and application forms. 'Sex' is banished, but the pursuit of a typology of persons based on the masculine and the feminine continues.[36]

How might agency be affirmed? Central to being human is the capacity to act in the world with deliberation and will. Common to all feminists is a critique of the sexualisation of agency that reduces woman to a child, a pet, a flower or plant, a sex object that is acted upon, rather than acting.[37] But agency is also often undermined in feminist accounts that emphasise how men and women are formed by institutions and forces beyond their control, or that stress a relational identity where the individual self is submerged in connections with others. Such notions prompted younger feminists to decry 'victim feminism' and insist instead on 'power feminism.'[38] In popular culture, this took the form of 'girl power,' where women were told, disingenuously, they can 'have it all': pursue societal norms of femininity and also have control over their destinies.[39] The naïveté of the girl power view, particularly in light of current cultural forces that expose women to sexual objectification in social media and new norms of casual sex, makes it especially critical that we attend to the disaffection with feminist politics that underlies it.

The question of what constitutes the self has been posed in other egalitarian frameworks besides feminism. Marx's concept of the person, for example, also seeks to understand the possibility of radical agency, even if his economic determinism is inadequate to the problem of sexual inequality, which has personal, sexual and cultural dimensions that cannot be reduced to property.[40] The problem of understanding agency in the context of unequal social relations can be informed by the Marxist idea of the social constitution of the self as derived from the idea of labour as a practical, creative activity. Labour is a process of objectification where, by cooperatively fashioning things out of nature, we fashion our identities. Under conditions of inequality, this process is distorted so that our capacity for agency is undermined, and we come to perceive ourselves as naturally incapable of agency. Yet although materialist thinkers who focus on the role of economic disadvantage are more cautious about the possibility of transformation, they are also more hopeful that relations between the sexes are shaped by historical factors that can be changed by political engagement.[41]

Sexist ideologies reproduce the experience of being a non-agent, but as we have seen, so too do feminisms that are unable to extricate themselves from dominant ideologies, manifest in Thomson's project of admitting women to a one-sided masculine model of agency, and in the cultural feminist revalorisation of the traditionally feminine. In contrast to these reified notions of agency, Marx takes the self to be grounded in the transformative practices of the community that enable autonomy and change. Thus although community is essential to the capacity of the individual to forge personality and define interests, not any community will do; illusory communities can set up new fetters, where the community takes on an existence independent of the individuals that comprise it.[42] Thus Marx, the critic of capitalism, nonetheless applauds the effect of capitalist upheaval that breaks up communities of hierarchy and coercion.

Connected with this is Marx's nuanced understanding of self-interest. His view that capitalism is an advance on feudalism is rooted in his unease with the idea of community as the guardian of its members and paternalistic models of transformation. Similarly, relations between children and parents, employees and employers, women and men, abound with examples of how 'the caring' may subsume the interests of 'the cared for' under their own when their respective interests are in fact at odds, or at least in tension. (It is revealing, perhaps, that the Christian idea of God's care for humankind is expressed with the metaphor of shepherd and sheep, which prompts some scepticism about a community of interests!) Thus just as Marx insisted in the 'Communist Manifesto' that workers should eschew a feudal conception of socialism that takes 'the almsbag' as its banner,[43] a feminism that takes 'care' as its slogan is similarly problematic if its real aim is to establish human equality under which all persons have significant scope for agency and autonomy.

This suggests that theories of sexual equality should abandon the attempt to ascertain the nature of sexual or gender identity. The project of delineating the human essence, isolating factors of 'nurture' from those of 'nature' from the moment of conception, would require infeasible laboratory conditions. In any case, sexual equality should not be reduced to biology; defining the persona of individuals according to, or in rejection of, biological characteristics, is at odds with the emancipatory goals of feminist equality.[44] 'What is woman?' is a question that, even if it admits of a reliable answer for the majority of women, cannot apply to all; and the answer will not get us any closer to removing economic, social, political and cultural barriers. As we noted above, Mill put the point well in proposing that instead of designing social institutions with innate differences in mind, deciding in advance who gets what opportunity on the basis of a person's sex, women and men should be allowed to get on with pursuing their projects and goals. Settling the nature of gender is unnecessary to achieve progress on the equality of the sexes. Broadening the scope of possible pursuits, for both sexes, and finding the means to make that possible, is the more appropriate goal.

## Dimensions of Wellbeing

Does this mean that the idea of care should simply be excised from a theory of equality? Or that Thomson's self-owning individual is irrelevant? Not at all; the relation between individual freedom and our connectedness with others remains crucial to a theory of sexual equality, though not in order to pin down the nature of the male or female self. An account of our social nature provides an important resource for the pursuit of equality. If we cannot be who we are without others, then some idea of reciprocity will undergird our egalitarian policies. Even the struggle for individual autonomy, as McNay notes, involves an understanding of how one is connected to others. At the very least, 'it is not possible to want autonomy, on the individual level, without wanting it for others and, therefore, its realisation cannot be conceived of in its full scope except as a collective enterprise.'[45]

The case of abortion is thus instructive in precisely the opposite way that Thomson intends. It does not illustrate that only contractually consented to obligations count; rather, it indicates the inevitability, in some sense, of one's connection with other beings. The unique experience of connectedness in pregnancy signals our common humanity and generates the imperative, as a being whose identity and flourishing is inconceivable without relations with other individuals, to be responsive to others' needs, be it those of offspring, neighbours, or desperate strangers.[46]

After two centuries of feminist debate, it may be that Wollstonecraft is a useful guide, not in her view that women should bear chief responsibility for the family, but in her insistence that the task of caring for others in the family is important work, requisite for inculcating the virtues of the public sphere. The domestic sphere is crucial for human fulfilment, and thus should be facilitated so that both men and women may share in its maintenance. That we are embodied and reproduce, that we need social relations for our constitution as persons, and friendship and love for our fulfilment, points to the vital role played by intimate relations for human flourishing.[47] We should not link these relations to a particular gendered identity, but rather, affirm their fundamental importance for all. To be fit for such work, women, like men, need the social support of education, political rights, the means of subsistence, and adequate childcare arrangements. Thus though the ethic of care is of qualified relevance for the ordering of public life, it is certainly an important dimension of human life that the public order should foster and resource.

Autonomy, too, will be central. Not only is the self-determining individual the agent of politics, politics must provide the conditions for self-determination in order for human beings to find wellbeing. Such conditions include adequate material resources for human health so that such agency is possible. But also, if we are to choose ways of living that will enable us to be self-determining persons, we need adequate cultural resources, educational opportunities and conditions of work. We all need, in Woolf's words, 'a room of one's own,' the conditions for autonomy.[48] An important feminist lesson is that a politics of equality must allow scope for both autonomy and care. If individuals are deprived of support for the latter, then it is more likely that the traditional sexual division of labour will persist, and the 'weaker sex' will end up as care's sole custodian. This is particularly likely given the significant tasks of caring for children, the elderly or those with disabilities, tasks that typically fall to women.[49] The upshot will be not only that women are denied opportunities for autonomy, but also that men are deprived of an important facet of human fulfilment.

Nussbaum has argued that it is possible to delineate the basic capabilities of human beings by addressing 'what activities characteristically performed by human beings are so central that they seem definitive of a life that is truly human?'[50] On this basis she identifies ten central human capacities, ranging from bodily health to the ability to form a conception of how to live, control over one's environment, and having attachments to others. These capacities are sufficiently broad, she argues, to cross cultures and count as universal, yet sufficiently open-ended to enable a variety of means for their realisation, depending on context and inclination. They are also 'transgendered,' open to men and women, although persons will vary in their interests and focus. Even if our desires vary, what makes life go well must refer to some idea of a fully human life where all capacities find an outlet.

Aristotle's idea of eudaimonia refers to fulfilment of this kind, where human beings realise their telos by developing the virtues. Although Aristotle's conception of such virtues might need some revision (we hope that warrior virtues, for example, should recede in importance) the idea that well-being involves the exercise of fundamental human capacities is no less applicable today. Marx too, for all his wariness about ahistorical, universal claims, was no less prepared, in his time and place, to claim that human beings realise themselves by exercising their capacity to engage in purposeful activity with others. Following Nussbaum and the insights of Marx, Aristotle and diverse feminists, we can say that in a fully human life one is cared for and cares for others and engages in creative activity in productive and public domains. The antinomy between autonomy and care, male and female, is thus diffused. The protection of this range of capabilities requires an ambitious egalitarian social policy, spanning matters of wealth and property, but also cultural and educational opportunities, the nurturing of emotions and the cultivation of friendship, to ensure that human beings are living flourishing lives.

Nussbaum, however, counsels moderation, insisting that it is not actual human functionings that should be secured but merely the capacity for such functionings. Government should not 'nudge or push people into functioning of the requisite sort, no matter what they prefer.' She adduces examples of the workaholic, the celibate, or the person who fasts, as people who have made choices that involve diminished functioning of some relevant kind or other, choices with which it would be wrong for the state to interfere.[51] She contrasts these ways of life with that of the 'double day' mother who did not choose to forfeit leisure and play. A self-declared 'political liberal' of a Rawlsian kind, Nussbaum contends that, in order to find agreement among 'reasonable' doctrines, it is important to 'refrain from asserting that non-autonomous lives are not worth leading, or even autonomy is a key element in the best comprehensive view of human flourishing across the board.'[52] In her more recent work she affirms again: 'to dragoon all citizens into functioning ... would be dictatorial and illiberal.'[53]

These qualifications to the capabilities approach are not as compelling as they might seem. If autonomy, for example, is a central capability, particularly important for women who have historically been denied it,[54] then it must involve what Nussbaum purports to reject: a comprehensive account in which 'autonomy and dignity' determine 'not only the core of the political conception but many noncore social and political matters as well.'[55] As she admits, if some form of functioning 'never arrives on the scene,' her list of capabilities 'are hardly even what they are.'[56] Capabilities are, after all, more than mere opportunities. The progress made by women illuminates the relation between capability and functioning. For it would be difficult to claim that once women were given formal opportunities to pursue the same paths as men, they in fact had the capability to do so; they needed to avail themselves of opportunities before they could be said to possess the relevant capabilities. This complex dynamic involves a number of factors. First, there is an evidence problem, in the sense that we do not know if someone possesses a capability if they never display its concomitant functioning. A second problem is how lack of confidence can cause one to believe one lacks a capability or the power to develop it. Finally, capabilities require their exercise in order to exist; they involve faculties that can atrophy unless used. Determining whether or not society has achieved the appropriate distribution of resources and opportunities will involve not just evidence of lack of obstacles to the development of capacities, but evidence of their manifestation.

Thus to return to the 'double day' mum (if we are to get clear on the distinction between workaholics and the overworked), not just capabilities, but also functionings must be brought into play. This is not to force people into pursuits, but to make an accurate diagnosis of relevant obstacles, and to devote efforts to their removal.[57] It is important not to take choices at face value, particularly if made within the context of a hierarchical culture. Friedman argues that 'cultural practices that violate women's rights are nevertheless permissible if the women in question accept them,'[58] but that seems too simple. As Chambers argues, disadvantage is not 'any less unjust' if freely chosen; an egalitarian society therefore ought to take measures to mitigate the effects of socialisation that encourages self-harming choices.[59] Contra Nussbaum, if large numbers of people forswore sexual intimacy, food or leisure, however voluntarily, we should nonetheless have concerns about their flourishing that prompt social redress, however cautious – as the word 'workaholic' implies, some freely chosen paths can have aspects of a pathology.

People can legitimately prefer one set of pursuits, be they work over family, or vice-versa. Our approach must be pluralist about value. Gender disparities themselves are not hard and fast evidence of inequality, since there can be statistical variations according to sex even under conditions of equality. Nature or nurture, it may be that a number of women prefer not to pursue the paths traditionally occupied by men. 'Glass ceilings' are difficult to perceive and overcome, in part because their very nature is hard to determine. Some may rationally decide to forswear the dizzying heights of professional success for the sake of having more time for the rewards of family life. Lack of female representation in top jobs is thus a complex matter. But well-rounded flourishing is something to strive for, and society should enable conditions of work so that family life is compatible with a successful career.[60]

We live in an age where we seek to subject all facets of human life to individual control, yet it remains that some aspects of human existence – such as dependency on others – are not a matter of autonomous choice. Some choices are costly and goods can be incommensurable. And thus, for example, if I am unlikely to garner academic laurels in the years my children are young and in need of my time, this may not be an inequity, but the measure of a life variously well lived. The focus on the actual deployment of capabilities in work, public life, love and play, that is, human flourishing, does not require that everyone display high-level functioning in all domains. We cannot have it all, or at least we each have to be reconciled to how our own particular 'all' excludes some indisputable, but incommensurable, goods.

When assessing the extent to which women have achieved human flourishing we need an appropriately nuanced, historical approach. In the twentieth century, women became legal persons, their sex officially irrelevant, only to find that as 'pregnant persons' they were not entitled to accommodation, and thus there later emerged a complex understanding of equality that takes account of the significance of gendered embodiment. A historical consciousness can engender a new perspective on the relation between women's struggles and those of other oppressed groups. Oppression is not inevitably the lot of women. We must eschew essentialism, not just in our understanding of human nature, but also in our understanding of oppression. Although women continue to be the unequal of men in many ways, they also have a history of achievement on which to build in eradicating other inequalities. Thus we may make steps toward the equal flourishing of all.

## Conclusion

Feminists have been preoccupied with the question of the identity of women. I have argued that in many ways this has been to the detriment of the pursuit of sexual equality. If we really want our daughters to have 'girl power' we must give up trying to settle the theoretical dilemmas of gender and consider instead the constituents of human flourishing and how capacities for well-being can be developed in both men and women. The ethic of care is not the province of women, and it is not a good model for a politics of equals. It is, however, a fundamental dimension of human existence, the product of choice but at the same time transcending it. And it is a dimension that self-determining citizens must seek to protect and support.

Thus gender per se presents no political imperatives. Equality between women and men, however, is an ideal that obligates society to enable individuals to engage in productive work, to care for dependent persons, to enjoy sexual freedom and to participate in political life. These are fundamental capabilities that require some minimum exercise in order for human beings to flourish: they give expression to Marx's idea of the individual as in need of 'all-round development.'[61] What measures must be taken to enable the exercise of these capabilities? I will not say much about this here, except to note that key obstacles to sexual equality remain economic, as men's and women's choices about working inside or outside the home are often determined by sex-differentiated job prospects and the high cost of childcare. At the same time, a person consigned to caring for children, even in the context of almost no access to opportunities for self-development outside the domestic sphere, may well be more fulfilled than the partner stuck in badly paid, non-autonomous and stultifying work outside the home. Thus the

Marxist focus on economic oppression, even if insufficient as an account of the origins of sexual inequality, remains well placed. Of course, sexual stereotypes, be they externally imposed or internally affirmed, remain an enormous challenge, and the gender impasse arises because of the difficulty of addressing them. But we may tackle them indirectly by focussing on social policy that enables a range of capabilities without prejudging which sex will display them.[62]

Equality is not the same as homogeneity, and human capabilities take diverse forms and will find diverse weightings among men and women even in a context of, if you will, androgynous flourishing. The point is not to dictate in advance what these might be, but to give men and women scope and support for activities in the private and public sphere essential to the development of their personhood. Human beings need to develop their capacities for forging caring relationships, for making contributions to the public welfare, and for autonomously choosing how to weigh all kinds of pursuits, unfettered by inequitable pay scales or sexual stereotypes. This requires a conception of equality that is linked to human wellbeing, the elaboration of which is the subject of this book. In the next two chapters we consider the reluctance of contemporary liberals to develop such a conception.

# Notes

1 M. Wollstonecraft, *Vindication of the Rights of Woman*, 126–7. Wollstonecraft, however, supposed that upon motherhood women would confine their activities to the domestic sphere, caring for children and the household.
2 J.S. Mill, 'The Subjection of Women,' 143–5.
3 See A. Bogdanov's wonderfully creative utopian novel, *Red Star*.
4 S. Firestone, *The Dialectic of Sex*.
5 J.J. Thomson, 'A Defence of Abortion,' 13.
6 C. MacKinnon, *Feminism Unmodified*, 94.
7 M. Fricker, *Epistemic Injustice*, 20.
8 R. Nozick, *Anarchy, State and Utopia*, 170.
9 'Defense of Abortion,' 11.
10 Whether the specificity of the abortion issue can be captured in terms of rights is addressed by R. Hursthouse, *Beginning Lives*, 194–217, and J. Finnis, 'The Rights and Wrongs of Abortion.'
11 See C. Overall, *Ethics and Human Reproduction*, 68–87.
12 T. Strong has suggested to me that our widespread use of birth metaphors – e.g. Marx's idea that capitalism 'gives birth' to socialism – indicates that the relation between mother and foetus is not so singular. However, we are unlikely to impute a mother-child relationship to the two societies in any substantive sense (see G.A. Cohen's critique of Marx's obstetric metaphors in *If You're an Egalitarian, How Come You're So Rich?*). Many animals give birth, but the relation of human mothers to their children is distinctive because it expresses our fundamental intersubjectivity, the development of which is crucial to distinctively human modes of life, and hence human flourishing.
13 See S. Lintott's compelling 'The Sublimity of Gestating and Giving Birth: Toward a Feminist Conception of the Sublime,' 237–50.
14 See M.A. Gilbert, 'Defeating Bigenderism: Changing Gender Assumptions in the Twenty-first Century.'
15 N. Fraser, *Justice Interruptus*, 176–7.

16 For example, 'man dives upon his prey like the eagle and the hawk; woman lies in wait like the carnivorous plant, the bog, in which insects and children are swallowed up.' S. de Beauvoir, *The Second Sex*, 407.

17 L. Irigaray, *This Sex Which Is Not One*, 30. See L. Alcoff, 'Cultural Feminism versus Poststructuralism: The Identity Crisis in Feminist Theory,' 3.

18 Kristeva famously vacillates on this, however, arguing that an essentialist ethic is to be transcended and that the special property of the female sex is its lack of identity altogether. See 'Woman's Time,' and Fraser, *Justice Interruptus*, 165–6.

19 S. Ruddick, 'Maternal Thinking,' 345. See also J. Benjamin, *The Bonds of Love*, E.F. Kittay and D. Meyers, eds, *Women and Moral Theory*, and E.F. Kittay, *Love's Labor: Essays on Women, Equality and Dependency*, N. Noddings, *Caring: A Feminine Approach to Ethics and Moral Education*. This approach continues to have influence; see A. O'Reilly ed., *Maternal Thinking: Philosophy, Politics, Practice*.

20 R. West, 'Jurisprudence and Gender,' 520–2. See also West, *Caring for Justice*.

21 J. Nedelsky, 'Reconceiving Rights as Relationship.'

22 See b. hooks, *Feminist Theory: From Margin to Centre*, S. Ahmed, *Transformations: Thinking through Feminism*, P.H. Collins, *Black Feminist Thought: Knowledge, Consciousness, and the Politics of Empowerment*, U. Narayan, *Dislocating Cultures: Identities, Traditions, and Third-World Feminism*.

23 L. McNay, *Gender and Agency*, 2.

24 Ibid., 53–4.

25 Ibid., 45.

26 Ibid., 151–5.

27 See B. Houston, 'Rescuing Womanly Virtues,' J. Grimshaw, *Philosophy and Feminist Thinking*, L. Segal, *Is the Future Female? Troubled Thoughts on Contemporary Feminism*, N. Fraser and L. Nicholson, 'Social Criticism without Philosophy,' 32–3; J.R. Richards, *The Sceptical Feminist*, 40, McNay, *Gender and Agency*, 11, 151; Fraser, *Justice Interruptus*, ch. 7; J. Kroeger-Mappes, 'The Ethic of Care vis-à-vis the Ethic of Rights: A Problem for Contemporary Moral Theory.'

28 T. Cockburn raises concerns that the ethic of care's political motivations might make it a poor model even for the care of children. See 'Children and the Feminist Ethic of Care.'

29 S.M. Okin, *Justice, Gender and the Family*, 101–9.

30 Ibid., 106–7.

31 See J. Butler, *Gender Trouble*, J. Butler, *Excitable Speech: A Politics of the Performative*, and S. Hekman, 'Subjects and Agents: The Question for Feminism.'

32 McNay, *Gender and Agency*, 68.

33 See D. Coole, 'The Gendered Self,' A. Stone, 'Essentialism and Anti-Essentialism in Feminist Philosophy,' 135–53, R. Braidotti, 'The Politics of Ontological Difference,' 102, H. Moore, *A Passion for Difference: Essays in Anthropology and Gender*, 20, D. Cornell, 'What is Ethical Feminism?' 93, and E. Spellman, *Inessential Woman: Problems of Exclusion in Feminist Thought*.

34 Coole, 'The Gendered Self,' 158–61.

35 G. Warnke's excellent introductory book on the subject, however, helpfully suggests that gender characteristics have different meanings for different people, and hence should not be regarded as uniquely determining of personal identity. See *Debating Sex and Gender*, 117.

36 Parenthetically, the impasse on gender is aggravated by the opaque way in which these problems are often posed. Whilst Thomson's reduction of pregnant women to rational choosers is overly simple, some of the poststructuralist social theory is notoriously complex; it seems ironic that arguments for human agency are at times couched in terms that threaten to render agency obscure.

37 Rousseau and Hegel are obvious examples, the former portraying women as infantile, the latter likening women to plants. See J.-J. Rousseau, *Emile*, 358 and G.W.F. Hegel, *Philosophy of Right*, 169.

38 N. Wolff, *Fire with Fire: The New Female Power and How to Use It.*

39 This is manifest in the Spice Girls and Madonna phenomena, the latter approvingly cited by C. Paglia in 'Madonna – Finally, A Real Feminist,' and the former inspiring at least one teenager manual, C. Plaisted, *Girl Power Get It! Flaunt It! Use It!*. The Nigella Lawson model, where the beautiful woman finds success in the kitchen, is another example: *How to Be a Domestic Goddess.* Some interesting critical literature is gathered in C. Schwichtenberg, ed., *The Madonna Connection: Representational Politics, Subcultural Identities and Cultural Theory.* The continuing influence of such views is evident in E. Zaslo, *Feminism, Inc.: Coming of Age in Girl Power Media Culture,* M. Meltzer, *Girl Power: The Nineties Revolution in Music,* R. Gill, and O. Koffman, 'I matter. And so does she: Girl power, (post)feminism and the Girl Effect.'

40 See, however, the following Marxian-inspired feminist views: Firestone, *The Dialectic of Sex,* MacKinnon, *Feminism Unmodified,* M. O'Brien, *The Politics of Reproduction,* N. Hartsock, 'The Feminist Standpoint,' and A. Jaggar, *Feminist Politics and Human Nature.*

41 Coole, 'The Gendered Self,' 151–5.

42 K. Marx and F. Engels, 'German Ideology,' 194–5.

43 K. Marx and F. Engels, 'Communist Manifesto,' 491.

44 See C. Koggel, *Perspectives on Equality,* 179–81.

45 McNay, *Gender and Agency,* 153. See also C. Taylor, 'Atomism.' For some interesting reflections on how the sexual division of labour might be redrawn, see F. Cancian, 'Gender and Power: Love and Power in the Public and Private Spheres,' and B. Honig, 'Difference, Dilemmas and the Politics of Home.'

46 As M. Barnes argues in *Care in Everyday Life: An Ethic of Care in Practice.*

47 A. Baier coins the term 'second persons' to articulate the idea of human beings as intrinsically dependent on others. See *Postures of the Mind,* 84. See also A. Jaggar, 'Feminism in Ethics: Moral Justification,' 225–44, and M. Friedman and A. Bolte, 'Ethics and Feminism.'

48 V. Woolf, *A Room of One's Own.*

49 M. Nussbaum, *Frontiers of Justice,* 168–70.

50 M. Nussbaum, *Sex and Social Justice,* 39.

51 Ibid., 43–4.

52 M. Nussbaum, 'A Plea for Difficulty,' 109–10.

53 Nussbaum, *Frontiers of Justice,* 171.

54 M. Friedman, *Autonomy, Gender, Politics,* 78. On the question of the authenticity of women's choices under conditions of sexist socialisation, see e.g. W. Brown, *States of Injury: Power and Freedom in Late Modernity,* D. Cornell, *At the Heart of Freedom,* D.T. Meyers, *Gender in the Mirror: Cultural Imagery and Women's Agency,* and N.J. Hirschmann, *The Subject of Liberty: Toward a Feminist Theory of Freedom.*

55 Nussbaum, 'A Plea for Difficulty,' 108.

56 M. Nussbaum, *Sex and Social Justice,* 43.

57 M. Weinzweig, 'Pregnancy Leave, Comparable Worth, and Concepts of Equality,' 71–101.

58 Friedman, *Autonomy, Gender, Politics,* 188.

59 C. Chambers, *Sex, Culture and Justice,* 129. A. Cudd's argument against Nozick's example of marital choice is apt here: *Analysing Oppression,* 130.

60 E.F. Kittay challenges the autonomous individual prototype in liberal thought – 'we are all at some time dependent' – in *Love's Labor: Essays on Women, Equality and Dependency,* 4, and E.F. Kittay and E.K. Feder, eds, *The Subject of Care: Feminist Perspectives on Dependency,* 2. See also Nussbaum, *Frontiers of Justice,* ch. 2, 3.

61 K. Marx, 'The Gotha Programme,' 531.

62 As O. O'Neill concludes in *Bounds of Justice,* 111.

# Part II
# Liberal Revisionism

# 4 Impartiality, Difference and Wellbeing

Ever since Mill made his eloquent argument for freedom of expression, political theorists have been concerned with the consequences of this freedom for social order. The problem of pluralism, how to reconcile citizens' different conceptions of the good in a single polity, emerges precisely because individuals are free to pursue their conceptions of the good. As Rawls puts it in *Political Liberalism*, 'How is it possible that there can be a stable and just society whose free and equal citizens are deeply divided by conflicting and even incommensurable religious, philosophical and moral doctrines?'[1] The answer, for many liberals, is to eschew any commitment on a range of matters of substantive value and to leave the thorny matter of human flourishing to personal choice.

In this chapter I examine Rawls's argument for a neutral state in light of the milieu of difference politics. I contend that although neutralist liberals like Rawls hope to meet the challenge of difference, they in fact render their theory more vulnerable. Rawls's ideas of reason, impartiality and cooperation are on the one hand indispensable for social life; without them the claims of difference threaten to destroy the possibility of social justice of any kind. However, these resources must be justified, ultimately, by reference to a substantive conception of the good, one that is in fact implied by Rawls's own argument. In order to further the liberal ideals of equality and autonomy that motivated what might be dubbed 'the neutralist turn,' we must focus, not on a political theory that disavows substantive values, but rather one that embraces autonomy and human flourishing.

## The Politics of Political Liberalism

Rawls's initial contribution to political philosophy centred on an argument for the redistribution of wealth. His later work, *Political Liberalism*, focuses on the problem of consensus in diverse societies, and is so called to contrast with 'comprehensive' doctrines which pronounce on 'what is of value in human life, as well as ideals of personal virtue or character' that bear on 'much of our non-political conduct.'[2] Typical comprehensive doctrines are the worldviews of fundamentalist religions, but Rawls contends that the liberalisms of Kant or Mill are also comprehensive because their political theories require that citizens subscribe to a liberal personal morality on the basis of certain moral views, concepts of the person, or metaphysics.[3] Political liberalism is narrower in scope, referring only to the question of the 'basic structure' of society, that is, a society's main political, social and economic institutions.[4] Further, political liberalism is less comprehensive, capable of being presented as independent of citizens' opposing religious and moral allegiances. Thus the politically liberal state is prohibited from espousing and promoting a liberal way of life. Rawls takes his approach to mark a departure from the aims of the Enlightenment project of 'finding a philosophical secular doctrine, one founded on reason yet comprehensive.'[5] This may seem a pragmatic course, since Rawls argues that in the face of diversity, the alternative – the imposition of community – would involve an intolerable level of force.'[6] But Rawls also advocates political liberalism on the basis of respect for citizens' deeply held moral views. A proper appreciation for the importance of forming and pursuing our own conceptions of the good requires that we do not repress some conceptions for the sake of a single, preferred one: neutrality is a means of protecting moral autonomy.[7]

Rawls restricts the scope of his theory in three other respects. First, in contrast to the impression of universality in *A Theory of Justice*, Rawls holds that justice as fairness applies only to a constitutional democracy.[8] Such a society is conceived as a 'fair system of cooperation over time, from one generation to the next,' where citizens do not consider their social arrangements to be dictated by a fixed natural order, or by a religious or aristocratic hierarchy.[9] Abandoning the rhetoric of the Archimedean point, the God's eye view to which *A Theory of Justice* aspired, here principles of justice emerge from society's public culture[10] (though not any public culture; Rawls's remarks about a Supreme Court and his rejection of parliamentary supremacy suggest that only America fits the bill[11]).

The second narrowing of scope is the 'political conception of the person,' people's public identity, the persona we take when deliberating about how the state should be administered, or when claiming our rights and honouring our legal obligations. Thus whilst individuals have two moral powers, the capacity for a conception of the good, and a capacity for a sense of justice,[12] it is the latter which is deployed in the public domain. Citizens may draw on their religious or moral commitments to reach an 'overlapping consensus,' but they can also appraise and revise these commitments and, if they are in conflict with political liberalism, put them to one side for the purpose of taking part in public institutions. Conceiving of themselves as 'self-authenticating sources of valid claims,'[13] citizens understand they may press their interests so long as they do not undermine the requirements of a political conception of justice.[14]

The third respect in which Rawls qualifies the scope of his theory follows from the idea of the public person; it is 'reasonable pluralism' and not pluralism per se which is to be accommodated by political liberalism. In a 'public culture of democracy' there will be a diversity of reasonable doctrines and moreover, it is from within those doctrines that a 'substantial majority of its politically active citizens' support 'an enduring and secure democratic regime.'[15]

The reasonable is an important benchmark throughout Rawls's argument. Parties to the original position are not just rational, in the sense of choosing effective means given their ends; this is, after all, something of a non-moral virtue and as such a slender resource for social life. 'Rational agents approach being psychopathic when their interests are solely in benefits to themselves.'[16] Reasonableness, in contrast, refers to a commitment to fair dealings, openness and good faith. Reciprocity is the essence of the reasonable; Rawls deems it a virtue that lies between the altruism of pure impartiality and the self-interest of mutual advantage. Reasonable persons 'desire for its own sake a social world in which they, as free and equal, can cooperate with others on terms we can all accept.'[17] Such persons affirm only reasonable comprehensive doctrines, that is, conceptions of the good which evolve from some tradition of thought, are more or less consistent or coherent, and are worked out by means of both theoretical and practical reason. Political liberalism counts as reasonable a number of views that are not liberal in the comprehensive sense; Rawls supposes that one can see a doctrine as reasonable without subscribing to it, thereby avoiding debate about which view of morality is true or acceptable, without endorsing some kind of scepticism. In dispute is not the existence of moral truth but the appropriateness of personal doctrines serving as a guide for public life and, in particular, the legitimacy of people being forced to give up reasonable doctrines to live by creeds other than their own.[18]

Rawls's confidence in the reasonable is such, however, that he contends that citizens will gradually coalesce around a set of political values. Justice as fairness may initially find only the tenuous support of prudential calculation (as, for example, the principle of toleration historically only garnered the acceptance of a 'modus vivendi' or mere co-existence). As political institutions are seen to function effectively, citizens' comprehensive doctrines begin to shift and reflect the values of the constitutional order. Once the 'rules of political contest' are firmly established, and public reason is seen to be the means of their application, a spirit of cooperation develops; a 'stable constitutional consensus' emerges. This in turn, deepens and expands to become an 'overlapping consensus' among citizens on the basis of their conceptions of justice. For Rawls, a hallmark of the resulting well-ordered society is some homogeneity in citizens' political views.[19]

All this looks like a rejoinder to communitarian critiques of *A Theory of Justice*.[20] In the 1980s 'justice as fairness' was targeted by critics like MacIntyre and Sandel for disavowing the pursuit of the good as an appropriate aim of political theory, whilst simultaneously smuggling in a certain conception of the good inherent in the idea of the rational, choosing self.[21] In this light, Rawls's strategy seems ingenious: he admits to the specificity of justice as fairness and its rootedness in a certain historical milieu, yet mounts a defence of the value of neutrality that is both principled and pragmatic. Weithman notes that this attenuated conception of liberal justice looks better able to promise stability than other more substantive versions;[22] and although stability might be deemed a mere practical concern, it is after all the precondition for any more substantive moral project committed to just social relations. Political liberalism respects individuals' pursuit of the good within the reasonable confines of the democratic tradition in which we find ourselves.

## Plurality and Difference

Since the communitarian assault on Rawlsian liberalism, a similar but distinctive critique has emerged from thinkers who stress, not the importance of community, but the salience of difference. In previous chapters we considered the claims of difference, that is, that a universal political order subsuming a diversity of social groups is a chimera, an illusory and self-defeating goal in the face of incommensurable identities and interests. Difference thinkers reject the ideal of a common conception of the good, but they share the communitarian suspicion of impartiality and the Rawlsian view that individuals should put their attachments to one side in order to cooperate in the political domain. The political orientation of communitarianism was a matter of some controversy, since it was unclear how seeing ourselves as, for example, 'intersubjective beings' might bear on matters like the distribution of wealth or the scope of liberty; indeed, it was argued that communitarianism implied a tradition-bound conservatism, where the community sets a way of life over which individuals have limited choice. The invocation of difference, in contrast, is an explicitly radical move, aiming to give power to the disadvantaged, and thus tackling Rawls's own ground of social justice. The difference response to Rawls is thus illuminating.

### Reason

Recall that political liberalism's starting point is reasonable and rational persons who cooperate in the institution of a liberal constitution and, eventually, a complex system of justice. Rawls is explicit that he is concerned only with normal functioning and 'puts aside' permanent disabilities that prevent people cooperating in society.[23] Minow criticises this approach:

> The views of mentally disabled persons, children and any others deemed to lack capacity for rational thought become relevant only through the imaginations of the 'rational' people who ask what they themselves would want if they were in the position of these incompetent persons.[24]

Children and mentally disabled adults pose special problems for a theory of justice because first, their lack of rationality makes it difficult for them to fend for themselves, and second, because the two groups are in many ways unlike. Whereas children are cared for as an interim measure until they reach adult reason, in the case of persons with intellectual disabilities, our concern is how to provide long-term care that is not an affront to their dignity. Thus we hope that resources go to children to develop their capacity to reason as they mature, whereas ongoing arrangements should be made to assist mentally disabled adults to live a life of self-respect.

It is odd, then, that Minow seems to baulk at any bald statement to the effect that mentally disabled people or children are in fact less rational than Rawls's ideal participants, suggesting instead that it is a matter of his theory 'deeming' it so. It seems undeniable that there will be classes of people for whom decisions are bound to be made by the 'rationally privileged,' even if we think that much consultation with, and regard for, the persons involved is required. Nussbaum's call for benevolence flags the role of third parties when it comes to attending to the interests of those lacking cognitive capacities.[25] Yet to heed Minow's appeal and attend to the interests of all members of our society, the weak as well as the strong, other forms of inclusive citizenship must supplement the model of agreement among the rational, however other-regarding they may be.[26]

The problem of difference also calls into question the role of reason in a fundamental way. If we take persons to be subsumed under incommensurable and conflicting identities, and not just economic resources but political power has been unequally distributed along these lines, then we face a history where reciprocity and fair dealings have been absent. This history is likely to have a legacy for the present; those who have been on the losing end may resist displaying the virtues of reasonableness, with the retort that these virtues have not been displayed in relation to them. As Laclau and Mouffe argue, such conflict would thus seem immune to resolution in light of the ideal of dispassionate reason.[27]

Difference theorists would resist casting the problem in terms of unreasonableness on the part of the disadvantaged, but there is a sense in which this is implicit in their case. Indeed, if we look at historical examples, it might be argued that it is a legacy of oppression, that is, unreasonableness on the part of the oppressing class can make for unreasonableness on the part of the oppressed, and this may persist even if the oppressors mend their ways and begin to establish a record of reasonableness. Lack of power may render disadvantaged people unable, or unwilling, to recognise and marshal effective ways of pursuing their aims. This is hardly an attractive proposition; the 'voice' of the oppressed should be recognised on its own terms, whereas attributing irrationality to the disadvantaged, like the idea of false consciousness, relies on a view that people do not always know their own interests.[28] That disadvantaged people respond to their situation in ways that seem irrational or unreasonable by some external criterion might call into question the legitimacy of the criterion itself.

A second, more abstract, objection to reason and rationality thus emerges. Minow broadens her complaint to criticise Rawls on behalf of those 'historically treated as incompetent.' Here Minow means that lack of capacity to reason is attributed to certain classes of persons by liberal theory. This is because the Rawlsian idea of detaching oneself from one's substantive commitments renders rationality 'deeply exclusionary.' Minow contends that there are many groups in society whose identity in fact involves a deep sense of attachment.

This more wholesale rejection of reason has its root in the feminist critiques we canvassed in the last chapter. Feminists have long argued that the ideal of reason has historically figured in political philosophy as a masculine capacity premissed on separation from the purportedly female domestic domain of care and reproduction.[29] Women, it was argued, are no less capable than men of quitting the domestic sphere for public reason, but more recently some have sought to reclaim the affective, 'feminine' domain, and its different moral voice.[30] Minow, too, complains that reason is the province of those who can more easily separate themselves from familial relations, specific to men of certain historical, ethnic and religious backgrounds.[31]

This conclusion, if accepted, might prompt one to call for a more inclusive conception of reason, but the force of this critique also casts doubt on the very idea of reason other than a mode of thinking specific to a culture, time, and place, in which case Rawls's ambition to find consensus among diverse citizens is misconceived. Moreover, if reason is a method for, as Young puts it, 'scaling bodies,' for manipulating persons, domesticating or ordering them by means of what Foucault calls a 'normalising gaze,' then not only is reason historically conditioned, but it is inherently oppressive and a poor resource for the pursuit of justice, if justice even remains as a plausible concept.[32]

## Impartiality

Related to the critique of reason is a critique of impartiality. We encountered this critique in Chapter 2, in Young's contention that impartiality is 'an idealist fiction.'[33] This argument reprises the Marxist idea that impartiality is ideological; the purported procedural justice of the rule of law, for example, disguises and thus legitimates the substantive unfairness of the capitalist order. However, the claim about ideology does not provide sufficient grounds for eschewing the ideal of impartiality. That one institution, A, serves to legitimate another, B, does not demonstrate that A is without value. Someone's cruelty might be masked by polite manners, but this is not sufficient to show that polite manners are without worth. One can take the view that the capitalist order be overthrown or reformed, whilst retaining a commitment to the institutions of impartiality that obscured the anti-capitalist enterprise.[34] Minow's insight that 'impartiality is the guise that partiality takes to seal bias against exposure' might prompt one to argue for genuine impartiality, rather than to reject its possibility.[35]

Here, however, the critique of impartiality is more thoroughgoing than a diagnosis of its ideological role. It is argued that the moral point of view must be situated, as exemplified, again, by care for loved ones in the home, historically associated with the female moral voice. We attend to others' needs more adequately if we permit fuller knowledge of their particular situation, and if we are not dispassionate but involved in their welfare.[36] This hearkens back to the socialist ideal of a society founded on fellowship and community rather than the abstract relations of disinterested citizens.

Moreover, impartiality is not only inferior to other modes of interaction; it is also unattainable. There is some overlap here with the critique of reason, which notes the futility of seeking the posture of distance required by rational thought. Impartiality, it is claimed, imposes a unity by means of single formula that subsumes concrete particulars, a unity that is achieved by means of a binary opposition where the universal is in fact just one principle asserted to the exclusion of others. Thus Derrida, for example, contends that 'one ensures phallocentric mastery under the cover of neutralisation every time.'[37] This argument can also take the form of a less abstract, sociological observation, which finds that our embeddedness in context and social relations render the pursuit of impartiality futile. Williams thus lambastes the 'myth of a purely objective perspective':[38]

> The godlike image of generalised, legitimating others ... too often reified in law as 'impersonal' rules and 'neutral' principles, presumed to be inanimate, unemotional, unbiased, unmanipulated, and higher than ourselves.

Young also contends that 'one has no motive for making moral judgements and resolving moral dilemmas unless the outcome matters, unless one has a particular and passionate interest in the outcome.'[39] In sum, the idea of impartiality is ideological, inferior, oppressive and impossible.

### Cooperation

Rawls stresses that society should be understood as 'a fair scheme of cooperation.' It might seem odd to oppose the idea of citizens seeking to get along with each other. However, it is argued that so long as it is premised on the false universals of reason and impartiality, cooperation is both a vain hope and a potentially oppressive demand. Thus Young calls for a 'democratic discussion where participants express their needs' and where no one appeals to a 'general interest' or 'speaks from an impartial point of view.' She urges a 'cultural revolution' which involves the 'politicisation' of the hitherto non-political, such as habits, feelings and expressions of fantasy and desire, which can assert 'the positivity of group difference' and allow 'affinities to develop across different groups.'[40] For her part, Minow supplants cooperation among the rational with a 'social relations approach' that emphasises the 'basic connectedness of people' and where we learn to 'take the perspective of another.'[41]

A yet more radical position finds the admission of difference to rule out cooperation all together. This position invokes a model of society riven by deep-seated divisions and antagonisms, where agreement is always tenuous and provisional. Foucault thus refuses to imagine a future without the fragmentation of diverse discourses, with the attendant imperative to resist. Mouffe draws on the idea of Schmitt's friend/enemy distinction to insist on the irreducibility of social conflict. Institutions might contest violence and domination, but they cannot hope to eliminate it. At best, diverse 'subject positions' of race, class, occupation or sexuality will come to provisional coalitions, crystallised into 'nodal points' of common resistance.[42] On this view, even the model of Rawls's 'modus vivendi' looks too ambitious.

## History and Neutrality

How fatal are these objections? Rawls seemed to anticipate them when he noted that 'the long controversy about toleration as the origin of liberalism' may seem 'dated in terms of the problems of contemporary life.' He insists, however, that ideals such as toleration remain relevant, so long as we understand 'what earlier principles require under changed circumstances' and insist that they are 'honoured in existing institutions.'[43] However, Rawls's historical preoccupations suggest that issues of substance divide him from his new critics. Take his example of the Reformation: there the problem was how to countenance more than one religion in a society characterised by the union of church and state. Religious toleration, in which the state prescinds from doctrinal commitment, underpins the 'modus vivendi' necessary for social order that could evolve into a more substantive and deeply held constitutional consensus. But many have questioned the idea that religious convictions can be sequestered away from one's political convictions. As Weinstock notes, some citizens face a heavier burden than others under the purportedly neutral Rawlsian regime.[44] The political liberal argument that 'respect for persons' intrinsic to the idea of being reasonable means religious citizens can appreciate the doctrine's scope for toleration[45] is not likely to assuage the discontent of the faithful who suspect that the reasonable is a cover for the secular.[46]

Moreover, advocates of difference call not just for the freedom to practice one's beliefs but for public recognition of identities. It is charged that coercion is implicit in the seemingly neutral postures of public reason, so that women forgo the domain of childcare in order to participate in a male-dominated workplace, disabled persons opt out of public services according to the 'universal' standard of the fully able person, or people of minority cultures check their habits and inclinations to live by the prevailing white norms. All too often in legal cases, political decisions and everyday confrontations with bureaucracies, reason seems but an instrument for manipulation where the disadvantaged are relegated to the realm of the non-rational, impartiality a mask behind which prejudice operates, and cooperation the pretence by which those without power are expected to easily conform to the habits and will of the powerful.

One remedy might be to develop Rawls's idea of primary goods, those goods we require for pursuing our moral conceptions, whatever they might be. Kymlicka suggests that along with such goods as rights and liberties, the good of membership in community should be added to the list, and it might be argued that the good of care be added also.[47] However, primary goods are understood in instrumental terms as the preconditions for an individuals' pursuit of his or her projects, be they communitarian or not, rather than essential to our identities as persons with attachments to others. More promising, perhaps, is Rawls's primary good of 'the social bases of self-respect' as an avenue for the inclusion of difference. But here too, critics' demands are for such far-reaching changes in public institutions to enable special arrangements for minority groups, that it is hard to see how these can be captured as discrete, instrumental goods possessed by individuals.

The target of difference is what we might call the ambition of emancipatory political theory. Taking a single identity, for example class in the Marxist case, is obviously vulnerable to charges of exclusion. On the other hand, if our theories of justice require assumptions about a 'view from nowhere' or an 'Archimedean point' or persons dissociating themselves from others or their commitments, then a liberal politics risks collapsing with its grandiose metaphysics.

One of the difficulties with the discourse of difference is the extent to which the terms impartiality, neutrality and objectivity are used interchangeably, all rejected for referring to an extra-human view, devoid of perspective or commitment. Rawls tries to distinguish among these terms: neutral refers to the posture of justice as fairness with respect to comprehensive doctrines, whilst the objective is the perspective agents must have in order to conceive and subscribe to justice as fairness. Rawls eschews the vocabulary of impartiality because it suggests an overly altruistic concern for the general good.[48] Neutral, though, is unfortunate, suggesting the implausible idea of 'neutering' one's identity, values or beliefs. The idea of the objective also intimates a subject-less perspective, even if Rawls insists on an 'in-the-world' conception to which human beings, with all their convictions and concerns, can realistically aspire.

The problems of neutrality, however, lie not just in matters of vocabulary. First is the problem of how deep is political neutrality, that is, whether its justification must be neutral. A second, related problem is the source of neutrality. The third problem is how extensive is neutrality, that is to what does it apply. Let us consider them in turn.

### The Depth of Neutrality

Some political philosophers have argued that neutrality itself must be defended in neutral terms, that we must have neutral reasons for being neutral. Ackerman, for example, endorses 'hard neutrality,'[49] which requires that the liberal be as noncommittal about the justification for neutrality as the matter of neutrality about the good life itself. On this view, policies need not be neutral in their effects, but justification for state policy must emerge from the commitments shared by all citizens, putting 'the moral ideas that divide us off the conversational agenda of the liberal state' to such an extent that justification is itself neutral.[50] Rawls's argument points to the importance of stability; neutrality is defended as what can garner success, and therefore sufficiently thin in its rationale as to be unproblematic in achieving agreement. In this, Rawls sometimes suggests that the argument for neutrality is neutral itself.[51]

More recent neutralists also seem to couch the issue in this way. Quong contends that liberalism is 'a solution to the fact that we cannot agree on the nature of the good life.'[52] Lecce also notes the pragmatic basis for neutrality: 'no one is asked to accept a lesser liberty for the sake of values that contravene her deepest convictions.'[53] Patten offers 'neutrality of treatment' as opposed to Rawls's neutrality of aim, whereby the state should not favour any view of how to live by means of an even-handed approach to diverse social groups,[54] also suggesting a thoroughgoing neutrality.

Being neutral about neutrality risks incoherence, however. Waldron contends that liberal neutrality is not rooted in moral scepticism, but has a substantive justification. The liberal is not neutral about the reasons for being neutral: 'One is always neutral in a particular dispute for a particular reason.'[55] As Dworkin put it forcefully: neutrality is required 'not because there is no right and wrong of the matter, but because that is what is right.'[56] Even Barry, an adamant neutralist, contends that the neutral state emerges from a substantive moral theory, not of how to live, but rather 'how we are to live *together*, given that we have different ideas about how to live.'[57]

Ultimately, neutrality is underpinned by the moral principle of respect for people's autonomy in developing their concept of how to live. Thus although Larmore contends 'we do better to recognise that liberalism is not a philosophy of man, but a philosophy of politics,' it is for the sake of respecting individual choice among contentious conceptions of how to live.[58] Thus the state is supporting individuals in living lives of value. In considering what paths to pursue, people to marry, or projects to undertake, individuals reflect on what is of value to them, and whether the way in which they have lived and plan to live properly reflects what they deem valuable. We try to choose our motivations, and not merely make choices in the service of our motivations. Revisability has its limits, however; we cannot change our conception of value so often that the conception cannot perform its role of shaping plans, rather than vice versa. We are 'enduring beings,' Waldron contends, seeking to make decisions that give content and meaning to our lives as a whole, and that build on and are integrated with past decisions.[59]

The idea that the state be neutral about a personal domain was first broached by Locke, who designated religion, questions of doctrine, individual salvation, beliefs and practices, as a sphere about which the state should be neutral. Mill widened this sphere of neutrality to include a myriad of choices about how to live. His rationale for this, however, was to bring human beings 'nearer to the best thing they can be,' a position that was premised on the idea, as Appiah argues, that it is 'objectively valuable' to be 'a certain kind of person.'[60] On this view, the liberal must be prepared to enforce the values of liberalism; he or she cannot be neutral about that.

Neutrality seems to have its limits in Rawls's view: justice as fairness is neutral in its aim with respect to comprehensive doctrines, but the effect of this aim is not neutral since 'the facts of commonsense political sociology' are such that some doctrines will gain more adherents than others.[61] But the only values at play in the aims of justice as fairness are procedural ones, such as consistency and impartiality. Yet it appears that Rawls has substantive reasons for endorsing neutrality. Fundamental moral ideas play a role: we are to live in a well-ordered society that provides a fair system of cooperation. Citizens are free and equal persons possessed of the capacities for a sense of justice and a conception of the good, given the moral importance of determining one's own way of life. Justice as fairness is objective because it produces a structure of reasoning that meets the criteria of rational inquiry, seeks to be reasonable, assigns reasons to agents in the world, and takes it as possible that reasonable persons can learn and master, not just the mechanics of practical reason, but the principles of justice that issue from the procedure of construction (i.e. the original position). These are all morally substantive reasons for Rawls's conception of political liberalism, that seem to be in tension with his insistence that a 'comprehensive' justification is off the table.

### Wherefrom Neutrality

The second problem is connected to the first; it is wherefrom neutrality, that is whether neutrality has a neutral source, derived from a 'God's eye view' or a view from nowhere, or can be understood as emerging from morally rich human practices. Again, the evidence is confusing, as we shall see. Rawls certainly attempts to leave behind burdensome philosophical baggage, insisting, for example, that the original position is but a 'device of representation,' a position we simulate in order to reason about principles of justice, rather than a metaphysical doctrine about the nature of the person. We are persons who, according to Rawls, cannot be imagined outside of our societies,[62] thus avoiding for example, the curious metaphysics involved in conceiving of the person as possessing both a personal standpoint and an impersonal one.[63] Rawls states:

> the objective point of view must always be from somewhere. This is because, as calling upon practical reason, it must express the point of view of persons, individual or corporate, suitably characterised as reasonable and rational. There is no such thing as the point of view of practical reason as such.[64]

Rawls goes further than simply debunking a burdensome metaphysics with an idea of human-made objectivity. Objectivity and the standards of justice turn out to be whatever emerges from our current consensus. Rawls's theory involves 'collecting settled convictions' from the 'public culture's shared fund' and citizens must view justice as 'derived from, or congruent with, or at least not in conflict with, their other values.'[65] Thus for Rawls, 'agreement in judgement, or narrowing of differences ... suffices for objectivity.'[66] This looks like more than the usual democratic proviso of any theorist, that the prescriptions offered cannot be put into practice without some kind of popular mandate. Here popular belief is in some sense constitutive of the prescriptions themselves. As Raz complains of the 'epistemic abstinence' of Rawls:

> whereas politicians, at least sometimes, try to secure agreement by convincing people that the principles underlying their proposals are true, Rawls abjures this argument, and seeks to secure agreement simply by pointing out that certain principles are already implicitly agreed to, or nearly so.[67]

This idea of justice as consensus is hard to square with the idea of standing back from the hurly-burly of human affairs to find an objective point of view, that of 'certain *appropriately defined* reasonable and rational agents' whose reasoning meets Rawls's criterion of 'success'.[68] Rawls goes so far as to say that one of the essentials of objectivity is that it is a point of view to be distinguished from that held by any agent; objectivity is thus determined by reference to an ideal potentially beyond real people's reach.

What are we to make of a neutrality which both is and is not defensible in neutral terms, which both is and is not beyond human experience? It is a poor answer to the problem of difference. The advocate of difference may suspect that a particular, advantaged perspective – that of the proverbial, able-bodied, heterosexual, secular and liberal white male, perhaps – can sneak in under the cover of Rawlsian objectivity, however contrary to Rawls's intentions. On the other hand, if Rawls ties his argument to practices current in contemporary liberal societies, his theory is vulnerable to the wars of difference in a more direct way. A theory founded on existing practices or currently held values runs the risk of being held hostage by power politics, where the advantaged are bound to win out. In taming justice as fairness, rendering it an interpretive theory of the actual practices of citizenship, Rawls becomes guilty of an undue optimism about not just the value of agreement on his terms, but the extent to which this agreement is in place. If this agreement is lacking, Rawlsian justice is in trouble.

Some interpreters of Rawls resist the idea of a minimal consensus based on the burdens of judgement and stress instead the idea of an ethical consensus that will exclude the unreasonable and the immoral.[69] If objectivity is an 'in-the-world' posture to which real agents must aspire and approximate, it must have a moral justification. This must be a justification that regulates our agreement, rather than trailing after it, however contrary, as Lister notes, to political liberalism's aim of finding agreement on a minimal 'qualified acceptability requirement' which rules out appeal to moral reasons.[70]

Thus Rawls must, in the end, abandon the artificial segregation of politics from comprehensive moral views about how we are to live. As Macleod puts it, it is 'better to argue about the merits of different purported reasons than to insist that sound political argument must be neutral about the good life.'[71] There is much about Rawls's theory, its insistence on the ideals of citizenship, moral reciprocity, autonomy and rationality that in fact suggests a comprehensive view. But Rawls's concern that principles of justice emerge from existing social sources means that the content of these principles is so attenuated as to refer only to something arbitrarily carved out as 'political.' No wonder that Rawls's liberal critics also fear a neutralism about neutrality itself.[72]

### The Extent of Neutrality

This brings us to the third problem, the extent of neutrality. Here there seems no ambiguity: political liberalism aims to exclude questions of substantive value about how individuals should live. However, Rawls's position has perfectionist elements. He notes that individuals tend to be motivated by an 'Aristotelian principle' that attributes greater value to more complex and demanding tasks.[73] Moreover, Rawls admits there may be perfectionist issues that are neither 'constitutional essentials' nor questions of basic justice but which might have 'fundamental importance.' Thus, 'national parks and preserving wilderness areas and plant species and laying aside funds for museums and the arts' might legitimately enter political debate, and the 'restrictions of public reason may not apply to them.'[74] Political values only 'normally' or 'typically' take precedence over the non-political. As Mulhall and Swift note, it appears that 'there are circumstances in which, even with respect to constitutional essentials and matters of basic justice, non-political [perfectionist] values might trump political ones.'[75]

These qualifications are a welcome admission about the role of human flourishing in public policy. Yet, lumbered with an arbitrary divide between the political and comprehensive, Rawls does not explain how the two might be connected or reconciled. Political theory and practice cannot consider what constitutes a life well lived beyond the matter of citizens' capacity to sustain liberal society. Should society promote the arts? Preserve historic architecture? Conserve green spaces? Inculcate values of political engagement in its adult citizens? For Rawls, bizarrely, none of these questions are properly political ones.

## Impartial Flourishing

Let us leave behind the dubious concept of neutrality, and its associations with the neutered, unreal person and a sphere beyond value. What of the more modest concept of impartiality, a posture of partial persons seeking to be fair? If impartiality is to be retrieved, its justification is not easily made by reference to a current consensus about political values, given the realities of difference. No more helpful is the view of Habermas, that consensus is available in some idealised communicative structure characterised by the frank, open exchanging of views.[76] From the perspective of difference, such a view puts the cart before the horse, since cultural identity renders persons unable to communicate in the way Habermas requires. The basis for impartiality must come from political theory itself; Rawls cannot avoid casting his position as a 'comprehensive doctrine,' suitably understood.

It is no solution, in either Rawls's terms or those of his radical opponents, to resuscitate some kind of foundationalism, a doctrine of truth or such like. But we can draw on the political ideas that have served us well, that have made the world a more just place, admitting that our understandings of these ideas remain incomplete. The moral justification for impartiality – that society should allow individuals to choose how to live because choosing how to live is a fundamental aspect of the good life – also suggests that impartiality should not impose a blockade on moral views, either as the justification for impartiality, or in the design of the environment in which individuals can be given impartial respect to make their own choices.[77]

Lister points out how marriage policy presupposes agreement on the value of human intimacy for wellbeing, even if we don't all avail ourselves of it, or its particular instantiation within marriage.[78] This 'higher order unanimity' tracks the independent objective value of marriage rather than vice versa. This is more ambitious than the conclusion that marriage is 'almost universally useful,' as Brake puts it.[79] An 'avoidance thesis' on the question of substantive value is doomed to failure given that the state's recognition of marriage cannot help but be founded on the role of marriage for human flourishing.[80] If neutrality was the aim, the state would be forced to get out of the marriage business altogether.[81] The campaign to extend marriage to same-sex couples is therefore a matter, not just of honouring rights to equality, but also enabling all to have the opportunity for this important source of human wellbeing.[82] Thus we can take the leap and commit to a conception of human flourishing, stating baldly that wellbeing comes from living a life of autonomy, self-determination and freedom from coercion, as well as the full development of one's capacities. An egalitarian theory strives to make such a life, what might be termed a life of 'self-realisation,' available to all persons. As Nussbaum emphasises, even those with mental disabilities have an interest in developing 'the full range of their powers' to enjoy the sort of independence 'their condition allows.'[83]

Rather than smuggling such ideals into a theory of justice as 'primary goods' that are instruments for pursuing our conception of the good, whatever it might be, these ideals are understood as features of the good itself. As Macedo remarks, there are 'better and worse ways of using our freedom.' It is fitting that liberal institutions 'help, in modest and gentle ways, to promote the ideal of autonomy, for that capacity helps make people more competent as liberal citizens and better able to flourish as persons in a liberal society.'[84] As we will see in subsequent chapters, this strategy need not run afoul of Rawls's worries about dictating a single way of living to all; the modern comprehensive doctrine has little in common with monistic conceptions such as theological ones from the past.

Such a position is both a scaling down from the heights of a God's eye view of rationality and a building up from the thin theory of value that emerges from the paltry resources of the current consensus on public reason. For the postmodernists are surely right that reason, in either guise, is in trouble, even if we do not want to join their dance on reason's grave. But simply consulting the current consensus denies us a critical perspective on our practices. Irrationality can afflict people's choice of means to realise their goals. Buying lottery tickets is not the most effective means of remedying poverty; martyr-like sacrifice of self will likely fail to promote the happiness of either the housewife or her family; taking drugs will not provide a real escape from the ghetto. If people feel trapped in their situations of powerlessness, they may act in ways that legitimate their situation or deploy fantasies of escape; such actions are understandable, but they are not rational. Marx's concept of ideology refers to how we can have self-deceiving beliefs that render inadequate social conditions more palatable. We should not assume that the oppressed enjoy some kind of epistemic privilege, as purported by Lenin's workers' vanguard, feminist 'standpoint epistemology' or critical race theory's epistemic injustice. Sometimes being an underdog helps one see the world aright; but sometimes it obscures the world.[85]

What is the role of impartiality in this account? To fit our picture, it cannot mean agnosticism about the good, nor can it mean a perspective beyond human experience. Impartiality is perhaps better able to accommodate such demands than the more grandiose, god-like terms of objectivity or neutrality; but impartiality still has something of the transcendent about it: a posture devoid of partiality. In what follows I hope to show how impartiality might be appropriately 'tamed.'

The debunking of impartiality often generates an implicit appeal to its ideals. When, for example, Marx declares that 'the ruling ideas are always the ideas of the ruling class,' he appeals to a communist alternative where ideas are not the effects of power. Such a vision is ruled out of court by postmodern interpretations, be it Lyotard's idea of incommensurable narratives, Foucault's contention that moral legitimacy is only provisionally enjoyed by oppositional discourses; or Rorty's view that the justification for political practices is simply the credo that 'this is the way we do things around here.'[86] None of these views inspire much confidence that we can be open to views other than our own. Indeed, this bleak picture of a world without impartiality likely produces a yearning for the recovery of that which is so quickly dismissed: a measure outside the particular perspective of any one party to repair intolerance and misunderstanding.

Moreover, the force of the critique of difference ultimately relies on the idea of impartiality in some sense. The appeals on behalf of disenfranchised groups call upon us to see their claims as legitimate, to take a more distanced view of our particular concerns in order to see the concerns of others aright. It is because of our commitment to the ideal of impartiality that the claims of the different command our attention, and it is because of the fact of difference that impartiality is required – we would not need impartiality if we were all the same.[87] The ideas of reasonableness, impartiality and cooperative communication owe their necessity to the difficulties that beset them. Impartiality thus figures as a regulative ideal because of our status as interested participants in political affairs.

Impartiality cannot, however, have imperialistic designs on the culture of society, reducing all political debate to mere adjudication, forswearing all questions of substantive value. Impartiality might seem to dictate abstinence on questions of the good or commitments to value; however, impartiality need not be at odds with perfectionist goals. Impartiality necessitates a pluralist conception of the good and thus public institutions should be impartial insofar as they permit us to pursue worthwhile commitments and values to the full, so long as they do not interfere with anyone else's pursuit. In other words, impartial institutions are a precondition of the good life, necessary for us to attain a life of autonomy, freedom from coercion and self-determination.

Impartiality is an important feature of the good. First, it makes sense to think of the good life as requiring a well-ordered, impartial society, not just in order to secure one the good, but because the good involves it being enjoyed by one's fellows. A good which is the fruits of, or consistent with, a partial, unfair society would thus in some sense be flawed as a good. Second, the good life is a life which is marked, not just by the fulfilment of one's capacities and goals, but where one has developed a moral consciousness, characterised by, among other things, some measure of impartiality.[88] Thus we can avoid the twin horns of Rawls's dilemma – the metaphysical implausibility of the idealised perspective versus the moral implausibility of the empirically given – by changing Rawls's framework in some subtle but important respects. Impartiality is an orientation in our current practices, rather than exemplified by them; both besieged and evolving, impartiality is a fragile, partial historical achievement on which we draw in political debate. And once we see how impartiality respects the individual freedom central to the good life, we can thence look to other ways in which society can further the conditions and possibilities of living well.

The dilemma of difference is precisely that the different are other than us, distanced from our concerns and unable to call upon our care in any intimate sense. And yet of course those who are different are also like us, human beings who require fair treatment. Thus we aim to design our public institutions so that we need not rely on the precarious moral attentions of particular persons, but are treated, however 'other,' as the same in worth and dignity in the public domain. The impartial treatment to which we are entitled as citizens is a politics of civility, a care and attention that, unlike the care of intimates, is generalised and abstract. Impartiality is civil in two senses. It is a mode of interaction appropriate to a certain space: a secular, public domain, be in it on a crowded bus or in a courtroom. And it is civil in the sense of being a form of decency, a mode of consideration, an expression of regard, which does not call up on us the unreliable and potentially patronising sentiments of charity, pity or care. Indeed, even as underrated a virtue as politeness has more than just an etymological affinity with politics, with the relation of citizens in the polis.[89]

Civility, of course, is a posture that we ought to take to all, and intrinsic to impartiality is the idea that it subsumes all citizens; it has an inevitable egalitarian aspect. Historically, impartiality's egalitarian aspirations were quite modest, referring only to how laws, however partial, applied equally to all. But a sharp distinction between formal and substantive understandings of impartiality is difficult to sustain. Impartiality carries with it an idea of fairness, and fairness invites us to ask whether a narrow, formal interpretation reflects the 'true' meaning of the concept, whether it enables ways of living that are consistent with its ideals.

Substantive justice, however, recedes in Rawls's later work. The difference principle, the redistributive maxim which dictates that inequalities must be to the benefit of the worst off, is downgraded, not a 'constitutional essential' since, unlike basic freedoms, it is less urgent, more difficult to find agreement about, and harder to ascertain whether it has been realised than questions of liberties and rights.[90] At the same time, the satisfaction of basic needs is stipulated as a precondition for constitutional principles,[91] what Rawls too casually refers to in the final restatement of his views as 'a property-owning democracy.'[92] In this 'new conversation,'[93] questions of substantive egalitarianism have thus been removed from the heart of the debate about justice, to be resolved either prior to, or after, the basic structure; moreover, the constitutional constraints put on political discourse make it difficult to raise such questions, let alone resolve them. Small wonder that commentators on Rawls complained that the egalitarian concerns of the difference principle had been muted: they play a 'secondary role,' contended Williams, end up being 'drowned out' as Okin put it, or have been downright 'abandoned,' according to Barry.[94]

Here Rawls's concern to base his theory on a consensus immanent in the political structure of liberal societies prompts some moves that again seem question-begging. It is not at all clear there is agreement in the United States that basic needs be met as a pre-constitutional essential, for the very reason that Rawls presumably thinks a more radical redistribution is too contentious to bear on the constitution. This suggests, again, that consensus looks like an unreliable measure; our position will have to be a more principled one, in which case questions of material position must be addressed in a deliberate way, not presupposed or postponed. Of course, the principles involved may come from current practices and ideas, but we will have to 'work them up,' both in terms of providing moral arguments for them, and in terms of expanding their range.

After all, if what people will agree to becomes our criterion, not only have we abandoned the terrain of social justice, but even Rawls's more modestly defined goals look tenuous. McCabe argues that liberals like Rawls end up being cowed by cultural diversity on all fronts. The fact that some people subscribe to fundamentalist religions opposed to teaching recognised science in public schools should not prompt us to give up on liberal education.[95] Why should cultural diversity prompt the liberal to abandon the pursuit of an equal society that enables its citizens to live full and rich lives? Moreover, if in fact it turns out that social and economic inequality are the result of cultural and material deprivation, then the egalitarian liberal should look to how the state might provide cultural resources that enable individuals to raise their level of flourishing. Here even Rawls's original theory of justice looks a problematic tool. As Sen has argued, the fact of difference may mean that an adequate, multi-faceted conception of equality dictates radical revisions to Rawls's original idea of primary goods; given the variations in people's capacities, it is hardly fair to secure for everyone the same index of primary goods to cover their needs as citizens.[96] Sen's criticism reminds us how the universal ideals of impartiality and public reason may require variegated treatment, diverse standards; just like the judge who applies a general law and then passes a specific sentence in light of the convicted person's situation, we must take account of the particular in order to impartially apply a universal standard of equality. In sum, an appropriate respect for difference should figure as an impetus for revising our understandings of equality, rather than postponing their consideration, as Rawls counsels.

## Conclusion

Liberal theory has tended to be couched in ways that fail to take seriously the problem of difference. The idea that cultural identity may require recognition is often reduced to a communitarian desire for a univocal community and a monistic conception of the good, and thus liberals such as Rawls provide a neutralist response that misses the mark. The problem of difference requires the retrieval of Rawls's earlier egalitarian concerns, placing them at the heart of a theory of justice, and expanding them to consider how we can better equalise access to the constituents of living well. If we are to attend to inequality, we must also retrieve the ideal of impartiality, castigated by difference exponents as both a metaphysical pretence and an undesirable political goal. In the face of a crisis of legitimation of liberal ideas in political culture, however, the defence of impartiality requires more substantive principles about equality and human flourishing than allowed by the Rawlsian constraint of neutrality. Our next task is to consider the work of another contemporary liberal who seeks to accommodate difference, this time by means of a philosophy of multiculturalism.

## Notes

1 Rawls, *Political Liberalism*, 133.
2 Ibid., note 1, 175.
3 Ibid., 78.
4 Ibid., 11.
5 Ibid., xviii.
6 Ibid., 37.
7 Ibid., 111.
8 Ibid., 311.
9 Ibid., 15.
10 Ibid., 8.
11 Ibid., 233.
12 Ibid., 19.
13 Ibid., 32.
14 Ibid., 29–35.
15 Ibid., 38.
16 Ibid., 51.
17 Ibid., 50.
18 Ibid., 59–61.
19 Ibid., 32 and 158–9. Some critics contend Rawls's project is better served by a 'convergence' rather than consensus interpretation. See F. D'Agostino, *Free Public Reason: Making it Up as We Go*, 30; K. Vallier, 'Convergence and Consensus in Public Reason,' 261–80.
20 Rawls, however, denies this, *Political Liberalism*, xvii n6; see also the discussion in S. Mulhall and A. Swift, *Liberals and Communitarians*, 167–70.

21 A. MacIntyre, *After Virtue*, and M. Sandel, *Liberalism and the Limits of Justice*.
22 P. Weithman, *Why Political Liberalism? On John Rawls's Political Turn*.
23 Rawls, *Political Liberalism*, 120, fn. 1.
24 M. Minow, *Making All the Difference*, 150.
25 Nussbaum, *Frontiers of Justice*, 145–7.
26 T. Scanlon, *What We Owe Each Other*, 177–87. The contemporary disability movement stresses including mentally disabled persons as citizens rather than patients. See B. Arneil, *Diverse Communities: The Problem with Social Capital*, 200–40; A. Beckett, *Citizenship and Vulnerability, Disability and Issues of Social and Political Engagement*, 162–91.
27 Laclau and Mouffe, *Hegemony and Socialist Strategy*, 122–7.
28 See J. Medena, *The Epistemology of Resistance*, 131.
29 See S.M. Okin, *Women in Western Political Thought*, C. Pateman, *The Sexual Contract*, G. Lloyd, *The Main of Reason: 'Male' and 'Female' in Western Philosophy*.
30 See Gilligan, *In a Different Voice* and Ruddick, *Maternal Thinking*, and writings by Irigaray and Kristeva compiled in Marks and de Courtivron, eds, *New French Feminisms*.
31 Minow, 152–3.
32 Young, *Justice and the Politics of Difference*, 124–30.
33 Ibid., 104, 112.
34 I make this argument in *The Concept of Socialist Law*, ch. 3.
35 Minow's book ends, surprisingly, with a gesture of this kind: *Making All the Difference*, 376, note 26.
36 Ibid., 382.
37 Quoted in D. Cornell, *Transformations: Recollective Imagination and Sexual Difference*, 95.
38 P. Williams, *The Alchemy of Race and Rights*, 11.
39 Young, *Justice and the Politics of Difference*, 104.
40 Ibid., 107, 153 and 163–73.
41 Minow, *Making all the Difference*, 379. See also Nedelsky, 'Rights as Relationships.'
42 C. Mouffe, 'Political Liberalism, Neutrality and the Political,' 322.
43 Rawls, *Political Liberalism*, xxviii–xxix.
44 D. Weinstock, 'A Neutral Conception of Reasonableness?,' 234–47. See K. Vallier, *Liberal Politics and Public Faith: Beyond Separation*, K. Greenawalt, *Religious Convictions and Political Choice*, T. Bailey, *Rawls and Religion*.
45 M. Nussbaum, 'Perfectionist Liberalism and Political Liberalism,' 37.
46 J. Bohman and H. Richardson, 'Liberalism, Deliberative Democracy, and "Reasons That All Can Accept",' 256.
47 W. Kymlicka, *Liberalism, Community and Culture*, 177; see Kittay and Feder, *The Subject of Care*, 193; and Nussbaum, *Frontiers of Justice*, 116.
48 Rawls, *Political Liberalism*, 50.
49 As H. Brighouse puts it in 'Is there a Neutral Justification for Liberalism?' 196.
50 B. Ackerman, 'Why Dialogue?' 16.
51 J. Rawls, *Justice as Fairness: A Restatement*, 184–6.
52 J. Quong, *Liberalism without Perfection*, 4.
53 S. Lecce, *Against Perfectionism: Defending Liberal Neutrality*, 265.
54 A. Patten, *Equal Recognition: The Moral Foundation of Minority Rights*, 115.
55 J. Waldron, *Liberal Rights*, 167.
56 Dworkin, *A Matter of Principle*, 203.
57 Barry, *Justice as Impartiality*, 77.
58 C. Larmore, *Patterns of Moral Complexity*, 129.
59 Waldron, *Liberal Rights*, 160–2.
60 Appiah, *The Ethics of Identity*, 27–8.
61 Rawls, *Political Liberalism*, 192–3 and *Justice as Fairness*, 154.

62 *Political Liberalism*, 27, 40–1.
63 T. Nagel, *Equality and Partiality*, ch. 2; see also T. Nagel, *The View from Nowhere*.
64 *Political Liberalism*, 116.
65 Ibid., 8, 11.
66 Ibid., 120.
67 J. Raz, *Ethics in the Public Domain: Essays in the Morality of Law and Politics*, 52.
68 Rawls, *Political Liberalism*, 111 (my emphasis), 119–20.
69 D. Estlund, *Democratic Authority, A Philosophical Framework*, 4, L. Wenar, 'Political Liberalism: An Internal Critique,' 32–62, M. Nussbaum, 'Perfectionist Liberalism and Political Liberalism,' 3–45.
70 A. Lister, *Public Reason and Political Community*, 9.
71 C. Macleod, 'Neutrality, Public Reason and Deliberative Democracy,' 175.
72 See R. Arneson, 'Neutrality and Political Liberalism,' and G. Crowder, 'Neutrality and Liberal Pluralism.'
73 Rawls, *A Theory of Justice*, 424–33.
74 Rawls, *Political Liberalism*, 214–15.
75 Mulhall and Swift, *Liberals and Communitarians*, 224.
76 As Habermas commends against the postmodernists in *The Philosophical Discourses of Modernity*, ch. 11–12.
77 C. Larmore makes the case for a substantive moral basis for liberalism, contra Rawls, in *The Autonomy of Morality*, 71. Contrast this with J. Simmons, *Justification and Legitimacy*, which goes further than Rawls in its attenuation of the moral justification for the state, in which authority depends simply on de facto acceptance.
78 Lister, *Public Reason and Political Community*, 161–6.
79 E. Brake, 'Minimal Marriage: What Political Liberalism Implies for Marriage Law,' 329–30.
80 C.A. Ball, 'Moral Foundations for a Discourse on Same-Sex Marriage, Looking Beyond Political Liberalism,' 1894.
81 M. Sandel, *Justice: What's the Right Thing to Do?*, 257.
82 See S. Macedo, *Just Married: Same-Sex Couples, Monogamy and the Future of Marriage*.
83 Nussbaum, *Frontiers of Justice*, 218. See also C. Lowry, 'Perfectionism for Neutralists,' K. Brownlee and A. Cureton, eds, *Disability and Disadvantage*, J. Bickenbach, F. Felder, B. Schmitz eds, *Disability and the Good Human Life*.
84 S. Macedo, 'Sexuality and Liberty: Making Room for Nature and Tradition?,' 87; and S. Macedo, *Liberal Virtues*, 263.
85 See L. Code, *What Can She Know? Feminist Theory and the Construction of Knowledge*, and Fricker, *Epistemic Injustice*; but see also S. Haack, *Manifesto of a Passionate Moderate*.
86 J.-F. Lyotard, *The Postmodern Condition: A Report on Knowledge*, and R. Rorty, 'Postmodernist Bourgeois Liberalism,' 80, and *Contingency, Irony and Solidarity*.
87 I am grateful to Neil MacCormick for suggesting this to me.
88 This is to render Rawls's claim that a sense of justice is one of our highest-order interests a more explicit moral requirement, rather than a quasi-empirical claim.
89 See M. Kingwell's stimulating essay, 'Is it Rational to Be Polite?,' 87.
90 *Political Liberalism*, 227–30.
91 Ibid., 7.
92 Rawls, *Justice as Fairness*, 135–40. Radical critics of capitalism, though conceding that Rawls 'says very little' about the democratic socialist implications of this idea, have pointed to its progressive implications. See M. O'Neill and T. Williamson, eds, *Property-Owning Democracy: Rawls and Beyond*, 3.
93 D. Estlund, 'The Survival of Egalitarian Justice in John Rawls's *Political Liberalism*,' 77–8.
94 B. Williams, 'Rawls Rethinks Rawls,' S.M. Okin, 'Book Review,' 1010; B. Barry, 'John Rawls and the Search for Stability,' 913.
95 D. McCabe, 'Knowing about the Good: A Problem with Antiperfectionism,' 316.
96 Sen, *Inequality Reexamined*, 8–9, 26–7 and ch. 5.

# 5 Equality and the Antinomies of Multicultural Liberalism

It is increasingly argued that states have a duty to protect minority cultures. This view reflects, as we've seen, the growing influence of the politics of 'difference,' where individuals are understood as bearing incommensurable identities based on race, ethnicity or gender. It also reflects the upsurge in demands for national self-determination, be it from indigenous peoples, Catalans, Scots or Quebecois. The influence of these developments is such that cultural rights might be viewed as a logical extension of the citizenship rights that enable citizens to be fully participating members of political communities. In the 1960s, Marshall claimed that twentieth-century 'social rights' to health, welfare and employment complemented nineteenth-century 'political rights' to the vote and to freedom of expression, which in turn extended the eighteenth-century model of 'civil rights' to fair judicial procedures.[1] Should cultural rights be understood as one more step in this process?

Whereas Rawls attempts to accommodate the politics of difference by narrowing liberalism's scope, Kymlicka urges a different strategy: he contends that cultural bias is inevitable to some extent and that this requires special arrangements for cultural minorities. The upshot might seem quite unRawlsian, but it remains that Kymlicka's multicultural liberalism affirms the Rawlsian project of state neutrality.[2] This chapter considers liberal arguments for, as Kymlicka puts it, 'group-differentiated citizenship'[3] and argues that the ideas of freedom and equality intrinsic to citizenship rights tell against extending rights to minority cultures in the absence of some normative assessment of the culture in question. Citizens should be understood to have an entitlement to culture in the broadest sense, as a constituent of equal wellbeing, since their capacity to be self-determining beings depends on a measure of cultural enrichment. Cultural enrichment may require the protection of endangered ways of life – such as those of minority cultures – but only if these cultures do not run afoul of citizens' wellbeing as autonomous individuals.

## The Value of Culture

Geertz holds that human beings are unique in possessing culture: we are suspended in webs of significance we ourselves have spun, and culture is 'just those webs'. Culture consists of 'interworked systems of construable signs,' a 'context' where 'social events, behaviours, institutions or processes' take place.[4] Of the many definitions offered by the *Oxford English Dictionary*, the closest to Geertz's concept is 'a particular form or type of intellectual development,' but most definitions indicate a normative aspect, such as 'the cultivating or development of the mind or faculties: improvement or refinement by education and training.'[5] The idea of improvement implies a hierarchical sense of better or worse cultures, and more or less cultured persons.[6] But we need not embrace such a hierarchical conception, deploying instead the idea of culture as a form of intellectual development or formation to acknowledge a diversity of cultures, whose importance is derived internally by their participants. Culture is a 'mode of life,' or, as Appiah puts it succinctly, the 'products of human work and thought,'[7] which, in Kim's words, permits 'the self-conscious evaluation of human possibilities in the light of a system of values that reflect prevailing ideals about what human life ought to be.' Because of its conventional, human-made character, culture is inevitably contrasted with nature, the biological, as the 'uniquely human means' by which the evolutionary process is affected.[8]

An important distinction is made between societal or national cultures, on the one hand, and immigrant or ethnic cultures, on the other. Societal or national cultures are the cultures of national majorities and minorities within a state, such as Aboriginal cultures, Quebecois culture and the dominant Anglophone culture in Canada, or Scottish, Northern Irish or Welsh cultures along with the English culture in the United Kingdom. Immigrant or ethnic cultures, on the other hand, refer to a heritage that individuals might keep in the process of electing to integrate within a national culture. Kymlicka uses this typology in order to distinguish entitlements, holding that only national cultures are entitled to cultural protection per se. However, it can be argued that, in certain cases at least, ethnic groups can have as much claim to being 'societal cultures' as national minorities: many people do not immigrate as a straightforward matter of choice, and the cultures of immigrant groups are sometimes stronger than those of national minorities.[9]

It is incontrovertible that people value culture. Cultures shape self-identity, contribute to self-respect, add meaning to individual actions, provide a sense of belonging, and foster intergenerational bonds.[10] In short, culture provides a secure sense of self that is necessary for agency of any kind. Languages, the media for citizens' participation in society, are sustained by cultures. However, a culture's relation to individuals' fulfilment is not always positive. Consider the fraught relations individuals have to cultures that abnegate or hold in contempt some of their values or aspects of their identities (e.g. their sexuality, attire, career ambitions, dietary preferences, and so on).

A prominent communitarian argument for protecting culture – the Quebec policy of cultural 'survivance' endorsed by Taylor – in fact permits measures that might hamper individual liberty in order to ensure that culture be preserved. On this view, the current generation can be entitled to bind

future generations to their culture; indeed, the culture itself bears such entitlements, rather than its members, who might otherwise disavow the policy
of cultural preservation.[11] This strategy of detaching culture from individual
interests respects culture, but it is in tension with the liberal emphasis on individual liberty, equality or indeed any other person-centred normative
criterion.

That individuals value or need culture may not entail that the state is obligated to protect a particular culture, let alone take steps to ensure its survival.
First, we need evidence that people's relation to their primary culture is a
special source of value that is central to a secure sense of self. It is true that
some people who lose their culture in a process of cultural decimation experience this as an assault on their very selves. Not only are they dispossessed of
their culture, they are also alienated from the majority culture (which after all
was likely responsible for the process of decimation); they are thus owed
measures of cultural recovery. In other cases, however, people lose their original culture and endorse a new one in a complex process that, whilst not the
outcome of a free choice, cannot be demonised as simply the result of oppression. The ways of life of the majority are hard to resist for individuals who
want to function and prosper in the society in which they live.

Of course, considerations about protecting things of value that are threatened
are not unique to culture. There are many ways of life, not necessarily connected to nationality or ethnicity, which are important to individuals and which
could count as quasi-cultural forms deserving of protection. Mining communities, fishing villages, cottage industries, traditional architecture, arts and
crafts, all figure in ways of life that give value and meaning to those who participate in them, and that risk being submerged by dominant, modern forms of
life. To which we can add a myriad of declining or moribund cultural forms that
people value, be they drive-in cinemas, greasy spoons or the cloister, which are
less likely to garner public favour. In light of this, the idea that the state ought to
protect a social form from extinction would seem to require a clear justification.
This suggests that criteria should be established to adjudicate the extent to which
cultural formation enables individuals to be self-determining and creative, to find
happiness, or to enjoy things of objective value. Such a strategy would be rooted
in an egalitarian argument that emphasises the importance of citizens' equal wellbeing. This is the position I will defend here.

## Liberty and Neutrality, Choice and Culture

Culture or ethnicity has had varying fortunes in the history of liberalism.
Many nineteenth-century liberals, such as Mill, were unabashedly Eurocen-
tric. A tradition of cultural liberalism, however, found expression in the work
of romantics from continental Europe, such as Fichte and Mazzini, and British
idealists like Hobhouse. These thinkers agreed that, as Kymlicka puts it, 'the
promotion of individuality and the development of personality is intimately
tied up with membership in one's national group.'[12] Since the Second World
War, however, liberals have avoided discussing culture, haunted, perhaps, by

the preoccupation with culture and ethnicity of Nazis and other racists, and until relatively recently liberals took a 'hands-off' approach to the problem of minority cultures, leaving it to individuals to join or leave, promote or neglect them.

Indeed, contemporary liberalism would seem ill-equipped to protect cultures, since its commitment to individual freedom suggests warding off, rather than fostering, interventions by social groups that might impede individuals' projects and goals.[13] The canonical liberalism of Mill focuses on the individual's liberty to choose how to live, a view that underlies Berlin's 'negative freedom,' whereby individuals are free insofar as they are unimpeded in their actions.[14] Dworkin holds that the state shows equal concern and respect for all citizens when it adopts a posture of neutrality about questions of value, thus rejecting as illegitimate 'external preferences' individuals might seek to impose on other people.[15] And as we saw in the last chapter, Rawls disavows 'comprehensive doctrines' that promote certain ways of life over others, even if they are liberal in character.[16] These neutralist views suggest that individuals should be free to choose cultures, but the state should be barred from actively protecting them. In his early work Kymlicka warned that communitarianism risked undermining choice, preventing individuals from living their lives 'from the inside.' Liberalism, in contrast, stresses the capacity, to choose one's way of life, and also to revise that choice.[17] Given that minority cultures are communities that seek to shape the choices of their members, it looks like the liberal critique of communitarianism[18] would also prompt a critique of policies of cultural protection; neutralist liberalism seems least likely to endorse a multiculturalist politics of group-differentiated citizenship.

In fact, however, a commitment to the protection of minority cultures has been a hallmark of contemporary liberalism. This is not just because of the post-Soviet alliances with defiant minorities that opportunistic liberal politicians have made in international politics. There are theoretical grounds, too, insofar as the emphasis on pluralist principles in many variants of liberal theory means that liberalism is hospitable terrain for what has been dubbed 'ethnoanarchism.'[19] But the most influential argument for the protection of culture is that of Kymlicka, the neutralist critic of community, who holds that where minority cultures are 'threatened with debasement or decay, we must act to protect' them.[20] For Kymlicka, the goal is 'secure cultural pluralism,' which can be assured without violating the requirements of neutrality. 'Cultures are not valuable in and of themselves, but because it is only through having access to a societal culture that people have access to a range of meaningful options.'[21]

This seems a curious position for two reasons. First, so much of what is constitutive of a culture is not merely instrumentally valuable (are Shakespeare or Caribbean dub poets valuable only as 'options' thrown up by the cultures in which they happen to originate?). Second, and more significantly, though societal cultures may provide access to a range of meaningful options, they can and typically do act to delimit the range of options available to individuals. Protecting culture therefore often involves measures that will discourage individuals from exercising their capacity to choose (indeed, that is often why protective measures are sought). This is obviously the case for cultures with fundamentalist traditions. Members of such cultures do not see the integrity of their culture as enabling choice. On the contrary, restricting choice is the purpose, rationale and consequence of reinforcing these cultures.

Kymlicka contends that we should try to render such cultures more liberal, noting that to take other cultures to be inherently illiberal and incapable of reform is ethnocentric.[22] Certainly, to consider cultures as 'no-go' areas when it comes to constructive criticism is not, as Taylor notes, a 'genuine act of respect.'[23] Cultures are typically hodgepodges of a variety of elements in which illiberal values are only a part; and hence illiberal cultures can be liberalised without destroying them. Phillips, wary of a multiculturalism that 'helps nourish cultural stereotypes,'[24] proposes that we adopt 'multiculturalism without culture,' dispensing 'with the reified notions of culture,' and seeking simply to address inequalities among cultural groups.[25]

Not all liberals, however, are at ease with this reformist agenda. Kukathas, in contrast, contends one is not protecting a culture if the culture in question is pressured to take on values outside of it. Groups can practice illiberal ways of life, so long as they offer a liberal right of exit.[26] Shachar's solution is to propose systems of joint governance, 'multiculturalist jurisdictions,' whereby authority over marriage and family law is shared between the state and minority groups, allowing individuals to opt out and seek state remedy in cases of unjust treatment, a system which better promises, she argues, 'transformative accommodation.'[27]

However, such systems promise further to entrench the position of those most vulnerable. As Chambers notes, on this view groups can 'implement unjust or unequal laws' that undermine individuals' ability to choose, yet are 'subject to state interference on an ad hoc basis' that nonetheless 'leaves the unjust law intact for others.'[28] Such proposals amount to what Green calls a 'checkerboard' liberal society, which cannot help but be insufficiently liberal however easily one can hop from illiberal to liberal square.[29] Moreover, it provides no solution to those who want both personal liberty and cultural identity. As Phillips notes, the right to exit 'does not provide enough protection to people living in oppressive conditions,' while failing to 'offer enough of a solution to those with a strong normative commitment to their cultural or religious group.'[30] The problem of 'minorities within minorities'[31] remains a challenge for the multiculturalist liberal who seeks both to protect and to change others' cultures.[32]

Lest the multiculturalist suggest we simply give priority to freedom-friendly cultures, it should be noted that the shaping of choice is intrinsic to culture, no matter what its content. The demand to protect culture is essentially a demand to encourage affiliation with that culture and discourage affiliation with others, essentially diminishing the possibility that certain exit choices will be exercised. For example, it is often said that today's Quebec, in contrast to the traditional, rural, Catholic society of the past, is a liberal society 'comme les autres' on the North American continent and thus that its nationalism is benignly liberal.[33] But it remains that Quebec nationalists seek to inhibit choice, particularly in the domain of language. Thus under Quebec law immigrants must send their children to French schools, shopkeepers must have French signs, and so forth. Choice is restricted, and with the aim of forestalling further choices of opting out of (or remaining in) Quebec's French culture.[34]

Although Kymlicka contends that 'our current ends are not always worthy of our continued allegiance, and exposure to other ways of life helps us make informed judgements about what is truly valuable,' his call is not for freedom to go beyond one's societal culture, but for freedom to move within it, choosing which features are worth developing, and which are without value.[35] The choices to pursue 'other ways of life' turn out to extend no further than the perimeters of our culture. This is a plausible empirical point: most of us do not consider quitting the culture in which we were brought up, and if our culture is taken from us our ability to choose may be hampered, however limited the choices it offered us. Culture is not a hobby that one picks up, tries out and decides to accept or reject. But, in that case, the rationale for protecting culture is not, after all, to assure an array of choices.

The argument that state support for culture is but a means of recognising everyone's interest in 'an adequate range of options' or the 'non-controversial value of a secure cultural pluralism'[36] skirts the issue of political neutrality about the good. The problem besets any purportedly neutral argument for protecting certain cultural forms. Dworkin similarly holds that state support for the arts does not reflect a preference for the arts in particular; such subsidies are merely a neutral effort at ensuring that the choice of the arts is available alongside other choices.[37] The idea of neutrality, however, becomes unrecognisable in such discussions. Talk of an 'adequate range' of possibilities fudges what is actually meant by adequacy. Liberal states do not subsidise all options that would otherwise be unavailable; they subsidise, dare we say, the 'good' ones, those conducive to self-determination, creativity and intellectual development: art galleries, rather than (arguably equally vulnerable) bingo halls.

Non-neutralist liberals are better placed to defend multiculturalism. Thus Raz offers a 'liberal case' for cultural rights that centres on the importance of culture for individual wellbeing. Culture determines the opportunities that give life meaning, facilitates social relations, and provides a sense of individual identity. Thus the state should not only repudiate 'a policy which forcibly detaches children from the culture of their parents,' but assure its citizens of 'unimpeded membership in a respected and prosperous cultural group.'[38] Raz contends that cultures are the 'precondition for, and a factor which gives shape and content to, individual freedom.'[39] Freedom here is reconceived as the prerequisite of agency. Similarly, though he frankly acknowledges that cultural identity has an uneasy relation with liberal values, Spinner-Halev argues that individuals 'need to be rooted,' and thus liberal societies should adopt a policy of 'pluralistic integration that protects cultural practices that are compatible with liberalism,' and which will 'work to break down cultural boundaries.'[40]

In sum, minority cultural rights protect the conditions for choice making in a minority culture, but they also inhibit the kinds of choices individuals may make. The case for minority cultural rights is difficult to couch with the liberal vocabulary of neutrality and freedom: as Phillips observes, 'wherever there are groups, there is always the potential for coercion.'[41] Influencing choice may not be a problem if one believes, as I will argue, that society should seek to further worthwhile pursuits and discourage lesser ones, on the understanding that a valuable life is an autonomous one. Such a position must involve a conscious effort on the part of policy-makers to enable individuals to live valuable lives, and this may require the protection of minority cultures. But this is not an option open to neutralist liberals who disavow the idea of influencing individual choice.

## Equality and Culture

There is another aspect to the idea of freedom of choice in the liberal tradition, and that is the principle of equality. Dworkin argues that equality is so crucial to the liberal ideal, that even the market should be understood as based on egalitarian principles. For Dworkin, persons and their plans of life should be given equal concern and respect; thus a 'liberal theory of equality rules out ... appeal to the inherent value of one theory of what is good in life.'[42] The unfettered market needs to be corrected to remedy undeserved inequalities, but its basic workings are egalitarian, insofar as it allows individuals equally to choose from a diversity of goods.[43] Kymlicka also focuses on egalitarian ideals in his argument for ensuring members of minority cultures have parity with members of dominant cultures. As he puts it, 'Some groups are unfairly disadvantaged in the cultural market-place, and political recognition and support rectify this disadvantage.' States embody cultures, at the level of language at least, but also in such things as public holidays or state symbols.[44] So refusing special rights to minority cultures violates the liberal requirement that the state be neutral amongst its citizens in order to treat them as equals. Without special cultural rights, members of many minority cultures face a loss which 'we cannot reasonably ask people to accept.'

This revisionist neutralism has found broad appeal among liberals. Indeed, in his recent work Patten argues that the liberal doctrine of neutrality should be reconfigured to ensure that the state is 'equally accommodating of rival conceptions of the good' for the sake of minority cultures.[45] All this suggests a potentially wide-ranging policy of cultural redistribution. In the case of ethnic groups, however, the rationale for group-differentiated rights is that they enable integration, by providing language training and combating discrimination and prejudice. This might require a number of exemptions and special measures in such cases as, for example, Sunday closing for shops, religious teachings, dress codes for school students and government employees. Kymlicka also suggests the revision of state symbols and calendars to avoid privileging some groups and disadvantaging others.[46]

A well-known objection to multicultural policies is that they promote inequality by isolating ethnic groups from the opportunities of the rest of society. Some British commentators warn against efforts to diffuse ethnic tensions by 'sleepwalking towards segregation.'[47] The objections to the politics of difference that we canvassed in previous chapters are apposite here. Against this, Kymlicka argues that policies adopted pursuant to the 1971 Multiculturalism Act have meant that Canada's record on racial equality and the integration of ethnic minorities is superior, in fact, to that of societies without such policies. The laboratory conditions for such findings are imperfect; it may be that multiculturalism has no such causal power and Canada's record can be attributed to other factors. Kymlicka stresses, though, that integration is the rationale for any policy of multicultural accommodation. Special arrangements for minority groups must pass two equality-based conditions: they must not allow one group to oppress another, and they must ensure that the group does not oppress its own members.[48]

Equality is bound to be a complex measure in cultural matters. Some cultures inevitably have a stronger presence than others in any given society. The number of adherents, their wealth, power and values, and the extent to which they instil their values in successive generations, will determine a culture's strength. In Canada, Aboriginal cultures, Polish culture, and Quebecois cultures do not enjoy equality with each other, nor do they enjoy equality with the dominant (that is, outside Quebec) Anglo-Canadian culture. But this does not necessarily call for political redress, and people's feelings on the matter will not decide the issue. As Ripstein puts it, 'we cannot decide which activities matter and how by considering how strongly people feel about them.... Instead ... we need some view about how important various activities and various sorts of injuries are.'[49] Only some cultures' weaker status raises questions for the political institutions of society, and only some cultures are unequal in ways that render their members unequal. In Canada, Quebec is an example of the former but not the latter, Aboriginal culture of both, and Polish culture of neither. Cultural inequality does not in itself settle the question of justice. As Moore puts it, 'people should expect to be in the minority at least some of the time, with regard to some matters. Simply being in a minority is not a form of oppression.'[50]

The aim of cultural equality cannot sidestep individual wellbeing in favour of the abstract goal of cultural survival. As noted in Chapter 2, the strength of a culture may actually bode ill for the equality of its individual members if the culture has inegalitarian customs.[51] Cultural equality also suggests anthropological naïveté – trying artificially to preserve culture in the face of a myriad of forces against it. We cannot equalise people's success in their pursuits.[52] We can, however, try to equalise the lot of those whose cultural identity renders them the unequal of others in relevant respects. In the case of Aboriginal people, particularly in Canada, we confront a record of poverty and disadvantage, a record of failure on the part of governments who have deployed significant funds to First Nations communities without achieving anything like equal wellbeing for indigenous peoples in comparison with white settlers. Remedying this inequality calls for cultural strategies, particularly in light of the failure of assimilationist policies of the past. Aboriginal peoples feel a strong connection to the remote communities in which many of them live, often in appalling social conditions, without clean drinking water, adequate housing or social support.[53] The Aboriginal case suggests that the roots of inequality are more complex than a simple matter of resources, even if material deprivation is incontrovertible.[54] What is at issue in cultural recognition is the restoration and affirmation of the sense of self-respect and self-worth that is essential for individuals to be the equals of others, along with adequate, targeted material investment in Aboriginal communities to ensure greater wellbeing.

It is possible, however, that cultural recognition will have no such egalitarian effect. The criterion of equality might in fact call for reform of traditional cultures, rather than their restoration. Or it might indicate a culture is past saving, that other alternatives should be adduced and promoted. As Buchanan puts it, we should be circumspect about our response to those who 'refuse to be rescued from their sinking lifeboat because it is *their* craft and because any other vessel seems alien and untrustworthy to them,' demanding 'timbers and pumps ... to shore up what we have every reason to believe is a doomed vessel.'[55] Moore points out that Buchanan's lifeboat analogy dissembles distinctive features of the cultural case: not only is the rescue vessel distinctively different from, perhaps alien to, one's own doomed lifeboat, it may also be the vessel of those who 'rammed and stole your boat in the first place, causing it to sink.'[56] Rescue might be possible, however, if integration and restoration go hand in hand. Acceptance on both sides can come if there is a reckoning with the historical record wherein the majority offers resources for both cultural restoration and integration to enable greater and more equal wellbeing for all. Aboriginal peoples' suppressed way of life, for example, offers an appreciation of our relationship with nature and our environment, and thus a process of cultural restoration stands to enhance human flourishing more generally. If we focus on the relation between culture and the flourishing of individuals, then both historical self-consciousness, and an appreciation for the wellbeing afforded by traditional ways of life, will facilitate a sensitive approach to disadvantaged cultural minorities.

One proposal to remedy inequality among cultural groups is special representation in government, whereby a certain number of seats in the legislature are reserved for the members of marginalised groups. Young argues that this allows for 'the assertion of a positive sense of difference by oppressed groups,' giving a voice to disadvantaged groups and promoting just outcomes.[57] Special representation has a history in Canada's federal system, where electoral districts are defined so as to ensure representation of regional 'communities of interest' in the upper house and the judiciary. Applied to cultural groups, Kymlicka contends such practices might also be seen as 'promoting civic participation and political legitimacy,' and 'alleviating the "sense of injustice" that arises' in the absence of 'effective representation.'[58]

The case of special representation underscores the distinction between national and ethnic minorities; the latter tend to seek greater representation in existing political institutions, whereas the former press for new, autonomous political institutions. This is to be expected, given that ethnic groups have grievances about exclusion from mainstream society, whilst national groups complain that they were forced to be included, as a result of conquest or colonisation. (Although, as we noted earlier, immigrants might contest the assumption that leaving their homelands was a matter of choice and demand autonomous political institutions too.) Minority 'communities of interest' based on geography have a case too because their position is structurally weak, irrespective of social attitudes or opportunities.

Special representation raises some of the same issues we encountered with the idea of redrawing electoral districts to favour racial minorities in Chapter 4. Such a policy suggests defeatism about society's capacity for equality, where representation is only possible on the basis of sharing the same repertoire of sociological characteristics,[59] that people are elected 'only to speak for their own group identity or interests, and never asked to address any wider concerns.'[60] As Kymlicka puts it, if some do a poor job of considering the perspective of others, then 'the solution is not to accept those limitations. Rather, we should fight against them.'[61] In the case of racial and ethnic minorities, ongoing progress towards greater equality can generate higher rates of representation without any special arrangements beyond more active recruitment by political parties, as already evident in liberal democracies. But in any case, that there are a goodly number of representatives of one cultural kind or another does not mean that individuals are well represented; group representation might encourage the false assumption that bearing an identity means one always acts on behalf of those who share it, a possible explanation for the disappointing evidence of continued poverty and racism suffered by Maoris in New Zealand, notwithstanding provisions for special representation.

Indeed, it may be that equality, strictly speaking, is of tangential significance for some cultural groups. Nationalist Scots or Quebecois may be prepared to give up some material wellbeing for the sake of political independence, justifying their cause by reference to historical entitlement rather than any equality that might result. True, Aboriginal struggles for land titles are linked to the quest for material enrichment, as evidenced by cases such as the Nisga'a people's successful claim to a significant parcel of land in British Columbia. Whether self-government provides material benefits for Aboriginal people is unclear, however, so the egalitarian case would need to be more nuanced about how political equality can generate the self-esteem essential to repairing generations of subordination. In the case of Quebec, there is doubtless a lot of nationalist bravado about the prosperity of a separate Quebec, but that is not the point of the enterprise. Moreover, the urge to separate from the wider society makes the benchmark for material advantage uncertain: with whom would a newly independent Quebec measure the equality of its citizens? All this is to suggest that even were we to attempt to defend cultural rights on egalitarian grounds, these would not necessarily be the grounds employed by advocates for these rights. As Raz puts it, there is a 'fundamental dialectical element' in liberal arguments that refuse to take cultures at their own estimation, endorsing reasons that 'are likely to vary from the reasons provided in most cultures for their value.'[62] We come again to the conclusion that the idea that minority cultures should be protected does not emerge in any straightforward way from the idea of equality as such.

## Culture in Common

Yet culture is hardly irrelevant to equality. Contemporary political philosophers influenced by multiculturalism tend to portray society as an empty shell that contains, in addition to individuals pursuing their choices, minority cultures with their distinctive values and preferences; society or community as such has no character or aims of its own. But if equality is germane to questions of culture, it will justify the protection of a common, if diverse, culture. By this I mean that citizens should have equal access to a common set of cultural resources, such as national language(s), education, the arts and leisure. This is so for two reasons. First, access to a common culture gives one access to other goods. Integration is not the same as assimilation; it is consistent with individuals retaining their diverse identities. Yet, all societies have a currency of success, and language is an obvious example where we do no favours by letting some opt out. Some American egalitarians worry that, though educators should be sensitive to African-American students' use of vernacular language, to go further and offer segregated instruction in 'ebonics', might in fact render black children less equipped to communicate in the public domain than their white peers.[63] Competence in a society's official language(s) is a precondition for equality (in Canada it is a requirement for the acquisition of citizenship). Second, a common culture is the background for state-provided social benefits. Miller argues that the nation-state embodies a 'common ethos,'[64] a public culture that marks out a set of interconnected people who can enlist in formal structures of reciprocity and mutual aid in light of a defined set of needs and interests.[65] Thus Anderson refers to the nation as an 'imagined community' that is conceived as a 'deep, horizontal comradeship,' a sense of obligation and trust that can transcend enlightened self-interest, sustaining systems of redistribution from which one does not directly benefit.[66] National feeling, on these views, is a necessary, if insufficient condition (consider the example of the United States), for policies of equality.

This might suggest an instrumental approach to culture and nationality, where a common culture is affirmed simply to supply the solidarity for principles of justice that are justified on independent grounds. However, my egalitarian conception of a common culture is not a mere means to an end, but is part and parcel of that end. On this view, egalitarian justice involves an idea of the public good as a project to which we have obligations and from which we derive wellbeing. Citizens understand themselves as related to other citizens, contributing and receiving social benefits. Membership in a society affords indivisible virtues like decency, tolerance, and humanity towards its less fortunate members. Wiggins points out how the 'solidarity of the human' is at the 'core of the ethical' and interlocks with the group camaraderie of the nation or family.[67] Thus it is not just national identity per se, but a particular community identity that involves a particular set of values. Of course, nationality is inegalitarian insofar as it excludes non-citizens from its purview.[68] For Pogge, what is needed is an international order designed in such a way that people 'disregard their private and local, including national, commitments and loyalties, to give equal consideration to the needs and interests of every human being on the planet.'[69] The responses of nationalist liberals, that the obligations of nationality need not rely on a denial of human equality, are unstable at best.[70] I explore these important issues later in the book.

For now, it is worth noting that a national policy of redistributing wealth inculcates in individuals the idea of helping co-nationals with whom they have a largely abstract relation, and that this is an auspicious basis for considering duties that might be owed to fellow human beings more generally. Rawls and Okin famously depict the family as a school of justice; perhaps the nation-state is something of a practicum. Indeed, countries with impressive records on egalitarian policy domestically are also among the most generous providers of foreign aid.[71] For the nation-state to be the basis for such redistribution it would have to cast off its original form as an ethnically homogenous community to become a porous, open-ended, 'polycentric'[72] association whose qualifications for membership do not depend on ancestry. And indeed, whilst the nation-state was designed to unite people by birth and blood, it has evolved to become more inclusive.[73] Bigotry is not unknown to new world or settler nations, but insofar as their very origin is premised on waves of immigration, they stand not as exclusive clubs, but as refuges from exclusivity and from the threats often presented by minority nationalities. Walzer holds up the United States for focussing not on ethnic but political ties,[74] and tying nationality to a politics of Americanness dispenses, at least in principle, with the xenophobia that characterises the nationality of say, Germany, where for a long time naturalisation decisions gave preference to those who could demonstrate that they were 'ethnic Germans.'[75] But a political exclusivity has its dangers. Consider the idea of un-American activities, the near monarchisation of the presidency, or the militaristic fetishism of the American flag.[76] Precisely how nationality can reject ethnic exclusivity whilst avoiding other pernicious forms of exclusivity needs further reflection.

Cultural traditions shape the character of a nation-state in a dynamic process, and the national character that results is malleable and changes over time. Canada evolved from having a distinctly British character to having what Europeans consider a largely American one, whilst its French character has been accentuated and a polyethnic ethos has emerged. This is the result of legislation to some extent (e.g. the official policies of bilingualism launched in the 1960s, multiculturalism in the 1970s), but mainly the vagaries of historical change – patterns of immigration, the decline of one empire and rise of another, the modernisation of Quebec, and so forth. The legacy of history –

e.g. the role of founding nations such as the English, French, and indigenous peoples in Canada – can be acknowledged in a self-conscious way that affords tolerance and inclusion of new cultures. What we have in common will thus be, in part, the acknowledgement of our differences, be they between the nations that constitute the multination state, or among ethnic groups that are integrated within. There is no single 'conception of the good,' even within the nations that make up the multination state.[77] To insist on a choice between a unitary conception of value or a multiculturalist conception is to force a Hobson's choice.

Thus a common, if variegated, culture need not be jettisoned to afford tolerance and inclusion. Canadians, for example, may be united by their participation in the 'Canadian conversation,'[78] but it cannot be a conversation that has no point, that comes to no conclusions, that refuses, even, to allow certain topics for discussion. Thus constrained, such a conversation would tell us nothing about why the integrity of the Canadian state matters, why the conversation should continue. The idea of a conversation has the advantage of stressing the open-endedness of shared values, how they are subject to interrogation, revision and adaptation. But this is compatible with the idea of a common culture, in which a cultural inheritance is modified by liberal and egalitarian ideals. Shared values, over which there can be democratic debate and conscious choice, is a far better prospect for equality than a focus on in-born identities. Liberals hope that multiculturalist policy demonstrates, as Kymlicka puts it, that 'Canada provides an important model of how a pluralistic country can live … in peace, civility and justice.'[79] But without a substantive normative framework for this pluralism, it is difficult to defend the arbitrary geopolitical entity that makes a country, to affirm that Canada, for example, is an entity whose integrity, consisting of certain values, however plural and open, is important. In the wake of the 'Brexit' referendum in the U.K., it seems important to appreciate the salience of a shared identity within a nation's borders, even if we must insist that it is an identity that is egalitarian, open, and inclusive.

Liberals resist considerations of historical tradition and the common culture of a nation, perhaps because they smack too much of communitarianism and the idea of ways of life are not entirely the province of individual choice. Why then make such an argument on behalf of multiculturalism? We could adduce the force of the Zeitgeist, which is decidedly on the multiculturalists' side. Thus Kymlicka proclaimed back in 2001 that 'there is no clear alternative,' that liberal culturalism, the 'clear consensus position,' had 'won by default.'[80] Given that the multiculturalist position is designed to counter injustice and oppression, it was bound to find the support of liberals. Many liberals are, after all, do-gooders, in both the best and worst senses of the term, and liberals' commitment to pluralism suggests a multiculturalist position, even if, unlike textbook pluralism, multiculturalism involves groups and members whose identities are not a matter of choice.

In sum, rights to culture must be derived from an understanding of the foundational role of a common culture. This is so for several reasons. First, if we accept multicultural arguments about the formative nature of culture, then this applies to a common culture as much as to minority cultures. Second, such a culture is not premised on a homogenous citizenry endowed with certain racial or ethnic characteristics, but rather admits of the complex history of dominant cultures whose impact is diffused and checked by ever new cultural influences and factors. Third, a common culture forms the webs of connection into which members of minority cultures must integrate to some degree. And fourth, a common culture, of however a minimal kind, renders the egalitarian project possible, for it sets out community, that is, relations of membership within which justice is not only pursued, but conceived.

## Equality and Value

An egalitarian society must have a common culture that enables its citizens to live well as self-determining persons. To be a self-determining being means to choose how to live, but also to make choices that further self-determination. Raz suggests that whilst we value autonomy because we value the capacity to choose the good, autonomy is fulfilled to the extent that the good is indeed chosen.[81] According to Raz, freedom derives its value from the purposes to which it is put: 'autonomy is valuable only if exercised in pursuit of the good.' Such pursuits, moreover, require 'social forms' that are 'morally sound' and a government which protects and promotes the wellbeing of people. If these social forms are found in a vulnerable, minority culture, then state redress is permissible. Cultures would be endorsed and protected in light of their significance for individuals' self-determination and capacity to live well.[82]

One autonomy-enabling social condition is freedom from interference. But this is insufficient. A second set of social conditions which enable autonomy are institutions that assure some minimum level of material wellbeing since, as we shall see, on our definition, one cannot be autonomous yet hungry or homeless. Finally, there are the possibilities provided by culture, in the widest sense of the word, including a culture of citizenship, which are premised on a plurality of autonomy-conducive choices. Society cannot avoid difficult decisions about what to support, but it should deploy grants, tax relief or public venues to support enterprises that provide valuable cultural possibilities. Thus to return to our example of Canada, the egalitarian project of cultural enrichment is manifest in state support for writers and artists, public funds for language teaching for immigrants whose native tongue is not English or French, as well as the provision of health insurance, labour legislation, pensions and social welfare provisions which protect citizens from the vicissitudes of the market.

What of minority cultures? Support for the languages of national cultures is essential and this means giving priority to vulnerable languages in certain contexts. Support for minority cultural practices will depend on the case for their value, and on meeting tests of equality and autonomy. Arguments for the preservation of culture for its own sake irrespective of individuals' interests, such as

Taylor's politics of recognition, are thus barred on my account. Moreover, the position outlined here puts other constraints on how we foster cultural diversity. It is not enough that a culture happens to be valued. If the state is to support a cultural practice, it must genuinely be of value, as well as widely accessible, open and consistent with freedom of choice.

A powerful objection to the idea that society should promote cultural pursuits that contribute to equality and autonomy is the likelihood of disagreement on such matters, given the reality of nationalist and multicultural conflict. Indeed, whilst neutralist liberals play down appeals to expediency in the context of disagreement about values, perhaps the attraction of their position lies in precisely such considerations, which account for much multiculturalist revisionism among liberals. Nevertheless, to acquiesce in the idea that it is impossible for society to make judgements about value overlooks important features of the cultural landscape, in particular, the vacuum left by neutralist liberals who refuse to consider the possibility of articulating common, if diverse, values. Affirming a common culture committed to autonomy and equality, which is made up of diverse sources, which is dynamic and open, and which contains self-defining cultures within it, will bring us closer to settling our cultural differences.

This possibility opens up when we consider the complexities of culture itself. Cultural pursuits are facilitated and undermined in invisible ways. As I argue later in this book, the market determines the availability of cultural options by the criterion of profitability, which cannot be understood as a straightforward expression of supply and demand. After all, consumers cannot vote on the context or effects of their choices about consumption, nor can they ensure that certain options are available to choose. One of the paradoxes of the contemporary interest in culture is that it coincides with a process of capital mobility that is rendering the world more homogenous, so that people from Naples to Nunavut imbibe the same popular culture. What I propose is thus a way of rendering the provision of cultural options open and accountable, in opposition to the closed and unaccountable ways in which cultures are affected by the global economy.

My focus has been on what the state is obligated to support, but this of course leaves all kinds of cultural possibilities free to develop and thrive without such assistance. There will be a plurality of cultural pursuits that the community will seek to promote, and many that will do well without state support. There is an immense variety of ways of living autonomously, and thus the culture of citizenship will be a pluralist one. What I propose is already instantiated to a considerable degree in contemporary liberal practice, which does support some ways of life and not others, subsidising ballet over bingo, or parks over drive-ins, to use our earlier examples. Where there is the most change is in our consciousness of, and sense of responsibility for, the cluster of normative judgements that justify decisions about state support for culture. Cultural understanding is an important aspect of my proposal, since I require that society reflect on matters of culture and value. Cultural possibilities are not the same as cultures, and our worries about an autonomy-threatening aspect of a culture should not deter us from supporting its benign aspects.

Perhaps the idea of protecting cultural possibilities seems naïve; you cannot protect the possibilities without protecting the source from which they came. But culture is a complicated phenomenon, whose contours are potentially more malleable than we might presume. Toronto, perhaps one of the most ethnically diverse cities in the world, put up street signs in certain districts designating 'Chinatown' or 'Little Italy.' No sooner were the signs up than the cultural boundaries shifted: old Chinatown is now largely a financial district, its community having moved westward and to prosperous suburban enclaves; Little Italy is now Koreatown. Efforts on the part of the state simply to recognise culture are sometimes clumsy and misconceived. Cultures remake themselves in surprising ways, and a simple strategy of preservation misses the mark. Consider the peculiar fact that Inuit printmaking was born in the modern era, making use of the dominant culture's technology, and catering to its demand. Or the fact that young Muslim women are taking up traditional dress to avoid sexual objectification, invoking the arguments of Western radical feminists. Or that efforts to downplay Christmas in the year-end celebrations at workplaces often meet with objections from non-Christians who had integrated a secular Christmas into their own religious calendars. Egalitarians must have a concern for culture, since culture is a constituent of living well, and they must seek to ensure that living well is equally enjoyed. Difference will of course thrive; varieties of, not just ethnicity or language, but talent and disposition, will see to that. But difference due to unequal access to culture is something the egalitarian society should seek to abolish, by providing the resources that enable access to culture, and by supporting valuable cultural possibilities.

## Conclusion

I have argued that culture has a significant connection to autonomy and equality. By this I do not intend the kinds of connections suggested by neutralist liberals in their embrace of multiculturalism. The protection of culture cannot be related to freedom if by that we understand freedom of choice, since cultural protection involves in some sense constraining choice. Equality cannot be the basis for protecting culture if by that we mean equalising cultures, since not only is that infeasible from a sociological point of view, but of questionable egalitarian value so long as it is individuals whose equality is at issue. I have contended that culture is relevant to equality in a much broader sense, since equal capacity for self-determination requires something like a common culture and a common commitment to support for culture. Kymlicka rightly comments that it would be 'a great intellectual, cultural and spiritual loss if Canada dissolved.'[83] If we frame questions of culture in the neutralist framework of much contemporary liberalism, however, where culture figures only as a feature of micro-communities within the state, we cannot even identify, let alone remedy, that loss.

Liberal ideas of equality and autonomy are relevant to the discussion of culture, but they must be seen as the fruits of a wider view of culture as a form of enrichment that depends on the political community for support. Equality requires that society foster cultural possibilities conducive to autonomy. Such a society affirms rights to culture, but within a framework of common citizenship that undergirds the equal entitlement of citizens to live autonomously and well. In the following chapters I build on this idea of a culture of citizenship to develop a theory of equal human flourishing.

## Notes

1 T.H. Marshall, *Sociology at the Crossroads.*
2 Although in his recent work on animal ethics, in collaboration with S. Donaldson, 'animal and human flourishing' and the 'flourishing of communities' are introduced as important criteria. S. Donaldson and W. Kymlicka, *Zoopolis: A Political Theory of Animal Rights*, 99, 165. M. Deveaux identifies Kymlicka as, though a critic of perfectionism, a comprehensive liberal; see *Cultural Pluralism and Dilemmas of Difference*, 130.
3 W. Kymlicka, *Multicultural Citizenship*, 47–8.
4 C. Geertz, *The Interpretation of Cultures*, 5, 14.
5 *Oxford English Dictionary*, 11th printing, 1247–8.
6 Appiah, 'Race, Culture and Identity: Misunderstood Connections,' 84.
7 Ibid., 83.
8 J. Kim, 'Culture,' 172.
9 *Multicultural Citizenship*, 96–7. See G.B. Levey, 'Equality, Autonomy and Cultural Rights,' 217. Kymlicka notes that in the Canadian context, the word 'multiculturalism,' which indicates the development of 'institutionally complete' cultures, is less suitable than a word like 'polyethnicity,' which suggests accommodating immigrant ethnicity within the public institutions of English and French culture. *Finding Our Way: Rethinking Ethnocultural Relations in Canada*, 59.
10 Kymlicka, *Multicultural Citizenship*, 89–90.
11 Taylor, 'Politics of Recognition,' 58.
12 *Multicultural Citizenship*, 51.
13 As V. Dyke complained in an early essay, 'The Individual, the State and Ethnic Communities in Political Society.'
14 I. Berlin, 'Two Concepts of Liberty.'
15 R. Dworkin, 'Foundations of Liberal Equality,' 115–16.
16 Rawls, *Political Liberalism*, 311, 337.
17 Kymlicka, *Liberalism, Community and Culture*, ch. 4.
18 Kymlicka is also critical of the perfectionism of Raz for similar reasons, urging the 'principle of neutral concern' over 'controversial public ranking of the intrinsic merits of competing conceptions of the good.' See ibid., 81.
19 G. Tamas, 'Socialism, Capitalism and Democracy,' 71.
20 Kymlicka, *Multicultural Citizenship*, 83.
21 Kymlicka, *Liberalism, Community and Culture*, 81.
22 *Multicultural Citizenship*, 94. Raz emphasises how the fact of accommodating a minority culture within a diverse society gives the culture scope for change, *Ethics in the Public Domain*, 171.
23 Taylor, 'The Politics of Recognition,' 68–70.
24 Phillips, *Multiculturalism without Culture*, 21, Narayan, 'Undoing the "Package Picture" of Cultures,' 1083.
25 Phillips, *Multiculturalism without Culture*, 42.
26 C. Kukathas, 'Are there Any Cultural Rights?,' 122.

27 A. Shachar, *Multicultural Jurisdictions: Cultural Differences and Women's Rights*, 121–4.
28 Chambers, *Sex, Culture and Justice*, 156. See also Benhabib, *The Claims of Culture*, 129.
29 Green, 'Internal Minorities and their Rights.'
30 Phillips, *Multiculturalism without Culture*, 157.
31 Eisenberg and Spinner-Halev, eds, *Minorities within Minorities*.
32 Muslims feel pressured to avail themselves of Sharia Law or risk deemed to have 'failed in their religious duties,' A. Eisenberg, 'The Debate over Sharia Law in Canada.'
33 See J. Carens ed., *Is Quebec Nationalism Just? Perspectives from Anglophone Canada*.
34 R. Whitaker, 'Quebec's Self-Determination and Aboriginal Self-Government: Conflict and Reconciliation?,' 198–9.
35 *Multicultural Citizenship*, 90–2.
36 Kymlicka, *Liberalism, Community and Culture*, 81.
37 Dworkin, *A Matter of Principle*, ch. 11.
38 Raz, *Ethics in the Public Domain*, 178.
39 Ibid., 163.
40 Spinner-Halev, *The Boundaries of Citizenship*, 155, 188.
41 Phillips, *Multiculturalism without Culture*, 176.
42 Dworkin, 'Liberalism,' 132.
43 Ibid., 132–3; Dworkin, *Sovereign Virtue*, 66–7.
44 Kymlicka, *Multicultural Citizenship*, 108–11.
45 Patten, *Equal Recognition*, 115.
46 Kymlicka, *Multicultural Citizenship*, 113–15.
47 See T. Phillips, 'Sleepwalking to Segregation,' Phillips, *Multiculturalism without Culture*, ch. 1; G. Levey, 'Equality, Autonomy and Cultural Rights,' 221.
48 Kymlicka, *Finding Our Way*, 70. This is affirmed in M. Wright and I. Bloemraad, 'Is There a Trade-off between Multiculturalism and Socio-Political Integration? Policy Regimes and Immigrant Incorporation in Comparative Perspective,' 77–95. However, K. Banting and W. Kymlicka, in 'Canadian Multiculturalism: Global Anxieties and Local Debates,' note the British context and raise some concerns, though with the conclusion that the Canadian case should not be confused with more worrying trends in Europe.
49 A. Ripstein, 'Context, Continuity and Fairness,' 217.
50 M. Moore, *The Ethics of Nationalism*, 114.
51 See the discussion in Chapter 2 on this point.
52 A point made by Rawls in *Political Liberalism*, 192–3.
53 A rash of suicides among young people in Attawapiskat First Nation, for example, is a symptom of the deep crisis facing Aboriginal people in Canada. See E. Lou, 'Five Facts on Canada Aboriginal Community Suicide Crisis.'
54 Thus 'genuine wealth' economists stress the importance of investments in social capital to improve human wellbeing in Aboriginal communities; see R. McGarvey, 'Money Alone Won't Solve the Attawapiskat Crisis.'
55 A. Buchanan, *Secession: The Morality of Political Divorce*, 55.
56 Moore, *Ethics of Nationalism*, 71, see also M. Moore, *A Political Theory of Territory*.
57 Young, *Justice and the Politics of Difference*, 99.
58 Kymlicka, *Finding Our Way*, 119.
59 Kymlicka, *Multicultural Citizenship*, 138.
60 A. Phillips, *Democracy and Difference*, 96 and *The Politics of Presence*, ch. 1–2. These considerations tell equally against Phillips's counter proposals for 'mirror representation.'
61 Kymlicka, *Multicultural Citizenship*, 140.
62 Raz, *Ethics in the Public Domain*, 182.
63 M.A. Johnson, 'The Ebonics Debate.'

64 D. Miller, *Nationality*, 74.
65 Ibid., 92–3.
66 B. Anderson, *Imagined Communities*, 7, 72.
67 D. Wiggins, 'Solidarity and the Root of the Ethical,' 260.
68 S. Scheffler, 'Liberalism, Nationalism and Egalitarianism,' 200.
69 T. Pogge, 'Concluding Reflections,' 298.
70 Y. Tamir, *Liberal Nationalism*, 100–2.
71 See Organisation for Economic Co-operation and Development (OECD), 'Sweden is a generous aid donor that has put development at the heart of its foreign policy.'
72 Tamir, *Liberal Nationalism*, 90.
73 E. Gellner argues that nationalism is a peculiarly modern phenomenon, attendant on mass literacy and public education, democratisation, social mobility and the diminution of privilege. *Nations and Nationalism*, ch. 4. H. Kohn makes a distinction between regressive and progressive nationalisms with the typology of 'Eastern' and 'Western,' the former xenophobic, the latter tolerant (though the typology itself looks xenophobic!), in *The Idea of Nationalism*.
74 M. Walzer, 'Pluralism: A Political Perspective,' 142–4.
75 J. Habermas, 'Struggles for Recognition in the Democratic Constitutional State,' 143–8; C. Gathmann and N. Keller, 'Return to Citizenship? Evidence from Germany's Recent Immigration Reforms.'
76 Tamir points to America to propose that nationality might be a more pluralistic basis for membership in community than shared values or beliefs. *Liberal Nationalism*, 90.
77 Ibid., 173.
78 J. Webber, *Reimagining Canada: Language, Culture, Community and the Canadian Constitution*, 9.
79 Kymlicka, *Finding Our Way*, 5.
80 Kymlicka, *Politics in the Vernacular*, 43, 48.
81 J. Raz, *The Morality of Freedom*, 133, 381.
82 Ibid., 381, Raz, *Ethics in the Public Domain*, 104.
83 Kymlicka, *Finding Our Way*, 177.

# Part III
# Equality and Living Well

# 6    What Equality Is and Is Not

In liberal democratic societies many people, philosophers and non-philosophers alike, will attest to a belief that equality is a good thing, or at least that inequality is bad. However, what we might call the 'equality consensus' is less clear about what equality means. Pretty much everyone will uphold the equal moral worth of individuals. But should people simply be accorded equal legal and political rights? Or should they also be made equal, in the sense of equal in their income, material resources or standard of living? Most would answer 'yes' to the first question, but the second provokes different responses. On the one hand, libertarians contend that we should treat people as equals by intervening only to stop those who threaten to interfere with others' equal rights to freedom. Respect for equality requires that we *not* redistribute property or income, as that would constitute interference in individuals' equal liberty. Radical egalitarians, on the other hand, believe that treating people as equals involves the redistribution of wealth, whether it be to achieve strict equality, to bring everyone to a level of sufficiency, or to improve the position of the worst off. They insist that material deprivation is at odds with the equality consensus.

In this chapter I defend the aim of material equality in light of three conceptual challenges that reflect the fundamental libertarian objection that the redistribution of wealth unjustly invades individual freedom. The first challenge is that egalitarianism is mired in a commitment to levelling down, where equality of resources is irrationally preferred over any other distribution even if it reduces the resources available to the better off at no benefit to the worse off. The second is the problem of talent; here it is charged that egalitarian distribution implies effacing, ignoring or even thwarting people's special capacities. The third is the matter of partiality, where promoting equality is taken to mean the elimination of any special regard the individual has for her own interests or those of particular others.

Levelling down, talent and partiality are large issues, each meriting sustained analysis; I bring them together here in order to show how they can all be illuminated by a flourishing approach to equality. The discussion will reveal, first, that equality is important precisely because of its effect on wellbeing, and second, that the egalitarian ideal is best served by aiming for equality in wellbeing, or human flourishing, rather than equality of goods or resources. Conceiving of equality in this way will enable us to see the truth in egalitarian views that are sometimes superficially dismissed as implausible.

## Levelling Down

The idea of equality of distribution, taken strictly, dictates that all individuals have the same amount of whatever it is that is to be equalised. On this view, equality entails a uniform pattern in which each person possesses as much as every other person and so we can arrive at an equal distribution by removing wealth from some to bring everyone down to the same level. But to attain equality by 'levelling down' is obviously problematic. Individuals seek to maximise their own resources, or ensure that their resources are not below some level of adequacy. But so long as others' shares do not affect one's own, it is unclear why one should care about them. Ultimately the rationale for strict equality looks like an aesthetic ideal of symmetry that is divorced from human interests, an odd goal for politics.[1]

The libertarian Nozick is famously critical of the redistribution of wealth for focussing on patterns of distribution, arguing that justice requires leaving individuals free to acquire wealth, however unequal the results.[2] Such libertarian squeamishness may seem beside the point, since the critic of levelling down objects to a particular pattern, strict equality, not egalitarian patterns in general. Strict equality nonetheless invites the well-known libertarian view that egalitarianism is simply a 'politics of envy,'[3] where the freely acquired property of some is taken away to sate the jealousy of others. Equality might leave the rich worse off, but it can leave everyone worse off too. An unequal distribution of resources that accords most citizens a good standard of living and a minority an excellent one is surely preferable to an equal distribution where all have an equal but paltry share. The horrors of strict equality are famously depicted in Vonnegut's story, 'Harrison Bergeron,' where a dystopian society eliminates advantage by forcing the beautiful to don masks, the athletic to be encumbered by weights, and the intelligent to receive radio signals that distract them.[4] Those who insist on strict equality seem motivated by a dog-in-the-manger attitude that resents others' benefits, an attitude widely denounced by philosophers as irrational.

Consequentialist reasons for rejecting levelling down focus on how it produces a decline in overall wealth without necessarily improving the situation of the worst off. Raz contends that strict equality lacks content, if it is concerned only that people have the same amount of x. We need an account about the value of x, in order to be concerned to redistribute it, and once we have that account, it is not clear why equality per se matters. Poverty, he argues, is bad for a person; thus there is something perverse about finding a society with widespread poverty (which is thus equal) superior to the society with pockets of poverty. Indeed, the perversity of equality means that the egalitarian will be moved to adopt policies of waste, since if pockets of poverty cannot be eliminated, then strict equality requires destroying concentrations of wealth to ensure equal poverty.[5]

Opposition to levelling down is such that much of the egalitarian literature repudiates strict equality, taking the view that egalitarianism is concerned with disadvantage rather than exactly equal distributions. The point was originally put by Frankfurt, who devised the idea of sufficiency as an alternative to equality. 'Sufficientarians' contend that what matters is that people not be impoverished, something missed in the folly of levelling down.[6] Frankfurt's deontological argument stresses that what is important from the moral point of view is whether everyone has enough, not whether everyone has the same.[7] Egalitarian redress attends not to the fact that some have less money than others, but the fact that 'those with less have *too little*.'[8] The moral wrong is not inequality, but the deprivation consequent upon inequality, and that is what motivates human compassion and efforts at amelioration.[9] Nagel contends that according to the principle of universal impartial concern, we should favour the worse off over the better off, but not begrudge 'advantages to the better off which cost the worse off nothing.' Strict equality, in contrast, means taking the side of some against others without improving their position.[10]

Building on Frankfurt's idea of sufficiency, Parfit coined the idea of giving priority, not to equality as such, but to improving the lot of the worst off, however costly that might be. This 'non-relational egalitarianism' refuses cost-benefit analyses; Parfit argues that benefiting people matters more the worse off people are, even if the worst off are harder to help.[11] This 'prioritarianism' is striking for its unfettered focus on individuals and how they are doing, pushing aside such considerations as their relative standing or what it would take to get them to do better.[12] It represents a more radical version of Rawls's argument that inequality is prima facie illegitimate, but permissible if it mitigates the situation of the disadvantaged.

In sum, there are consequentialist and duty-based reasons for rejecting levelling down conceptions of equality. The consequences of strict equality are bad insofar as they worsen some people's situations without improving others, and there is nothing fair about undermining some people's standing without improving the standings of others. Strict equality fails by the criterion of Parfit's 'person-affecting claim': equality is only important if it affects individuals' rights, freedoms, happiness or dignity, but a policy of strict equality, in contrast, can mean levelling down to achieve a symmetrical pattern to no particular person's benefit.

All this might suggest we should abandon the concept of equality. Putting the debate in terms of a choice between an irrational preoccupation with levelling down or a focus on the elimination of the deprivation of worst-off individuals suggests equality as such is beside the point. Yet dispensing with substantive conceptions of equality undermines an ideal that animated egalitarian political arguments in the first place, including arguments for the elimination of deprivation. To see what is at stake in this ideal, let's take another look at levelling down.

## Equality and Wellbeing

Strict equality can be defended on deontological grounds: equality is just, even if it fails to produce any good consequences. Temkin argues that inequality is bad even if it is not bad for any particular person. Equality, like retribution, has value when no one derives any wellbeing; thus wrongdoers should be punished despite there being no people for whom it matters (e.g. the punishment is not known, or the wronged community ceases to exist). Temkin contends that inequality is always in some sense unfair, and thus can prompt a sense of injury; it is unfair that some are blind and others are not, even if we should not therefore blind the sighted. 'Equality is not all that matters. But it matters some.'[13] On this view, equality should be given prima facie, if not overriding, importance. Cohen contends that arrangements of strict equality are always just, though other considerations might outweigh justice. Equality is the baseline just position, but there might be justice-mitigating considerations such as the Pareto-efficiency criterion where inequality is permitted if one or more persons improve their situation without worsening the situation of anyone else.[14]

Putting the problem in terms of a trade-off between the justice of equality and other values enables us to see, contra Parfit, the persisting value of equality. The pitfall of the trade-off approach, however, is that equality becomes an abstract, special good, isolated from, and defeated by, other values, and thus far removed from considerations of human wellbeing. In cases of conflict, equality therefore risks consistently losing out to other human goods. If equality is to survive as an ideal of distributive justice, it must be connected to the wellbeing of persons.[15] Casal astutely notes that once we satisfy the criterion of sufficiency (or priority), so that deprivation is ameliorated and all have enough, there may still be added value in achieving equality. The truth of the positive thesis, that people should not be impoverished, does not demonstrate the negative thesis, that no other distributional requirements are necessary. It is not 'a matter of indifference how to distribute benefits in excess of those required to attain sufficiency.'[16] Rather, equality continues to have value even if we grant the primary importance of attending to disadvantage. As Moss remarks, 'even if equality is to be valued "merely" because of its instrumental features, this does not mean that there is not a very strong reason to promote equality.'[17] Aiming for sufficiency, or targeting only the worst off, may mean that we set our sights too low.

If the equal society moves to a purportedly Pareto-optimal inequality, but the now relatively disadvantaged are also members of a historically disadvantaged group, then the moral picture looks more complex and not so optimal after all. For Phillips, 'inequalities that derive from the privileging of particular groups of people and/or particular types of work are unjust and should be eliminated.'[18] Wolff concludes from this that there are certain cases where an exclusive benefit should be eliminated even if this will not seem to benefit anyone, so as not to 'send messages of deep political inequality.'[19] Scanlon points to the 'strong egalitarian' case for strict equality which centres on 'the belief that it is an evil for people to be treated as inferior, or made to feel inferior' which is always a risk where there are differences of wealth, whatever the circumstances.[20] O'Neill adduces 'distinctively egalitarian concerns with the badness of servility, exploitation, domination, and differences in status,' in contrast to 'certain kinds of fraternal, egalitarian social relations,' which mean that disparities of wealth always carry with them social costs.[21] Inequality has an impact on social relations: it fuels disparities in political influence as well as mistrust, subservience, disrespect and the corruption of values.[22]

All this suggests that losses in 'social equality' are always at issue when we depart from economic equality.[23] It is a misnomer to dismiss the interest in strict equality as a pernicious 'levelling down,' once we understand that it is never the case that giving extra to some will have zero adverse effects on others. Reducing inequalities, even where the reduction does not immediately materially benefit the worst off, is thus not a pointless obsession but a genuine means of remedying the disadvantages of inequality, given that 'all or almost all gains in equality involve a benefit of some kind to at least some individuals.'[24] Pareto-optimal cases of inequality would seem hardly to occur, given the consequences of economic inequality, however nuanced, for social relations and the dynamics of power. Furthermore, material inequalities tend to snowball: a move to inequality, though initially costless for the now less equal, generates imbalances of power that can eventually lead to distributions that are morally problematic. Scanlon points out that there is much at stake when wealth is unequal: 'Those who have greater resources than others … can often determine what gets produced, what kinds of employment are offered, what the environment of a town or state is like, and what kind of life one can live there.'[25]

Thus, even if it seems that a minority can enjoy extra benefits with no harm to the majority, such benefits sometimes, perhaps always, entail worsening the situation of those excluded from them. Wolff warns against the 'cancer' of levelling down, with its assumption that advantage always entails deprivation, and that equal distribution should prevail every time. Egalitarians should not foster the resentment of others' good fortune disdained by libertarians. But for all that, it remains that inequality itself has 'cancerous' tendencies. Once we take the counsel of moral individualism and think about what it is that we are trying to make more equal, we can see that inequality is to be eliminated because we believe in the equal moral worth of persons, and we want the distribution that enables all individuals to develop and realise their personhood, to live a fulfilling life. Indeed, if we focus on people's wellbeing, it seems arbitrary not to add to the task of eliminating disadvantage the more demanding goal of promoting equality.[26] Contra Temkin, an equal pattern is not pursued for its own sake, but it remains the prima facie just position, since without evidence to the contrary, we can assume that any departure from it will worsen the situation of some party or other – that is, negatively affect their wellbeing – and hence that there must be wellbeing justifications for departing from it.

This is straightforwardly apparent in two areas of public policy: private health care and private education. Even if the quality of an initially equal system of publicly provided medicine is at first unaffected by the arrival of private medicine, the public system can suffer in the long term, degenerating into a last-resort source of health care for those unable to afford private medical care. Public facilities will decline and their staff will leave, as nurses and physicians seek out better pay and opportunities in the private system. In the case of education, the existence of fee-paying schools may mean a decline in the quality of public education due to the departure of academically and economically privileged students (although it has also been suggested that in some cases the public system benefits from the high standard of private schools[27]). Nevertheless, even if superior private schools do not directly affect the quality of the public system, in a world of finite resources and opportunities such schools will likely afford its graduates better positions, thereby furthering inequalities in resources, status and power. The idea that inequality is costless for the less advantaged is challenged by such examples.

A focus on wellbeing illuminates how *both* inequality and levelling down are wrong for the same reason: people have fewer goods than they would, and should, otherwise have. It's because goods are good, so to speak – that is, they provide wellbeing – that we want more of them. That is why we perceive the wrongness of an unequal distribution of goods, and the wrongness of removing goods from some people simply because they cannot be equally shared. It does not follow from the claim that inequality is wrong that any equal distribution is better than any unequal one. As Christiano and Braynen put it,

> What the egalitarian must say is that every non-egalitarian distribution is unjust because it is not equal. Only equality is fully just. But the egalitarian need not say that every egalitarian state is better than every non-egalitarian state.[28]

The wrong of inequality, of relative deprivation, in fact gives us grounds, in certain situations, to prefer unequal shares to equality.

It remains that an inequality of goods, even without serious deprivation, can have a deleterious effect on persons. This is because people value goods and would like to have as much as they can, and feel injured by others having more. Thus departing from the prima facie just pattern of strict equality is in fact a kind of 'cancer' that can infect a community of persons, generating loss of self-respect, fatalism about one's prospects, reduced trust and civility, indeed alienation from one's fellows to an extent that produces violence and violation. Equality is not always to be preferred to inequality, but inequality, if egregious enough, can damage wellbeing, and thus it makes sense to prevent or limit the extra benefits some can accrue; measures sometimes dismissed as 'levelling down' are not always an impediment to wellbeing that the ideal of equality, properly understood, seeks to promote.[29]

## Luxury, Scarcity and Positional Goods

The insight that not all inequalities are material in kind produces challenges for distributive justice. Wellbeing inequality is complicated by, for example, the nature of aesthetic goods that bear a complex relation to equality. Gourmet cooking, historic architecture and antiques are not only unequally distributed, but their origins are embedded in unequal social relations. Yet for all that they can provide wider benefits. Nagel finds it an 'undeniable and widespread fact of life,' that people get 'vicarious pleasure' from the 'lives of luxury and taste led by others, at a level which is possible only for a few because of its costs.'[30] We can steer away from Nagel's spectator model, however, to see how examples of luxury and taste can contribute to widely available forms of enjoyment. Ordinary folk can enjoy living among, if not in, grand houses. We can visit art collections, if not own them. We can buy cookery books inspired by great chefs and try out their recipes, even if we cannot afford to frequent their restaurants. Similar examples are ersatz versions of antique furniture and costume jewellery that copies real gems. Thus people take pleasure in fine things, the finest of which are beyond their reach.

Many luxuries emerged when Western societies were encased in rigidly unequal social structures. Universal suffrage and the welfare state, along with the production of cheap consumer goods and the emergence of mass markets, meant that distribution, though still unequal, could be characterised by greater access to aesthetic goods. But such goods are not equally divisible, and thus distribution should allow for diversity. Jane opts for an old house in a lovely part of town, Joan collects Venetian glass, Jill likes to eat out often, whilst Jan has a season ticket to Tottenham Hotspur at White Hart Lane: each recognises the incommensurability, given the exigencies of scarce resources and the demands of equality, of a single person having access to all such goods. Thus we have a rich public culture of variegated projects and products, supporting diverse yet also more equal wellbeing.

Positional goods are goods whose value involves exclusivity and the conferring of status, on not everyone having a Porsche[31] or a posh accent. Insofar as a good's value is parasitic on relations of inequality, it is not congenial for an egalitarian distributive scheme. However, in other cases, non-ownership is not the same as non-enjoyment: rare objects of beauty can contribute to the wellbeing of many people. Furthermore, a flourishing approach recognises that some wellbeing is better than none, and thus eschews the dog-in-the-manger view that seeks to eliminate wellbeing simply because it is not equally enjoyed. Redistribution must, at a minimum, result in securing extra benefits for the disadvantaged and if it does not achieve this, then it should not be pursued; the spectre of Bolsheviks trashing the art collections of the bourgeoisie is a salutary reminder of the unethical implications of a strict egalitarian measure. It would be a particularly damning example of levelling down if we got rid of the beautiful because not everyone could own it.

These considerations indicate a cultural rationale for allowing disparities of wealth under certain conditions. Once all are assured an adequate standard of living, giving people extra rewards if they work harder or longer, or at more unpleasant or difficult tasks, might pay social dividends. This is consistent with extra or arduous work being deserving of extra income as compensation, in order to acquire further means of enriching one's life. Cohen calls such cases 'special burdens,' which restore equality of wellbeing if the over-worked lead an 'oppressive existence.'[32] He gives the example of overworked surgeons, but the surgeon's work has benefits that might mitigate some, at least, of her or his burdens. Lower-status, onerous and less fulfilling jobs are better candidates for special-burden compensation, e.g. oilrig workers, office cleaners, or those who do shift work. Extra rewards for arduous and stressful work would correct inequality, generate greater productive capacity, and may further enable some to acquire and protect cultural resources of value that would have a trickle-down effect.

This is not to license incentives. Rawls permits incentives with the ration-ale that although they produce inequality, they mean greater productivity and thereby raise everyone's standard of living; in their absence we would all be worse off. Cohen points out that this argument allows individuals to proceed on an ethic of selfishness in their private lives that contradicts their public commitment to the worst off.[33] The disadvantaged would benefit more if the enterprising forewent their extra enrichment and yet continued to be highly productive. Moreover, incentive arguments take for granted that narrowly selfish, monetary interests will always be a principal motivation for human beings. Human flourishing may be best served by opportunities for leisure, since it is leisure rather than financial reward that is often at issue for the overworked, and which is crucial to discovery and creation.[34] And human beings might care about – or under the right conditions come to care about – producing goods because of the intrinsic interest of the work or its contribu-tion to society. Many people in high-paying jobs are doing work that satisfies them such that they would, if they were honest, be happy to do them without extra remuneration.[35] If citizens espouse values of fellowship, regard for others and a culture of common wellbeing, equal distribution, indeed equal flourishing, is the background condition for their own wellbeing.[36] Pessimistic assumptions about human nature may turn out to be correct, and society might have to settle for incentive schemes to achieve the level of pro-ductivity necessary for any move towards equality. But this is a roadblock that should not be set up in advance, in case the route proves rocky. Let's test the road first: it may be smoother than we think.

Thus, to address the challenge of the levelling down problem, we will need a more nuanced measure than goods or resources in order to assess how indi-viduals are doing, whether they are fulfilling their potential, living well, are autonomous and contented. Society should create social conditions that enable equal wellbeing, and where some have more wellbeing than others, this should be a target for egalitarian remedy so long as it does not mean decreasing some people's wellbeing with no benefit for others. This follows from Christiano's insight, 'If it were not true that more well-being is better than less, then there would be no point to equality.'[37] Thus, though there is some injustice in some having more than others, a flourishing account cannot permit the removal of flourishing for the sake of mere symmetry; equality is not always better than inequality. Wellbeing is an indeterminate principle;[38] there will always be chal-lenges in deciding how resources are to be distributed in order to render people equal in their wellbeing. We should aim for the distribution that brings everyone to an adequate level of wellbeing, ambitiously understood, and that maximises wellbeing even when it cannot be equalised, so long as inequality truly has no negative impact.

## Talent

Unequal talent might seem a thorn in the side of the equal society. Plato's Republic, with its community of different classes of persons based on aptitude, some of whom are involved in political life while others merely protect or service it, is a disturbing model for egalitarians. Yet even if we seek, following Marx, to break down the division of labour and allow individuals access to a variety of tasks, people will be more suited for some pursuits rather than others, and not all pursuits are equally enjoyable. Equality is a problematic ideal if it demands the elimination of displays of superiority of all kinds, as we saw in Vonnegut's society where even talent is levelled down. In Rawls's idea of the natural lottery, people's assets are a matter of luck for which there should be no financial reward.[39] Beyond his concession to incentives, Rawls does not address the question of how talent might be recognised and developed. I noted above that, in most societies today, work that is more likely to be fulfilling – autonomous, stimulating, creative and publicly esteemed – is typically more highly remunerated, compounding the injustice. But this means that on a wellbeing model, even if inequalities of talent are severed from economic reward and there is genuine equality of opportunity, unequal talent can persist as a problem for the society that seeks equality. Thus Nagel concludes that perfectionists' commitment to developing 'maximum levels of excellence' is anti-egalitarian, 'recognising and exploiting the natural inequalities between persons, encouraging specialisation and distinction of levels in education, and accepting the variation in accomplishment which results.'[40]

Yet the talented among us provide discoveries, ideas and works of art that enhance our culture, shape our society's institutions and practices, and improve our standard of living, health and quality of life. The public culture that is produced by the great achievements of the few seems a genuine case of 'trickle down' that can be justified on egalitarian grounds, where talent provides benefits to which the less endowed nonetheless have access. Nozick's famous 'Wilt Chamberlain' thought experiment, where basketball fans voluntarily transfer resources to a talented basketball player in order to watch him play, is suggestive here.[41] The example's power comes from our intuitions about the value of the development and display of athletic skill, but this does not mean talented persons are entitled to a disproportionate share of society's wealth. Rather, it is because all human beings are entitled to a life of wellbeing that, though Chamberlain is not entitled to be richer than everyone else, he is entitled to develop and express his talents. Everyone's access to opportunities for developing talent should be as unfettered as possible, so what Fishkin calls 'bottlenecks' to success can be reduced or eliminated. This means appreciating the complexity of the definition, manifestation, and development of talent, and the ways individuals end up on different paths in life that can lead to significant differences in their lots.[42]

There is thus an egalitarian principle for encouraging the development of exemplary talent: as Galston puts it, 'the full development of each individual is equal in moral weight to that of every other.'[43] We owe it to everyone, however talented, the opportunity to enjoy the wellbeing that comes from fulfilling her potential, and the exceptionally talented can enhance the wellbeing of others. There is no egalitarian benefit in the elimination of opportunities for the development and recognition of unequal talent, but contra Nozick, we should not compound natural inequality with material inequality, be it overpaid sports stars or, the corollary, overpriced tickets for sporting events. Public criteria determine that 'my technical competence may entitle me to a position as a brain surgeon. It does not follow that I am entitled to half a million dollars a year.'[44] Of course, it may be that talent is in some instances a catalyst of 'special burdens', as we discussed above – special talent equips one to perform a job that is particularly onerous and for which one may merit special compensation.

The equal society would not, however, be without honours. Displays of excellence, in all walks of life and not just in the domains that traditionally confer prestige, should be honoured in accordance with how excellence contributes to the wellbeing of others. Honours enable the community to express its gratitude to fellow citizens, and the honoured individuals to take pride in the contribution they have made, without being a vehicle for personal enrichment.[45] Honours thus help maintain the distinction between talent and material wealth. Walzer contends that the harm of inequality lies in its spill-over effects, e.g. when unequal wealth begets unequal political power. He thus proposes 'spheres of justice,' where the distribution arrangements in one domain are insulated from those of others.[46] However, not only is economic inequality likely to taint human relations, such as those of trust and fellowship, economic inequality tends to generate inequality in other domains.[47] Finally, it is not true that economic inequality only matters if it has a wider impact; significant disparities of wealth in themselves are counter to the equal human wellbeing that is properly our aim.[48] Thus ascribing a role for honours does not mean that an inequality of 'separate spheres' is to be permitted.

## One's Own

The feminist slogan 'the personal is political' was coined to signal the need for public scrutiny of unjust personal relations, in particular the power husbands have historically held over wives. However much the family home is a setting for valuable intimate relations and a refuge from the burdens of the public domain, it is also a site of power that should answer to the demands of justice.[49] The family is relevant to justice in another sense: individuals can transmit their advantages or disadvantages to loved ones in significant ways, often in tension with society's egalitarian policies. Nonetheless, when individuals have personal loyalties that are in conflict with the public commitment to equality, these loyalties should not simply be overridden. The domain of intimates has special, valuable qualities that must be permitted some scope in the pursuit of egalitarian ideals.

Nagel formulates this problem in terms of a conflict between the impartial and partial standpoints occupied by individuals, a 'division of the self' that is difficult to reconcile. On the one hand we experience the world from our individual points of view, and have concerns and attachments that are 'extremely important' to us, and on the other hand we can think about the world in abstraction from our particular place within it, and recognise the sense in which everyone's life matters as much as one's own.[50] We are able to conceptualise the impersonal standpoint by thinking about how having one's own interests and desires is something we share with others. Nonetheless, there are occasions when the commitment to others seems to call upon sacrifices of the personal to which the individual is reluctant to accede. What is needed is a shift in motivation, Nagel says, so that although people 'still want material comforts, good food and vacations in Italy,' they would 'not feel right about these things if other members of their society could not afford them.'[51]

Nagel's conflict between standpoints results in a division of labour between the societal and the individual, premised on the 'irreducibility' of the personal view which is 'always present alongside' the impersonal standpoint. But this suggests an odd detachment from the project of equality on the part of individuals, and Nagel admits that his view has poor prospects for integration. On his account, motivating human beings to support radical institutions of redistribution that limit the options of their personal lives remains a challenge: 'an acceptable combination of individual and political morality remains to be invented.'[52] Thus some have concluded that such ambitions might be relegated to 'how the world should be rather than what social institutions should be like,' as Scanlon puts it.[53]

In his provocatively entitled, 'If You're an Egalitarian, How Come You're So Rich?,' Cohen insists on bringing the egalitarian's personal motivations in line with his or her public commitments. According to this argument, egalitarians should consider parting with significant amounts of personal income to redress inequality, and moreover, be motivated in their everyday lives by the plight of the less fortunate. Cohen argues that our egalitarian commitment should shape not just our conformity to the rules, but the scope of the rules, and our willingness to give up personal resources to render the less fortunate more equal.[54] Estlund has countered that the importance of the personal tells against Cohen's insistence that a theory of justice should go beyond institutions and shape the choices of individuals. In order to allow scope for personal commitments to family and friends, people should be free to refuse to take positions unless remunerated at a level to help honour such commitments. Estlund adduces examples such as siblings who have unequal family burdens or couples where one person faces sacrificing his or her career ambitions for the sake of the other.[55]

Adjusting pay scales in light of such prerogatives, however, would do violence to an egalitarian order. For such cases enable some to take advantage of their privileged market position to blackmail society into higher reward. This is so no matter how valuable the personal purposes that motivate the wealth-seekers.[56] We all have such personal commitments, and it seems unfair that only those who are in a position to demand high salaries should be in a position to honour them. It is possible that, like the compensation for arduous work that imposes special burdens, an egalitarian scheme would provide recompense for special obligations. But it would be a license for a rampant and unfair escalation in the hierarchy of wealth, with deleterious effects on wellbeing, if highly skilled people could bargain for high pay, whatever their motives. Enabling people to care for their loved ones should be a responsibility of the equal society, but it is not best discharged by allowing individuals to exploit market advantages.

Brighouse and Swift discuss the relation between egalitarian commitments and parent-child relationships. They contend that in decisions about children's education, egalitarians should support state-provided education and send their children to state schools. Only when a child's wellbeing is suffering significantly in the state-provided system is the parent justified in placing the child in a private school.[57] In general, however, parents should forbear from certain activities of 'illegitimate favouritism' that advantage their children. Thus: professional parents should not participate in 'take your child to work' days which 'potentially entrenches socially stratified roles' and highly intelligent children who are already more likely to succeed should, prima facie, not have bedtime stories read to them if that will particularly advantage them.[58] Partiality can, however, play a role as a check on the egalitarian principle, so for example, reading bedtime stories is permitted as an 'overriding moral consideration,' given the 'familial relationship goods' that are involved.[59]

Even the egalitarian society that succeeds in mitigating the conflict between personal and public commitments will nonetheless have instances where these commitments are at odds. An egalitarian pay scale that permits no special pleading, or that seeks a healthy work-life balance, cannot wholly remove the genuine conflict between family attachments and public obligations when it comes to allocating time, for example. Should I go to the community meeting or should I spend time with my children? In the absence of measures that coerce people's participation, such questions will persist in an egalitarian society. It is important that we recognise that value pluralism, essential to any adequate conception of wellbeing, admits of dilemmas and (modestly) tragic choices, where some good must be lost for some other good. Political versus personal decisions are but one species of such difficulties.

The problem of such motivational conflicts indicates how important it is that we design society's institutions so as to secure, as much as possible, equality in people's material positions. The literature on personal obligations and prerogatives in the domain of justice tends to take as its context that of the unequal society which requires remedy, a situation that produces this motivational conflict. Far from overriding personal obligations, the equal society should make it possible for individuals to pursue their projects without a sense of constant unease about whether they have done enough for others. Society would be structured so that social institutions, not voluntary donations or individual displays of conscience, ensure the wellbeing of citizens. Indeed, well-designed institutions should mean that there is very little persisting inequality that fails at the bar of justice.

Williams's critique of utilitarianism is apposite here. Williams argues that utilitarianism requires that the individual become a channel for the input of aggregate aims of society and the output of maximising satisfaction, thus becoming alienated from 'his actions and the source of his action in his own convictions.'[60] Analogously, if we treat equality as a pattern of holdings, then we are tempted by the idea that we simply apply this pattern to human decision making at all levels, again doing violence to individuals' integrity as they are reduced to equality maximisers, channels for an impersonal value.[61] This problem arises with Cohen's egalitarian ethos, which can hector individuals to do more for equality even where fully instantiated egalitarian institutions exist.[62]

A different picture emerges with my flourishing view. It is because among our personal commitments are precisely the principles of the egalitarian society in which we live, making up an egalitarian ethos in which we believe we must take 'direct responsibility' for justice,[63] that we care about social arrangements that best realise equality. Individuals topping up, ad hoc, the distributive justice meted out by the state, with the attendant problems of potentially patronising social relations, as well as inconsistent and contingent results, are among the reasons for preferring that institutions do the job.[64] Our egalitarian ethos should centre on the aim of equal human wellbeing, and as such seek, among other things, to avoid the debilitating effects of constant soul-searching, and the inadequacies of individualised remedies for social justice. Thus, although there is not a cognitive division of labour when it comes to one's own wellbeing and distributive questions, the citizen needs social structures in place that make it possible for the commitment to equality to be so assured that other commitments can be pursued with purpose and vigour.

Wellbeing is not served by saddling individuals with impossible choices about the people and pursuits they love versus their political ideals. A flourishing approach to egalitarianism can therefore provide a better answer to, for example, the problem of parents' partiality for their children. Familial relationship goods have, as Segall puts it, 'absolute value.'[65] These goods are exemplified by activities shared by parents and children that are constitutive of human flourishing, and as such are to be, not rationed and minimised, but encouraged and fostered, within an egalitarian institutional context that assures us that such goods can be pursued guilt-free.

This strategy differs from that of other critics of Cohen, such as Tan, who reject the 'trans-institutional' approach for a disjunction between public and private domains, where equality is the province of institutions, removed from the everyday lives of citizens.[66] If we treat equality as a pattern of holdings for which the individual has responsibility only when, as it were, wearing his or her citizen-hat, as Tan and Nagel suggest, then we have a system of equality that is presented as an alien intrusion on one's ideals and values, a poorly grounded and precarious alternative. This problem persists in other models, where principles of justice make demands on the personal yet permit what critics (with some concession from Cohen) call an agent-centred 'personal prerogative' that allows certain exceptions to the pursuit of equality.[67]

On the wellbeing model it is for the sake of equality that we give individuals space to pursue their projects and to nurture important others, because it is wellbeing that we are seeking to improve when we try to make people more equal. Equality itself contributes to a person's wellbeing, and though one may understand this in light of reasoning along the model of abstraction that Nagel proposes, this is not to hive off egalitarian values from one's own, but to count equality as among one's personal commitments. It would do violence to one's integrity if equality were treated as alien to personal fulfilment. Indeed, individual wellbeing involves equality in the sense that even the richest person's quality of life must involve living in a society where others live minimally well too. Thus we return to some of the considerations adduced in the levelling down question.[68] Being rich amongst the destitute is not a high quality of life, and if one is impervious to this claim, then there is a sense in which one is thereby living a lesser life. Dworkin puts it thus: 'everyone is insulted by a political and economic system dedicated to inequality, even those who profit in resources from the injustice';[69] another way of expressing Marx's communist ideal of how 'the free development of each is a condition of the free development of all.'[70]

Contemporary egalitarianism is too preoccupied with material goods, understood as having an inherent competitive structure. But the ideal of the equal society seems inextricably bound up with a conception of community where members do not see themselves as rivals for goods. Moreover, in the egalitarian society what is of value is not just material in kind; as Wolff puts it, 'enjoyment of what can be shared rather than privately consumed' is central. The experience of nature or culture, conversation, friendship or physical activity, are all vital constituents of human flourishing. On a wellbeing account, many goods that contribute to our wellbeing are social, where, as Tawney puts it, 'to divide is not to take away.'[71] On this view, individual wellbeing depends on membership in a certain kind of community.

Thus human flourishing can be hampered by inequality, no matter where one is in the economic hierarchy.[72] The perfectionist Hurka notes some of the considerations we observed earlier in relation to strict equality: cooperation with one's fellow citizens goes more smoothly when citizens are secure and educated, and social relations will be more amicable without the condescension, servility, resentment and arrogance that attend class divisions. Further, 'a society of material equals is unlikely to be one in which people's main aims are monetary.'[73] People's aims centre on the accumulation and preservation of wealth where there is inequality and anxiety about financial security. In such contexts, individuals avoid worthwhile but non-remunerative pursuits, and pursuits with intrinsic worth are typically approached instrumentally in terms of the wealth they might generate. Thus the disadvantaged are burdened by anxiety and fear, and the fabulously rich can find their values to be corrupt and shallow.[74]

This point need not be given an extravagant interpretation where the rich benefit so much by living among equals that the goods and opportunities they must forfeit in the name of equality pale in comparison. It is difficult to compare such disparate goods as, on the one hand, the benefits of superior character, bonds of community, pleasure at the diminution of others' hardship, with, on the other, the benefits of extra resources, such as fancy holidays, grand houses or luxury goods. And if these goods could be weighed against each other, there would be cases where advantaged individuals would claim to benefit more from the latter. However, considerations about the benefits of equality for the previously advantaged are not the main justification for egalitarianism (just as Marx's claim that the propertied, too, were alienated under capitalism, though important, does not figure as the main argument against capitalist exploitation). Thus, in contrast to perfection-dominated arguments in which equality is merely a 'tendency' favoured by perfectionism,[75] human flourishing must meet the bar of justice, that is, the principles of equality. Moreover, given flourishing's non-material components, all of us benefit from a society where equality in material distribution generates genuine community.

## Conclusion

This chapter noted that beneath the equality consensus there lurks some grave doubts about the radical position on economic equality. These doubts were distilled into three problems: the spectre of levelling down; the place of superior talent; and the role of personal attachments and commitments. I have suggested ways in which these challenges can be overcome. Strict equality is not ludicrous, but its attainment is only relevant insofar as human wellbeing is at stake. Sometimes human wellbeing requires departures from strict equality. Superior talent should be cultivated and recognised, but it should not enable a disproportionate share of wealth; a conception of egalitarianism in terms of wellbeing enables us to develop talent without developing disparities of wealth. The wellbeing of the talented, and of the rest of us who might enjoy the fruits of that talent, enables us to understand how strict equality of wealth is not necessarily the best way to realise the egalitarian ideal. Finally, the problem of how to weigh the demands of one's principles against personal attachments should be understood as symptomatic of an unequal society in particular. We seek to render individuals more equal in order to resource them in their pursuits, and to enable their full enjoyment of them. A focus on wellbeing rather than goods is helpful in resolving the dilemma of public and private.

Equality of individuals' moral worth is a constant ideal; material equality, however, is more complex. Inequality is prima facie wrong; it is a kind of injustice. But the story cannot end there. The principle of equal human well-being, and our interest in living well, determines permissible inequalities in light of their capacity to add to people's wellbeing. This means a radical redistribution of wealth from the advantaged to the disadvantaged, but not always with the result of strict equality. Wellbeing is a criterion by which we can both justify strict equality under certain well-defined conditions, as well as call for departures from strict equality when those conditions do not obtain.

One reason why egalitarians have been saddled with the problems of strict material equality is the focus on property and material goods, a preoccupation inherited from the libertarian conception of persons as owners and possessors. Egalitarian goals must refer not to what people have, but how they fare, in an ideal society. Moral individualism, prompted in part by libertarian critiques, is indispensable in determining what distribution best promotes individual well-being and the social culture with which individual wellbeing is inextricably connected. Egalitarianism is a contextualist ethics, even if it is also a principled one, but though universal lessons are hard to draw, we can distil our findings into a helpful image. Justice, equality and wellbeing are like points on a triangle: one starts with justice, which demands strict equality;[76] equality is then modulated by qualitative considerations about wellbeing; high levels of wellbeing that are unevenly enjoyed, the fruits of serious economic disparity, must then answer to the court of justice and the egalitarian principles which justice entails. Individual wellbeing depends on justice, since one's ability to enjoy wellbeing involves a just context where the development of one's projects and personal pursuits is unfettered by anxiety about their inegalitarian preconditions.

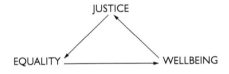

*Figure 6.1* Justice, equality and wellbeing

In sum, I have sought to address three vexing challenges to the ideal of material equality in order to sort out, in some preliminary way, what equality is and is not. I have argued that a radical egalitarian position with plausible accounts of the problems of levelling down, talent, and partiality can be achieved if we conceive of equality in terms of living well. There remains, of course, a great deal to work out in the project of defending the egalitarian ideal proposed here. Does desert or responsibility have any role in a conception of equality, or are citizens entitled to resources even if they refuse to contribute to their production or make poor choices? If wellbeing is understood along perfectionist lines, does this not risk elitism and paternalism, vices commonly supposed to be contrary to egalitarian views? And how might a wellbeing approach to equality address problems of global justice? These questions are the subject of the chapters that follow.

# Notes

1 Depicted in Y. Zamyatin's dystopian novel, *We.*
2 Nozick, *Anarchy, State and Utopia*, 155–60.
3 Ibid., 229.
4 K. Vonnegut, 'Harrison Bergeron.'
5 Raz, *The Morality of Freedom*, 225–9.
6 P. Casal provides this helpful characterisation in 'Why Sufficiency Is Not Enough,' 297–8.
7 H. Frankfurt, 'Equality as a Moral Ideal.'
8 Ibid., 146.
9 R. Crisp, 'Equality, Priority, and Compassion,' 758.
10 T. Nagel, *Equality and Partiality*, 69.
11 D. Parfit, 'Equality or Priority?' 103–6.
12 Ibid., 100–1.
13 L. Temkin, 'Equality, Priority and the Levelling Down Objection,' 154–5.
14 G.A. Cohen, 'The Pareto Argument for Inequality,' 164. Cohen concedes that inequality might be a matter of 'damage limitation' in real-world scenarios where productivity is only possible if the talented get greater incomes; see Cohen, *Rescuing Justice and Equality*, 84.
15 I. Hirose contends that economists' 'aggregate' view shows that the wellbeing of the better off 'counts negatively' in the 'overall goodness of affairs,' once we consider how wellbeing is determined by relational factors, *Egalitarianism*, 79.
16 Casal, 'Why Sufficiency Is Not Enough,' 307.
17 J. Moss, *Reassessing Egalitarianism*, 18.
18 A. Phillips, *Which Inequalities Matter?*, 68.
19 J. Wolff, 'Levelling Down.'
20 T. Scanlon, *The Difficulty of Tolerance*, 214–16.
21 M. O'Neill, 'What Should Egalitarians Believe?,' 130.
22 J. Stiglitz notes how severe inequality produces civil conflict, criminality, instability and lack of cohesion in *The Price of Inequality*, 84. Even where people have adequate incomes, the spectacle of the very rich produces a society-wide consumerism where we 'work more to maintain our consumption relative to others'; working hard 'for the family' paradoxically means we spend less time with the family and family life deteriorates, 105–6. See also F. Neuhouser, 'Rousseau's Critique of Economic Inequality.'
23 See D. Miller, 'Equality and Justice.'
24 O'Neill, 'What Should Egalitarians Believe?' 146.
25 Scanlon, *The Difficulty of Tolerance*, 205.
26 P. Gilabert, *From Global Poverty to Global Equality*, 167–8.
27 C.M. Hoxby, 'Do Private Schools Provide Competition for Public Schools?'; D. de la Croix and M. Doepke, 'Politics and the Structure of Education Funding.'
28 T. Christiano and W. Braynen, 'Inequality, Injustice and Levelling Down,' 34.
29 See Hurka, *Perfectionism*, 178.
30 Nagel, *Equality and Partiality*, 138.
31 Thus the Janis Joplin song: 'Oh lord, won't you buy me, a Mercedes Benz; my friends all got Porsches, I must make amends...'
32 Cohen, *Rescuing Justice and Equality*, 55–8. S. Scheffler discusses the problem of individuals being 'overly burdened' in his defence of Rawls in 'Is the Basic Structure Basic?.'
33 Cohen, *Rescuing Justice and Equality*, 36.
34 Hurka, *Perfectionism*, 171.
35 W. Galston, *Liberal Purposes: Goods, Virtues and Diversity in the Liberal State*, 207.
36 G.A. Cohen contends an ideal of justificatory community motivates egalitarians who thus set themselves an 'interpersonal test' whereby 'we do not make policy

*together* if we make it in the light of what some of us do that cannot be justified to others.' See Cohen, 'Incentives, Inequality and Community,' 351.

37  T. Christiano, *The Constitution of Equality: Democratic Authority and its Limits*, 33.

38  Ibid., 24.

39  Rawls, *A Theory of Justice*, 74.

40  Nagel, *Equality and Partiality*, 135.

41  Nozick, *Anarchy, State and Utopia*.

42  J. Fishkin, *Bottlenecks: A New Theory of Equal Opportunity*. See my 'Bottlenecks to Flourishing and the "Road Less Travelled" in Political Philosophy.' C. Chambers notes the snowballing of advantage in 'Each Outcome Is Another Opportunity: Problems with the Moment of Equal Opportunity,' 383.

43  Galston, *Liberal Purposes*, 193.

44  Ibid., 206–7. It is worth noting that, 25 years after Galston made this remark, the figure would now be much higher.

45  This is not to replicate the Stalinist cult of the 'Hero of Socialist Labour' that justified abysmal working conditions and punitive practices for the less productive. See V. Shlapentokh 'The Stakhanovite Movement: Changing Perceptions over Fifty Years,' 259–76. Russia is reputed to be reviving the practice and contemporary capitalism is not immune – consider the 'employee of the month' ritual designed to spur greater productivity. Honours would need to be designed so they are a genuine means of expressing the community's esteem for talented and hardworking contributors.

46  Walzer, *Spheres of Justice*, 12.

47  A. Swift, 'The Sociology of Complex Equality.'

48  See B. Barry, 'Spherical Justice and Global Injustice,' 70.

49  The slogan was coined in the 1970s but well developed by Okin in *Justice, Gender and the Family*.

50  Nagel, *Equality and Partiality*, 18.

51  Ibid., 126.

52  Ibid., 129.

53  T. Scanlon, 'Justice, Responsibility and the Demands of Equality,' 86.

54  Cohen, *If You're an Egalitarian, How Come You're So Rich?*, 128, 149. See also *Rescuing Justice and Equality*, 117. L. Murphy also makes an interesting argument for the claim that 'all fundamental normative principles that apply to the design of institutions also apply to the conduct of people,' in 'Institutions and the Demands of Justice,' 251.

55  D. Estlund, 'Debate: Liberalism, Equality and Fraternity in Cohen's Critique of Rawls,' 99–105.

56  M. Otsuka comes to the same conclusion in a trenchant argument from a left-libertarian perspective in 'Prerogatives to Depart from Equality,' 112.

57  H. Brighouse and A. Swift, 'Legitimate Parental Partiality,' 43–80. Their recent book, *Family Values: The Ethics of Parent-Child Relationships*, explores these issues more broadly within the context of the family. See also H. Brighouse and A. Swift, 'Parents' Rights and the Value of the Family,' H. Brighouse, *School Choice and Social Justice*, A. Swift, *How Not to Be a Hypocrite: School Choice for the Morally Perplexed Parent*, S. Brennan and R. Noggle, eds, *Taking Responsibility for Children*, D. Archard and C. Macleod, eds, *The Moral and Political Status of Children*.

58  See A. Swift, 'Justice, Luck and the Family: The Intergenerational Transmission of Economic Advantage from a Normative Perspective,' 270. See also S. Segall, *Equality and Opportunity*, 164.

59  Swift and Brighouse, 'Legitimate Parental Partiality,' 57; see also the same discussion in *Family Values*, 129–32.

60  B. Williams, 'Critique of Utilitarianism,' 116–17.

61  K.C. Tan makes this objection, though without drawing my conclusions about equality's relation to human wellbeing, in 'Justice and Personal Pursuits,' 28.

62 Though Cohen thinks that in addition to the effective coercive rules of institutions, a just society's ethos involves 'a structure of response lodged in the motivations that inform everyday life,' rather than rules which 'severely compromise liberty if people were required forever to consult such rules.' Cohen, *Rescuing Justice and Equality*, 123. Nonetheless, this is more demanding than the position ventured in 'If You're an Egalitarian' where our personal obligations arise because of inadequate institutions.

63 Murphy, 'Institutions and the Demands of Justice,' 271.

64 I explore some of these problems in 'Begging.'

65 See Segall, *Equality and Opportunity*, 166.

66 Tan coins the 'trans-institutional' label for Cohen's view and subjects it to critique in 'Justice and Personal Pursuits,' 29. See also K.C. Tan, *Justice, Institutions and Luck: The Site, Ground and Scope of Inequality*, 53, 19–49.

67 See S. Scheffler, 'Is the Basic Structure Basic?' 120. Cohen makes the concession in *Rescuing Justice and Equality*, 61.

68 Scanlon, *The Difficulty of Tolerance*, 202–18, M. O'Neill, 'What Should Egalitarians Believe?.'

69 Dworkin, *Sovereign Virtue*, 280.

70 Marx and Engels, 'The Communist Manifesto,' 491.

71 R.H. Tawney, *Equality*, 291; J. Wolff, 'Fairness, Respect and the Egalitarian Ethos Revisited,' 338.

72 For example, A. Sen notes that 'shared communal benefits' of basic education 'which may transcend the gains of the person being educated.' *Development as Freedom*, 128. The relation between equality and human wellbeing is charted in R. Wilkinson and K. Pickett, *The Spirit Level: Why More Equal Societies Almost Always Do Better*.

73 Hurka, *Perfectionism*, 179.

74 Ibid., 172–9, 172; see A. MacIntyre, *After Virtue*, 188, on playing chess and instrumental rationality.

75 Hurka, *Perfectionism*, 189.

76 Segall similarly argues that egalitarianism should adopt a rule of thumb where unequal distributions always require a justification in *Equality and Opportunity*, 31.

# 7 Human Flourishing and the Use and Abuse of Equality

Why do we condemn economic inequality? Unequal distribution of wealth can have the effect that some people are poorly housed, badly nourished, ill educated, or uncultured, among other things. In other words, inequality leaves some less 'well off' than others, and thus when we seek to make people more equal our concern is not just resources or property but how people fare under one distribution or another. We care about inequality because of its effect on people and we lose interest in problems of inequality if the putatively unequal are doing equally well in their quality of life.[1] Ultimately, the answer to the question 'equality of what?' is flourishing, since whatever policies or principles we adopt, it is flourishing, or wellbeing, that we hope will be made more equal as a result of our endeavours.

Flourishing is not, however, the focus of most egalitarian theories. Most egalitarians avoid ideas such as living well or the good life, focussing on goods, income or resources – on the instruments of flourishing, not flourishing itself.[2] This is because most contemporary egalitarians are neutralists, who are uneasy with ideas of what counts as a life well lived. The idea of flourishing presupposes that we can delineate, in some more or less objective way, living well from living badly, in order to promote the former and discourage the latter. Neutralists contend that social policy should play no role in the matter of plans of life. Individuals' freedom to choose how to live should be respected and political theories that seek to promote living well are illiberal.

In the last chapter I noted how a focus on flourishing sheds light on some of the challenges facing egalitarianism. This chapter sets to making a case for what follows: a flourishing account of equality. I take up Arneson's suggestion that there might be 'conceptual room ... within the space of perfectionist views, for political principles that are nonelitist, recognizably liberal, and egalitarian'[3] to capture the philosophical context and general features of an egalitarianism centred on the idea of flourishing. First, I will show that the flourishing approach has historical antecedents in socialist writings from Morris to Marx to Beveridge; second, I will discuss the influence of some contemporary egalitarians such as Sen and Nussbaum. Finally, I will argue that a focus on flourishing can address the problem of individual responsibility that so vexes contemporary egalitarians.

The human flourishing approach I defend here may be called 'egalitarian flourishing' or 'egalitarian perfectionism.'[4] These terms are controversial. As we noted in the last chapter, equality per se is often not the goal of thinkers dubbed egalitarian; egalitarians are typically concerned to make people more equal, not fully equal. The metric of flourishing, we shall see, poses special problems as something to be distributed in equal quantities. Nonetheless, my approach insists that equality per se, understood as equality of flourishing, is the proper aim of egalitarianism. As for perfectionism, it too might be thought to be misleading. Gaus's remark that perfectionism involves 'making others more perfect in our own eyes' is a typical but distorted perception of the view.[5] In what follows, I hope to correct familiar misunderstands of what perfectionism entails. First, it is usually taken as a unitary ideal, whereas I will argue that flourishing takes many forms. Second, it is assumed to imply coercion, which I eschew. And third, it is supposed that perfection per se – some absolute, flawless state of excellence – is the theory's goal, a supposition I also reject. These themes emerge in the following chapters.

## The Aesthetic Road to Equality

The idea that public policy should seek to render levels of human flourishing more equal might seem at odds with the lack of interest in equality of contemporary perfectionists such as Sher, who discusses the idea largely to reject it,[6] or Raz, who as we noted in the last chapter, finds equality a misguided ideal. The perfectionist tradition is thought to focus on enabling great achievements for the gifted – promoting superman over the herd, as Nietzsche put it – rather than extending wellbeing to the many.[7] At most, perfectionists are interested in equality for instrumental reasons, as a means of achieving perfection. Thus Galston contends that a conception of equality 'is needed to move from the individual good to public institutions and policies.'[8] Hurka suggests that egalitarian policy serves perfectionist goals, and thus perfectionism has a 'strong but defeasible tendency to favour material equality.'[9] The position I seek to advance, in contrast, begins with egalitarian premises and then argues that what we seek to equalise is flourishing.

The concept of egalitarian flourishing or egalitarian perfectionism might seem peculiar to contemporary ears. But there are historical precedents. Indeed, the entire nineteenth century egalitarian tradition has perfectionist assumptions. For the socialist aesthete Morris, there was no tension between perfectionism and egalitarianism.[10] Morris's design house – Morris, Faulkner and Company – sought to create 'art for life,' and much influenced by the art of the Middle Ages, looked to traditional manufacturing for an aesthetic beautiful in form, useful in practice, and fulfilling in its creation. This conception of art was a broad one, figuring in 'all labour in some form or other.'[11] Thus even before Morris became engaged in political debate, his aesthetic ideals, in their very emphasis on cooperative labour, artisans and decorative art, had a populist, and in some sense egalitarian, aspect.[12]

Morris's aesthetic was at odds with nineteenth-century trends, not only the taste for ornate decoration and methods of mass production, but also the imperatives of the capitalist economic system. Traditional crafts, the preservation of green spaces, respect for historical architecture, were at risk if wealth was in the hands of the few. The revitalisation of the arts required society to challenge 'the privilege of private persons to destroy the beauty of the earth for their private advantage'; so that the arts could be 'the common possession of the whole people.'[13] Morris is often said to have anticipated the philosophy of Britain's National Trust, whose aesthetic aims are bound up with egalitarian policy: care of England's historic buildings requires public stewardship, which in turn entails the principle of public access. As Octavia Hill proclaimed when she founded the National Trust in 1907: 'The need of quiet, the need of air, the need of exercise, and the sight of sky and of things growing seem human needs, common to all men.'[14]

Like his mentor Ruskin, Morris came to see the constitutive link between egalitarianism and human flourishing, given capitalist inequality's deleterious impact on people's wellbeing. 'A very inequitably divided material prosperity' meant that men and women 'work as laboriously as ever they did,' but have 'lost the solace that labour once provided,' that is, 'the opportunity of expressing their own thoughts to their fellows by means of that very labour.' The result was the diminishing of the valuable: 'cheap market wares,' 'mere scaffold-poles for building up profits.'[15] Thus Morris's aestheticism, 'an act of rebellion against an ugly age,'[16] became a political struggle for equality centred on the idea of wellbeing.

Morris understands wellbeing objectively, independent of people's subjective views. As evidenced by the titles of his lectures, 'How We Live and How We Might Live,' 'Useful Work *versus* Useless Toil,' 'True and False Society,' Morris's idea of social justice assumes a conception of objective value. Inequality not only makes us 'sweating and terrified for our livelihood,' it robs the poor of the 'true ideal of a full and reasonable life.' Socialism will not be realised until:

> workers get out of their heads that they are but an appendage to profit-grinding, that the more profits that are made the more employment at high wages there will be for them, and that therefore all the incredible filth, disorder, and degradation of modern civilisation are signs of their prosperity.[17]

Inequality had so degraded human beings that their choices were bound to be bad; reduced to a 'skinny and pitiful existence' the worker 'scarcely knows how to frame a desire for any life much better than that which he now endures perforce.'[18] Moreover, the rich, too, can be badly off, leading a life that is 'empty, unwholesome and degraded.'[19] In embracing the hope for 'a new and higher life for all men,'[20] Morris supposed that one could pronounce on the kinds of lives people ought to live, a matter beyond the ken of most people.

Morris is not unusual among nineteenth-century socialists in his desire to marry perfectionism with egalitarianism. Marx took the view that the remedy of inequality was bound up with a conception of wellbeing and the ideal of 'communist man.' Marx's critique of inequality is also a critique of alienation, an inherently perfectionist concept, referring, not just to the unfairness of economic hardship, but the distortion in values such hardship imposes. Thus Marx's case against capitalism centred on its affront to the 'nobility of man,'[21] the way in which relations of private property make people 'stupid and one-sided'[22] and how money causes the 'overturning of *individualities*.'[23] Economic inequality is wrong because it degrades human beings, robs them of dignity, self-determination and the ability to develop their capacities. Work, which should distinguish human beings from other species and be the source of human fulfilment, becomes an alien activity, a mere means to satisfy external needs. Marx's concept of exploitation, whereby owners appropriate the product of workers, like the idea of alienation, is also focussed on how workers' ability to live well is undermined by capitalist relations of production.[24]

At the core of Marx's perfectionism is the concept of 'species being' that refers to human beings' unique capacities and potential: how we participate in 'conscious life activity,' in which our productive powers, our 'working up of the objective world,' enable us to form things 'in accordance with the laws of beauty.'[25] Our unique capacity to labour, what Marx contended distinguished the 'worst architect' from the 'best of bees,'[26] is the result of essential human characteristics that include, as Leopold notes, consciousness, intentionality, language, co-operation, tool use and tool making, productive activity and creative intelligence.[27] According to Marx, in labour we duplicate ourselves, 'intellectually but also actively,' and therefore contemplate ourselves in the world we have created.[28] Communism restores to us our free, creative activity so that our labour becomes 'not only a means of life but life's prime want,' making possible the 'all-round development of the individual.'[29] The latter notion acknowledges that human needs are diverse. As Leopold notes, they include fellowship and community; moreover, Marx's idea of human flourishing embraced such things as recreation, culture and emotional satisfaction, in addition to his insistence that 'fulfilling work is central to the good life for human kind.'[30] Morris was a follower of Marx, and pored over (though he admitted with some difficulty) what he reverentially referred to as the 'great work' of *Capital*.[31] One commentator contends that Ruskin's ideas provided a natural route to Morris's socialism that Marx's writings served to confirm.[32] Indeed, it may be said, with a pleasing irony, that in the 1880s Morris anticipated ideas about labour in Marx's '1844 Manuscripts,' not published until long after Morris's death.

Morris's ideal is not without problems. First, his antipathy to mass manufacture was paradoxical, since it meant that only the affluent could afford his labour-intensive goods. It is ironic that only today are Morris-decorated artefacts, be they only mugs or tea towels, within the means of most people and this is precisely because they are mass-produced. A second and related problem is Morris's backward-looking aesthetic (which prompted him to declare, following Ruskin, that Oxford had been 'destroyed' by nineteenth-century development) and his focus on aesthetic endeavour that produces art for life.[33] In his preoccupation with decorative arts, tapestries, furniture and wall coverings, Morris seems to rule out the modern, individualistic aesthetic of the single work produced by the great artist in a way that is detrimental to a pluralist conception of human flourishing. Yet, however controversial we might find Morris's aesthetic ideals, we have much to learn from his conviction that the struggle for equality should aim to improve human wellbeing and that beauty is constitutive of a flourishing life.

It was not just socialists who believed the community should foster worthwhile ways of living. We are so used to thinking of Mill in terms of a hackneyed harm principle that we overlook the perfectionist aspects of his thought. But as Appiah points out, a 'my-freedom-ends-at-your-nose antipaternalism' fails to capture Mill's concern for human development. In 'On Liberty' the 'cultivation of individuality' emerges as society's ultimate aim: 'What more or better can be said of any condition of human affairs, than that it brings human beings themselves nearer to the best thing they can be?'[34] The idea that society should enable individuals to live well continued to animate liberalism after Mill. Hobhouse considered the idea of a common culture vital to his liberalism when he wrote in 1911 that

> mutual aid is no less important than mutual forbearance, the theory of collective action no less fundamental than the theory of personal freedom ... we regard liberty as primarily of social interest, as something flowing from the necessities of continuous advance in those regions of truth and of ethics which constitute the matters of highest social concern.[35]

Thus when early twentieth-century egalitarians married their ideal of equality to the principle of a public responsibility for the good life, they were helping themselves to a widely accepted view. Tawney, for example, affirmed Morris's evolution from aesthete to socialist when he argued that egalitarianism followed from perfectionist ideas about the state:

> the association of culture with a limited class, which is enabled by its wealth to carry the art of living to a high level of perfection, may ... preserve culture, but it cannot extend it; and, in the long run, it is only by its extension that, in the conditions of to-day, it is likely to be preserved.[36]

For Tawney, a concern for 'the perfecting of the individual,' meant 'an outlook on society which sympathised with the attempt to bring the means of a good life within the reach of all.'[37] In the 1930s Laski's egalitarianism also stressed the promotion of value; he criticised the preoccupation with 'material acquisition' because it 'fails to make response to those spiritual springs of discontent' where 'the masses' find 'their rest hours so void of the sense of creativeness or power.'[38]

Socialists accordingly conceived their goals in terms of the constituents of flourishing. In the Fabian call for a National Minimum, for example, the distribution of leisure counted as much as the distribution of income, since it would enable individuals to 'nurture and express their individuality.'[39] Beveridge, one of the architects of the British welfare state, spoke of a postwar 'battle' against the 'giants' of injustice. The perfectionist terms of his argument are striking: he refers to the amelioration of squalor and the elimination of idleness, rather than simply increasing income or resources. For Beveridge, the new commitment to the state provision of social welfare involved the aim of elevating human fulfilment, capacities and character.[40]

We now have two ways of conceiving the relation between equality and human flourishing. On the first, equality is valued instrumentally, as a means of protecting the constituents of human flourishing; the good is promoted where there is public stewardship and its corollary, public access to the valuable and other egalitarian measures. But on the second, equality itself is an ideal, which is specified in terms of enabling more equal wellbeing. The answer to the question of what it is we are trying to make more equal is flourishing, an answer that was – it appears – commonsensical for egalitarians in Morris's time and sometime thereafter.[41]

## Neutralism v. Perfectionism

As we noted in the Introduction, the publication of Rawls's *A Theory of Justice* set the terms for political philosophy after the subject had languished for most of the twentieth century, and those terms have tended to eschew perfectionism. It is worth recalling again that Rawls's position is not devoid of perfectionist elements. He agrees with Aristotle that individuals are motivated by the idea that challenging tasks are more valuable,[42] and he admits that the restrictions of liberal neutralism may be waived for such cases as national parks and funding for the arts.[43] Nonetheless, the idea of neutrality about the good in contemporary liberal discourse has become prominent under Rawls's influence: conceptions of the good are susceptible to controversy and should be relegated to the domain of personal choice.[44] Egalitarian philosophers since Rawls tend to define the metric of distributive justice in terms of the means to individuals' ends, things that, as Rawls puts it, 'a rational man wants no matter what else he wants.' Under conditions of fair equality of opportunity, once goods (which include non-material goods) are allocated according to a just principle of distribution, whether people flourish or not is taken to be a matter of their own responsibility; as Rawls puts it, 'it is assumed that the members of society are rational persons able to adjust their conceptions of the good to their situation.'[45]

Neutralists may differ on whether autonomy is the rationale for their views, or whether neutrality must forswear even autonomy as a value. For Dworkin, the ideal of equality necessitates neutrality: showing equal concern and respect to people extends to their conceptions of how to live. The 'beer-drinking, television-watching' citizen's plan of life should not count for any less than the plan of life of the intellectual or the aesthete. Indeed, Dworkin goes so far as to see the market, not normally celebrated for its equality, as an expression of egalitarian principle, insofar as each person's preference stands as good a chance of success as that of any other. 'A liberal theory of equality rules out ... appeal to the inherent value of one theory of what is good in life.'[46] People should be free to decide what kind of life they want to pursue with their fair share of resources.[47]

A notable exception is the influential work of Sen, which seeks to provide an objective measure of the quality of life in his analysis of equality. Sen argues that focussing on equitable shares of goods fails to consider how 'what goods do for people' is subject to enormous variation because of the differing circumstances of people's lives.[48] His answer to 'equality of what?' is therefore not goods or preferences for goods, but 'functionings,' or capabilities to achieve functionings.

> Living may be seen as consisting of a set of interrelated 'functionings', consisting of beings and doings.... The relevant functionings can vary from such elementary things as being adequately nourished, being in good health, avoiding escapable morbidity and premature mortality, etc., to more complex achievements such as being happy, having self-respect, taking part in the life of the community, and so on.[49]

This approach departs from 'resourcist' views that, Pogge notes, are concerned with distributive patterns regardless of how a given distribution of resources 'correlates with persons' differential capacities to convert such resources into valuable functionings.'[50]

Those who argue that the state is obligated to compensate for non-material inequalities sometimes appeal to the criterion of satisfaction or happiness. Welfarist criteria have the attraction that they focus on the effect of egalitarian measures; making people, as Dworkin puts it, 'equal in what is really and fundamentally important to them.'[51] We can avoid starting-gate problems where, after an initially equal distribution, some are stranded as a result of bad luck or mismanagement, since we are always monitoring how people are doing with their goods. And we can take account of how people vary in the goods they need in order to attain the same level of satisfaction; e.g. in order to enjoy the same basic level of mobility, Bill needs a wheelchair and modifications to his house, whilst Mary has no such needs.

The satisfaction criterion also implies, however, that we are obligated to provide extra resources to ensure equal satisfaction for those who have expensive tastes, or are easily bored or restless, if these are predilections over which individuals have no control. This is Cohen's view, one that he derives from the Marxian maxim of each according to his needs, where irresistible tastes are deemed analogous to unchosen needs.[52] Thus Sebastian gets subsidies for caviar to attain the same level of satisfaction as Homer, who is content with cheesies. This view naturally provokes scepticism. Dworkin, for example, argues that people should take responsibility for the satisfaction they extract from goods, and that egalitarian distribution should therefore focus on resources rather than welfare. The lover of 'plovers' eggs,' to use Dworkin's example, must bankroll his own enthusiasm.[53]

Sen rejects satisfaction in favour of the criterion of functioning for a different reason; namely, concerns about the quiescence of the disadvantaged. Desire fulfilment can give a distorted measure of wellbeing because of the problem of 'entrenched deprivation,' where the disadvantaged person adjusts down his or her expectations, goals and desires. 'The extent of a person's deprivation, then, may not show up in the metric of desire-fulfilment, even though he or she may fail to be adequately nourished, decently clothed, minimally educated and properly sheltered.'[54] One can become accustomed to disadvantage, just as one can take privilege for granted and feel discontented. Thus cheery Tiny Tim seems to have plenty of welfare even if the affluent but miserable Scrooge, an inefficient converter of goods into happiness, leaves Tim with few resources. It is a poor theory of equality that reinforces the effects of unequal distribution and concludes that the demands of equality are met simply because the poor are undemanding.[55]

## Constituents of Flourishing

Sen does not, however, directly tackle what I take to be the root of the problem infecting many alternatives to the criterion of satisfaction, which is their agnosticism about value.[56] Indeed, Nussbaum, who with Sen elaborated the capabilities approach, flatly denies that their critique of Rawls extends to his neutralism: 'the Capabilities Approach ... is a form of political liberalism, it is not a comprehensive doctrine of any sort.'[57] We noted in Chapter 3 that Nussbaum emphasises this point: 'respect for people and their choices' means that 'capability, not functioning, is the appropriate political goal.'[58] Mistakenly rejecting perfectionism on the grounds that it espouses a unitary conception of how to live, she concludes that 'we understand that respect for one's fellow citizens as equals requires not building the state on the ascendancy of any one particular comprehensive doctrine of the purpose and meaning of life, however excellent.'[59]

But Rawls's schema is inadequate not just because of what Sen calls its 'goods fetishism' that fails to take account of the impact of goods on persons. The neutralism of egalitarian positions in the Rawlsian tradition is also a serious defect. Primary goods are inadequate as an egalitarian measure because appeal to them fails to address the question of what counts as doing well, an assessment of the purposes to which goods are put. What is bad about being poor is not simply having less money than other people, but being deprived of the constituents of a valuable life. Sen, however, is reluctant to defend the perfectionist implications of his argument. This is manifest in his move to emphasise capability rather than its exercise, i.e. functionings, in order to give scope for choice, including bad choices detrimental to full functioning. The idea of capability focuses on the accessibility of x, y, and z, even if people only opt for x; it leaves people free to decide what capabilities to realise.[60]

Sen and Nussbaum are wrong to drop functioning for capability for two reasons. First, though freedom to choose is an aspect of wellbeing, wellbeing per se is also a matter of actual achievement.[61] Wellbeing involves not just access to a fulfilling life, or the capacity for such a life, but living it. It would be a paltry ideal of 'communist man' if it meant he merely had the opportunity to hunt in the morning, fish in the afternoon, criticise after dinner, but opted instead for lying on the couch.[62] It is in the nature of social class, for example, that a culture of fatalism and low expectations can be transmitted across generations so that people fail to flourish even when they have capabilities they lacked before. Often we need to do things in order to be able to do them. Nussbaum concedes, then, that there are cases when 'the absence of a function is really a sign that the capability itself has been surrendered.'[63] Moreover, we cannot determine whether there is genuine equality of opportunity without reference to the extent to which outcomes are in fact equal; as Sen admits, functionings have at least a data-collection advantage in that they are more easily observed.

It thus makes sense to take functioning – or, better, flourishing – as the object of egalitarian policy. As Arneson notes, there are clear cases where we should seek achieved wellbeing over opportunity for wellbeing if the result is a higher quality of life.[64] This is especially obvious for certain functionings, like health, which are valuable irrespective of people's choices.[65] This is not to say that the state should simply eliminate the possibility of failure; this would in fact undermine flourishing, which sometimes necessitates struggle, not effortless success. But where there are trends of failure to achieve flourishing, social policy should consider whether there are environmental causes that might be repaired.

The second advantage of a focus on functioning, or actual flourishing, lies in its ambition. Cohen faulted the capabilities idea for 'athleticism,' i.e. linking distributive justice to active engagement when the amelioration of disadvantage – e.g. feeding a hungry baby – need not require agency.[66] In this, he was making the cogent (and congenial) point that functionings are what is really at stake in disadvantage, rather than opportunities or capabilities to function. But 'athleticism' is suggestive. If we focus on mere access to functioning, our egalitarian commitment may whittle down to the simple satisfaction of basic needs. Active engagement with the world, creative labour and participation, as conceived by socialists such as Morris, are vital aspects of wellbeing. Nussbaum and Sen's capabilities include, after all, not just subsistence, but uniquely human capabilities for creation and participation.

Thus actual flourishing, in all its forms, should be our focus if we seek to render people more equal. The constituents of flourishing can be grouped into three categories. First, there is the ability to choose, as much as is possible given degrees of mental competence, how to live; for most people, a non-autonomous life falls short as a flourishing existence. A second constituent of wellbeing is objectively worthwhile pursuits, for there are better and worse ways of living and even the freely chosen pursuit can be defective. Finally, personal contentment is an important feature of flourishing, since freely chosen objective pursuits are inadequate sources of wellbeing if the person derives no pleasure or fulfilment from them. As Sher puts it, 'we can hardly deny that happiness, pleasure, and enjoyment are among life's goods.'[67] Though the valuable does not necessarily produce pleasure, this should not entail an austere version of perfectionism where pleasure figures as 'an accretion,' relevant only insofar as worthy pursuits tend to produce it.[68] How much weight to give each component is a tricky question; ideally each – autonomy, objective value and happiness – should have equal weight, but this is impossible to measure and there will be tradeoffs, though one would cease to count as flourishing if any one component is too lacking.

Some egalitarians have gone so far as to call for concepts of recognition or democratic equality to express the idea that wellbeing is derived from participation in one's community rather than mere possession of goods.[69] Although these formulations are to be praised for including important constituents of wellbeing besides material things, their weakness is their preoccupation with citizenship and the regard of others, to the neglect of economic inequality per se, which is after all important in its own right for determining how people live. One's public standing is relevant to wellbeing, but the wellbeing afforded by creative work or cultural pursuits, to offer some examples from Morris, let alone having one's basic needs met, have little to do with political engagement or recognition, and a life well lived may forgo any such democratic claims or interests. One might simply agree with Oscar Wilde that the problem of socialism (or deliberative democracy, for that matter) is that it takes too many evenings. Democratic conceptions of equality suffer from a dogmatism about human flourishing.[70]

The flourishing conception has classical philosophical antecedents. For Aristotle, happiness or eudaimonia refers to the idea of fulfilling our capacities: activity, using our reason, in the pursuit of excellence. The ancient Greek conception of 'the good life' is clearly a long way from the hedonist conception promoted by beer commercials and popular culture, but as noted in Chapter 1, Aristotle was convinced that living well involved contentment and bodily pleasures.[71] Marx's view that individuals actualise themselves through labour is similar in its emphasis on the development of human potential that produces feelings of wellbeing.[72]

It follows that wellbeing involves more than the satisfaction of biological needs. People need food, shelter, and health, but they also need education, friendship and love, participation in public life, play and sport, experiences of nature, culture, and opportunities for intellectual reflection in order to enjoy wellbeing.[73] Indeed, it may be that once a threshold of physical wellbeing is met, improvements in wellbeing derived from such pursuits are more important.[74] Nussbaum's views seem rather Janus-faced here: she supplies an ambitious list of capabilities that seem inherently tied to perfectionist views of human fulfilment, yet as we have seen, is adamant that her approach has no truck with conceptions of the good.

Egalitarians sometimes suggest we should aim to make people equal in all the constituents of human happiness, and where this is not possible, compensation should be provided. Shoeless Joe is poor, but has love and friendship. Conrad is rich, but has no friends. A life without friends is unequal to that of most human beings in a way that has a particularly negative impact on human wellbeing. Public provision of opportunities for social interaction can be seen therefore as an equalising policy that might take precedence over the provision of additional wealth. Scholars in the new discipline of 'Happiness Studies' stress the connection between subjective wellbeing and what might be dubbed 'worthy' pursuits such as walking rather than driving, or seeing friends rather than shopping.[75] Smith warns against being 'seduced by oversimplified conceptions of happiness as a matter of "feeling good," ' since there is 'a range of goods that we value and relish' that enable us to live life in 'all its fullness' and that involve struggle or exertion, not pleasure per se. Interestingly, however, much of the recent literature provides empirical evidence to suggest that contentment has less to do with hedonism and more to do with the Aristotlean conception of striving towards fulfilment than one might have thought.[76]

The nineteenth-century French utopian socialist, Fourier, considered inequality in love and sex an injustice and proposed that in utopia, the unattractive and uncharming would be romanced and befriended by those more fortunately endowed, an idea adapted by the Bolshevik Kollontai.[77] This is an extreme version of what Roemer, paraphrasing Marx's idea of 'communist man,' calls the 'socialist person' assumption, where conditions of equality nurture more comradely individuals who willingly contribute to the community.[78] Fourier's ideas have been reprised in Van Parijs's idea of compensation to losers in love who fail to find marriage partners.[79] This may seem ludicrous, as if individuals' lives are wholly the responsibility of society, to be manipulated and massaged. Yet it seems indisputable that disadvantage is not just a matter of shortfalls in income. One source of wellbeing is, besides access to economic capital, the opportunity for social capital, that is, networks of cooperation, voluntary associations and community activities that reward participants with relations of reciprocity and greater human fulfilment. For example, as we become more aware of the impediments to flourishing posed by lack of support for those with disabilities, it is particularly clear that focussing on economic inequality alone is an inadequate response. The alienation that can be experienced by people on the autism spectrum, for instance, suggests that what is required is adjusting the 'neurotypical' social conditions that assume a certain model of 'normal' human interaction, in order to make it possible for everyone to flourish. The flourishing model is able to avoid the pitfalls of both the satisfaction and resources approaches by focussing on how people live.

Nonetheless, we can live under ideal conditions for flourishing and still fail to flourish. Lack of human relationships might be the inevitable result of certain kinds of character or inclinations. Some of us are like Eeyore in *Winnie-the-Pooh*, determined to take a grim look on life. Others are like the lazy aristocrat Oblomov in Russian literature: slothful persons who fail to make the most of our potential.[80] Character may be the result of remediable environmental factors – family background, schooling, class position or deprivation – but no society, however successful its policies, can wholly eliminate glumness or sloth. A flourishing approach must therefore accept some inevitable shortfalls in flourishing.

## Thresholds of Flourishing

Flourishing itself is, as Christiano puts it, 'an indeterminate principle,'[81] and cannot be strictly equalised. Nonetheless, we can attend to levels of flourishing to determine whether shortfalls are the result of conditions that can be improved by public policy. We need a demanding set of expectations as well as an imaginative preparedness to see the environmental roots of wellbeing deficits. Public policy can address a culture of anomie or alienation that breeds loneliness by providing opportunities for social interaction and community, or support to families to help raise children who are loved and lovable. These ideas look like radical departures from neutralist orthodoxy, but they are in fact practiced in many liberal democracies where it is assumed that the state should enable citizens to live well. Policies we take for granted include: state funding for museums, theatres, orchestras and parks; social programmes to improve diets and levels of physical activity in schools, but also increasingly in workplaces; local government initiatives providing support for new parents, the elderly or the chronically ill; funding for sports and heritage. Cities, in particular, are impossible to imagine without a myriad of measures, be they as mundane as zoning, that have as their criterion human wellbeing.

Strict equality is ruled out by my position because flourishing by its very nature cannot be precisely calibrated, let alone equalised. More needs to be said, however, about the idea of greater equality of flourishing. Critics of perfectionism will accuse my egalitarianism of an untenable tension between a commitment to equality and a commitment to flourishing: which takes precedence? What about the problem of talent, the challenge we encountered in the last chapter, where some individuals stand to reach very high levels of flourishing compared to those of others? And what of those whose capacities fall short of the norm? These questions seem to thwart the project of equalisation.

We can call this the Mozart problem: giving extra music lessons to Mozart compared to his unmusical peers would divert resources away from the untalented to the talented, on the supposition that it would produce greater excellence and perhaps greater flourishing. Our intuitions in such situations might indeed favour the provision of special resources to the talented, but then equality of flourishing seems at risk. It is tempting to dispel the tension by drawing an analogy with need, where unequal needs necessitate unequal distribution. Musical people need extra resources to develop their musicality, just as the chronically ill need more medical resources than the healthy, along the lines of Marx's argument in the 'Critique of the Gotha Program.' For Marx, unequal provision is the way to realise equality, given human diversity.[82] But the Mozart case is not strictly analogous to that of the chronically ill, since at issue is not extra resources that restore some to 'normal' levels, but rather that enable some significantly to exceed the norm. Those of average talent may complain that perfectionist policies simply compound an existing inequality. Giving more resources to the talented Mozart not only increases his flourishing relative to others because he gets better; it is also the case that Mozart exercising his talents raises the standards by which we measure flourishing, so that his bested rival, Antonio Salieri, for example, no longer sees himself, or is seen by others, as flourishing. The talented are turned into mediocrities by the flourishing of the more talented.

One way of addressing these issues is to adopt a threshold approach. This is Nussbaum's strategy to deal with 'capability failure.' She proposes two thresholds, the first a threshold for the capability to function for a basic human life, which, once secured, should be supplemented by a second threshold for capability for a good human life.[83] If everyone reaches the second threshold, society can then allow for unequal levels of capability beyond the threshold. There are many attractions of thinking of flourishing in terms of thresholds. First of all, it prevents levelling down problems. The state secures equal threshold flourishing, attending to the needs of those who are less able than the norm, but it can also seek to maximise flourishing beyond the threshold, attending to the needs of those who are more able. Another attraction of the threshold strategy is it avoids taxing individuals with the onerous project of maximising equal flourishing, a problem we identified in the last chapter. A third attraction of thresholds is that they allow an accommodation of the Mozart problem that does not forsake equality altogether; maximisation of aggregate flourishing is subject to egalitarian conditions. On the flourishing model, our interest in equalising wellbeing derives from the principle that more wellbeing is better than less. And so the threshold strategy will allow for some to enjoy a higher level of wellbeing than others only if this does not bring about disadvantage. All must reach a threshold of flourishing, understood as a high level of flourishing to which all are entitled. We permit unequal allocation of resources and unequal flourishing so long as the threshold is met. Hurka mocks the idea of a threshold for its tension with excellence: 'The terms "perfectionism" and "excellence" hardly connote contentment with the moderately good.'[84] But egalitarian perfectionism is unabashed on this point; it focuses on flourishing as what we seek to make more equal, and thus gives up on maximising excellence if this sacrifices some for others. However, so long as society meets a high threshold of equal flourishing, the position is prepared to moderate equality in order to provide opportunities for excellence.

In the Mozart case, one person's unusually high level of flourishing means those who lack the talent of a Mozart can nonetheless derive enormous fulfilment from, if not performing his music, then listening to it. Moreover, for all Salieri's grievances, the high flourishing of Mozart nonetheless benefits other musicians by taking music to a new level, so that those who come after him are inspired and motivated to reach a new standard. The relevant threshold thus rises accordingly. One should see the development of talent in this light too. Of course, it must be stressed that equality of flourishing can also have beneficial secondary effects: all of us stand to flourish more in the equal society than in the society where we are witness to deprivation and misery. However, the spillover egalitarian effects of excellence and equality are subsidiary considerations. We seek equal flourishing to ensure that even those who are disadvantaged in talent and ability have an adequate level of flourishing, and we direct resources to the talented to enable them to fulfil their potential.

Where is the threshold? I have suggested that the threshold should be high; an egalitarian position that centres on flourishing as opposed to merely surviving will aim for more than meeting basic needs. Equality would be undermined if the threshold is set too low, contenting ourselves with low levels of human attainment. As Nussbaum puts it, we must go beyond 'mere human life to the question of good life, the level we would really like to see a human being attain.'[85] However, setting the threshold too high can make it difficult to achieve equality. A high threshold means great diversity below the threshold, and the task of bringing people up to the threshold might centre on those close to the threshold, where a small effort can bring enormous results. The result, though it maximises total flourishing, or brings about the most improvement in flourishing, may be a yawning and worryingly irremediable gap between those left at the bottom and those at the threshold. Below the threshold, we should seek to ensure that the worst off find their levels of flourishing improved first. Lowering the threshold would help society focus on the worst off, and ensure that improvements to the flourishing of the most disadvantaged. But too low a threshold will permit a great deal of inequality above its limits.

Rather than a two-threshold approach, a staggered threshold strategy would enable us to render people as equal as possible. That is, to reach our ambitious threshold, we must first focus on equal achievement of flourishing at a low threshold, then moving on to raise individuals to a higher threshold, and then higher, and so on. This allows us to take into account transitional considerations. That way we have an ambitious level of flourishing whilst retaining our focus on equality, avoiding wide disparities of flourishing. As the situation of the worst off is improved, so the threshold must be constantly nudged upwards to bring the disadvantaged to increasingly higher levels of flourishing and reducing the gap between them and their more advantaged fellow citizens.

A familiar objection to any egalitarian measure is the problem of severely disabled persons who require an enormous amount of resources in order to secure modest gains in flourishing, with the consequence that resources are so depleted that everyone else is unable to rise above the threshold. It is for this reason, among others, that I do not incorporate a straightforward prioritarian or difference principle approach that always targets the worst off. Like Nussbaum and Arneson, I concede a qualification to the threshold approach, in which its requirements can be relaxed if total human flourishing would otherwise be severely reduced.[86] We must recognize, of course, the desirable prospect of ever higher equal flourishing, given innovations in health, social policy, urban planning and egalitarian principles.

Nonetheless, our attitude to distribution above the threshold cannot be unaffected by our egalitarian convictions. Moreover, even below the threshold we will encounter Mozart problems, since bringing everyone to an adequate level of flourishing involves taking into account the special talents of some individuals, the development of which is necessary for adequate flourishing. A familiar example of 'topping up' a threshold for the few is the provision of enrichment programmes for 'gifted' children in state-funded schools who would otherwise have low levels of flourishing. We might think that so long as the public school system provides an adequate level of resources to mainstream schooling, it is fair to deploy extra resources for exceptionally bright children. But this position would depend very much on the facts of the case; an extraordinarily generous provision for the gifted may be unfair given its long-term effects, especially if we could instead provide special education for children with disabilities to significantly improve their levels of flourishing.

In sum, the task of equalising flourishing is best achieved by means of a staggered threshold approach, which seeks an ambitious level of equal flourishing by means of improving flourishing, as much as is possible, at a base level and then raising it in stages, to ensure that the flourishing of the worst off is constantly improved. The requirement that we attend to the worst off should be relaxed, however, if aggregate flourishing threatens to be seriously diminished. Though the threshold approach suggests a lack of interest in equality above the level of sufficiency, and a lack of interest in perfection below sufficiency, in fact both considerations continue to play a role throughout the distributive model. The aim is equality of flourishing, but also the maximisation of flourishing, within certain egalitarian constraints.

## Responsibility and Wellbeing

The problem of individual contribution is a serious challenge to the ideal of equality. Failures of contribution can take many forms; there are those who have a diminished or no capacity to contribute, and there are others who contribute less than they are able. Anti-egalitarians pejoratively dub the latter 'shirkers,' 'free-loaders,' or 'spongers' because they benefit from others' contributions without contributing their share. Perfectionist egalitarians may seem particularly vulnerable on this issue, perhaps generalising from their own enthusiasm for work (work which in Morris's case, at least, was both interesting and lucrative), to assume that the equal society would consist of industrious and fulfilled persons sustaining equality through their contributions. How much people contribute compared to what they receive has often been thought a mere 'detail of the countinghouse' to use Tawney's evocative expression.[87] Yet unconditional income means that self-reliance might atrophy and responsible citizens end up subsidising the costly ways of life of irresponsible citizens, thereby producing an inequality of contribution that is unfair.

Putting the question baldly, are the lazy entitled to the fruits of the industrious? Egalitarians, resisting the Victorian idea of the 'undeserving poor,' might counter with another, equally crude question: Should anyone starve? Marx's slogan, 'from each according to his ability, to each according to his needs,' makes a clear separation between contribution and distribution. (It is worth noting that under Stalin, Marx's heady utopianism was overturned with the ominous warning, 'those who do not work do not eat.') There is a conundrum here: it would be an unjust society that abandoned its unproductive members, and yet it would be an unjust society where some shirk a duty to contribute. Moreover, both societies cultivate impoverished relations of responsibility and reciprocity; neither admits that enabling the welfare of others is a duty of citizenship.

A well-known example of an argument for equality without duties of contribution is the 'welfare for surfers' credo of Van Parijs. Van Parijs calls for an unconditional social minimum that ensures support for individuals who refuse to work. If we respect individual choice, then we must not make social welfare contingent on making choices that are productive. Van Parijs argues that an unconditional basic income is simply a fair allocation of individuals' collective assets to which all have equal entitlement. Moreover, human diversity is such that it would be difficult to find a fair way of rewarding the degrees of 'disutility' different kinds of work impose on individuals.[88] Thus Van Parijs bites the bullet: lazy surfer though he may be, he is entitled to a social minimum, producing an egalitarian position unlikely to win support from the industrious or affluent. Van Parijs makes no demands of the lazy, but he is demanding of the hardworking:[89] under-contributors can only be looked after if there are willing over-contributors. The upshot may be political disaster; it may also be unfair. Moreover, an unconditional largesse that asks nothing of citizens also shows little respect for individuals' capacity for self-discipline and responsibility in directing their lives. It is thus understandable that the Right derides the 'Nanny State,' where the nourishment of the nursery is always on offer, and Nanny is barred from scolding squanderers of social welfare.

One solution is to modify a theory of distribution in order to take into account considerations of luck and responsibility. Rawls sought to mitigate the position of the worst off, and though this task presupposes fair equality of opportunity, it does not set any conditions for the amelioration of disadvantage. Dworkin, in contrast, argues that a hierarchy of reward is justified only if it is the outcome of freely chosen decisions.[90] The influence of this argument is such that the vast majority of contemporary egalitarians, however diverse, have been dubbed 'luck egalitarians' for favouring a metric that distinguishes between 'option luck' – features of one's lot that are shaped by choice – and 'brute luck' – features of one's lot that are immune to choice.[91] Even welfarist egalitarians such as Cohen, who take exception to Dworkin's resources metric and are sympathetic to the idea of compensation for deficits in satisfaction due to expensive tastes, agree with Dworkin that redistribution should zero in on 'accidental inequality.'[92]

This approach assumes that we can distinguish between outcomes that are chosen and those that are not. Yet prudent decision-making skills might be among the results of Rawls's 'natural lottery,' for which one cannot take credit or blame.[93] The brute luck/option luck distinction is hard to draw if economic condition affects choice-making capacity; bad choices may result from economic disadvantage, not the other way around. Poorly paid employment can engender a desire for gratification that is unavailable at work and fatalism about the prospects of prudent investment in the long-term. Why not, then, blow one's pay on a Saturday night to compensate for the drudgery of the week even if it leaves nothing for a rainy day?[94] The familiar 'culture of poverty,' where poor people are acculturated into a set of fatalistic attitudes and practices, discourages people from taking steps to improve their lot.[95] It seems harsh to condemn the imprudent to impoverishment, particularly if initial bad decisions produce a class-divided society with lasting intergenerational effects. Furthermore, in today's economy, where there is a dearth of secure and rewarding work, and many are inevitably condemned to the ranks of the 'precariat,' society's responsibility for the badly off, the underemployed and unfulfilled, seems particularly salient.[96]

Some luck egalitarians might agree that the choices made by poor people are the result of disadvantage, and thus the consequences that ensue are best thought of as bad brute luck. This would be a political variation of Scheffler's metaphysical claim that luck egalitarians are working with an implausible conception of free will and the capacity of the person to make choices without influence.[97] Indeed, if we reflect on the circumstances of one's life, it is hard to draw a hard-and-fast line between that which is the result of conscious choice, and that which is beyond one's control.[98] Cohen coined the idea of 'access to advantage' to enable a more fine-grained conception of genuine choice, without the distortions of disadvantage. The problem of 'adaptive preferences,' in which one endorses a bad choice where it seems no other is available, is relevant here.[99] However, if one presses these strategies, so that apparent choices are largely in fact instances of brute luck, the option luck/brute luck divide starts to seem of mere polemical value in warding off right-wing challenges to the principle of redistribution. We put the cart before the horse if we attribute 'bad luck' to those outcomes we think of as unjust rather than deploying luck as a criterion for justice. If the egalitarian insists that disadvantage is in fact almost always the consequence of disadvantaged circumstances, then the idea of luck appears to be beside the point.

Moreover, assuming it were possible, the task of discerning precisely which disadvantages merit amelioration and which do not would involve intrusive surveillance. This is not just an implementation problem, but one of principle about what social relations are inherent in the egalitarian ideal. Critics argue that the assumptions behind these measures of 'shameful revelation' seem to be derived from a libertarian suspicion of sharing with others, especially distasteful in a society whose egalitarian ambitions are bound up with principles of mutual respect and social solidarity.[100] Policing the home life of welfare recipients, designating expenditures through a coupon system, insisting that people submit to training or report for work – such measures disrespect the privacy and self-determination of individuals. Arneson therefore says we should 'downplay' desert and focus instead on the moral requirement of giving aid.[101]

Desert could be marshalled, not to determine entitlement to human flourishing, but to shed light on what counts as flourishing. Mill contended that there are cases where 'help perpetuates the state of things which renders help necessary,'[102] although recent studies suggest that guaranteed income may have no such effect.[103] The egalitarian flourishing approach, however, need not take a stand on this issue since, whatever the case, desert is a poor criterion for distribution, at least below our threshold, because it is simply unjust to withhold aid to the needy. However, feeling deserving of resources – which comes from being productive – is a significant constituent of wellbeing. Not being hungry, of course, is a more important source of wellbeing than feeling deserving of food. Yet getting and feeling that one has earned what one is getting is better than just getting. Moreover, as Sher argues contra luck egalitarianism, respect for autonomy often involves allowing people to shoulder the costs of life's contingencies that are difficult to separate into the categories of the chosen and unchosen.[104] Rendering flourishing more equal is not necessarily a matter of eliminating the setbacks of life, whatever their source. Thus there are wellbeing grounds for a community to refuse to pick up the tab for bad choices. Individuals will not learn how to make good choices, they will be reluctant to choose goods that require deferral of gratification, and they will not learn the virtues of reciprocity and responsibility. Human flourishing therefore is best achieved, not by foisting good choices on people, or manipulating them to make good choices, but by helping them to become 'good choosers.'[105] The wellbeing conception indicates the importance of providing conditions that enhance choice-making capacity.

Quong contends that perfectionists demand that citizens provide others 'with the aid or resources they need in order to achieve a flourishing life' which means that some are not required to 'take responsibility for their own ends and adjust their expectations in light of the resources they are entitled to.'[106] However, this supposes that a flourishing account of equality treats the parties to distributive justice like patrons in a restaurant, who merely order up the dishes they fancy. This is ruled out by the threshold mechanism I presented above. It is also ruled out by the nature of flourishing itself, which is an objective measure, and in which active contribution is an important constituent. Egalitarian flourishing therefore cannot help but be, as Quong puts it, 'sensitive to considerations of individual responsibility.'[107]

On this view, we should consider the matter of individuals' contribution, not in order to punish the under-contributors, but to help them enjoy more fulfilling lives. Working gives structure to one's life, exposes one to different experiences and people, provides scope for cooperation and interaction with others in the public domain, enables one to develop skills and earn respect for them, to become self-directed, self-controlled and ethical.[108] Being responsible is thus a crucial basis for self-respect and furthers human wellbeing. Instead of a sink-or-swim approach to equality that punishes the less productive, we should see non-contribution as itself a form of disadvantage, a shortfall in flourishing.

Moreover, contributors should not resent the under-contributors, but rather appreciate the complex nature of wellbeing. The community that radical egalitarianism presupposes requires that all see themselves as full participants with duties of mutual aid, something that Cohen, for all his luck egalitarian inclinations, also underscored in his discussion of socialism.[109]

Luck egalitarians tend to be neutralists who are ill placed to consider how responsibility is a constituent of living well. Egalitarian perfectionism enables a more constructive approach that, discerning a lack of flourishing, seeks not humiliation, but the bolstering of the means of self-respect. Furthermore, the idea of human flourishing better realises what Dworkin calls the 'challenge model,' where living well is akin to an inherently valuable skilful performance bound up with being self-determining, developing one's capacities and talents and finding self-mastery:[110] living the Morris life, if you will. Contra Dworkin, however, responsibility is compatible with social institutions that enable citizens to live well. Indeed, why not emphasise the responsibility of the more productive to assist the vulnerable members of their community; as Arneson puts it, 'the special responsibility of the individual to fashion her own good life is fully compatible with the responsibility of other people to boost her prospects of attaining the good.'[111]

Dworkin makes the insightful point that injustice insults and diminishes the self-respect of citizens, the rich as well as the poor. If we are seeking equality in living the good life, and if the good life is in some sense a life of self-mastery, then queuing for income does not render the beneficiary the equal of others. This is worth bearing in mind when considering the problem of 'welfare bums,' who as the phrase suggests, live lives that are in some sense contemptible.[112] Yet productivity is not necessarily constitutive of living well; some might venture that the pleasure-seeking grasshopper has a better appreciation of the good life than the toiling ant.[113] The flourishing model takes a broad view of what constitutes a contribution to society. Once we steer away from the allocation of goods and focus instead on the constituents of flourishing, we can give up productivist obsessions to embrace a wide-ranging view of the worthwhile. Some flourishing persons are not economically productive, but they develop talents or interests that make for a fulfilling life; the artist is an obvious example, but so is the person with intellectual disabilities who would like to participate in society in a meaningful way.[114] On this view unlike, say, the hermit or couch potato, the much-mocked surfer, whose vocation requires application and skill, is a potential candidate for living well, although the flourishing approach also suggests the surfer is missing something if he or she fails to contribute to society altogether.[115]

Finally, we should stress the phenomenon of the undeserving rich – people whose wealth is the result of inheritance, dividends, mere ownership of assets. In our haste to come to terms with the problem of the alleviation of poverty without any effort on the part of the poor, we can easily overlook how many of the wealthy are undeserving of their wealth and moreover, fail to contribute to society. As a Canadian socialist leader once put it, there are 'corporate welfare bums.'[116] Moreover, easy access to income can mean lives that are pre-occupied with the status conferred by luxury goods, lives that are aimless, frivolous, devoid of projects, falling far short of genuine human flourishing. Hurka notes, 'if it is corrupting to receive a welfare cheque ... should it not also be corrupting to receive an inheritance or dividend cheque?'[117] The problem of responsibility, wealth, and flourishing is not uniquely applicable to the disadvantaged.

## Conclusion

The welfare state has marked both the triumph of the egalitarian vision of Morris and its disappointment. On the one hand, access to the means of subsistence now stands as a fundamental right in Western liberal societies, and it is difficult to imagine the commitment to redistribution of wealth, however unevenly assured, ever disappearing. On the other hand, this commitment is, in even its most ambitious forms, limited: evident in only some, privileged parts of the world; and under considerable pressure to limit its scope to the provision of opportunities, severed from ideas about improving how people live. I have argued that equality should focus on human flourishing, and that this focus will best address the problem of individual responsibility that besets contemporary egalitarianism. It remains to consider whether a flourishing account can respect the freedom of individuals that is presupposed by the idea of holding them responsible for their choices. The question of perfectionism and paternalism is the subject of the next chapter.

## Notes

1 I am following D. Parfit's position that egalitarianism must be premised on a person-affecting claim. See 'Equality or Priority?,' 103–6.
2 But see the policy-oriented study, J. Baker, K. Lynch, S. Cantillon and J. Walsh, *Equality: From Theory to Action*, which focuses on resources, but also human interests such as love or learning.
3 R. Arneson, 'Perfectionism and Politics,' 39. S. Lecce, in 'Should Egalitarians be Perfectionists?,' 133–4, accuses egalitarian perfectionism of giving priority to perfection over equality, but I hope to show that this charge is answered with an account that starts with the principle of equality and then advances a flourishing metric.
4 V. Haksar makes an interesting case for a link between equality and perfectionism that centres on the perfectionist potential of Rawls in *Equality, Liberty and Perfectionism*; my account takes a different tack.
5 G.F. Gaus, 'Liberal Neutrality: A Compelling and Radical Principle,' 162.
6 G. Sher, *Equality for Inegalitarians*.
7 'The herd is a means, no more!,' F. Nietzsche, *The Will to Power*, 766.
8 Galston, *Liberal Purposes*, 192.
9 Hurka, *Perfectionism*, 189.
10 Something of which bourgeois enthusiasts of Morris's contribution to drawing room decor are usually unaware, or tend to ignore. Given the phenomenon of New Labour, it might be said that the British Left in recent times often looks like it is more inspired by Morris wallpapers than Morrisian socialism!

11 Morris, 'How We Live and How We Might Live,' 21; Morris, 'The Aims of Art,' 84.

12 Of course, though the production of art in the Middle Ages was cooperative, consumption was restricted to an elite.

13 Morris, 'The Socialist Ideal,' 256.

14 See National Trust, UK, *Playing Our Part: National Trust Annual Report*.

15 Morris, 'Art and Socialism,' 193, Morris, 'How We Live and How We Might Live,' 14.

16 P. Stansky, *William Morris*, 17.

17 Morris, 'How We Live and How We Might Live,' 22.

18 Morris, 'How I Became a Socialist,' 281. The inhabitants of Nowhere also lament that 'the once-poor had such a feeble conception of the real pleasure of life.' W. Morris, *News from Nowhere*, 121.

19 Morris, 'How I Became A Socialist,' 281 and 'How We Live and How We Might Live,' 10. See also Morris's pitying portrait of the privileged Judge Nupkins in *The Tables Turned, or Nupkins Awakened*.

20 Morris, 'Dawn of a New Epoch,' 123.

21 Marx, 'Economic and Philosophic Manuscripts of 1844,' 100.

22 Ibid., 87.

23 Ibid., 105.

24 Ibid., 74. J.B. Glasier draws a divide between Marx and Morris in *William Morris and the Early Days of the Socialist Movement*, 142–50. But see E.P. Thompson, *William Morris: Romantic to Revolutionary*, 747–50.

25 Marx, 'Economic and Philosophic Manuscripts,' 76.

26 Marx, *Capital*, 344–5.

27 D. Leopold, *The Young Karl Marx*, 225.

28 Marx, 'Economic and Philosophic Manuscripts,' 76.

29 Marx, 'Critique of the Gotha Programme,' 531.

30 Leopold, *The Young Karl Marx*, 225, 278.

31 Which Morris read and re-read to such an extent that in the course of less than two years it was so worn that it had to be rebound. See A.L. Morton, 'Morris, Marx and Engels,' 7, 1, 45.

32 Ibid., 46.

33 Morris scholars debate the extent of Morris's medievalism; many see his aesthetic ideas as the inspiration for modernist architecture and design that focuses on comfort and simplicity.

34 J.S. Mill, 'On Liberty,' 82. Appiah, *The Ethics of Identity*, 27.

35 L.T. Hobhouse, *Liberalism*, 67.

36 Tawney, *Equality*, 117.

37 Ibid., 114.

38 H. Laski, *Democracy in Crisis*, 265.

39 See B. Webb and B. Hutchins, 'Socialism and the National Minimum,' and B. Jackson, *Equality and the British Left: A Study in Progressive Political Thought: 1900–64*.

40 W. Beveridge, *The Pillars of Security*, 16.

41 In his critique of perfectionism Quong notes in passing that neutralist liberalism is relatively new; see *Liberalism without Perfection*, 7. S. den Otter illuminates the perfectionist cast of the British liberal tradition in *British Idealism and Social Explanation*, 168–75.

42 Rawls, *A Theory of Justice*, 424–33.

43 Rawls, *Political Liberalism*, 214–15.

44 See Quong, *Liberalism without Perfection*, 7. But as Arneson retorts, 'In the same spirit of neutrality, should government refrain from pursuing policies justifiable only by appeal to controversial conceptions of the right?,' 'Liberal Neutrality on the Good: An Autopsy,' 195. For some trenchant critiques of the controversy argument, see J. Chan, 'Legitimacy, Unanimity and Perfectionism,' 21; S. Caney,

'Anti-perfectionism and Rawlsian Liberalism,' 258; S. Clarke, 'Contractualism, Liberal Neutrality, and Epistemology,' 635.

45 Rawls, *A Theory of Justice*, 94.
46 Dworkin, 'Liberalism,' 132; S. Lecce 'Contractualism and Liberal Neutrality: A Defence,' 538.
47 Dworkin, *Sovereign Virtue*, ch. 1 and 2.
48 Sen, *Development as Freedom*, 70–1, 88–9.
49 Sen, *Inequality Re-examined*, 39.
50 T. Pogge, 'Can the Capability Approach be Justified?,' 194.
51 Dworkin, *Sovereign Virtue*, 31.
52 G.A. Cohen, 'On the Currency of Egalitarian Justice,' 923.
53 Dworkin, *Sovereign Virtue*, 52.
54 Sen, *Inequality Re-examined*, 42, 54–5.
55 Sen, *Development as Freedom*, 62–3. T. Scanlon concurs that welfare's subjectivism should be qualified by the discrimination between important and unimportant interests. See 'Value, Desire and the Quality of Life.'
56 C. Lowry makes an excellent case for thinking that 'the question of capability and neutrality is a live one' in Sen's work in 'Beyond Equality of What: Sen and Neutrality,' 229. The eschewal of neutrality would make perspicuous Sen's 'rationale for preferring the capability approach over resourcism' which Pogge complains is 'obscure.' See Pogge, 'Can the Capability Approach Be Justified?,' 204.
57 M. Nussbaum, *Creating Capabilities: The Human Development Approach*, 92.
58 M. Nussbaum, *Women and Human Development*, 87. See also A. Sen, *The Idea of Justice*, 235–8.
59 Nussbaum, 'Perfectionist Liberalism and Political Liberalism,' 22.
60 Sen, *Inequality Re-examined*, 51–3. Lowry contends that Sen holds, not that Rawls has no interest in the impact of primary goods on persons, but that Rawls too easily assumes that mere possession of primary goods is a sufficient indicator of equality. See 'Beyond Equality of What,' 229–30.
61 In a similar vein, T. Hurka argues that the capability approach should include choosing as a functioning in its own right. 'Capability, Functioning and Perfectionism,' 155–6.
62 Marx and Engels, 'German Ideology,' 160.
63 Nussbaum, *Women and Human Development*, 93.
64 Arneson, 'Perfectionism and Politics,' 62–3.
65 Nussbaum, *Women and Human Development*, 91.
66 G.A. Cohen, 'Equality of What? On Welfare, Goods and Opportunities.'
67 G. Sher, *Beyond Neutrality: Perfectionism and Politics*, 229.
68 Hurka, *Perfectionism*, 26.
69 N. Fraser, 'Social Justice in the Age of Identity Politics: Redistribution, Recognition and Participation,' 30–1, 48–55; E. Anderson, 'What Is the Point of Equality?' 313.
70 Wolff, 'Fairness, Respect and the Egalitarian Ethos Revisited,' 349; C. Schemmel, 'Why Relational Egalitarians Should Care About Distributions,' 3.
71 Aristotle, *Nichomachean Ethics*, 1153b16–1154a6.
72 Thus Marx speaks of how the elimination of private property allows the 'emancipation of all human senses,' 'Economic and Philosophic Manuscripts of 1844,' 87–8.
73 A point stressed by Nussbaum in *Women and Human Development*, 75; and *Creating Capabilities: The Human Development Approach*, 33–4; see also J. Wolff and A. De-Shalit, *Disadvantage*, 38–40.
74 J. Griffin, *Wellbeing*, 52–3.
75 See D. Gilbert, *Stumbling on Happiness*, D. Nettle, *Happiness: The Science Behind Your Smile*, R. Layard, *Happiness: Lessons from a New Science*, R. Frank, *Luxury Fever: Money and Happiness in an Era of Excess*.

76 R. Smith, 'The Long Slide to Happiness,' 202.
77 C. Fourier, *Harmonian Man*, ch. 1, 4, and 5, A. Kollontai, *Love of Worker Bees*.
78 J. Roemer, *A Future for Socialism*, 110–11.
79 R. Arneson, 'Equality and Equal Opportunity for Welfare,' 231; and P. Van Parijs, *Real Freedom for All*, 125–30.
80 I. Goncharov, *Oblomov*.
81 T. Christiano, *The Constitution of Equality*, 33.
82 'One worker is married, another not; one has more children than another, and so on and so forth,' Marx, 'Critique of the Gotha Program,' 530–1.
83 Nussbaum, 'Human Capabilities, Female Human Beings,' 81.
84 Hurka, 'Capability, Functioning and Perfectionism,' 159.
85 Nussbaum, 'Human Capabilities, Female Human Beings,' 82.
86 Nussbaum, *Sex and Social Justice*, 43; Arneson, 'Perfectionism and Politics,' 56.
87 Cited in W. Kymlicka, 'Left-Liberalism Revisited,' 13.
88 Van Parijs, *Real Freedom for All*, 97, 162.
89 Just as Fourier relied on the over-contributions of the beautiful.
90 R. Dworkin, *Sovereign Virtue*, 73–8. This contrasts with traditional meritocratic views; see D. Miller, *Principles of Social Justice*, ch. 9.
91 See Anderson, 'What Is the Point of Equality?,' R. Dworkin, 'Equality, Luck and Hierarchy,' S. Scheffler, 'What Is Egalitarianism?,' Arneson, 'Equality and Equality of Opportunity for Welfare,' G.A. Cohen, 'On the Currency of Egalitarian Justice,' J. Roemer, *Theories of Distributive Justice*.
92 Cohen, 'On the Currency of Egalitarian Justice,' 907–10; see also Cohen, *Rescuing Justice and Equality*, 7–8.
93 R. Arneson, 'Egalitarianism and the Undeserving Poor,' 332.
94 As Stompin' Tom Connors put it, 'The girls are out to bingo and the boys are getting stinko, we think no more of Inco on a Sudbury Saturday Night' (Inco was a Canadian mining company in operation for much of the twentieth century).
95 Hurka, *Perfectionism*, 170. See M. Harrington, *The New American Poverty*.
96 G. Standing, *The Precariat: The New Dangerous Class*, 3–25.
97 See S. Scheffler, 'What Is Egalitarianism?,' 17–19; and 'Choice, Circumstance, and the Value of Equality,' 10–14.
98 G. Sher notes examples of 'unhappy outcomes that are the results of people's choices, yet are not themselves chosen,' in *Equality for Inegalitarians*, 30.
99 Cohen, 'On the Currency of Egalitarian Justice,' 917; *Self-Ownership, Freedom and Equality*, 253–5.
100 Wolff, 'Fairness, Respect, and the Egalitarian Ethos.'
101 Arneson, 'Egalitarianism and the Undeserving Poor,' 349–50.
102 Mill, 'Principles of Political Economy,' quoted in ibid., 335.
103 See R.C. Fording and W.D. Berry, 'The Historical Impact of Welfare Programs on Poverty: Evidence from the American States.'
104 Sher, *Equality for Inegalitarians*, 125.
105 Note J. Waldron's argument against paternalism: 'I wish … that I could be made a better chooser rather than having someone on high take advantage (even for my own benefit) of my current thoughtlessness and my shabby intuitions,' 'It's All for Your Own Good.'
106 Quong, *Liberalism without Perfection*, 121, 125.
107 Ibid., 125.
108 As Arneson says, 'for most poor people, having a job is good for you whether you think so or not,' 'Egalitarianism and the Undeserving Poor,' 348.
109 G.A. Cohen, *Why Not Socialism?*. See C. Sypnowich, 'G.A. Cohen's Socialism: Scientific but also Utopian,' 28; N. Vrousalis, 'Jazz Bands, Camping Trips and Decommodification: G.A. Cohen on Community,' 142–3.
110 Dworkin, *Sovereign Virtue*, 253–76.

111 Arneson, 'Liberal Neutrality on the Good,' 200; C. Armstrong, *Rethinking Equality: The Challenge of Equal Citizenship*, ch. 4.
112 Dworkin, *Sovereign Virtue*, 280.
113 See B. Suits, *The Grasshopper: Games, Life, and Utopia*.
114 J. Elster goes so far as to defend those who 'prefer the passive pleasures of contemplation', *Making Sense of Marx*, 522.
115 A. Glyn argues that a 'Participation Income' that covers everybody involved in 'a wide range of activities not limited to paid work that contribute to society,' could turn out to exclude so few people that a universal Basic Income would be an 'administrative matter.' See his *Capitalism Unleashed*, 182.
116 The phrase was coined by David Lewis, former leader of the New Democratic Party of Canada. See his *Louder Voices: Corporate Welfare Bums*; also Wolff, 'Fairness, Respect, and the Egalitarian Ethos Revisited,' 340.
117 Hurka, *Perfectionism*, 185.

# 8   Autonomy and Living Well

Can a theory of equality focussed on human flourishing respect individuals' freedom to choose? The view that we should hold people responsible for their choices, discussed in the previous chapter, follows from the idea that we should respect people's interest in making choices. Given that people can make choices detrimental to their flourishing, a flourishing approach to equality faces a conundrum: on the one hand, the focus on flourishing suggests people need direction on how to live; on the other, since choice is a constituent of flourishing, flourishing seems undermined by such direction.

In this chapter I examine the controversy about autonomy and flourishing to show how it is possible both to promote the good and leave individuals free to choose it. I argue that autonomy is integral to wellbeing, but a poor cultural environment can undermine autonomy and society therefore should seek to provide favourable conditions for choice. The result is a concept of egalitarian flourishing that not only is consistent with autonomy but also conducive to it; more conducive, indeed, than rival, neutralist liberal positions.

## Paternalism and Perfection

The complaint that perfectionism is paternalistic is a familiar one. First comes the charge that perfectionism is committed to a monological conception of human flourishing that precludes diversity. This is followed by the charge that perfectionism is coercive. The perfectionist might appear to have an easy answer to the first charge in Marx's ideal of communist man, who as we noted in Chapter 1, will 'hunt in the morning, fish in the afternoon, rear cattle in the evening,' and 'criticise after dinner.'[1] However, Marx's ideal does not describe the diversity of pluralism, so much as a variegated yet single way of life – the Morris way of life, if you will, given Morris's example of a life devoted to a variety of creative activities.[2] Nonetheless, if one enjoins more than one kind of activity, one must countenance differences in people's choices about how to arrange their pursuits. Morris recognised, for example, the extent to which people live in common with others 'may differ pretty much according to our tendencies towards social life,'[3] and argued that inevitable 'varieties in temperament'[4] and differences in 'capacities and desires'[5] would cause individuals to pursue a variety of ends, a fortunate fact in light of a finite store of resources.

Indeed, the objection that perfectionism commits us to promoting a single conception of the good is hard to take seriously. Debates about perfectionism have been ill served by the assumption that the alternative to neutrality is a preoccupation with, as Quong puts it, 'some particular ideal' of what constitutes a good life.[6] Wellbeing takes diverse, sometimes incommensurable forms. Although value-nihilism is ruled out by perfectionism, value-pluralism is not.[7] Some perfectionists may be bigots and xenophobes, but there is considerable ideological space between neutrality about the good and what Dworkin castigates as an 'ethical intolerance' of all conceptions of the good but one's own.[8] Raz, for example, argues that pluralism and tolerance are necessary because complete moral perfection is unattainable: whichever form of life one pursues, there will be 'virtues which elude one because they are available only to people pursuing alternative and incompatible forms of life.'[9] Just as Marx noted that treating diverse human beings as equals requires an unequal distribution that apportions according to different human needs, so must we recognise that talents and interests are diverse, and thus human flourishing is multifarious in character. Wellbeing figures as what we might call a 'diverse universal,' a common goal that can be realised in many different ways.

These considerations about pluralism do not, however, settle the second aspect of the paternalism critique – that perfectionism involves coercion. Even if egalitarian perfectionists conceive of the good pluralistically, they might still advocate restrictive measures to ensure that we choose from among its forms. As Sher notes, choice can be restricted in various ways: explicit coercion in the form of punishment or the threat thereof – a clear case of unfreedom; the use of non-rational methods of persuasion such as subsidies and taxes; and finally, efforts to institutionalise and enable worthwhile pursuits.[10]

Neutralist liberals sometimes suggest that perfectionism is wedded to the first form of choice restriction, whereby people are forced to subscribe to certain ways of life.[11] Yet coercion is at odds with both flourishing and equality. Coercion was in fact one of the grounds for Morris's critique of capitalism: 'while you live,' he lamented, 'you will see all round you people engaged in making others live lives which are not their own.'[12] Socialists should help people discover their wants, encourage them to want more, challenge them to want differently, and to envisage a society of the future in which people, freed at last of necessity, might choose among different visions of the good.[13] Indeed, one cannot live the good under coercion. As Hurka says of governments: 'they can supply the necessary conditions of their citizens' perfection, or conditions that make this perfection more likely, but the sufficient conditions are beyond their power.'[14]

Coercive measures adopted for non-perfectionist reasons can, of course, turn out to have perfectionist effects. For example, the sanctions of the criminal law can induce people to make better choices about how to live. Sher concludes from such examples that perfectionists can countenance coercion in certain circumstances.[15] Yet although some sanctions might have perfectionist implications, the basis for such coercion is a standard liberal one about preventing harm to others. Thus even if such prohibitions have the result that people do not participate in unworthy activities, the presence of such perfectionist consequences does not demonstrate that liberal public policy adduces legitimate perfectionist grounds for coercion.

What of restricting choice through the use of non-rational methods of persuasion? A flourishing approach to equality seems at odds with this approach too. We only know what the good is in light of reasons. Choosing the putatively good without understanding why is a poor basis for good choices. Moreover, even the more benign examples of the restriction of choice – the use of incentives, and attempts to institutionalise and enable worthwhile ways of living – are problematic where they undermine our capacity to make reasoned choices.

Perhaps, however, we give choice too much weight. Choice represents the individual's ability to be self-determining, to be autonomous. Autonomy is valuable, certainly, but is it the only value? Other things may be more important; sometimes, it may be argued, actually living the good is more important than having freely chosen the bad. Conly argues that autonomy has been 'overvalued' and that the state should interfere with autonomy in order to prevent harm. We use our autonomy with the aim of making good choices, and that aim may be better realised by state intervention that limits autonomy.[16] Sher also ventures: 'Even if promoting other values invariably undermines autonomy, why must governments always resolve the dilemma in autonomy's favour?'[17] Indeed, the idea that other things are valuable besides autonomy follows from our understanding of autonomy itself, which after all is exercised in order to achieve certain valuable ends.

The example usually invoked here is that of compelling children to learn music. Even if Mozart was forced into playing the piano as a child, his valuable contribution to music far outweighs an early forfeit in autonomy. However, the compulsion of children is a standard exception to liberal principles because children are not yet capable of making decisions in full knowledge of their consequences. We must consider whether the autonomy of mature persons can be violated to ensure they make valuable choices. It seems that adults can be induced to choose a valuable pursuit, thus being non-autonomous in the initial choice, but come to appreciate the pursuit's value and thereafter choose it autonomously. This is particularly so if the infringements of freedom are minor and the gain in value significant. Some perfectionists insist that what matters is autonomous choice of not all ends, but the 'encompassing ends' that shape a life.[18]

Anti-perfectionists complain that efforts to influence choice 'artificially distort' choosers' opportunity costs,[19] treating them 'as if they lack the ability to make effective choices about their own lives.'[20] For these critics, even the most gentle of interventions in individuals' choices constitutes an illegitimate thwarting of their personhood. However, living autonomously is an elusive idea: it involves freedom from the interference of others, but it also refers to the exercise of a type of freedom, a moral freedom of self-determination. We do not live autonomously if we live lives that are purposeless, empty, plagued by ignorance and lethargy, even if no one stands in our way to do otherwise. Autonomy is more than a mere means to personal fulfilment; the ideal of self-creation implicit in autonomy suggests that an autonomous life is an end in itself. As Taylor puts it, freedom means not just doing what you want, but ensuring that 'what you want doesn't run against the grain of your basic purposes, your self-realisation.'[21] We should see autonomy in terms of self-realisation, something that can be diminished by bad choices. Thus as we noted last chapter, Morris argued that conditions of inequality meant the disadvantaged person 'scarcely knows how to frame a desire for any life much better than that which he now endures perforce.'[22]

Scanlon's 'value of choice' theory maintains that choice is not valuable as such. Choice has value where the individual is in a position to make good decisions about how to live, and because the ability to direct our own lives is an essential feature of self-respect and dignity. Scanlon contends, however, that some people are ill prepared to make good choices and thus society should tackle the context in which choices are made.[23] If the individual is not in a position to make good decisions, choice loses its weight. As Raz notes, the opportunity to choose the bad is not one we value; where the choice is bad, the fact that we made it is no consolation.[24] Indeed, that we chose the bad seems more tragic than if it had been foisted upon us.

## Markets and Values

This suggests that more benign ways of affecting choice – incentives and social institutions that promote the valuable – can be permissible. The idea that perfectionism inevitably involves violations of autonomy suggests that our ways of life must be either immune to influence or putty in the hands of others. Such views involve a false understanding of the nature of agency, wherein individuals are only freely choosing if untouched by social influences. Of course, one's life goes better, as Kymlicka puts it, if one is 'leading it from the inside, according to my beliefs about value.'[25] However, our desires, tastes, even needs, are shaped within a social context, moulded by a myriad of influences. One cannot 'make people's lives better against their own convictions.'[26] A life cannot be lived any other way but from the 'inside,' but who one is 'on the inside' is affected by her situation on the outside, the influence of a social milieu.

Thus the debate about choice must take account of this modest 'social thesis.'[27] The idea of responsiveness to reasons, at the heart of our ideal of autonomy, involves a conception of the person with grounds for choice beyond the self; the choosing self is not pure will, but a being who considers how to act by reflecting on external sources of information. The tastes of friends, the values of parents and those with authority or influence, formative experiences in one's life, superficial factors such as the symbolic value of a pursuit, all contribute to choices about how to live.[28] In this we must, as Bakhurst puts it, 'wean ourselves off the idea that the self is something purely inner and psychological.'[29]

In market societies, many of these factors are the effect of advertising, product differentiation, brand promotions, packaging or 'imaging' and are not conducive to choices made on the basis of good reasons. Indeed, what Quong calls 'the paternalizee's capacity to effectively advance his or her own interests'[30] is certainly undermined by profitable enterprises in the market. The market is touted for supporting the neutralism of the liberal state because its exchanges are conducted according to the supposedly contentless measure of profitability, but this in fact makes for significant consequences for the kinds of values one can pursue. The effects are often deleterious for human flourishing, even measured on a simple scale of expressions of satisfaction.[31] Moreover, market actors who influence choices are not typically held to public account or democratic control. Thus it is particularly damning of neutralist positions that they continue to evoke the 'marketplace of ideas' in making their case.

Kymlicka uses the metaphor of a 'cultural marketplace' to defend the 'free association of individuals' who can forge shared cultures or good ways of life; thus 'social perfectionism' is to be preferred to 'state perfectionism.'[32] This position is at odds with Kymlicka's multiculturalist views, discussed in Chapter 5. In his argument for special rights for minority cultures, he rejects the possibility of the neutral 'cultural marketplace,' contending that without state intervention some are disadvantaged in the pursuit of valuable ways of life.[33] However, on the general question of the state's role in promoting good ways of living, Kymlicka insists on a neutralist position preoccupied with individuals' capacity to pursue their plans of life without state interference. Confronting sources of the good that are vulnerable or threatened, such as natural wilderness areas or historical artefacts, he agrees the state should offer support, not because these are sources of valuable options, but for the sake of neutrality, so that these pursuits remain options for future individuals: 'Even if the cultural marketplace can be relied on to ensure that existing people can identify valuable ways of life, it cannot be relied on to ensure that future people have a valuable range of options.'[34] Dworkin adopts a similar strategy. He suggests that funding for the arts, though apparently at odds with liberal neutrality, is permitted to provide 'complex and diverse' cultural forms. Thus society should, as 'trustees for the future complexity of our own culture,' protect the 'structure of our intellectual culture' rather than 'particular aesthetic events.'[35]

It is misleading, however, to insist on a contrast between identifying the good, which is the province of the cultural marketplace, with preserving the options this marketplace throws up, which falls to the community. The reasons to think that the market will fail to preserve what has antecedently been selected as valuable are also the reasons to think the market will fail to permit the identification of the valuable in the first place. The political community cannot ensure a 'valuable range of options' without determining what the valuable might be. There will be many options that are threatened, and not all of them can or should be protected. Protecting the valuable requires action that counteracts the market and its 'myopic bias.' Thus the Marxist economist Kay points to the 'utter irrationality' of capitalism as a 'mode of satisfying human needs' evident in 'urban decay' and other social ills.[36] The failings of the market are not therefore limited to inequalities of distribution, as egalitarian liberals tend to suppose.

Moreover, in an age of sophisticated communications, private enterprise has taken advantage of the astonishing mobility of capital and consumption. As we noted in Chapter 5, the result has been an increasing homogeneity, as much of the world's population consumes the same fast food, hums the same popular songs, and wears the same casual clothing. Equality is not uniformity; for us to flourish equally, we need a variety of cultural options. This is important for self-determination, whereby meaningful choice – not just consumer's choice in a context of market options – is intrinsic to an autonomous life. As Arneson points out, given the pernicious forces at work undermining choice, 'one does not exhibit disrespect for a person by treating her in accordance with principles that she actually rejects, but that she would accept if she were fully rational.'[37] These principles must be carefully deployed, but this can be done non-coercively, pluralistically, and in light of the need for a social context that enables autonomous choices for flourishing.

## The Old Fogey Problem

There persists the worry that, though neither unitary nor coercive, the values of the flourishing approach are exclusive in another sense. For all its potential as an egalitarian bulwark against the destruction of value by the market, a focus on flourishing remains vulnerable to what I call the 'old fogey' critique, which detects an old-fashioned, snobbish, or elitist conception of value or 'taste' in the idea that society should enable lives of value. In what follows I explore the extent to which fogey or conservative values might inform a flourishing account of equality, looking at first, the progressive impact of conservative cultural criticism, and second, the conservative themes to be found among some progressives.

One of the first examples of the progressive impact of conservative ideals is found in the thought of Ruskin, art critic and mentor of Morris. Ruskin contended that he was, like 'my father was before, a violent Tory of the old school,'[38] holding that human government was simply the 'executive expression of Divine authority,'[39] a hierarchical model of paternal rule.[40] For Ruskin, the superior should have the power 'to guide, to lead, or on occasion even to compel and subdue their inferiors.'[41] However, Ruskin's conservatism also involved an obligation to preserve relations of community and benevolence, in opposition to the market-driven imperatives of self-interested individualism. The origins for this lay in his aesthetic views, in which he stressed that works of beauty could not be separated from the social conditions in which they were made. And it was the prevailing social conditions – characterised by 'degradation and deathfulness to the art-intellect'[42] – that increasingly became his focus. Thus society should seek the 'careful preservation and just division' of the riches that is produced by humanely organised work.[43]

This mingling of the conservative and the radical is exemplified again in MacIntyre's work. Informed by Aristotle on the one hand and Marx on the other, MacIntyre takes aim at the 'science of human behaviour' that purports to be neutral about value in order to secure 'manipulative power.'[44] Conservative themes are also manifest in Marcuse's critical theory that likens American capitalism to fascism, and notes the paradoxical role played by aristocratic privilege:

> The fact that the transcending truths of the fine arts, the aesthetics of life and thought, were accessible only to the few wealthy and educated was the fault of a repressive society. But this fault is not corrected by paperbacks, general education, long-playing records, and the abolition of formal dress in the theatre and concert hall. The cultural privileges expressed the injustice of freedom, the contradiction between ideology and reality, the separation of intellectual from material productivity; but they also provided a protected realm in which the tabooed truths could survive in abstract integrity – remote from the society which suppressed them.[45]

For Marcuse, the cultivated European refugee transplanted to southern California, there was a genuine loss in mass culture's suppression of aristocratic values, even if he had no truck with the inequality those values presupposed.

That the anti-commodification cause of egalitarians should find allies among conservatives is exemplified in Cohen's essay 'Rescuing Conservatism.' Cohen defends the conservative attitude that seeks to preserve 'that which has intrinsic value,' explaining that 'some things must be accepted as given ... not everything can or should be shaped to our requirements.'[46] Elsewhere Cohen argues for a socialist system of distribution based on 'communal reciprocity' that rejects the mutual provision of market society which is 'only a by-product of an unmutual and fundamentally *non*reciprocating attitude.'[47] Cohen contends traditional conservatives and socialists find common cause against 'market mania,' manifest in ideologies like 'Thatcherite Toryism' that stand as 'a great betrayal of conservativism,' in their failure to recognise what Marx saw so well: that 'capitalism so comprehensively transforms everything,' including itself.[48] British 'large-C' Conservatives since Thatcher 'blather on about warm beer and sturdy spinsters cycling to church and then they hand Wal-Mart the keys to the kingdom.' This is why working class communities will find that, as Cohen puts it (perhaps with Ruskin in mind), 'small-c conservatism is a buffer against *in*equality.'[49]

Cohen notes the affinity of his views with the conservative Oakeshott, though he decries the latter's 'tendency to put truth in the service of antidemocratic reaction.'[50] Oakeshott expressed an explicit commitment to the idea of a life well lived and a wariness of market forces that might seek to undermine it. He took aim, after all, not just at central planners, Fabians, social democrats and socialists, but also at Thatcher's and Hayek's neoconservatism. He decried the embrace of 'productivity,' and rejected Hayek's 'plan to resist planning.'[51] He did not fully understand how the scrupulously neutral liberal state that restricts itself to overseeing the play of market forces in determining value is likely to risk the sale of culture to the highest bidder, but there are certainly intimations of this in his work. Thus conservative ideas such as those of Oakeshott may be marshalled, for example, in a project of public education that, as Bakhurst puts it, enables 'autonomy and the opportunity to live a worthwhile life, to engage in productive work, to benefit from satisfying leisure and to enjoy happy relationships with others.'[52] This involves the community identifying the valuable, and taking steps to preserve and transmit it through educational policy, by establishing strictures against unfettered development, and providing public access to cultural forms.

The essence of the 'old fogey' position on human flourishing is a disapprobation of certain values and ways of life and a respect and esteem for other, contrasting ones, particularly those of the past. The aim is that as many people as possible disavow the bad and avow the good, rather than that the good be preserved for the privileged. Indeed, this view can find support from egalitarian views such as Sen and Nussbaum's capabilities approach, particularly Nussbaum's ambitious list of capabilities that refer to a variety of aesthetic, recreational and social goods.[53]

Beyond some general guidelines, what counts as a source of wellbeing will be subject to lively debate in a democratic society, among fogeys and hipsters, conservatives and progressives.[54] The egalitarian society should aim to inculcate an appreciation for the worthwhile, to forge common understandings of valuable ways of living, and this will involve esteem for ways of life inherited from the past.[55] A concern for flourishing means we must be pluralists about the good, finding value in a variety of traits, activities and practices, and that we stress our role as autonomous thinkers on questions of value, the precondition for which is the give and take of critical debate. Taking up Mill's call for liberal toleration of human diversity, Sher claims that perfectionist policies should 'leave ample room for "experiments in living."' Enabling us to flourish requires, as Sher put it, 'an especially uncompromising commitment to freedom of thought and expression.'[56] In short, human flourishing necessitates an appreciation of our cultural inheritance, but also critical reflection on, and lively debate about, in Oakeshott's words, the 'conversation of mankind.'

## Whither Perfectionism?

If the individual is embedded in a complex weave of social factors, it is poor sociology to conceive of the neutral state as enabling an unfettered autonomy that ensures individuals enjoy absolute authority over judgements of value. And poor sociology makes for poor ethics, since refusing to exert political influence on the social environment leaves it open to all kinds of other influences, less worthy in their goals, and less transparent and democratic in their methods. The contrast should not be between individuals free to choose under a regime of neutrality as opposed to individuals rendered unfree by perfectionism, but rather between individuals whose choices are constrained by an unaccountable market as opposed to individuals whose social environment is regulated by representative political institutions that facilitate autonomous choice.

If by coercion we mean society rendering some choices more attractive than others, then egalitarian perfectionism is guilty as charged, but then so is just about any polity. Liberal societies today encourage some ways of life and discourage others, in state support for the arts and education, and lack of support for, or discouragement of, other leisure activities such as the consumption of alcohol. Taxation, wherein the state's need to raise revenue is channelled into levies on certain kinds of goods, is an obvious example of such 'coercion,' one that Mill himself defended. In the absence of full equality, however, sales tax has regressive effects, and the taxation strategy is often prompted by moralising views that seek heavy-handedly to direct choice in ways that are not necessarily in keeping with the values of perfectionism. In some domains – smoking, food, alcohol – there seems an excessive, puritanical perfectionism which Morris, the plump, pipe-smoking and wine-drinking lover of beauty, would never have countenanced.[57]

Thus the question is probably not whether perfectionism, but whither, since it is difficult to imagine any society not taking an interest in the values – however private – of its citizens. What methods, then, can the egalitarian perfectionist deploy to enable citizens to live well? I have argued that out and out coercion, punishment or threats to punish, are inadmissible on the grounds that they violate autonomy. However, our social thesis holds that influence is inevitable, and thus the responsible course is to embrace influence and to use it carefully, publicly and transparently, guiding by incentives, education, and providing resources to institutions that offer pursuits of value.

The most important way in which an egalitarian conception of flourishing can enable citizens to live well is equality itself. The argument for equality's positive effects on flourishing has been powerfully made in the work of Wilkinson and Pickett, who contend that 'reducing inequality is the best way of improving the quality of the social environment, and so the real quality of life, for all of us.'[58] Their study surveys the correlation of inequality and a host of indicators of poor wellbeing such as obesity, violence, teenage pregnancy, depression, low educational performance, impoverished community life and social relations, a high incidence of punishment and imprisonment, low mental and physical health, and high rates of drug use. They conclude:

> If you want to know why one country does better than another, the first thing to look at is the extent of inequality. There is not one policy for reducing inequality in health or the educational performance of school children, and another for raising national standards of performance. Reducing inequality is the best way of doing both.[59]

A striking feature of this research is the strategy of moving from the distribution of income to questions of wellbeing. The authors speculate on the cause of the interrelation between equality of income and quality of life, beginning by recognising something like the social thesis I proposed earlier, where individuals are shaped by the milieu in which they live, be it cultural understandings, friendship and community, recognition of status, or stable and secure interactions in civil society. Inequality undermines that milieu, causing instability, mistrust and alienation, all of which have further negative consequences for wellbeing.[60] It is interesting how this influential work takes for granted that what is of fundamental interest is how well people live; once an economic minimum is in place, income distribution is only relevant as a means to this more important goal.

One example that illuminates the relation between equality and perfectionism is the folly of the American 'war on drugs.' Bad choices are often made because people are vulnerable, disadvantaged, under-educated, oppressed or alienated, prey to easy comforts, mind-numbing pleasures or imprudent choices. Taking addictive, health-adverse narcotic substances is one such bad choice. 'Law and order' conservatives in the United States have argued that tougher measures are required to stop the traffic and use of illegal drugs. The opposing view usually maintains that people should be free to pursue whatever conception of the good they choose, however misjudged.

Our considerations about the conditions for choosing well should qualify this stark contrast. Many take drugs, knowing of their dangers, because they suffer from an addiction in which drug-taking is a compulsive behaviour, and cannot really be described as the result of autonomous choice.[61] In the ghetto or the slum, many become addicted to drugs out of hopelessness, in the belief they have no other option; they make what we might call a non-choice. Of course, in the unequal society, drug addiction may also be the lot of the relatively privileged. People can feel alienated despite access to wealth: the bored suburban housewife who relies on what the Rolling Stones called 'mother's little helper' or the pressured investment banker addicted to cocaine. On the conception of egalitarian flourishing, coercion is the wrong response to the irrationality of drug addictions. Society should instead seek to remedy the social conditions that cause people to find these choices reasonable.[62] This may involve some compulsion; if the addicted person is no longer autonomous, she might properly be required to undergo rehabilitation to restore her autonomy, even if this means a suspension of choice in the short term.

At the same time, a more open attitude to drug use as a potential Millian experiment in living under certain specified conditions, is invited by the flourishing approach. Egalitarians will nonetheless take an interest in the choice to use drugs, how it responds to, and can cause shortfalls in, human flourishing, and thus be in a better position to discern the social conditions that might prompt damaging drug use. A commitment to autonomy as a central feature of living well, coupled with an egalitarian concern for the deprived social conditions that produce choices inimical to such living, yield an argument for attending to bad choices without banning them.

Thus we might as a community decide to create an environment that fosters good choices in order to enhance our autonomy. This is not the view that autonomy may be restricted if that will produce good consequences.[63] Sunstein makes an influential case of this kind with his 'nudge' idea where social welfare is improved by 'libertarian paternalist' measures. This view suggests that autonomy is valuable only instrumentally, in terms of its epistemic advantages, and is thus easily sacrificed if these advantages do not obtain. My view does not treat autonomy instrumentally in that way. However, I find more congenial Sunstein's supplementary claim, that 'helpful choice architecture' can organise the inevitable context of choice to enhance our choice-making capacity, given human beings' limitations of time, interest and attention.[64] Indeed, if we are prone to 'mindless choosing,' subsidies and rewards could help us choose more mindfully, safeguarding our autonomy, not undermining it.[65] There is thus a good case for careful policies of 'moral environmentalism,' to structure the plethora of unaccountable influences on our options.[66]

We have noted how the liberal tradition was long comfortable with certain perfectionist ideas. Thus Hobhouse insisted that we should not coerce people for their own good, not out of indifference to the good, but because we value it and know coercion cannot secure it. He also insisted that our concern for the good requires us to arrange social conditions so people will elect to live good lives.[67] And indeed, the sense of connection we have with others, expressed in the idea of solidarity, paradoxically involves respect for the individual's space that others may not invade.[68] Neutralists are not neutral about everything – it is inevitable, according to Rawls, that public policy whose justification is neutral about questions of the good life will have non-neutral consequences when put into action. But restricting neutrality to the justification or aims of public policy is nonetheless hard to sustain. Autonomy itself, as Macedo notes, is from a liberal perspective, not 'simply one ideal of life among others.'[69] Even Rawls, though he divorces political liberalism from more 'comprehensive' doctrines, concedes that our measure of political institutions makes reference to their efficacy in human flourishing, maintaining that political institutions are 'just and good' to the extent that they allow 'worthy ways of life.'[70]

Dworkin's position is a particularly interesting example of cracks within the neutralist position. In his later work, he explains how we are concerned that our lives be a success, not in the paltry sense of succeeding in satisfying our given interests, but on the loftier criterion of fulfilling our 'critical interests,' the interests we 'ought to have,' and government should 'act to make the lives of those it governs better lives.' Dworkin 'does not rule out the possibility' that 'the community should collectively endorse and recommend ethical ideals not adequately supported by the culture.' Nor does he rule out compulsory education and other forms of 'short-term, non-invasive' regulation. He allows for 'short-term educational paternalism that looks forward, with confidence, to free and genuine endorsement.'[71]

Nonetheless, Dworkin retains his old squeamishness: 'Paternalism is misguided because it wrongly treats convictions as limitations or handicaps.' Genuine endorsement, we are cautioned, cannot be the product of being hypnotised, brainwashed, or frightened. The agent's endorsement is not 'the result of another person's thoughts being piped into his brain.' Individuals cannot use the law to 'forbid anyone to lead the life he wants, or punish him for doing so,' out of a belief that a person's ethical convictions are 'profoundly wrong.'[72] Dworkin encourages individuals who possess 'strong convictions' instead to 'campaign for the good as they see it.'

We are unlikely to thank Dworkin for the insight that it is wrong to beat up people if we disapprove of their pursuits. Such truisms are hard to avoid, perhaps, in a society that has, historically, moralised on the one hand about Americanness and on the other about not imposing morality, where the idea of the good life is pulled between images of consumer satisfaction and bible-thumping notions of salvation. Dworkin is exercised by the possibility of repressive moral views being enforced on others; indeed, the example he uses most often is an antipathy to homosexuality. This may account for why, though giving scope for the community to encourage the good life, he also indicates the community should refrain from doing so. Yet equality requires mechanisms for enriching the public domain, not so that we can coerce sexual minorities into living by the majority's code, but to foster a cultural environment that enables a range of worthwhile choices. Presumably, Dworkin would have fewer problems with public educational campaigns that promote tolerance of diverse forms of sexuality. Inequality is, after all, relevantly manifest in the kinds of lives people are acculturated to pursue. We shouldn't snub the beer-drinking, television-watching citizen, and certainly we shouldn't force him to give up his pleasures. But we might think about how society can render more accessible other kinds of pleasures that would facilitate a variety of models of living well.

Recall Dworkin's attack on the idea of a social obligation to provide the means for satisfying expensive tastes, noted in the last chapter. Dworkin portrays these tastes as the frivolous pursuits of the few; his example of a penchant for plover's eggs is revealing. But what of tastes for a wholesome natural environment, a culture of civility, the preservation of historic buildings, access to the arts? These goods may be costly, but they merit support, not so the elite might enjoy them, but so that they may be accessible to all. They are constituents of the public good, a rich and diverse cultural environment that enables a plurality of genuinely valuable choices. Dworkin's argument portrays the individual as a consumer in an idealised marketplace, making unfettered choices in full knowledge of their effects. There is no mention of the deleterious effect that real markets have on human pursuits, where the loftiest goods are victims of market failure, economies of scale, the exploitation of resources, the commodification of culture.

Egalitarian flourishing need not involve paternalistic meddling or brutal coercion; it requires only a social commitment to enabling a plurality of worthwhile ways of living, by redistributing wealth and regulating the market, subsidising threatened goods, and educating and informing citizens so that their choices are the product of rational decision-making. In sum, egalitarian flourishing aims to render human wellbeing more equal, not only by redistributing wealth, but also:

i   protecting vulnerable sources of value to ensure they are available for individuals to pursue: a policy of stewardship;

ii improving access to sources of value to ensure they are available to individuals regardless of income: a policy of accessibility;

iii encouraging the pursuit of the valuable by means of education and subsidies: a policy of incentives.

## Art and Freedom

We have seen how an aesthetic critique was the impetus for Morris's egalitarian ideas. Indeed, much of the pre-Rawlsian egalitarian tradition assumed that the pursuit of equality was connected to enabling broader enjoyment of beauty. However, it is precisely the aesthetic aspect of the idea of human flourishing that might arouse the suspicions of contemporary liberals, who contend that we court the danger of destroying the individual self-expression inherent in artistic pursuits, or rendering fundamental questions of equality a trivial matter of taste.

Controversy over Morris's aesthetic predilections illuminates this question. Critics contend that his ideal of medieval artisanship romanticised the past and dismissed the modern, showing itself hostile to individualistic forms of expression, and betraying an illiberal, monocultural view of value.[73] The problematic relationship between socialism and art was evident in the twentieth century. Historically, when Marxists have sought to politicise the aesthetic, the result has been aesthetically and politically disastrous. Soviet-style state socialism, for example, deployed the Marxist conception of the epiphenomenal nature of art to press art into the service of propaganda.[74] This had a deleterious effect on art itself, as evidenced by Stalin's imposition of a crude socialist realism.[75] And it made for injustice, brutally suppressing freedom of expression, and manipulating art to dissemble this injustice, so that the aesthetic became an exercise in myth-making carried out without dissent by artists-cum-propagandists.

There are other, more promising, radical approaches to art, such as those of the Frankfurt School, which maintain that emancipation and human well-being have an aesthetic dimension. Art and the imagination play a critical and subversive role in a context of injustice as an 'anticipatory illumination,'[76] a 'dissenting force,'[77] 'bringing untruth to consciousness of itself'[78] or widening the scope of those who might participate in its production.[79] The aesthetic thus serves several important functions for egalitarianism. First, art's capacity to enhance human life reminds us how flourishing comprises more than the satisfaction of basic, material needs. Second, the aesthetic offers a sphere of intrinsic, non-instrumental value, a counter to political theories focussed on property, goods or utility. Of course, one can trade or invest in art, but truly appreciating art involves understanding it as a non-commodity. Third, the aesthetic involves the idea of creativity and the role of individual freedom to enable creation, giving scope for autonomy.

Fourth, the aesthetic unleashes the utopian, and thereby the inspiration and vision for political change. Returning to Morris, his beautiful artefacts implicitly suggest an alternative future, and his literature explicitly invokes utopian possibilities. Morris subverts the distinction made by Engels between 'scientific' and 'utopian' socialism, finding some kind of utopian vision indispensable for the socialist project. Dreams of the beautiful are a stance from which to criticise, but they also provide us with a refuge that nourishes the hope one needs to fight injustice.[80] Thus Morris's idea of beauty became, not just a stance of revulsion, but also an impetus for change. He was not just 'the idle singer of an empty day,'[81] but a practical man, a 'moral realist,' to quote a non-philosophical use of the term,[82] who took stock of his experience in the world to present 'the *datum* which all our adventures, worldly and other-worldly alike, must take into account.'[83]

Finally, the aesthetic sheds light on the anti-subjectivism inherent in the flourishing account of equality. The idea of the beautiful is a useful antidote to mere taste that relegates critical assessment to the vagaries of individuals' desires. Theorists intent on debunking the idea of truth have sometimes invoked aesthetic devices from literary theory to refer to a non-rational or sublime realm of discourse where meaning is constructed rather than found.[84] The result is a relativism with which Morris, with his firm ideas about what constitutes the beautiful and the ugly, would have had little patience. We might take issue with Morris's dismissal of rival aesthetic views, but not the importance of the pursuit of the truly beautiful, a pursuit that requires freedom to explore a variety of aesthetic forms. For Morris, one could sensibly talk about the education of desire toward the truly fulfilling, so that we should have, for example, nothing in our homes that we 'do not know to be useful or believe to be beautiful.'[85] It is in this light that we can understand Morris's concern to distinguish between dream and vision,[86] and his awareness that the route to 'the change beyond the change'[87] would involve, not just protest and struggle, but the painful matter of acquiring new attitudes and values.

Morris's combination of utopian and realist views about art helps give content to the concept of a perfectionism that eschews coercion. The sorry history of radical efforts at directing art demonstrates the futility of compelling people to realise particular goods or particular forms of art. We can give artists a framework for artistic activity, an education in the history of art and in artistic technique, satisfactory working conditions and good materials, some remuneration or subsidy. But it would be self-defeating to direct artists to produce certain works of art, as though aesthetic perfection could be created by means of an impeccably designed paint-by-number kit. Similarly, in our pursuit of wellbeing more generally, contra the scaremongering of anti-perfectionists, the role of the community will be to provide, not a substantive conception, but a framework for the pursuit of the many ways of living well.

One critic of perfectionism complains that either the theory is monistic about the good, or, if it is pluralist, too abstract to be of any use since it provides no 'precise ranking' of diverse goods to guide public policy.[88] Such a view seems to hold perfectionism to a standard of applicability not demanded of other political philosophies. The flourishing account sets out general principles for what constitutes wellbeing: it is a tripartite conception that includes objectively worthwhile pursuits, autonomy, and contentment, and as such it generates a set of sources of flourishing identified in the previous chapter. Beyond that, however, the question of what good to promote, and when, belongs properly in the domain of democratic debate in light of the particulars of the case, not abstract theorising; thus the opera house is built in one context, and the stadium in another.

## Adventures with Excellence

It is often supposed that when the artist aspires to create beauty, he or she is striving for excellence, something that is by definition attainable only by the few. Certainly excellence is central for many perfectionist theories. Doubtless this is in part because 'arete,' the Greek term for 'virtue' is also translated as 'excellence' in order to capture the sense of human self-realisation. Galston, for example, refers to the 'excellent individual,' 'human excellence' and different 'conceptions of individual excellence' ranging from that of Locke, Kant and romanticism.[89] Hurka also refers to 'routes to excellence' and 'opportunities for excellence.'[90]

In the last chapter's discussion of thresholds of flourishing, excellence was shown to have a fraught relation to equality. Excellence is inevitably and inherently comparative, and thus hierarchical or exclusive in the sense that to be excellent is to be superior to the average. As educators well know, if all students are ranked as alpha, then the term loses its meaning. Even if, as Hurka contends, 'there are many excellent activities,' the term excellence suggests a society more concerned with some reaching the pinnacle than ensuring all reach a threshold.

Furthermore, excellence is at odds with flourishing. It is hard to think of people actually living their lives with this goal in mind. Neither my relation to my family nor my efforts at philosophical insight are best described as activities engaged in the 'pursuit of excellence,' but rather trying to do things well. Excellence can distract us from the value inherent in an activity, rendering an activity instrumental to some extrinsic good, seeking an apex of achievement, a laurel or accolade, analogous to the way in which, as perfectionists often complain, market reward renders many worthwhile activities instrumental.

The word, excellence, though, in any case, has been taken over by such a wide array of cultural sources that one could argue it has become flabby, quite the opposite of demonstrably superior to the achievements of 'the herd,' and thus unable to exert its discriminatory force. Consider the role of the word 'excellent' in teen flicks of a generation ago, as in 'Bill and Ted's Excellent Adventure' or the mantra 'Wayne's World, Wayne's World, Party Time, Excellent.' 'Excellent', like 'cool' or 'awesome,' has played a distinctive role in youth discourse, where, just as 'cool' has nothing to do with temperature or 'awesome' with being humbled before greatness, 'excellent' no longer refers to a summit of value. These terms simply mean a general approbation, an expression of preference, nothing more specific than the hurrah valuation in emotivist theories of ethics.

The problem is compounded by more cynical uses of the word excellence in corporate settings. It is prominent in the world of business executives, human resources offices, advertising and marketing. Sadly, the cynical use is also found in higher education, a favourite among administrators. Government has adopted a policy of creating 'centres of excellence' among Canada's universities; and research-granting organisations describe their standard as one of excellence, a criterion dependent on, among other things, previous success in getting grants. Here the word's capital depends on its association with the exclusive, but its ubiquity in the corporate-speak of academic institutions to facilitate the imperatives of managerial success has made the word seem common and tawdry.[91] The tragic impact on university students, the 'excellent sheep,' is that they feel they must 'choose between learning and success.'[92]

Thus autonomy, the value at the heart of our argument, is undermined by the cult of excellence. Critical thinking, self-direction, the ability to reflect upon and choose how to live, is in conflict with a culture that treats learning as instrumental to status and acceptance. In these cases from contemporary culture, excellence might have been denuded of its austere, exclusive associations, but it is hardly more favourable to an egalitarian policy. Though ideological, the term's aim continues to be to single out the few among the many, however poor its criteria for doing so. In all these variants, excellence has little role in a theory of human flourishing that seeks critical distance from the institutions and imperatives of the market in order to enable persons to live genuinely, and equally, well. In sum, human flourishing – living well, contentedly, autonomously, and as an equal with one's fellows – is not best conceived using the devalued currency of excellence.

## Principles of Egalitarian Human Flourishing

In light of the arguments of the past three chapters, we can now formulate some general principles about egalitarian human flourishing:

1   A theory of equality should focus on the quality of people's lives. Resources are a crucial source of wellbeing, but the reason we seek greater equality in the distribution of resources is in order to better equalise human wellbeing.
2   Flourishing is both a subjective and objective measure, and a mix of three ideas: being able to choose how to live; living a life that involves self-mastery and objectively worthwhile pursuits; and personal contentment.
3   Flourishing differs from standard accounts of distribution that deploy a measure of equality that is also the thing that is equalised (e.g. resources or primary goods). Society should seek higher and more equal levels of human flourishing, yet flourishing itself cannot be exactly calibrated and thus resists precise distribution, let alone equalisation. A flourishing approach, in its focus on human wellbeing, will eschew levelling for its own sake.

4   Egalitarian policy should promote a social and cultural environment conducive to wellbeing. Society should foster good choices about how to live by means of support for egalitarian policies for the arts, education, nature, and culture more generally.[93]

5   One reason why flourishing itself cannot be equalised is that it depends on subjective factors such as psychological disposition (the Eeyore problem). We can live under ideal conditions for flourishing and still fail to flourish. A flourishing approach should, nonetheless, consider all shortfalls in flourishing as potentially within the scope of public policy.

6   Egalitarian flourishing is able to avoid egalitarian approaches that risk a harsh justice for the irresponsible, as well as perfectionist approaches that prove paternalistic. Active, contributing and autonomous individuals flourish on this account, and thus the shirker is understood as a have-not in need of inculcation in living well. Respect for individual freedom is addressed by a conception of autonomy, coupled with a social thesis, which justifies improvements to the cultural environment to enable better-informed choices conducive to self-determination.

## Conclusion

Political philosophy has been badly served by the neutralist preoccupation with abstinence on questions of value. Liberal egalitarians criticise alternative views for focussing on 'the good,' with the implication that such views assume there is only one good, and that people should be compelled to live it. A life of value, I have argued, comes in many forms and our efforts in pursuing it are, contra the idea of uninfluenced choice, affected by many factors. The aesthetic dimension of flourishing underscores how self-direction is central to human wellbeing, and how the political community must provide the context for both art and flourishing to thrive, without getting mired in the dubious value of 'excellence.' In seeking to enable worthwhile choices, society is simply acquitting itself of a social thesis, whereby the environment that shapes decisions about how to live is rendered transparent, accountable, and conducive to human wellbeing. How we should understand the idea of the public good that undergirds the flourishing argument for equality, and how this project might be deployed in the global context, where inequality is most stark, are important questions. These are the subjects of the next two chapters.

## Notes

1   Marx and Engels, 'The German Ideology,' 160.
2   So varied and prodigious was his pursuit of the good that his physician said that Morris died from 'simply being William Morris, and having done more work than most ten men.' F. MacCarthy, *William Morris: A Life for Our Time*, vii.
3   Although he added, 'for my part I can't see why we should think it a hardship to eat with the people we work with,' 'How We Live and How We Might Live,' 23.

4 Morris, 'True and False Society,' 234.
5 'How We Live and How We Might Live,' 16.
6 Quong, *Liberalism without Perfection*, 15.
7 S. Wall, *Liberalism, Perfectionism and Restraint*, 18.
8 Dworkin, 'Foundations of Liberal Equality,' 118. Barry invokes the Thomist way of life as a foil to his idea of impartiality, rather stacking the deck: *Justice as Impartiality*, 72–9.
9 Raz, *The Morality of Freedom*, 395–6.
10 Sher, *Beyond Neutrality*, 61.
11 Gaus contends that the wrongness of coercion underpins the argument for state neutrality in 'Liberal Neutrality,' 138.
12 *News from Nowhere*, 147.
13 Thompson, *William Morris*, 806.
14 Hurka, *Perfectionism*, 152–5.
15 Sher, *Beyond Neutrality*, 69.
16 S. Conly, *Against Autonomy: Justifying Coercive Paternalism*, 16. See also S. Conly, 'Three Cheers for the Nanny State.'
17 Sher, *Beyond Neutrality*, 57.
18 Hurka, *Perfectionism*, 152–5.
19 Lecce, *Against Perfectionism*, 122–3, 134.
20 Quong, *Liberalism without Perfection*, 106.
21 C. Taylor, 'What's Wrong with Negative Liberty,' 147.
22 Morris, 'How I Became a Socialist,' 281.
23 T. Scanlon, 'The Significance of Choice,' 73–8, 84.
24 Raz, *The Morality of Freedom*, 381, 412.
25 W. Kymlicka, *Contemporary Political Philosophy*, 216.
26 Dworkin, 'Foundations of Liberal Equality,' 118.
27 See Taylor, 'Atomism.'
28 For a sample of views, see D. Bakhurst and C. Sypnowich, eds, *The Social Self*.
29 D. Bakhurst, *The Formation of Reason*, 64.
30 Quong, *Liberalism without Perfection*, 83.
31 This is borne out by some interesting recent work in economics – A. Offer, *The Challenge of Affluence: Self-Control and Wellbeing in the United States and Britain Since 1950*; P.A. Victor, *Managing without Growth: Slower by Design, Not Disaster*; Frank, *Luxury Fever*; see also the 'happiness studies' works listed in Chapter 7, note 76.
32 Kymlicka, *Contemporary Political Philosophy*, 246–8.
33 Kymlicka, *Multicultural Citizenship*, 113. For Patten, 'neutrality of treatment' means that 'the state's policies must be equally accommodating of rival conceptions of the good.' *Equal Recognition*, 115. See also the role of flourishing in Donaldson and Kymlicka, *Zoopolis*, 99; 165.
34 Kymlicka, *Contemporary Political Philosophy*, 247.
35 Dworkin, *A Matter of Principle*, 232. Elsewhere Dworkin remarks in passing that the imposition of taxes to finance museums is an example of how 'government acts properly when it coerces people in order to protect certain values.' *Life's Dominion: An Argument about Abortion, Euthanasia, and Individual Freedom*, 154. H. Brighouse concludes that if liberals want to justify funding for the arts, they may have to give up 'the neutrality constraint,' 'Neutrality, Publicity and State Funding of the Arts,' 63. Quong insists that demand should dictate the provision of cultural goods, which should be paid for 'at the point of consumption.' *Liberalism without Perfection*, 90–1.
36 'Myopic bias' is Offer's expression in *The Challenge of Affluence*, 74. See also G. Kay, *The Economic Theory of the Working Class*, ix.
37 Arneson, 'Liberal Neutrality on the Good,' 213.
38 J. Ruskin, *The Works of John Ruskin*, 35, 13.
39 J. Ruskin, *Unto this Last, Political Economy of Art, Essays on Political Economy*, 80.
40 Ibid., 10.

41 Ibid., 160.
42 Ibid., 20.
43 Ibid., 137.
44 MacIntyre, *After Virtue*, 78–83.
45 H. Marcuse, *One Dimensional Man*, 58.
46 G.A. Cohen, 'Rescuing Conservatism: A Defence of Existing Value,' 149.
47 Cohen, *Why Not Socialism?*, 45.
48 Cohen, 'Rescuing Conservatism,' 168.
49 Ibid., 173.
50 Ibid., 170.
51 M. Oakeshott, *Rationalism in Politics and Other Essays*, 26. See also A. Gamble, 'Oakeshott's Ideological Politics: Conservative or Liberal?,' 166–7; D. Villa, 'The Cold War Critique of Political Rationalism,' 323–4; and W. Galston, 'Oakeshott's Political Theory: Recapitulation and Criticisms,' 224.
52 Bakhurst, *The Formation of Reason*, 159.
53 Nussbaum, *Women and Human Development*, 75.
54 A. Lister suggests that an 'anarchical default' might be rejected for all policies and 'some fairly strong forms of perfectionism' would be legitimate, so long as they are reached democratically in 'Public Justification and the Limits of State Action,' 157.
55 Heritage conservation districts such as Barriefield Village in Ontario involve a principle of stewardship for the public good which restricts homeowners' freedom of choice in altering their properties. See R. Cardwell, B. Carr and C. Sypnowich, eds, *Barriefield: 200 Years of Village Life*.
56 Sher, *Beyond Neutrality*, 138.
57 Consider the charming encounter between the hero and the child shop clerks in the matter of a hand-crafted pipe and tobacco pouch in Morris's utopia, *News from Nowhere*, Chapter VI.
58 Wilkinson and Pickett, *The Spirit Level*, 29.
59 Ibid., 29–30.
60 Ibid., 31–45.
61 R. Goodin, *No Smoking*, 25–8.
62 D. Husak, and P. de Marneffe, *The Legalisation of Drugs: For and Against*, 29. 'If you're living in a poor neighbourhood deprived of options, there's a certain rationality to keep taking a drug that will give you some temporary pleasure,' according to C. Hart, interviewed in J. Tierney, 'The Rational Choices of Crack Addicts.' See Hart's fascinating study, *High Price: A Neuroscientist's Journey of Self-Discovery that Challenges Everything You Know about Drugs and Society*, and another provocative work, G. Heyman, *Addiction: A Disorder of Choice*.
63 'What we need to do is to help one another avoid mistakes so that we may all end up where we want to be,' Conly, *Against Autonomy*, 2.
64 C.R. Sunstein, *Why Nudge?*, 137–8.
65 R. Thaler and C.R. Sunstein, *Nudge: Improving Decisions about Health, Wealth and Happiness*, 43.
66 S. Wall, 'Moral Environmentalism,' 93–5.
67 Hobhouse, *Liberalism*, 76. Mill famously qualified his harm principle in the later chapters of 'On Liberty,' confronting challenging examples of self-inflicted serious harm, such as gambling and alcoholism.
68 This is something that emerges in Wiggins, 'Solidarity and the Root of the Ethical,' 260. See also, cited in ibid., 243, P. Foot, 'Morality, Action and Outcome.'
69 Macedo, *Liberal Virtues*, 263.
70 Rawls, *Political Liberalism*, 210.
71 Dworkin, *Sovereign Virtue*, 128, 274.
72 Ibid., 274, 283, 269.

73 L. Davis, 'Morris, Wilde, and Marx on the Social Preconditions of Individual Development,' 719–32, 725–7.
74 G. Lukacs, 'Appearance and Essence.'
75 See R. Robin, *Socialist Realism: An Impossible Aesthetic*.
76 E. Bloch, *The Utopian Function of Art and Literature*, 146.
77 H. Marcuse, *The Aesthetic Dimension*, 8.
78 T. Adorno, 'Cultural Criticism and Society,' 28.
79 W. Benjamin, 'The Author and Producer,' 230–8. See also I. Gallagher, 'William Guest Goes Shopping.'
80 Thompson, *William Morris*, 672–5, 802.
81 W. Morris, 'The Earthly Paradise,' 437.
82 Thompson, *William Morris*, 717.
83 C.S. Lewis, 'William Morris,' *Rehabilitations*, 55.
84 See S. White, *Political Theory and Postmodernism*.
85 W. Morris, 'Hopes and Fears for Art,' 76.
86 See R. Williams, 'Utopia and Science Fiction.'
87 A phrase from W. Morris, 'A Dream of John Ball,' 257.
88 D. Weinstock, 'Neutralizing Perfection: Hurka on Liberal Neutrality,' 52.
89 Galston, *Liberal Purposes*, 229–32.
90 Hurka, *Perfectionism*, 171.
91 See B. Readings, *The University in Ruins*, 3, 21–43. S. Lukes's dystopian satire, *The Curious Enlightenment of Professor Caritat*, 48–9, makes fun of the research maximisation strategies of contemporary universities when the hero is asked for the weight, in kilos, of his academic contributions.
92 W. Deresiewicz, *Excellent Sheep: The Miseducation of the American Elite and the Way to a Meaningful Life*, 3.
93 Consider obesity, a cause of diminished flourishing, prevalent among economically disadvantaged people, and how it might be tackled by policies that encourage physical exercise and the consumption of healthy food. The debate initiated by the British celebrity chef, Jamie Oliver, about the quality of school meals, is interesting in its concern for, not just healthy eating, but also the aesthetics of good food.

# 9 Equality and the Public Good: Local and Global

Conceiving of equality in terms of human flourishing requires improving disadvantaged people's share of material resources, but it also involves enhancing non-material features of people's situation. In particular, I have argued that if we are to make people's level of flourishing more equal, we must attend to the cultural environment in which people live. Individual choice is affected by a myriad of external influences, and thus the egalitarian society should promote worthwhile ways of living by fostering a culture that encourages good choices and discourages bad ones. The equal society equitably distributes human goods, the constituents of flourishing, but it also fosters a social fabric that improves individual wellbeing.

The human flourishing approach to equality has both small-scale and large-scale applications. It is a truism that one's lot in life is to a large extent determined by where one is born: into which family and in what part of the world. Disparities of wealth among persons is constituted by the have and have-not contexts in which people find themselves, e.g. if they are raised by a family with or without resources, good or bad parenting skills, and if they live in a developed or underdeveloped, just or unjust, tolerant or prejudiced, society. Both family and society are facts about a person that he or she cannot control; we are powerless to change either parentage or birthplace. They stand as morally arbitrary factors and moreover, their arbitrariness intersects, since some parts of the world have institutions that seek to ameliorate familial disadvantage, whilst others leave such disparities untouched, or even entrench their salience. It is thus not surprising that contemporary egalitarian debate is increasingly focussed, on the one hand, on the micro-issues of family, schooling and parenting, and on the other, on the macro-issues of nationality, global justice and cosmopolitan ethics.

The contingent features of nationality and family confirm the importance of shifting emphasis from resources to a variety of sources of human flourishing. After all, nation and family supply not only material advantage or disadvantage; they also supply human relationships, cultural practices, institutional supports and social life; they determine, to some extent, one's income, but also one's education, physical fitness, acculturation, aspirations and self-esteem. People are unequal not just in their levels of income or property, but also in reference to a myriad of constituents of human flourishing, many of which are, of course, crucially connected to levels of wealth.

The idea that society should promote a culture favourable to human flourishing raises the thorny problem of 'the public good.' If, as this book has argued, we should seek to make people's shared environment conducive to choices that enable human flourishing, it seems inevitable that we would seek to further the public good. In this chapter I will first consider the different conceptions of the public good, dispelling the idea that the term invokes some supra-individual entity. Second, I will show that the public good, typically regarded with suspicion by liberal egalitarians as a harbinger of conservative traditionalism, is in fact central to equality's pursuit. Finally, I will argue that the public good can mitigate the inequalities of both family and geography. As an egalitarian concept, the public good is concerned with objective criteria for flourishing that can further global egalitarian goals.

## Public Goods and Private Benefits

The idea of the public good is mired in ambiguity. One conception of the public good draws on the idea of a shared understanding of value. That is, the public good refers to those goods that are identified as valuable for a society's members – e.g. public transit, art galleries, etc. – via a process of public discussion and consensus. This first understanding is the precondition for a second, in which the public good refers to those goods that a society decides to provide publicly, zeroing in on the public good's source in public institutions – such as publicly funded health care or free music lessons provided by public schools – which are nonetheless enjoyed by individuals, perhaps even privately. A society might have a commitment to the arts as a public good but nonetheless not concern itself with public availability, providing opportunities only for the artistic geniuses, or letting the market determine prices for artworks or gallery tickets, or doing nothing to acculturate people to appreciate art.

Two further understandings refer directly to public access: on the third, the good is public when it is accessible to all, e.g. by open entry to parks or museums. A fourth conception considers a good to be public in virtue of its metaphysical character as a good that is non-excludable and not a possible object of distribution, such as clean air. This understanding brings to the fore a controversial feature of the public good, the problem of free riders who fail to contribute but nonetheless enjoy public goods – e.g. she who avails herself of clean air while engaging in practices that cause air pollution. Such goods also cause collective action problems since people are reluctant to bear the cost of goods that others can enjoy for free.

Fifth, the public good might be thought to refer to something that is good for the public per se, an abstract entity with its own integrity, composed of such properties as civility, stability and lawfulness. Such a good would be the property of the social whole, of society, and thus an abstraction that cannot be distributed to individuals, nor necessarily of interest to them. As such, it is an entity that has moral entitlements to which individuals' interests might be sacrificed, as in: 'personal freedom must sometimes be sacrificed for the public good.'

Not surprisingly, in light of this variety of understandings, the very idea of the public good is controversial, seeming inimical to both methodological and ethical individualism, where the relevant units of analysis, the agents or victims of moral rights and wrongs, are individuals rather than supra-individual entities. Margaret Thatcher's famous remark that 'there is no such thing as society' is an extreme version of the suspicion that 'the public' is an abstraction incapable of having goods. It is even more problematic than the much-derided idea of 'the people' that, though potentially repressive, at least refers to human beings, notwithstanding Mill's astute objection that 'the "people" who exercise ... power, are not always the same people as those over whom it is exercised.'[1] In Chapter 6 it was argued that equality is only valuable in light of its effects on persons. Just as equality derives its value from its impact on the flourishing of individual persons, so too, good cannot devolve upon a non-agent or non-subject – 'the public.' Nonetheless, methodological individualists can concede that there are publicly provided and publicly available goods, since the equal society requires socially organised systems of distribution of such things as income, education or health care, but they might baulk at the idea of a public good per se. The connotation of a supra-individual abstraction might be mitigated by restricting the idea to a public good, or public goods, plural, rather than *the* public good.

Raz defines *a* public good in terms of its accessibility to all: 'A good is a public good in a certain society if and only if the distribution of its benefits in that society is not subject to voluntary control other than each potential beneficiary controlling his share of the benefits.'[2] For Raz, public goods that are consumed, like water and air, are only contingently public, since it is theoretically possible, given the right technology, to apportion their benefits individually. Inherent public goods, in contrast, refer to 'general beneficial features of a society,' such as the fact that it is tolerant or cultured. Raz's conception of inherent public goods straddles our fourth and fifth definitions, since what distinguishes inherent goods from contingent ones, according to Raz, is both the essential non-exclusivity of their enjoyment among members of a society and their intrinsic value.

Raz's view does not entail any kind of anti-humanism, where the value at stake does not bear on the wellbeing of persons, an objection, as we saw in Chapter 6, Raz himself makes of the idea of strict equality. Inherent goods enrich people's lives; both the goods themselves and the lives they enrich are intrinsically valuable. For example, art and the life enriched by art are both valuable.[3] Indeed, goods are inconceivable without human beings to create, define, acknowledge, and enjoy them. Raz remarks:

> It is a public good, and inherently so, that this society is a tolerant society, that it is an educated society, that it is infused with a respect for human beings, etc. Living in a society with these characteristics is generally of benefit to individuals.[4]

Certainly the egalitarian conception of human flourishing offered here is committed to the view that the value of the public good lies in its connection to individual wellbeing.

One could go further and hold that the public good is not only of benefit to individuals, but that the only reason to provide it is that individuals so benefit. There is no tension between the view that a good is intrinsically valuable, or valuable for its own sake, and the view that its value is essentially related to human wellbeing. Education, for example, is valuable for its own sake, in the sense that an education is not merely instrumentally valuable, but its value could not be elucidated without essential reference to the way it enriches individual lives.

The controversy arises because we are accustomed to thinking of the public good in communitarian terms. Communitarians like Sandel call for a conception of the person as a social being, which entails a political project that focuses on tradition and a common conception of the good.[5] Liberals, in contrast, focus on the individual's capacity to choose how to live, and a political structure that enables the individual to distance him or herself from traditional ways of life in order to pursue his or her own conception of the good. The communitarian critique prompted Rawls to retort that liberalism should be 'political not metaphysical.'[6] Liberals complain that it is unclear what impact the preoccupation with community has on the central question of politics, the distribution of power among persons through rightly ordered social institutions. Worse, they argue, the emphasis on community generates a substantive politics that confirms the traditions of the community and thus threatens to be conservative, illiberal, backward looking and inegalitarian.

Rousseau's defence of the general will famously puts the common good before individual interests. He contends:

> There is often a great deal of difference between the will of all and the general will; the latter considers only the common interest, while the former takes private interest into account, and is no more than a sum of private wills.[7]

That community might overtake the flourishing of individual persons is particularly evident in Taylor's endorsement of the 'survivance' model of recognition politics that we encountered in Chapter 5. For Taylor, steps should be taken to preserve a threatened cultural community even if no individual member of that community cares about its preservation.[8] The common good, a shared conception of the valuable, is thus not contingent on questions of access, since a good can be held in common without being apportioned among persons, let alone apportioned evenly or fairly.

In an encyclopaedia entry on 'the public interest,' Weale states that the public interest means 'the interests of the members of a society considered in their broadest relations,' referring to the supply of indivisible goods, like clean air, or the preservation of aspects of a collective identity, like a language.[9] The first example is one where all members of society equally share in an incontrovertible good, but the latter example of language is one where many might not find themselves interested in, or benefiting from, what is identified as the public interest. The difficulty with the phrase 'public interest' is that, like the public good, it again suggests the communitarian idea of a supra-individual entity, which may or may not involve the interests of particular individuals. On the other hand, understanding the public good's instrumental value for individual interests does not mean that individuals should treat it merely instrumentally. One risks destroying the goose who lays the golden egg if one treats the public good as a mere vehicle for one's interests, and a public that is replete with value of benefit to individuals must be given special protection from exploitation by individuals.

An emphasis on flourishing or perfectionism seems inevitably communitarian in some sense. Perfectionists certainly ascribe to the community the role of contributing to, or facilitating, the valuable. Hurka speaks of policies that lead to 'richer, more vital societies.'[10] Sher decries a 'coarse and vulgar public culture.'[11] Galston speaks of 'public morality' and 'public' or, as Macedo also contends, 'liberal' virtues.[12] The relation these public goods bear to individuals is a complex matter. Galston and Macedo are concerned about the kinds of virtues needed to sustain a liberal society, rendering it stable and secure, e.g. loyalty and tolerance, suggesting a supra-individual entity to which individuals must contribute. But it is individuals who possess the virtues in question; moreover, the social entity to which they contribute is, qua liberal, one that exists to protect individuals' interests, particularly the individual interest in autonomy. Nonetheless, there is a strong strain of (American) patriotism here, where the individual has an obligation to display certain virtues, not principally for the direct contribution such virtues make to his or her wellbeing, but in order to sustain the state, understood not just as an instrument of human wellbeing, but as an end in itself. Thus, however liberal Galston's civic republicanism, it is nonetheless communitarian in its conception of value, where contributing to the flourishing of the state is expected of all citizens, and where the wellbeing of the state takes precedence over the interests of individuals.

A different concept of the public good emerges in the ideas of Hurka and Sher. Their concern for the character of society is not for a social whole whose importance transcends that of puny individuals. In fact, they have little interest in such communitarian ideas. Rather, they are concerned to foster excellence and thus with the question of how certain commonly held values shape the pursuits of individuals and the ways in which they live. Sher notes that if a public culture is 'crude, one-sided, or distorted, then our ability to recognise what goes on within and among people will be crude, one-sided, or distorted, too. And this cannot but diminish our ability to attain a whole range of fundamental goals.' Similarly, Hurka worries about the 'general, cultural loss' that comes from some talents not being developed. It is the impact of culture on the ability of individuals to live well that prompts him to suggest policies on behalf of culture, not the other way around.[13]

Of course, the preoccupation of Sher and Hurka with the living of excellent lives, though individualised, does not bear on the distribution of excellence, that it be equally or widely available. They are, in a sense, insufficiently attentive to the 'public' aspect of the public good. It is interesting, then, that it is the liberal Galston who, in his emphasis on liberal virtues, the purpose of which is the polity's wellbeing, tends to run afoul of liberal individualism, whilst it is the Aristotelians who, for all their objectivism about value and lack of interest in distributive justice, nonetheless focus on individual wellbeing. Both camps, however, are inadequate on egalitarian grounds: what is needed is a conception of the public good that makes clear its role in eliminating disadvantage that inhibits equal human flourishing.

In what follows, I will draw on the diverse senses of the public good to develop a concept that makes the public good's impact on individual persons paramount. This account is communitarian, but only insofar as the community is instrumental to human interests. Much liberal anxiety about the public good arises from a failure to appreciate the idea's potential to enable individual wellbeing. The public good is, I argue, properly construed as a precondition for the promotion of individuals' greater and more equal flourishing.

## The Public Good and Equal Citizens

The public good thus derives its value from its contribution to enabling individuals to live flourishing lives. It remains to be seen how it can help render individuals more equal. In what follows I elaborate on six considerations in which the public good has an egalitarian impact on human flourishing.

### Social Being

The first sense in which the public good enables equal flourishing is what in earlier chapters we have dubbed the social thesis, the obvious sense in which flourishing is predicated on social being. Human beings are social creatures, 'intersubjective' persons, as Sandel puts it.[14] To be a person requires social interaction, care and love from family members, education and acculturation, a social context and form of life that comes from the community.[15] As Aristotle famously puts it: 'he who is without a polis … is either a poor sort of being, or a being higher than a man.'[16] Society, and hence some kind of public, is thus a precondition for agency and individual integrity, for the development of human self-consciousness, even for rational life.[17]

Thus though individuals should be protected from social intrusions that threaten freedom, given our nature as social beings, the social is a necessary component of any account of human flourishing. This of course offers only a minimal sense in which equal flourishing and the public good are connected: the social thesis merely stipulates that the public good, in the sense of the good of our connection with the public domain, is a precondition for equal flourishing; it does not show how the public good will help us flourish equally.

### The Amelioration of Disadvantage in Social Life

The second consideration follows from the first and addresses more directly the principle of public provision of goods to ameliorate disadvantage. Earlier chapters have stressed that human flourishing is something about which there is a fact of the matter; chronic alcoholics are not flourishing, even if they claim to enjoy their freely chosen lives of drunkenness. Thus flourishing is not determined simply by people's preferences, even though self-determination and contentment are features of genuine flourishing. Flourishing is, as Appiah puts it, a 'more-than-want-regarding notion.' Moreover, flourishing involves improving, progressing: 'deferring to our current desires can only leave us as we are.'[18]

How can the public good, or public goods, contribute to flourishing? For starters, the community provides the good of the public realm itself, a common sphere of interpersonal engagement. There will be inherent public goods from which we all benefit; a society of tolerance, aesthetic apprecia-tion, civility, which enjoys low levels of pollution and high levels of health, is one in which all individuals are more likely to flourish. We also need social interaction, friendship, and community and there are disparities in these things, just as there are disparities in income. As we noted in previous chap-ters, it turns out that once essential material conditions obtain, the social dimensions to a person's life are more important than affluence in making a person content.[19] Some of us are disadvantaged in the capacity for social interaction and thus public provision of opportunities or support for social life constitutes a policy of equalisation. The state cannot find friends for the friendless, but a robust conception of the public good will involve an imagi-native approach to the problem of community in modern, complex societies, facilitating local communities, clubs, societies, public lectures, festivals, and so on, as well as attending to social handicaps and problems of alienation.

### The Public Good – Singular and Plural

As we have underscored in previous chapters, the diversity of valuable social opportunities underscores that flourishing, though objective, is not unitary. Given that flourishing can take many forms, the idea of a single public good may seem misleading. The public good consists of an array of public goods, spanning a range of, often incommensurable, sources of value. The pluralism of the public good is essential for it to perform an equalising role, not forcing everyone into the same mould, but enabling all to fulfil their diverse potentials.

Thus the egalitarian society will provide a whole complex of public goods, promoting social practices that aim to foster the flourishing of persons physic-ally, mentally and socially, which can be given the more general and abstract designation of 'the public good,' singular. On an egalitarian flourishing account, the public good refers to a common commitment to the background conditions for human flourishing which feature in the public domain. This complex of goods that make up the public good consist of some which are good for all and accessed by all (e.g. clean air), and others which may not be of interest to all (e.g. art exhibitions). Human beings benefit from a common commitment to diverse sources of human wellbeing. Thus the public good, far from an anti-individualistic communitarian abstraction, contributes to people's flourishing.

## Egalitarian Decision-Making

The public good has an equalising effect because it involves an emphasis on participation in public institutions. Citizens, whatever their means, can participate as equals in the definition and creation of public goods in order to promote equality. What constitutes the public good should be forged through public debate, rather than private market decisions; democracy, according to Hobhouse, 'founds the common interest on the common will.'[20] The good life is accountable to a democratic public, which can make decisions about, for example, how waterfronts might be developed, whether to build a theatre or a museum, the location of ice hockey rinks, public transit policy, and so on, in an open and transparent forum. Public goods include people, who together reflect on their common commitment on value, thereby countering trends of declining opportunities for social interaction in large, market societies.

Utilitarians and their critics have refined the idea of preference satisfaction with notions like higher pleasures,[21] informed desires,[22] global desires,[23] or an objective list of sources of wellbeing, in order to capture the idea of a higher, ethical interest.[24] Appiah humourously synthesises such views into the idea of a 'Maxi-me,' another version of oneself with full information and unimpaired reason.[25] Identifying what is good means going beyond people's actual desires, but to find institutional resources for genuine goods, we must return to the world of real people who, equipped with access to information, leisure and opportunities, are our only resource for making decisions. Moreover, respect for persons and the principle of autonomy means institutions should enable self-determination about questions of the good. The ideal of democracy gives us no other option but to rely on public deliberation. This does not rule out the delegation of public power to experts or those with special authority to help devise policy and advise elected representatives – e.g. arts councils, heritage committees, child welfare boards, etc. The public good gives authority nonetheless to the community as a whole to delineate the constituents of flourishing.

The public good necessitates transparency and accountability, rather than tradition or the authority of the wise, as is implied by some communitarian conceptions of the common good, and moreover, instead of leaving the provision of opportunities for flourishing to the contingent outcomes of mysterious market forces. As noted in earlier chapters, the market is seldom criticised for being paternalistic; on the contrary, it is often idealised for the array of choices it offers consumers. Yet the operations of the market are not subject to the conscious control of ordinary people. What to produce and where, the social relations of production, questions of sustainability and respect for the environment: these are just some of the relevant decisions of the private sector that are generally not subject to public accountability.

A process of community deliberation is inherent in the idea of the public good. It is a fair way of proceeding, but it is also the best way of approximating the idea of objective public goods, where we seek to identify the truly good, not just what is taken for good, in order to improve flourishing and render it more equal. Of course, the public can be mistaken, and what is taken for good can fail to map on to what is truly good.[26] Yet the idea of the public nonetheless carries with it an idea of going beyond the personal or private, contingent or subjective choice, in order to establish policies that must meet a test of legitimacy and are thus subject to justification.

### Public Provision of Sources of Wellbeing

The principle of egalitarian decision-making leads to another, about the egalitarian impact of public goods. The project of the welfare state has centred on mitigating economic disadvantage by establishing institutions in the public domain that contribute to flourishing. Public coffers finance social welfare, but social welfare is public in another important sense: it renders the sources of flourishing public in nature. Converting private goods into public goods has been pivotal to the modern egalitarian project: publicly provided social welfare rather than private charity, public medicine rather than private medicine, and public schools as opposed to private schools.

An important feature of many of these public goods is that they are available to all citizens in the form of universal programmes; they are not means tested and thus the economically advantaged and the disadvantaged have equal access to them. Many advocates of universal programmes have noted their salutary impact on equality.[27] Participation on the part of privileged persons – who are well educated, articulate, aware of their rights and how to press for them – means that the public good has effective advocates. Goods that are exclusively public and universal are likely to prosper if they are not in competition with the private sector for resources and commitment. Finally, universal public goods are superior to targeted goods because if all citizens make use of them they are without stigma and therefore ameliorate inequality more effectively.

This is not to conjure up the idea that the private domain is to be eliminated, as is the guardians' lot in Plato's *Republic*. So long as children are raised in families, the priorities of parents can still have a profound effect on individuals' life chances. It is undeniable that the institution of the family is a source of inequality. However, the family is also an important sphere of human wellbeing, and my argument does not propose that we do away with family life; despite the variety of childrearing abilities, children do well living with their parents.[28] Short of egregious neglect, we tend to assume that

parents are entitled to make choices that may diminish their children's prospects. Callan puts it, 'just because a particular option is educationally bad it
does not follow that parents have no right to choose it.' For example, coerc-
ing parents into providing music lessons to their talented children rather than
acquiring fancy cars seems to go against our understanding of the family as in
some sense an autonomous sphere (with certain limitations – e.g. if fancy cars
took precedence over feeding one's offspring).[29]

The public good is thus an essential remedy for the dilemma wherein families facilitate flourishing but do so unequally. Public goods can be deployed
to make available public options for flourishing to compensate for shortfalls in
the private options provided by families. At the height of the British welfare
state, for example, there was public provision of music lessons as well as competitive sports teams in schools, so that the curriculum provided musical and
athletic opportunities for children that mitigated disparities in parents' where-
withal or inclination. There has also been subsidised 'school dinners,' hot
meals at lunchtime to compensate for lack of nutrition at home but which are
consumed by all school children.[30] Though we would expect the egalitarian
flourishing society to have far less disparity among families, disparity is not
wholly eliminable. A common yet pluralistic understanding of flourishing,
which includes goods like literature, art, music, physical activity and nature,
can help people disadvantaged by family background by making these goods
widely available in social institutions, imposing negligible, if any, costs, in
non-intimidating and encouraging forms. The aspiration to a public conception of the good is both egalitarian and communitarian in ways that enable
individuals to flourish.

## A Community of Equals

Finally, the public good can serve egalitarian purposes by uniting us in community in such a way that we understand each other as fellows, comrades in a
common project, united in an ethos of equality. This may seem like an ambitious goal, given the diversity of any society. The centrifugal tendencies of
many multi-national and culturally diverse societies points to the difficulty of
enforcing national unity with an ambitious vision of national values.[31] Yet a
point frequently made throughout this book is that, contra neutralist liberals'
claims about the illegitimacy of substantive conceptions of value in the public
domain, liberal societies in fact deliberate about, and promote, the public
good. Moreover, also contra to the liberal neutralist view, we have affirmed
that such perfectionist efforts presuppose pluralism about the good. Benign
paternalism is manifest in the many ways in which public spending subsidises
the worthwhile – libraries, galleries, museums, or parks. These endeavours
can transcend the differences of culture, language and ethnicity that may
divide a society; they are thus valuable sources of social unity.

There is, after all, as we noted in Chapter 5, a deep connection between
the public good and national identity. National institutions are an obvious
framework for shared membership. Moreover, in conceptualising the public

good, national character will certainly affect how we understand the precise forms of human flourishing. Indeed, scholarship about justice is often ridden with nationalist assumptions: e.g. Sunstein's claim that people's interests involve 'a conception of political freedom having deep roots in the American constitutional tradition.'[32] Distinctive cultures, languages, customs and values are bound to shape the public good, even if human beings share fundamental interests regardless of nationality. Thus, aesthetic fulfilment is a universal feature of human flourishing, yet certain kinds of aesthetic pursuits will be favoured in one society, but of no interest in another.

Indeed, when it comes to actual instances of perfectionist policy-making, the national might not be particular or local enough. Considerations of well-being are particularly apt at the municipal level. Concern for human flourishing in all its diversity motivates support for parks, skating rinks, swimming pools, libraries, music festivals and craft fairs. Schools are community hubs and their properties recreational spaces, as well as places of education, and thus school closures raise all kinds of difficult questions about human well-being in local jurisdictions.[33] City councils regulate the affairs of municipalities in a variety of ways, be it zoning, licensing of businesses, controlling traffic, designating heritage properties, even regulating hotdog stands and taxis, all of which are done with an eye to the wellbeing of the urban community. It would be impossible to describe all this activity by local governments in terms of neutrality about the good; considerations of the constituents of living well are central to these decisions.

Neutralist liberals overlook the municipal level in their arguments against perfectionism, but local government is a striking example of the inevitability of perfectionism in public policy. That it does not attract controversy is interesting; perhaps it is because cities have limited coercive powers that liberals do not flinch at their prerogative to promote the good, however pluralistically and modestly. Or perhaps liberals are more confident of a consensus about the good at the local level than the national, where citizens have more in common and community seems more feasible. This is not to say that the public good can only be literally, local. After all, cities require provinces, states, and national governments for infrastructure, income, support and resources. Higher levels of government provide the conditions for local conceptions of the public good, and seek to shape and influence them. Nonetheless, local government is replete with instances of the politics of the public good.

## Exclusive Publics and Global Equality

I have argued that the project of making human flourishing more equal involves a conception of the public good. There may be doubts, however, about the compatibility of the idea of the public good with global equality, given the lack of equality in the global context, and scepticism about the prospect of a global consensus about the public good that might facilitate equality in many disadvantaged parts of the world. We began this chapter by noting that arbitrary advantage and disadvantage had a micro source in the family and a macro source in nationality. In the case of the private domain of families, a rich conception of the public can be an important antidote to the maldistribution of the constituents of flourishing, offsetting the poor resources, values and opportunities that some face simply in virtue of who their parents are.

However, mitigating that other source of arbitrary inequality, that of the society into which we are born – whether it is affluent or poor, just or unjust – is a different matter. The idea of the public good might seem to entrench the privileges of the lucky parts of the world, and do nothing for less fortunate societies. What is the fate of individuals who live in societies where ideas about the public good are distorted or atrophied, or limited in their accessibility – at odds with equality, rather than furthering equality of human flourishing?

If the public good is articulated only in a national context, within a circumscribed territory, the prospects for a global public good look bleak. This is particularly manifest in the arguments of some political theorists who emphasise the importance of one's particular national affiliation. Miller makes the case:

> Bearing a national identity means seeing oneself as part of a historic community which in part makes one the person that one is: to regard membership as something one has chosen is to give way to an untenable form of social atomism which first abstracts the individual from his or her social relationships and then supposes that those relationships can be explained as the voluntary choices of the individual thus abstracted.[34]

It is true that we may feel partiality for our co-nationals insofar as we share not just a common territory, but common institutions, values and history. Thus, as we noted in Chapter 5, it is argued that 'patriotic priority' or national partiality produces the social cement necessary for a people to identify egalitarian policy as part of a public to which they have a duty of contribution.[35] (It seems relevant that the provision of competitive sports in the English state school system centred on games such as cricket and football, important features of the English cultural identity.) It might well be the other way round, of course: social justice generates the solidarity that makes for compatriot preference.

Miller goes on to defend the idea of the nation in terms of its entitlement to 'compatriot preference' given that nations, their institutions and citizens, should be understood as primarily responsible for themselves, arguing against 'the cosmopolitan view that our responsibilities to the world's poor are in principle exactly the same as our responsibilities to our fellow-citizens.'[36] For Miller, though nations are responsible for wrongdoing to other nations, this follows from the special relationships within nations of 'identifying with compatriots, sharing their values, and receiving the benefits that national communities provide.'[37]

Considerations of justice suggest that the national complexion of the public good remains an arbitrary affair. Why should *these* people in particular, and *these* specific practices, be the locus of a person's concerns? Patriotism is fundamentally contingent – I could as well have ended up on the other side of the world and feel loyalty to another nation; indeed that is the experience of many immigrants. And why care for the many millions of one's fellow citizens with whom one shares no other relation than citizenship? We do not have face-to-face relations with foreign peoples, but nor do we have such relations with our fellow citizens.[38] Partiality is much more defensible when it comes to the family – swapping my son for another, perfectly serviceable object of affection is unthinkable, but there is no such impediment in the case of one's co-nationals, the identities of which, given patterns of immigration, do change. Nor does partiality seem at issue, therefore, in my swapping my support for a cause that affects the benefits of my fellow Canadians for one that benefits a different constituency.

A morality of preference for co-nationals thus seems a paltry justification for withholding from contributions to the have-nots elsewhere who are not fortunate enough to be within the ambit of our particular public good.[39] Tan contends, 'While cosmopolitanism must allow space for patriotism, it need not be expected to allow space for the entire range of conventional patriotism.'[40] Political philosophy should attend to the predilections of citizens, but they should not simply defer to them, particularly if it means licensing injustice. Calls for a 'careful balance' between nationalism and cosmopolitanism are thus salutary.[41]

Some have argued that the national community be jettisoned for a conception of international citizenship, taking the view that nations inevitably tend to be 'ethnarchies' whose territory marks an exclusive, but arbitrary, moral concern.[42] As we noted in Chapter 5, however, those societies with the most developed sense of a national community in the form of obligations to members by means of progressive social policy, ambitious programmes of socialised medicine, childcare, pensions and welfare entitlements, are also the nations with the most generous policies of foreign aid. Our elaboration of the public good as consisting in objective goods, genuine in some universal sense, essential to the flourishing of all human beings, should apply across borders. The egalitarian impulse that prompts the idea of the public good applies globally. Internationalist ideals underlay nationalist republicanism in its origins: the idea of national affiliation merging into 'wider moralities'[43] was at the heart of the nationalist ideals of Mazzini, for example, who envisaged the 'brotherhood of man' as the basis for the unification of Italians.[44]

Affirming the idea of a national community, therefore, need not entail rejecting the cosmopolitan view. It is a false polarity to say either we look after our own, or exhaust our resources to look after needy others beyond our borders. We look after the weak and vulnerable in our societies because of egalitarian principles that generate a sense of obligation, a conviction about our duties to fellow human beings that extends to those in need of care, within and beyond our borders. And a robust sense of the constituents of wellbeing that prompts us to go beyond biological need at the local level, to resource local libraries, swimming pools and parks, will also underwrite initiatives to provide the means of life abroad, be it clean drinking water, or again, more ambitiously, schools, libraries, and recreational facilities. Yes, the local contribution to conceptualising and applying the public good is challenging to translate into cosmopolitan terms. History leaves its mark; it shapes who we are, and it produces the institutions we cherish in our conception of the public good. But membership, though particular in its realisation, can be understood as something objectively worthwhile for all, and thus requiring the reallocation of global resources. As Mason argues, it is a generalisable value that we each should belong to, and participate in, the public life of particular communities.[45]

## Global Public Goods

The idea of 'global public goods' has been developed in the field of international relations to address problems of distributive justice among peoples. In this context, global public goods are defined as 'outcomes that tend toward universality in the sense that they benefit all countries, population groups and generations.'[46] The idea's premiss is that people in advantaged countries are obligated to consider the impact of their activities on less advantaged parts of the world. There are public goods that people in other countries can enjoy without contributing to their cost, but also public bads, cases of negative externalities, where the costs of goods are distributed beyond national borders.

The vulnerability of public goods to under-provision, where people are reluctant to provide goods that others can enjoy without cost, is exacerbated at the international level, given that the effects of externalities can be both remote and profound. In an interconnected world, the benefits and burdens of public goods extend far beyond those who initiated them. Theorists of international justice are concerned about maintaining the provision of global public goods when the drive to privatisation renders universal goods more vulnerable. Sen argues that global public goods – the product of exchange and interdependence in a variety of economic and social spheres – compel us to reject conceiving justice in the naïve terms of a grand universalism where borders and territory are irrelevant. But nor can we opt for a national particularism that is merely supplemented by international relations, where justice is the province of national states, or at most, national states in concert. A global focus underscores how human beings have plural affiliations or multiple identities that criss-cross nations, territories and generations.[47]

Once we see how pursuits conducive to human flourishing are valuable to people outside of our compatriot identity, we can understand how we are morally required to share our advantages with those beyond our borders. This emerges with the idea of a 'rooted cosmopolitanism' whereby we qualify our patriotism with cosmopolitan obligations, so that affect for the local can generate duty to the global,[48] and so our local practices meet some cosmopolitan criterion of value, relevant, in a rudimentary way at least, to the amelioration of disadvantage in other societies.

Global public goods take controversial forms: free trade regimes, systems of knowledge, financial markets, environmental protection and public health, peace and security. One might expect anti-perfectionist assumptions to guide these discussions, in which the content of global public goods is assumed to be largely instrumental, supplying only the background conditions – economic, environmental and social – necessary for individuals to make choices about how to live, without seeking to influence those choices. However, interestingly the largely economics literature does not rule out the idea of common sources of human flourishing, referring to both instrumental and intrinsic goods without much differentiation. For example, in Samuelson's classic formulation, public goods encompass both national defence and outdoor circuses.[49] Perhaps economists do not sweat over the perfectionist issue: what is good is merely a matter of what garners market demand or citizens' support; its public character is not a value question, but a matter of the structure of the good and how it is accessed. Further, qualms about paternalism might not be relevant in a context where individuals freely partake of a good, not at the behest of the provider of the good, but rather, oftentimes contrary to the provider's wishes, who feels cheated by free riders who consume the good without contributing to its cost. Thus economists take for granted that public goods match the preferences of consumers without agonising over the character of choice formation or people's real interests.[50]

Although the economics literature does not explore, let alone argue for, the perfectionist aspects of the concept of global public goods, they are evident in international cultural policies. Under the aegis of the UNESCO World Heritage Sites, a variety of historic locations, ranging from the streets and canals of Venice, to the Alhambra palace in Granada, to the Rideau Canal system of Eastern Ontario, are deemed valuable and to be protected. They exemplify the qualities of global public goods, where the costs of conservation are local but the benefits are global. When cultural artefacts – buildings, works of art, books, treasures – are vandalised or destroyed, it counts as a form of cultural genocide with universal adverse consequences, a loss for humanity as a whole (e.g. the Taliban's destruction of ancient Buddha statues in Afghanistan, the Nazis' burning of 'decadent' art, the looting of museums during civil wars).[51] The case for a global commitment to the preservation of such goods relies on a flourishing account of value, where the products of human creativity are goods that are a source of wellbeing for all peoples, to be maintained to enable broad access to their benefits. Cultural heritage is said to be 'an end in itself' that 'enriches' and 'empowers' people. Even if heritage buildings could be replaced with an attraction that would generate more visitors or more wealth, such a move would be neither justified nor desirable: 'We must look for the intrinsic value of the cultural heritage above and beyond what it is likely to generate in terms of tourist dollars.'[52] This means an unabashed defence of the objective value of historic architecture, monuments, parks, museums and galleries.

Environmental economics has pioneered this way of thinking about public goods. Although clean air is a means to more substantive ends, other environmental goods such as green spaces and biodiversity must be articulated in terms of their non-instrumental, intrinsic value, to be conserved against forces to exploit and destroy them. Cited criteria include such ideas as 'nonextractive use value,' 'aesthetic value,' 'recreational value,' or 'option value,' that is, the value from 'maintaining the option of taking advantage of a site's use value,' or even more extravagantly, 'nonuse value,' the value 'that people derive from the knowledge that the site exists, even if they never plan to visit it.'[53] The idea of the public good is helpful in extending our outlook beyond our compatriots in that it fixes on the constituents of wellbeing, context-dependent but also universal in value and, ideally, open to all. Have-not peoples suffer deficits in wellbeing not just because of physical brutality or economic deprivation. Economic deprivation is often a root cause of lack of wellbeing in other domains, but disadvantage cannot be understood solely in terms of income. Have-not peoples are also worse off because they lack cultural and social sources of wellbeing; they may be illiterate or ill-educated, without leisure or culture, isolated or alienated.

Discussions of global justice seldom focus on the ways in which a society acculturates its citizens through policies relating to physical and mental health, opportunities for culture, and so on. Rather, the literature alights on disparities in income or wealth, or extreme forms of degradation such as the violation of human rights. The ways in which cultural privilege is transmitted are well known in the literature about families, but not much discussed in the context of global justice, where the literature tends to concentrate on transfers of wealth and the import of liberal freedoms, or institutions of democracy. The latter is manifest in the civic republican tradition that centres on acculturating individuals to become better citizens, displaying liberal virtues of tolerance and autonomy, helping to sustain a free and democratic order: ensuring that citizens have, as Skinner maintains, 'the capacities that enable us willingly to serve the common good, thereby to uphold the freedom of our community, and in consequence to ensure its rise to greatness as well as our own individual liberty.'[54] Liberal philosophers interested in public education and democracy also zero in on the instrumental value of literate, autonomous and cultured citizens, who have 'the ability to deliberate, and hence to participate, in conscious social reproduction,'[55] a theme in the statist communitarian views we surveyed earlier in this chapter.

These instrumental versions suit a foreign policy bent on stability, wherein liberal democratic institutions are exported to disadvantaged (and politically extremist and terror-prone) parts of the world. Such a policy improves institutions in the affected countries, but it also furthers the interests of Western societies who seek security in relations with hostile, authoritarian powers. The task is not easy, and thus democracy is often at the centre of acrimonious and violent military conflict. The irony of imposing democracy through force has not been lost on many commentators (and, sadly, not just commentators). Building democracy is hardly likely to succeed unless it is part of a general project of enabling people in their own projects to become self-developing, seeking to increase their own levels of flourishing.

It may be wise to separate the project of democratisation from that of the constituents of wellbeing sought by cosmopolitan justice. This is not because the two are unrelated: it is clear that democratic participation is a feature of wellbeing and that democratic participation can be, as Sen argues, a promising route to wellbeing's achievement.[56] But though the idea of the public good does not forswear democratisation, it should take its chief task to be inherently individualistic and focussed on the flourishing of persons. That is, the public good should be oriented to furthering the wellbeing of individuals who, as an aggregate, contribute to, and partake of, the public good. To this end, the concept, however universal in its basic constituents, must be particularised contextually in order to tackle the wellbeing or flourishing of particular peoples so that an ambitious programme of global equality comes into view that concerns itself with wealth and civil liberties, but also other, often neglected, constituents of human flourishing. Once social justice is broadened beyond borders and beyond income to focus on global public goods, it can generate international commitments that rival the loyalty of co-nationals, but also help to thwart the pernicious counter-enlightenment ideologies spreading around the world today.

Whether or not this sense of a general humanity can generate a universal political order, with representative institutions, rights of citizenship and voting, remains to be seen. There are many ways in which the larger setting threatens to replicate the worst shortcomings of the national – voter apathy, excessive bureaucracy, and so forth – and it seems unlikely that the shortcomings of national citizens will be corrected at the global level. Some European cosmopolitans have been hopeful,[57] drawing on the example of the European Union, where national identity must jostle with a pan-national identity. The European model has an impressive record of commitment to foreign aid, but it has not won the hearts and minds of its electoral body. With voter turnout ever declining, 42.54 per cent, in 2014,[58] the idea of a political entity beyond the nation that commands allegiance from diverse peoples is a hard sell, manifest in the 'exit' sympathies of a range of Europeans, from British Tories to Greek Marxists. The legitimacy of a European polity that might override the decisions of a democratically elected national government, be it Brussels's austerity dictates or regulation of cheese, has prompted a call for reaffirming national sovereignty, evident in the recent Brexit referendum victory. The project of global distributive justice and global public goods is best not tethered to an ambitious project of global democracy. Nonetheless, global human flourishing requires the building of institutions that both respect local decision-making and facilitate international cooperation.

## Conclusion

I have defended the idea of the public good as central to a conception of equality that seeks to minimise disparities in human flourishing. We should not be squeamish when confronting the idea of the public good; properly understood, it is neither metaphysically peculiar nor politically conservative. The public good refers to features of a society that are provided by the community, collective in their conceptualisation and provision, yet essential to individual wellbeing. In an egalitarian theory, the public good consists of a myriad of particular goods that improve individuals' lives. What is shared of the public good will be some, if not all of: the common understanding of its value, the good's source in our public institutions, its indivisible character, its open access, and the shared conception of its ideals. The raison d'etre of the public good, however, must ultimately be the actual enjoyment of individuals of the constituents of human flourishing.

A conception of egalitarian human flourishing relies on a commitment to the idea of the public good that is universal in scope and application yet also, and inevitably, capable of accommodating the customs and practices of a particular community. As such it is able to counter the myopia of a self-regarding patriotism, in order to generate global obligations, whilst allowing for the self-governance of disadvantaged countries in their efforts to eliminate inequality. The public good is an important feature of the project of egalitarian human flourishing and its power is such that it is pivotal to the realisation of the egalitarian ideal, both locally and globally. In the next chapter we will consider more closely the challenge of cosmopolitan duties for a theory of egalitarian human flourishing.

## Notes

1 Mill, 'On Liberty,' 6.
2 Raz, *Morality of Freedom*, 198.
3 Ibid., 200–1.
4 Ibid., 199.
5 Sandel, *Liberalism and the Limits of Justice*.
6 J. Rawls, 'Justice as Fairness: Political Not Metaphysical.'
7 J.-J. Rousseau, 'The Social Contract,' 185.
8 Taylor, 'The Politics of Recognition.'
9 A. Weale, 'Public Interest,' 725.
10 Hurka, *Perfectionism*, 168.
11 Sher, *Beyond Neutrality*, 212.
12 Galston, *Liberal Purposes*, 289.
13 Sher, *Beyond Neutrality*, 213–14; Hurka, *Perfectionism*, 168.
14 Sandel, *Liberalism and the Limits of Justice*, 62.
15 Otherwise we are little more than animals, as tales of abandoned children suggest. See H. Lane, *The Wild Boy of Aveyron*, L. Malson and J. Itard, *Wolf Children and The Wild Boy of Aveyron*.
16 Aristotle, *Politics*, 5.
17 See Bakhurst, *The Formation of Reason*, 8.
18 Appiah, *The Ethics of Identity*, 157.
19 See the works in 'happiness studies' listed in Chapter 7, note 76.
20 Hobhouse, *Liberalism*, 116.
21 Mill, 'Utilitarianism,' ch. 2.
22 C. Sunstein, 'Preferences and Politics,' 12.
23 Griffin, *Wellbeing*, 147.

24 D. Parfit, *Reasons and Persons*, 497–9.

25 Appiah, *Ethics of Identity*, 175.

26 Rousseau makes this point about the general will.

27 B. Rothstein and E.M. Uslaner, 'All for One: Equality, Corruption and Social Trust.'

28 Brighouse and Swift, *Family Values*, 96–7.

29 E. Callan, *Creating Citizens*, 203–4.

30 I am grateful to David Bakhurst for supplying me with this example based on his experience growing up in London in the 1960s and 70s. These policies have ebbed and flowed since then: L. Tickle and A. Bawden, 'Cuts could serve up an end to free healthy school dinners for infants.'

31 See K. McRoberts, *Misconceiving Canada: The Struggle for National Unity*, especially ch. 10.

32 C. Sunstein, 'Preferences and Politics,' 13. A striking example of American-ness in the discussion of values and patriotism is the collection, J. Cohen, ed., *For Love of Country*.

33 Where I live the unsuccessful campaign to save Kingston Collegiate, our downtown high school and the oldest in Ontario, centred on, not just children's education, but also the school's contribution to community life.

34 Miller, *On Nationality*, 59–60. Miller goes so far as to conclude that the religious architecture of minority groups should be prohibited: 'Majorities and Minarets: Religious Freedom and Public Space.'

35 Ibid., 70–2. See also R. Miller, 'Cosmopolitan Respect and Patriotic Concern,' C. Wellman, 'Relational Facts in Liberal Political Theory: Is there Magic in the Pronoun "My"?,' C. Taylor, 'Why Democracy Needs Patriotism.'

36 D. Miller, *National Responsibility and Global Justice*, 231.

37 Ibid., 265.

38 Appiah, *The Ethics of Identity*, 216.

39 C. Jones, *Global Justice*, 170.

40 K.C. Tan, *Justice without Borders: Cosmopolitanism, Nationalism and Patriotism*, 145.

41 J. Couture and K. Nielsen, 'Cosmopolitanism and the Compatriot Priority Principle,' 193.

42 See D. Kostakopoulou, *The Future Governance of Citizenship*, 196–8.

43 Ibid., 200.

44 G. Mazzini, 'Europe: Its Condition and Prospects,' 266.

45 A. Mason, 'Special Obligations to Compatriots,' *Ethics*, 107, 1997.

46 I. Kaul, I. Grunberg and M.A. Stern, 'Defining Global Public Goods,' 16.

47 A. Sen, 'Global Justice: Beyond International Equity,' 120.

48 See Appiah, *Ethics of Identity*, ch. 6 and Couture and Nielsen, 'Cosmopolitanism and the Compatriot Priority Principle.'

49 P. Samuelson, 'Diagrammatic Exposition of a Theory of Public Expenditure.'

50 M. Desai, 'Public Goods: A Historical Perspective.'

51 R. Lemkin coined the term 'genocide' and applied it to the killing of human beings, but also the destruction of their culture, including artefacts. See his *Axis Rule in Occupied Europe: Occupation, Analysis of Government, Proposals for Redress*. See also D. Nersessian, 'Rethinking Cultural Genocide Under International Law,' R. Bevan, *The Destruction of Memory: Architecture at War*.

52 I. Serageldin, 'Cultural Heritage as Public Good: Economic Analysis Applied to Historic Cities,' 241.

53 Ibid., 245–6.

54 Q. Skinner, 'The Paradoxes of Political Liberty,' 197.

55 A. Gutmann, *Democratic Education*, 46.

56 Sen, *Development as Freedom*.

57 D. Archibugi, *The Global Commonwealth of Citizens: Toward Cosmopolitan Democracies*.

58 Compared to 62 per cent in 1979 when the EU was established; see Euractive. com, 'It's official: Last EU election had lowest-ever turnout.'

# 10 Cosmopolitans, Cosmopolitanism and Human Flourishing

Debates about equality tend to take as their context the relations among citizens in a single society. Yet as we noted in the last chapter, problems of inequality obviously go beyond a particular territory or country. The equality gaps that concern us are no longer, as they were a hundred years ago, only between rich and poor persons within a country, but also between rich and poor peoples: problems of inequality are most egregious between the 'haves' and 'have-nots' in the international context. And yet we lack the capacity to redress global injustice: institutional resources, human motivation and the concepts of political philosophy all tend to presume the predominance of the nation-state paradigm. As one prominent commentator puts it, 'liberal goals are achieved in a liberalised societal culture or nation.'[1] Thus perhaps the toughest test of an egalitarian theory is what it can contribute to the promotion of equality, not among citizens, but around the globe.

Few egalitarians would dispute that richer peoples have duties of redistribution to poorer peoples. The question is the extent of these duties of global justice, particularly in comparison to the duties of domestic justice. Consider the following example. Suppose an Englishman is on holiday in Spain. Walking along a deserted beach, he hears the voices of two men, crying out from the sea. 'Help! For Gawd's sake, help!' is one. 'Aidez-moi! Mon dieu, aidez-moi!' is the other. Two men are drowning and begging for assistance, but our Englishman fears he cannot save them both. Would the demands of 'compatriot preference' dictate that he should save his fellow Englishman and allow the Frenchman to drown?[2] This seems a despicable conclusion. Yet most people would agree that nationality is the basis for a sense of connection that generates special obligations with the result that one's co-nationals, particularly disadvantaged co-nationals, come first. The policy of looking out for one's own is bolstered by the view that the distant disadvantaged are better served if they are left to help themselves, a policy that respects their capacity for self-determination. Others argue that nationality is arbitrary and that there is no reason why an adequate egalitarian theory should not be global in scope, with no regard for borders or territory.

In the face of this difficult tension, I argue in this chapter that the human flourishing approach can illuminate problems of international justice. Last chapter we noted how the concept of the public good had global application.

Here I zero in on human flourishing's role in remedying global inequality. Focusing on rendering human flourishing more equal will enable us to find a middle course, which affirms our cosmopolitan duties whilst recognising the inevitable and valuable role of a culture of self-determining citizenship. If we are to make human beings in the world more equal, then we must consider how cultural practices affect human flourishing.

## Cosmopolitanism v. Cosmopolitans

The idea that individuals and nations have obligations of justice to non-nationals has been dubbed 'cosmopolitanism.' The history of this word makes it a rather curious choice. In the past, to be cosmopolitan was to be a certain kind of person marked by diverse cultural influences. The term could imply either praise or denigration. On the one hand, cosmopolitanism was a form of privilege, connoting the well travelled and culturally sophisticated, contrasted with the provincial and naïve; cosmopolitanism was an admirable but perhaps elite aesthetic. On the other hand, the cosmopolitan was also the target of xenophobia, disrespect, mistrust, even racism. Cosmopolitans were regarded as foreign, 'dirty,' and decadent, associated with Jews or 'Bolsheviks,' whom bigots sought to exclude.[3]

The cosmopolitanism of global justice, in contrast, is an ethical perspective. The current usage builds on the word's etymology, 'kosmos,' meaning world or universe, and 'polis,' meaning state, conjoined to refer to a global state that would institutionalise an international moral order. This kind of cosmopolitanism has a certain political cast, affirming a concern for the wellbeing of persons outside one's milieu in a spirit of indifference towards their particular cultural practices. Prejudice has no part of contemporary cosmopolitanism, but nor does enthusiasm for the exotic. As Jones puts it, cosmopolitanism is a moral perspective that is impartial, universal, individualist and egalitarian, the fundamental idea of which is that 'every human being has a right to have her or his vital interest met, regardless of nationality or citizenship.'[4]

This is a contrast between what might be dubbed cultural worldliness and moral worldliness, the former interested in the distinctive contributions of different cultures, the latter interested in moral duties to persons irrespective of cultures. The two are often muddied in current debates among political philosophers, however, since defences of cosmopolitanism often refer both to the aesthetic ideal of a 'citizen of the world' who savours cultural diversity, and the moral ideal of international obligations. Thus in a critique of nationalism, Waldron appeals to 'the cosmopolitan self' who lives a 'freewheeling cosmopolitan life' in which he or she 'learns Spanish, eats Chinese, wears clothes made in Korea, listens to arias by Verdi sung by a Maori princess on Japanese equipment, follows Ukrainian politics, and practices Buddhist meditation techniques.'[5]

For Waldron, such a conception of the person is better able to respect the autonomy of the individual who can choose and revise how to live, irrespective of ethnicity or nationality. But not just personal freedom is at stake;

Waldron also implies a cosmopolitan ethic is an antidote to the 'cultural exclusiveness' and 'ethnic sectarianism' which have produced global injustice.[6] Elsewhere, liberal political philosophers have drawn on this ideal of the cosmopolitan self to make an argument for international justice. Thus Appiah refers to the 'cosmopolitan patriot' who is attached to home, but takes 'pleasure from the presence of other, different places that are home to other, different people.' Such a perspective also produces a commitment to the 'equal dignity of all persons' and 'the notion of human rights – rights possessed by human beings as such.'[7]

There are some genuine tensions, however, between the cosmopolitan aesthetic and cosmopolitan ethics, or cultural worldliness and moral worldliness. First, the beautiful and the moral are not the same thing, and indeed there is always the potential for a conflict between the two. Beautiful things can be the result of unjust arrangements, and thus the values of cultural worldliness will sometimes be at odds with those of moral worldliness. (Consider the child labour that produces splendid Oriental carpets.) The cosmopolitan person's enthusiasm for cultural creations might involve a certain indifference to the circumstances of their origin. Cosmopolitan ethics, in contrast, insists on the priority of justice, regardless of aesthetic considerations, and perhaps at their cost.

A second difference is thus the attitude to difference itself. Whereas neither perspective is one of loyalty to one's own, the cosmopolitan aesthete enjoys diversity; the cosmopolitan ethicist, on the other hand, calls for a universal standard. Finally, a third difference is each position's relation to inequality. It might be noted that the cosmopolitan is typically a privileged person, who has access to foreign travel, some knowledge of art and the means for enjoying it, who possesses sophisticated tastes and a cultivated, open mind. This is evident in the enthusiastic endorsement of cultural worldliness on the part of what must be admitted are relatively privileged persons, usually from relatively privileged societies: e.g. academics, who have opportunities for the cosmopolitan way of life that most people lack. And those who express mistrust of cosmopolitanism, however bigoted and pernicious their views, might well be giving expression to a resentment of cultural inequality that is spawned by unjust material inequality.

The cosmopolitan mode of life thus seems awkwardly paired with cosmopolitan justice. Moral worldliness seeks the mitigation, if not elimination, of disparities of wealth; instead of being the fruit of disadvantage, it seeks to be its antidote. The fact that people in wealthy parts of the world enjoy a high standard of living whilst people in poor parts of the world can barely survive is denounced as morally repugnant. And thus those of us who lead cosmopolitan lives are obligated to share our wealth with those parts of the world in which we take a cosmopolitan interest. In light of all this, global justice is perhaps poorly described as a 'cosmopolitan' position, given the long association the term has with positions of privilege.

Might, however, the morally worldly need some kind of cultural worldliness? That is, does the pursuit of global justice require a focus on the constituents of human flourishing, constituents that involve precisely those matters of cultural value emphasised by the cultural cosmopolitan? I believe that the current usage of cosmopolitanism as a moral perspective in fact requires some recourse to the original, non-pejorative idea of cosmopolitanism as a mode of life; global justice involves some idea of cultural evaluation. In what follows I will argue that current arguments for moral worldliness must in fact resort to cultural worldliness.

## Global Egalitarianism

Rawls's theory of justice has been an important inspiration for theories of global equality. Recall that *A Theory of Justice* argues for the redistribution of wealth in light of the arbitrariness of circumstances that determine one's level of advantage. This is captured with the thought experiment of the original position, where behind a 'veil of ignorance,' I do not know what kind of person I will be in the society I am designing, and thus self-interest dictates I come up with principles of justice that protect the worst off. As we saw in the last chapter, the idea that levels of wealth and resources are the result of arbitrary and undeserved factors seems ideal for capturing the contingency of being born with one citizenship or another, and the consequent impact this can have on one's material position.[8]

Indeed, it might be suggested that Rawls's theory works best on the international stage. After all, in the context of a single, affluent national polity, the idea that my ability to be wealthy or poor is the unmerited byproduct of a 'natural lottery' is vulnerable to a variety of objections derived from concepts of free will, desert and responsibility. But to be born in a poorly governed, drought-stricken and impoverished country as opposed to an affluent liberal democracy truly does seem to be a matter of plum bad luck. As Brighouse puts it: 'National membership is for the most part morally arbitrary. We did not choose our nationality from a range of serious options any more than we chose our race or sex, or the class position of our parents.'[9] Pogge notes that the past fifty years have

> culminated in unprecedented economic inequality between the most affluent tenth of humankind and the poorest fifth. What makes this huge and steadily growing inequality a monstrosity, morally, is the fact that the global poor are also so incredibly poor in absolute terms. They lack secure access to food, safe water, clothing, shelter, basic education and they are also highly vulnerable to being deprived of the objects of their civil and political human rights by their governments as well as by private agents. Some 18 million of them die prematurely every year.[10]

Thus many theorists of international justice have applied Rawls's arguments to the problem of global inequality. Some global egalitarians go so far as to defend a 'global difference principle' in which inequalities between human beings across the globe are only justified if the worst off benefit, thus calling for a dramatic redistribution of wealth from the haves to the have-nots.[11]

Rawls himself, however, resists such radical global interpretations of his argument. In *The Law of Peoples*, he contrasts his position with that of cosmo-politans who take national boundaries to have no mitigating effect on efforts at distributive justice. Rawls counsels respect for national diversity: societies, their institutions, values and policies, are various and not all societies can be reasonably expected to accept any liberal principle of distributive justice. He insists that in the global context, our measure should not be a 'global egalit-arian principle' but rather a mere 'duty of assistance'; our target is not to engi-neer equality but rather to 'assist burdened countries to become full members of the Society of Peoples and to be able to determine the path of their own future for themselves.' The duty of humanitarian assistance is restricted as a 'principle of transition' that takes as its aim improvements in the management of the disadvantaged country's economy.[12]

These three principles: a duty of assistance rather than strict egalitarian principle; aid towards full membership in a global community rather than global equality; and a posture of transition rather than longstanding com-mitment, have attracted considerable controversy. For many egalitarians, Rawls's global principles betray the ideals of his original theory of justice. Tan laments that whereas Rawls finds an individual's lot arbitrary in the domestic arena, in international politics, Rawls assumes a communal unit of analysis, forcing individuals to shoulder the burden of their country's lot. In effect, individuals are held accountable for their country's inadequate domestic policies, whether or not they played a role in formulating them.[13] Rawls thus ends up retracting his egalitarianism, lowering his sights in the global context and leaving inequality intact within societies other than his own as well as the inequality between his society and others.[14]

There are some obvious obstacles to exporting Rawls's principles of justice to other disadvantaged peoples. One difficulty is the identity of the relevant parties. Are the haves and have-nots individuals or nations? Given that some have-not nations possess pockets of great affluence, affluence that in some cases surpasses that of the well off in have nations, it is uncertain who should contribute to whom. Thus Rawls's concern that nations pull themselves up by their own bootstraps responds in part to the problem of internal mal-distribution. Holding countries responsible for their own distributive woes is a way of dealing with the complexity of whom to target in trying to equalise global wealth. Moreover, remedy for the maldistribution of wealth within a country is a burden that may be infeasible for third parties to shoulder; it is perhaps also unfair to expect them to do so. Nonetheless, Rawls's argument has the paradoxical upshot that individuals in poor countries who are far worse off than the worst off in his own country are entitled to less, not more, amelioration.

How might we resolve this stalemate about the ambitions of global justice? The root of the difficulty, I contend, is Rawls's metric of primary goods. Rawls's difference principle seeks to attend to the worst off's share of primary goods that include such things as wealth, income and property. On the one hand, this metric is mobile and easily redistributed globally. Hence radical global Rawlsians have no difficulty envisaging ambitious reallocations of resources from the rich to the poor. On the other hand, there is great uncertainty about the effect of such redistribution. After all, as I have argued, people's ability to live well depends on more than just access to goods. How they acquire the goods and what they do with them are also crucial in determining how well they live. There are cultural factors here that the cosmopolitan person's more strongly evaluative, cultural approach can help identity. Thus our criterion of human flourishing can enable a more perspicuous debate about the extent of egalitarian obligations on a global scale.

## Equality of What and for Whom

We have seen that there are two issues pertaining to the problem of how we should conceive of equality in the international arena. The first is what metric should be used to measure inequality and its amelioration. This is the problem of 'equality of what,' which is acutely difficult to answer in the global context, where people vary so much in their circumstances and interests. Another tough issue is the extent of equality; that is, how far our equalising policies should extend, and how ambitious they should be. Here again we confront a challenge that is all the greater when situated in the international arena, where the disparities are so overwhelming and the task of remedy seems almost infinite. Let us first address the question of what to equalise.

It is instructive that Sen's call for a shift in focus in egalitarian argument to the criterion of capabilities was launched in the context of impoverished societies outside the Western liberal democratic, capitalist framework.[15] We noted in Chapter 7 how one rival approach, equality of welfare, which centres on experiential states or the satisfaction of preferences, has the advantage of focusing on the subjective impact of redistribution. How the person fares with their allocation of goods, their level of satisfaction or contentment, certainly seems a relevant consideration in the matter of equality. However, welfarism suffers from taking people's ambitions at face value. People's preferences and plans of life can take the shape that they do precisely because of the distorting effects of unequal distribution. 'The extent of a person's deprivation, then, may not at all show up in the metric of desire-fulfilment, even though he or she may be quite unable to be adequately nourished, decently clothed, minimally educated and properly sheltered.'[16]

This problem is manifest in attitudinal comparisons on a global scale, between the materially advantaged in a society of hyper-consumerism, alienation and neurosis, which can indicate a shortfall in welfare, compared to the materially disadvantaged in the close-knit and protective community who are happy with little.[17] On the other hand, a resources or goods approach, though it has the advantage of seeking a fair distribution of wealth regardless of people's preferences, suffers from an inability to attend to the particularities of the source and effect of inequality. Focusing on equitable shares of goods fails to take account that 'what goods do for people' will be subject to enormous variation because of differing circumstances in how people live. These circumstances are personal, social and environmental. They include nutritional needs, disease and disability; location and the attendant physical factors of climate, famine, and natural disasters; as well as the cultural impact of location in the form of norms, customs and expectations, gender relations or family structure.[18]

It should be apparent that these considerations are particularly relevant when comparing the position of persons globally. An interpersonal comparison of capabilities that allows for contextual factors has a paradoxical effect on the demands of redistribution in the international context. On the one hand there are grounds for making significant redistributions in order to take account of the serious shortfall in capabilities that results from the particular circumstances of deprived persons in developing countries. Yet on the other hand it is true that the developing context might have a more modest minimum to achieve the same level of capabilities. Sen notes when considering the effect of 'social exclusion' on human capabilities:

> The need to take part in the life of a community may induce demands for modern equipment (televisions, videocassette recorders, automobiles and so on) in a country where such facilities are more or less universal (unlike what would be needed in less affluent countries), and thus imposes a strain on a relatively poor person in a rich country even when that person is at a much higher level of income compared with people in less opulent countries.[19]

Sen stresses how, compared to a goods approach, his metric of capabilities can pinpoint precisely what is at issue when diverse people are poor.

We have seen in earlier chapters how the human flourishing approach takes a more radical stand than does Sen on the question of the neutralism of schemas such as Rawls's. Instead of capability or opportunity for flourishing, my focus is on flourishing or wellbeing itself, a partly objective, partly subjective measure. It is apparent that poverty is significant because of the impoverishment of wellbeing that it produces. We need to consider the universal constituents of human flourishing, particularly in cases of global justice, in order to understand our global obligations to those leading lesser lives.

This book has identified the constituents of flourishing as autonomy, worthwhile pursuits and personal contentment – suggesting an ambitious approach to equality, where wellbeing is understood to involve more than just the physical means of life. People need the basic necessities such as food, shelter, and health, but they also need social and cultural goods, education, leisure, friendship and love. The ideal of active engagement with the world, creative labour and social interaction, as conceived by socialists such as Morris, are vital aspects of wellbeing even if mere survival does not depend on them. As we saw, human flourishing itself cannot always be equalised. In the global context it is particularly obvious that whether one person is flourishing or not will depend on the conditions in which they live – adequate provision of material resources, health, education, access to culture, nature and leisure. Some conditions, though vital to living well, can only be fostered by political measures, not provided by them. For example, it is probably fair to say that the most important factor in determining whether people flourish, besides having enough to eat, is the presence of friendship and love in their lives. But these cannot be guaranteed by state policy, though I have suggested that providing opportunities for fellowship is not beyond the purview of public policy. People's personalities, however, are not wholly the province of social mitigation.

Another legitimate kind of variation in flourishing is cultural. Here we should deploy the cultural cosmopolitan's criteria of value, sensitive to cultural difference yet convinced of universal norms that can be applied to different cultures. The attention to context is to be distinguished from a relativism that eschews the possibility of an objective understanding of flourishing in the first place. One should defer to local standards where they pose a genuine framework for wellbeing, but the ideal of flourishing nonetheless involves certain objective features. The idea of universal constituents of human flourishing requires that we not simply acquiesce to the local, since it may be that local practices contribute to shortfalls in flourishing. For example, agencies such as Oxfam focus on development projects where women are trained in new skills and acquire new capacities of self-determination in order to lead small-scale economic enterprises that respond to needs in their communities. This is an illustration of how the ideal of flourishing can serve to elevate and extend local understandings, rather than be cowed by them. Thus although the actualisation of flourishing will be shaped by the practices of a particular community, the constituents of flourishing are universal. The concept of flourishing thus must both have recourse to local norms as well as being prepared to transcend them.

We are thus concerned to ensure, as much as possible, that people actually exercise their capabilities. Egalitarian policy may have to settle for aspiring to equalise the conditions of flourishing, but the extent to which this aim is realised will be assessed, in considerable part, by whether people actually flourish. Thus I have insisted throughout this book that we cannot be content with an emphasis on the potential to flourish. Although the social conditions of flourishing are most amenable to political change, we aspire to create those conditions precisely so that people should flourish and the measure of our success in so doing must be an increase in actual flourishing.

In the global context, where a history of deprivation can condition one's choices, egalitarians should be especially wary of lowering their sights to the mere availability of possibilities for human flourishing, rather than flourishing per se. I have noted that even if conditions are improved, the effects of disadvantage can be long lasting. A culture of low expectations and fatalism about life prospects can persist across generations long after the original disadvantaging conditions have been ameliorated. Cultural conditions can build upon material conditions so that remedying the latter, the original source of disadvantage, might not improve disadvantaged persons' levels of flourishing.[20] It is important that we attend to flourishing itself to ensure that there are not additional measures that must be taken to encourage people to take advantage of conditions conducive to flourishing.

## Flourishing Providers

The emphasis on human flourishing is also an important corrective to the welfare and resources metrics from the point of view of those who are giving aid to the disadvantaged in far-flung corners of the globe. Merely handing over resources will be an unsatisfactory method of meeting one's global egalitarian obligations. Donors will want to see the effects of their contributions on the wellbeing of disadvantaged persons. From the point of view of outsiders concerned about the effect of aid, the standard of satisfying preferences will be of interest only if preferences are directed to the realisation of objective goods. As Cohen argues, egalitarians rely on an ideal of community, where justice requires individuals to contribute for the sake of the satisfaction of needs other than their own. This is not just a pragmatic consideration; it is inherent in the very enterprise of egalitarianism.[21] And it is only intelligible if understood in terms of individuals who care not just about who has what, but how they are doing with their respective shares, whether they are able to derive flourishing from their share of resources.[22]

The problem of the global donor thus provides additional motivation for the flourishing approach. That many international charities take pains to inform their donors of the effects of their donations bears out the importance of the flourishing perspective. It might be objected that although the donor's perspective is relevant on strategic grounds, since satisfied donors are more likely to be generous, the satisfaction of the well off is hardly a criterion for a normative theory of global equality. Why should the matter of the redistribution of global wealth be held hostage by the views of the globally advantaged?

I think, however, that it is not an illegitimate intrusion of realpolitik to consider the perspective of advantaged persons who seek to contribute to the improvement of the globally worst off. For the idea of global justice depends on a concept of reciprocity where in virtue of our common humanity we have obligations of redistribution to those, not only as in the case of citizens, we have never met, but also who are culturally remote. So it is important that the connection between donors and recipients of global egalitarianism is well forged. Moreover, there is a particular respect in which the interests of such persons are a way of calibrating the success of the egalitarian enterprise. People who part with their resources to help others will want to know that their efforts are effective. To that extent, their concerns are in harmony with the egalitarian project, and can contribute to a high bar of achievement, rather than pose a constraint on the ideals of egalitarianism.

Nonetheless, we should attend to the perspective of the global donor with some caution. The decision to make charitable donations can be determined by the sympathies of the moment; made conditional on paternalistic proselytising; skewed by the distractions of other causes and the temptations of self-interest. Thus the perspective of the global donor can be no more than a supplementary consideration in matters of international obligations to remedy inequality. However, insofar as global redistribution requires an appeal to the well off to contribute to the less well off, a flourishing perspective promises to be more effective than others.

All this suggests the importance of thinking about global flourishing not just in terms of inter-state transfers, as Rawls's law of peoples proposes. Such a strategy makes the pursuit of global justice an abstract, bureaucratic affair, to be summarily discharged. This is not to say that states do not play a vital role in the redistribution of wealth. Rather, the global policies of states should be viewed in terms of the discharging of obligations of particular persons, citizens of one country who also understand themselves as part of a global humanity to whom they owe obligations, which merit successful realisation rather than token gestures. Thus thinking of particular persons whose interests are bound up with the pursuit of global justice, and whose own flourishing depends on the successful deployment of the capability to be just, directs us to consider how global justice must be accountable, its efforts scrutinised and its results subjected to improvement and revision.

How stringent should be the demands on the highly flourishing in one country to contribute to those who fail to flourish in another country? The moral worldliness of political cosmopolitanism would suggest an almost limitless obligation. If human flourishing is the primary value, it is difficult to provide grounds for why the flourishing of one's compatriots matters more than the flourishing of persons far away. Thus a human flourishing concept of moral worldliness seems to confirm the imperative to provide aid wherever it is needed, regardless of borders or territory. Moreover, insofar as we are concerned that people flourish not just in terms of bodily health, but also in the cosmopolitan's criterion of cultural wellbeing, with scope for human interaction, music, art, and enjoyment of nature, it would seem that the bar for global redistribution is very high indeed.

This understanding of egalitarianism in terms of the conditions of flourishing will be cautious about grand universal standards whose ambitions are difficult to realise. However, the focus on flourishing, which takes account of the degree to which a redistribution of resources is successful in actualising greater equality of flourishing, is prepared to be more ambitious than other metrics. Once we seek the genuine improvement of the lives people live, we find ourselves raising the bar of equality, undertaking far-reaching aid projects and global redistributions in order to further human flourishing. Does this mean that national territory is irrelevant in matters of global justice? It seems to have no place in terms of minimising the obligations of affluent people to provide aid to deprived non-nationals. Does it have any role, however, for the deprived non-nationals themselves? Here we will find that cultural worldliness gives us a more complex picture.

## Self-Determination and Universal Flourishing

Thus far the idea of cultural worldliness has figured in our argument for global egalitarianism insofar as our focus is the conditions which cause people to have impoverished lives, a measure that necessitates cultural criteria, not just the criteria of income and goods. The ethics of international justice thus requires a culturally attuned approach. The resulting idea of egalitarian flourishing, even if it focuses on the particular conditions that impede flourishing, rather than goods and resources per se, nonetheless indicates a massive transfer of such goods and resources between different parts of the world, regardless of nationality.

The marriage of moral and cultural worldliness, however, involves two aspects of human flourishing that bring nationality back into the picture: self-government and cultural diversity. First, let us consider the problem of self-government, or the relation between human flourishing and responsibility. In discussions of egalitarianism in a local context, it is often argued that redistribution should be conditional on the blamelessness of the have-nots. That is, only inequality that is the result of bad luck, as opposed to bad choices, should be ameliorated. The lazy, the irresponsible, the foolish or self-indulgent do not merit the aid of their fellow citizens. In a similar vein, Miller has voiced a powerful objection to the idea of cosmopolitanism, which focuses on the salience of national boundaries. For Miller, a theory of global justice needs to understand our fellow human beings '*both* as agents capable of taking responsibility for the outcomes of their actions *and* as vulnerable and needy creatures who may not be able to lead decent lives without the help of others.'[23] Miller goes on to argue that given have-not countries bear some responsibility for their disadvantage, advantaged countries' obligations should therefore be more narrowly remedial, in light of the requirements of fundamental human rights.[24]

This hard line on what in the domestic context is often called the problem of 'welfare bums' conceptualises it as a tradeoff between human need on the one hand and the virtues of responsibility on the other. Of course, some deploy the criteria of responsibility and reach different conclusions: Pogge's position is that responsibility lies wholly with the citizens of affluent countries whose governments have contributed to global institutions that made other countries poor.[25] Tan amplifies this view with a luck egalitarian argument that generates a demanding understanding of global justice, whereby deprivation is largely the result of factors beyond the control of its victims, particularly place of birth.[26] These are 'natural and arbitrary facts' which institutions then 'systematically translate' into 'significant advantages for some and disadvantages for others.'[27]

A flourishing approach, in contrast, is able to offer a more unified strategy that doesn't hive off meritorious cases from the unmeritorious, avoiding the controversy between Miller and Tan as to where exactly that line should be drawn. Instead, as we saw in Chapter 7, enabling people to act responsibly and resourcefully is part and parcel of improving the situation of the worst off. That is, personal responsibility is among the things we are trying to improve, rather than a countervailing principle that checks or mitigates egalitarian improvement. Simply joining the queue for social assistance does little for a person's capacities, resourcefulness or initiative, let alone self-respect or dignity. The advantage of the flourishing approach is that it recognises the importance of more qualitative criteria of flourishing and failure to flourish. This is no less applicable to problems of global poverty. My flourishing approach takes stock of Miller's anti-cosmopolitan case for a narrower understanding of global justice. On my view, aid policies should be tied to measures that enable self-improvement, not to 'cut off' poorly administered peoples from the largesse of the better-off, but to enable them to improve their institutions and policies and thereby improve their flourishing, both in the form of effective self-government, and in the form of superior outcomes.

Our efforts to remedy inequality, in taking a flourishing approach, will aim to enable people to improve their own lot. This does not mean taking no interest in how people run their economic, social and political affairs, as Rawls's standoffish law of peoples indicates. Faced with the real political difficulty involved in helping needy people with whom one has no substantive relationship, not even the abstract one of citizenship, it is tempting to beat a hasty retreat to a minimalist position as Rawls does. How to give aid in a way that avoids violating self-determination yet succeeds in genuinely improving human flourishing is a real dilemma. But rather than simply dispatching parcels of aid, however generous or paltry, and turning our backs, those of us fortunate to live in the have regions of the world must actively contribute to flourishing by recognising the role of the have-nots in improving themselves. We cannot remedy global inequality just by throwing money at the problem; we need to understand, work with, and improve the local institutions, practices and policies that will be the vehicle for remedying disadvantage. With technological support, resources, training and guidance, people will achieve both self-governance as well as other constituents of flourishing – high levels of education, better nutrition, etc. – that such governance aims to achieve.

This brings us back to the point about cultural variation of the objective constituents of flourishing. Given cultural diversity, it is important that communities have some autonomy in the administration of aid from abroad. A given community is likely to understand the particulars of their case, the specific needs and challenges that hinder the flourishing of their people. Local problems will need local solutions in a fundamental sense. So it is important on grounds of an egalitarian conception that encompasses local culture and self-determination as features of human flourishing (as well as practical effectiveness), that disadvantaged people have a role in determining their own fates. And the cultural cosmopolitan who insists on the value of the variety of cultures in the world will be the first to point out that the stuff of one culture cannot be easily supplied by another.

One of the features of global inequality is the cost it imposes on cultural diversity. The economic dominance of America, for example, means not only that the world's wealth is unevenly distributed, but also that the cultural practices of underdeveloped countries are vulnerable to the behemoth of Western consumerism. As Tan warns, 'not only are the cultures of poorer countries not regarded highly by the richer ones, but the cultures of the latter are threatening to drive out the culture of the poor even in their own countries.'[28] Thus in our understanding of global egalitarianism as seeking to improve people's flourishing, we are better able to appreciate the cultural shortfall imposed by economic disparities. All this means that, although advantaged peoples are not entitled to put the interests of their fellow citizens first, disadvantaged peoples are not best helped by unconditional largesse on the part of the advantaged: self-determination, self-help and cultural autonomy are important features of human flourishing that limit foreign aid to policies and projects that seek to enable self-improvement on the part of disadvantaged persons.

This emphasis on self-direction might seem to evoke the spectre of relativism. That is, if we want to let people shape their own destinies as part of the process of improving flourishing, then we will be committed to a hands-off approach to cultural practices, abstaining from judging the merits of one culture in light of our own. This brings us to another concern about the role of culture and morality in cosmopolitanism, that is, how much we want to address violations of universal criteria like the fundamental human right to not be tortured or maimed, the principle of equality between the sexes, the importance of scope for personal choice about how to live, freedom of expression, and opportunities for political participation. Attending to flourishing requires that we be sensitive to the nuances of a different context, not just to accommodate cultural diversity, but also, when it comes to fundamental aspects of human flourishing, to take a critical stance on cultures. This follows from our earlier discussion of how flourishing has objective constituents, even if it admits of cultural or subjective variation.

Global justice cannot be a no-strings-attached shuffling of resources. If we want to raise the level of flourishing in economically impoverished parts of the world, we will also need to attend to how different parts of the world are impoverished in the ways in which people live, and that includes their democratic and liberal opportunities. Of course, the commitment to the role of democratic participation as a constituent of human flourishing means that Western democrats cannot simply march into other parts of the world with a new 'white man's burden' of cultural imperialism, this time liberal democracy rather than Christianity. As Tan argues, such a stance must remain committed to the principle of self-governance: 'the motivation for change must be internal and outside involvement must aim primarily to realise the aspirations of oppressed individuals.'[29] In sum, there is an egalitarian obligation on the part of citizens of the world to defend the fundamental interests of vulnerable people, wherever they are, in light of universal criteria, yet qualified by principles of self-help and local knowledge.

## Conclusion

In this chapter I have sought to apply the concept of egalitarian flourishing to the vexing problem of global injustice. I have argued that such an approach attends to the global scope of what is dubbed 'cosmopolitanism' in contemporary political philosophy, whilst appreciating the cultural interests of the 'citizen of the world,' the cosmopolitan. This marriage of ethical principles and an appreciation for modes of living, or what I have called moral worldliness and cultural worldliness, gives us a number of advantages over neutralist approaches to egalitarianism.

First, such an approach can better understand the dimensions of inequality in distant parts of the world, which have particular circumstances, needs and challenges that cannot be conceived or addressed simply in monetary terms. Thus flourishing is what is unequal and it is flourishing that we seek to improve in our global egalitarianism as we target the unequal conditions that produce unequal wellbeing. Flourishing is an objective measure, insofar as we can set out universal constituents such as health, education, political participation, friendship and family. But how these constituents are to be understood and realised will depend enormously on the particular context and subjective situations of the people involved. Second, the concept of flourishing enables us properly to expound the relation between the haves and have-nots. The redistribution of global resources requires a sense of reciprocity wherein donors can understand the impact of their contributions and assess their effectiveness, as well as involve themselves to the extent that they can facilitate the development of worst-off peoples.

Third, flourishing helps to stipulate the extent of global redistribution. The well-off are obligated to contribute to the worse-off not to equalise wealth; given human diversity it is unclear what that means, let alone what purpose it serves. Rather, lack of flourishing, and in the first instance, severe shortfalls of flourishing, are the target of our redistributive policies. Connected with this is a fourth consideration that concerns the stringency of the obligation to redistribute global wealth. The flourishing perspective emphasises the role of self-governance and self-help in attending to disadvantage in countries other than our own. This is a principle that emerges from the idea of equalising social conditions in order to improve wellbeing, since policies that impart skills and further local institutions enable the self-direction that is essential to living well.

Fifth, human flourishing is affected, of course, not just by lack of resources or opportunities, but also by oppression. And thus the global egalitarian finds the flourishing approach useful in its insistence that we seek not just the redistribution of wealth but also the furtherance of fundamental human rights, in order to improve the human flourishing of people in societies other than our own. Again the self-help idea is important here, since our strategy should not be a kind of moral imperialism that bulldozes its way through sovereign territories to fix human rights, but rather a strategy of enabling the internal movements that seek social change.

Finally, the argument of this chapter presents a challenge to theories of equality, offering a radical and ambitious conception of what it is we are seeking to equalise in the form of the conditions of human flourishing.

However, such a conception must also be offered with a more modest view of the role of egalitarian political philosophy. Human flourishing may be a demanding measure for equality, but it is hardly a straightforward one; it does not supply us with a simple formula or yardstick. Ultimately, the task of rich peoples providing aid to poor peoples is political, a task to which philosophy can only offer a framework for understanding. I hope to have clarified egalitarianism in this chapter by providing a demanding yet nuanced project of equalising the conditions of human flourishing around the world. How to effect egalitarianism globally nonetheless remains a matter of will and action in light of particular circumstances.

We live in a world characterised by enormous disparities of wealth and property, of health, self-respect, and the development of human potential. The moral worldliness of contemporary arguments for cosmopolitanism must be paired with cultural worldliness to give scope to the non-material aspects of human flourishing and sensitivity to the diversity that culture presents. It is an unequally flourishing world and it is by focusing our theory and practice on the social conditions that impede the flourishing of persons that we will better achieve the global justice that, for all the successes of egalitarian movements in certain, privileged parts of the world, continues so desperately to elude us.

## Notes

1 Kymlicka, *Politics in the Vernacular*, 216.
2 P. Singer originated this kind of example with the idea of a drowning child who can as easily be saved in one's locale or on the other side of the world. See 'The Drowning Child and the Expanding Circle.'
3 Paradoxically, 'cosmopolitan' was also a Bolshevik term of abuse connoting disloyalty to Russia, bourgeois class origins or dilettantish tastes.
4 C. Jones, *Global Justice*, 15–17.
5 J. Waldron, 'Minority Cultures and the Cosmopolitan Alternative,' 95.
6 Ibid., 113.
7 Appiah, 'Cosmopolitan Patriots,' 22, 25.
8 Rawls, *A Theory of Justice*.
9 H. Brighouse, 'Against Nationalism,' 379.
10 T. Pogge, 'Human Rights and Human Responsibilities,' 185.
11 C. Beitz, *Political Theory and International Relations*, 143–53; T. Pogge, *Realising Rawls*, ch. 6.
12 J. Rawls, *The Law of Peoples*, 118.
13 K.C. Tan, *Toleration, Diversity and Global Justice*, 179.
14 Ibid., 165.
15 Sen, *Development as Freedom*.
16 Sen, *Inequality Re-Examined*, 42, 54–5.
17 Sen, *Development as Freedom*, 62–3.
18 Ibid., 70–1, 88–9.
19 Ibid., 89–90.
20 The idea of 'racial stigma' captures this phenomenon; see G. Loury, *The Anatomy of Racial Inequality*.
21 Cohen, *Why Not Socialism?*, 39–45.
22 This is particularly evident in the response of individuals in Western countries to

the Syrian refugee crisis, who are concerned about the wellbeing of the people they sponsor; that they are housed, clothed and fed, that they find work, learn the local language, that their children integrate into schools, etc.

23 Miller, *National Responsibility and Global Injustice*, 237.
24 Ibid., 166.
25 T. Pogge, *World Poverty and Human Rights*, 139–45.
26 Tan, *Justice, Institutions and Luck*, 173–4.
27 Ibid., 15.
28 Tan, *Toleration, Diversity and Global Justice*, 120.
29 Ibid., 137.

# Conclusion
## A Utopia for Mortals

This book has argued that a political philosophy of equality should focus on human flourishing. Human flourishing is what is ultimately important in ameliorating disadvantage. Instead of insisting on a metric of resources or goods – the means towards, rather than the end of, wellbeing – we should consider how well off individuals are, in the fullest sense, and adopt measures that enable both greater equality, and greater overall maximisation, of wellbeing. Wellbeing consists of objective goods, autonomy and contentment, all of which contribute to people's quality of life. What really matters when we seek to make people more equal is that they are living well.

In the 1990s egalitarianism found itself facing challenges from a broad range of perspectives that came under the umbrella of identity politics, all casting doubt on a common project of enabling equality. I have argued that liberal theories of equality that focussed on the polity's neutrality on questions about value failed to meet the challenges of these perspectives. The best prospect for renewing equalitarianism is to forge a politics that is explicit about the relation between valuable ways of living and the amelioration of disadvantage. This approach arises in the context of relations of inequality within Western societies, but it has relevance for the gravest examples of inequality in a globally unjust world.

My human flourishing account of equality, or egalitarian perfectionism, confronts a number of controversial issues. Neutralist liberals accuse perfectionists of being coercive, intolerant and paternalistic and these charges would seem especially problematic for a theory of equality. I have sought to show that perfectionist ideas of wellbeing, though often portrayed as the province of elitist and illiberal doctrines, can be oriented towards improving the lot of the worst-off in ways that respect, indeed promote, liberal principles of autonomy and responsibility, and shed light on vexing issues of global justice.

After Rawls's theory of justice, many liberals allied themselves with socialist ideas about the redistribution of power and resources, producing an exciting debate about how the principle of equal distribution can be related to ideals of liberty. The price for this, however, was the prevalence of a liberal insistence on agnosticism about the good that drew egalitarianism away from ideas about living well. Indeed, the focus on neutrality was such that even the idea of equality was often displaced as debates about consensus, difference,

democracy and recognition came to dominate political theory. Political philosophy became preoccupied with questions of the self and culture. I have
insisted that culture is relevant to equality, but not just for multicultural politics. We must take seriously the importance of culture more generally for the
fulfilment of human capacities and the equality of citizens. Our measure in
politics should be human flourishing, and culture is a crucial factor in such
flourishing.

My case draws on some of the ideas of Morris, the Victorian aesthete and
socialist, whose work as an artist inspired his political commitments. This may
seem a surprising choice, but I would like to emphasise again that Morris's
views about living well as equals were hardly eccentric. The tradition of political philosophy from the Ancient Greeks onwards assumed the centrality of the
question of how we should live. And the modern egalitarian tradition, from
socialists like Marx to progressive liberals such as Mill and Hobhouse, assumed
that the equal society would enable its citizens to live well. Indeed, I would
venture that we will look back on the neutralist liberal era as an aberrant and
unfortunate chapter in the history of egalitarian political philosophy, at odds
with the tradition of conceiving social justice with reference to ideas of wellbeing, the public good, and community that are so central to the ideal of equality and the hope of its realisation.

We should not forsake the ambitions of the progressives of our past
century by settling for a make-do politics that metes out benefits to vocifer-
ous interest groups but takes no interest in a culture common to citizens.
Equality is furthered not by holding the line, excluding questions of value, to
protect individuals from each other, as neutralist liberals presuppose. The task
of making decisions about value is of course not an easy one, and critics are
right that controversy and disagreement are inevitable. We have, however,
found a remarkable degree of agreement in our liberal societies, demonstrated
by public support for education, the arts, libraries and literacy, the conservation of green spaces, the preservation of historic buildings and institutions. If
we refuse to make decisions about our public culture consciously and democratically, we will find cultural possibilities will be decided for us, by the economically and socially powerful, or by the iron forces of the market.

A Morris-inspired theory of egalitarian flourishing might be parodied as
'workers of the world unite, you have nothing to lose but your chintz!'[1] But
the idea that inequality enslaves one to false values or condemns one to an
ugly life – that, as Morris put it, 'men in civilised societies are dirty, ignorant,
brutal,' and this, too, can be judged 'unfair'[2] – is an important counterbalance
to the prevailing political culture of neutralism and moral scepticism. Moreover, Morris's egalitarian sensibility makes for a perfectionism that is neither
coercive nor unitary. Equality thus requires, not just access to the means of
life, but the acculturation of individuals to live well. Moreover, there are
good grounds to think that greater equality would in fact bring with it the
enculturation that enables us to determine our fates and fulfil our capacities.
As Morris reminds us, 'Art is long and life is short; let us at least do something
before we die.'[3]

Many issues remain about the account of egalitarian flourishing expounded in this book. It is the nature of political philosophy that in addressing one question we at the same time end up posing new, unanswered ones, both conceptual questions about ideals and their justification, and practical questions about feasibility and implementation. Thus I close my inquiry in the knowledge that much more needs to be done. In this final chapter, I highlight some of the issues that arise from my account in order to provide preliminary suggestions as to how to think about them. The issues at stake can be grouped around a general, conceptual question that is at the same time a question about the very relation between theory and practice: the question of utopia.

## Utopia and Utopianism

The position defended here might well be identified as utopian, in the sense that it aspires to an unreachable ideal. First, it purports to ground political theory in a conception of worthwhile ways of living, a subject about which there is notorious disagreement. Second, it seeks to improve persons, rather than take them as we find them. Third, it invites the objection made so often of utopianism, that its unrealistic aspirations will generate a politics that is at best paternalistic, at worst authoritarian. My responses to these objections, presented above, focussed on the relationship between equality and living well, the central role of autonomy in human flourishing, and the inadequacy of the market as a forum for determining value, in contrast to public forums such as democratic institutions. Is this utopian?

Utopianism is an elusive phenomenon to articulate. Utopia has been defined as an 'ideally perfect society whose members live the best possible life,' or an 'imaginary ideal society.' As such, it is assumed to be beyond the reach of actual practice, and theories that are 'utopian' are deemed unrealistic or improbable: reflecting a 'tension between philosophical ideals and the practical realities of society.'[4] Some claim that utopianism has both inspired and plagued progressive thought since the Jacobins of the French Revolution.[5] The Jacobins inaugurated a modern politics where the pursuit of progress and emancipation makes for a kind of blindness: first, the progressive's faith in canonical egalitarian ideals can be so unshakeable that they become impervious to revision; and second, the progressive can become oblivious to the moral costs of his or her ideals. The ends, particularly progressive ends, are taken to justify the means. Such dogmatism goes hand-in-hand with the conceit that a single theoretical approach will get things right, once and for all. Thus utopian political philosophies can be curiously apolitical, assuming that their contribution will remove the need for political disputes thereafter.

Connected with this is an urge to transparency or disclosure, wherein full membership in a just society removes the need for checks on politics, countervailing considerations in the pursuit of justice. The idea that we can have our cake and eat it too is illustrated by the insightful critiques of the classic assumption in political theory that there is a trade-off between equality and liberty. Progressives trenchantly argue that equality is the precondition for liberty, that liberty is an egalitarian entitlement and requires egalitarian conditions. This is a compelling view, but the idea that there can never be tension between liberty and equality is a simplistic further step, which has a distinctly utopian character.[6]

The right-wing objection to utopianism is well known. Conservatives such as Burke counselled that politics could only build on existing customs and traditions, and that human beings should not take bold leaps into an unknown future.[7] This epistemological point was made again by postwar critics of the welfare state such as Hayek, who insisted that only individuals possess knowledge, and thus that 'social engineering' or indeed central planning of any kind inevitably produces ill-informed and tyrannical policies.[8] Pessimism about human knowledge for such conservatives is coupled with pessimism about human nature, the idea that we are too selfish – too preoccupied with, as Hobbes says, 'obtaining power after power that ceaseth only until death'[9] – to be permitted to aspire to anything more than stability and order in our political arrangements.

Of course, socialists who aspire to a 'scientific' basis for their politics, such as Marx and Engels, also scorn utopia. There is paradox in this, given their obvious radical aims. However, for Marxists, radicalism is thought to follow from a good grasp of political reality – it is the moderates who are utopian. Marxists' critique of the rival views of 'utopian socialists' emphasised how social change is not produced by coming up with good ideas, but must emanate from existing historical processes. The contrast between utopian and scientific socialism first appears in the 'Communist Manifesto' in which Marx and Engels castigate socialists such as Owen and Fourier for being utopian in their methods and goals. These early socialists were utopian because

> they reject all political, and especially all revolutionary, action; they wish to attain their ends by peaceful means, and endeavour, by small experiments, necessarily doomed to failure, and by force of example, to pave the way for the new social Gospel.[10]

For Marx and Engels, the 'fantastic pictures of future society' were 'painted' by utopian socialists when the proletariat was 'still in a very undeveloped state.'[11] According to the doctrine of historical materialism, genuine social change requires that the working class seize the opportunities presented by the increasing crises of capitalism, rather than conceiving of revolution as an act of mere will and the realisation of good ideas. This doctrine also rejected the idea that the communist future could be foretold in advance. Marx scoffed at 'recipes for the cookbooks of the future,' claiming that again, historical context would yield political principle.[12] Engels amplified this argument thirty-one years later in 'Socialism: Utopian and Scientific' where he contends that, in contrast to the utopian approach, 'socialism became a science thanks to Marx.'[13]

It is interesting to note a 'realist,' anti-utopian strain in political thought is prominent on both the right and the left. For the conservatives, attention to history constrains change, for the socialists, it provides opportunities for change. Yet both camps stress it is utopian for political action to be blind to historical circumstance. There is wisdom in these views. Political philosophers should be sensitive to the constraints of the societies in which they live. 'Ought implies can' is almost a truism, particularly relevant in the domain of politics. However, existing reality must not be allowed some kind of automatic legitimacy. Political pragmatists can be prone to either resisting change, as in its conservative variants, or waiting for the ideal opportunities for change to happen, the tendency of some Marxists. Both risk conferring moral value on the given, even if, in the Marxist case, it is as a necessary stage that will inevitably be transcended. Political philosophy cannot be reduced to mere assent to the world as we find it, or where the laws of history will take it; it must be a normative enterprise, concerned with human progress and social improvement. Thus Cohen trenchantly argues that justice and equality should be 'rescued' from 'facts' that diminish the ambition of normative political theory.[14]

Political philosophy is distinctive in that, in its effort to address the normative question of how we are to live in common, it cannot escape an empirical reality that throws up, for example, problems of scarcity, human nature, the dynamics of social change. The more radical our political philosophies, the more they seek to transcend this empirical reality. To that extent they inevitably risk looking unrealistic or ungrounded in the facts of politics and power. But the value of human-led emancipation is evident in many instances of genuine social progress, in which human beings have figured as not just the objects, but also subjects, of change for the better. It is irresponsible to not demand that we think and rethink how the world might otherwise be, that we 'face the strange,' as David Bowie put it. A political theory that seeks to dispense with utopian objectives, the aspiration to an ideal, is paradoxically, utopian itself, because it betrays a naive optimism about the world as we find it. Utopia per se is of course not a live option; the ideal society will always be beyond the grasp of flawed mortals. But some kind of utopian imperative, such as the quest for human flourishing, is essential to the very task of political philosophy.

Rejecting Cohen's ambition to divorce political philosophy from considerations about facts, Miller argues that a political philosophy 'for earthlings' must be thoroughly action guiding, whereby we 'allow the unavoidable limitations of the earthly city to shape our understandings of justice' in order to 'mark out a road down which we might travel.'[15] The alternative, as he eloquently puts it, is 'political philosophy as lamentation' which 'places justice so far out of the reach of human beings that nothing we can practically achieve will bring us significantly closer to the cherished goal.'[16] For Miller, the latter breeds a posture of resignation, which finds the real world hopelessly 'contaminated.'

However, the options for the egalitarian need not be so stark. Miller's impatience with conceptual claims about moral ideals might be said itself to betray a spirit of resignation. Political philosophers should maintain a healthy degree of scepticism about the feasible to ensure their analyses perform what Swift calls 'a crucial practical-evaluative role,'[17] not in order to forswear application, but better to understand when the exigencies of application call for a degree of moral sacrifice. Resignation is rather the peril of the political philosophy whose moral compass is derived solely from real-world considerations. We need to retain an idea of utopia as an aspiration, to ward off what Estlund calls 'utopophobia,'[18] without dispensing with a sober understanding of where the real world falls short, why it does so, and how its shortcomings might be ameliorated.

How then do we continue the quest for what Morris called the 'earthly paradise,' and affirm the utopian aspiration without falling prey to utopianism? First, we must not be cowed by appeals to democracy in a political theory of egalitarian flourishing. Second, the concept of privacy is vital in the ideal equal society. Third, for all the talk of perfectionism, as I have noted in earlier chapters, my philosophy of equality is best understood as seeking improvement in human flourishing, not perfection per se, conscious of the finitude and frailty of human existence. I will consider each of these themes in turn to venture an appropriately utopian conception of equality as human flourishing.

## Philosophers and Democrats

A prominent theme in much recent political theory is the idea of finding agreement among citizens. This is apparent in contractualist approaches that derive political principle from the agreements – usually hypothetical – among individuals, an example of which is the work of Rawls, and also the influential school of deliberative democracy, which seeks to build political principles on the properly constituted practices of political discourse. The latter holds that if our democratic institutions are sufficiently inclusive, sincere, open and principled, then good policy will follow.[19] It is indisputable that the political theories of intellectuals and academics will ultimately succeed or fail in the hands of the people at the ballot box. And there is much that political philosophers can do – though our record thus far is hardly stellar – to render our philosophical claims comprehensible and compelling to a wider public. I believe, however, it is a confusion to build into the criterion of acceptability of a political theory the extent to which the theory finds acceptance. Conflicts of interest, power struggles, lack of imagination, fatalism and stupidity, all contribute to distortions in the deliberations or agreements of existing publics that only lower our sights in political philosophy.

Deliberative democrats are quick to reassure us that their conception of democracy is not just rule of the people, but rule of the people under the right conditions – political judgement must be the fruit of fully informed, open, sincere and reasonable deliberation. But this seems somewhat underhand: egalitarian political theorists posit idealised democracies that incorporate philosophical standards of justification, with the aim, one suspects, of producing the very theories of justice the theorists had already formulated. To put faith in consent is unrealistic, but the problem is not solved by rigging consent to produce right results. Democracy as a method is a way of showing respect to citizens, giving them authority in their common political affairs; it enables a broad consultation of diverse views, and it gives power to the people. These constitutional issues are different, as Christiano insists, from the matter of what policies are actually chosen.[20] Weinstock complains that the idea of specifying the character of democratic debate means that 'the challenge of moral pluralism has been not so much addressed as circumvented.'[21] Moreover, such approaches tend to water down politics, lowering the bar on important questions of value. Political philosophers are obligated to confront difficult questions about how to live well and they must accept that the people may not agree with the philosophers' answers, perhaps because those answers were not put convincingly, or were insensitive to questions of context, or were just plain wrong. At the same time, the people can make mistakes, in which case political philosophy is especially important as a counter to error, rather than seeming slavishly to reproduce it by incorporating democratic criteria for its values.

Radical political theory has notoriously supposed there might be an end to politics, e.g. with Marx's idea of the withering away of the state upon the full flowering of socialist relations of production and social life. This idea stems from a tendency in some radical thought to seek the elimination of conflict and dispute. The ideal also plays a role in some of the deliberative and contractualist perspectives, as well as the discourse on difference, which aim to transcend the opposition of interests and perspectives. But here we find true utopian folly, if the hope is to denude politics of controversy, and moreover, a view that threatens to be illiberal. In much of this work there lurks the hope that if we could only hear other voices aright, dialogue would be possible and differences overcome or transcended. At the same time, contemporary political theory seems to hold up political engagement as a universal goal, as the telos of a human life, the criterion for equality. This might also emanate from the deliberative perspective, insofar as it subsumes questions of justice to the imperative of democratic participation. But it is precisely because of the human diversity that makes politics inevitable that we should ensure that politics is, to some extent at least, optional, and allow for the possibility that not all of us find our flourishing in democratic engagement. That would be, after all, the democratic thing to do.

## Privacy and Equality

Privacy is often thought of as in tension with the pursuit of equality. Certainly if intrinsic to the idea of privacy is an unqualified title to private property, immune to interference, then the conflict with egalitarianism is obvious. The idea of personal freedom is often couched in terms of implying a right to the accumulation of wealth so claims to property and privacy may in certain cases overlap, but the connection is not a necessary one. Whilst a personal domain is essential for privacy to be respected, such a domain need not be owned. A peeping tom invades the privacy of a guest or housesitter as much as that of an owner or tenant.

Privacy is doubtless something of a modern, in many ways Western, construction. Its importance for modern individuals is such that our living space is configured with several senses of privacy in mind: the locked door of the bathroom behind which one attends to the body; the study, sometimes called the 'den,' to which one retreats for solitary contemplation; or the ideal in middle-class households of one bedroom per child to encourage children to develop into autonomous selves. But its recent vintage, or its role in contemporary unequal relations, does not show its lack of value. As we saw in Chapter 3, Woolf's feminist call for a 'room of one's own' demonstrates how even those members of society, subject to exploitation behind the cover of 'privacy,' also find the concept a fundamental precondition for autonomy and human flourishing. The closet is a refuge in the context of oppression, in which case the elimination of oppression would, we hope, remove the conditions that gave rise to the need for retreating to a private domain to hide one's true nature, for dissembling. But it gets things backward if we focus on the dissembling itself; moreover, it violates the principle of respecting persons' privacy. Society should respect individuals' choices about how much to disclose or share with their fellows.

However much the public good is nurtured, and egalitarian flourishing promoted, we live among each other as strangers, not intimates, whose mode of social interaction, as I have noted, is best thought of as civility. The root of civility is the Latin word for city, and thus, as one historian of etiquette notes, it represented the reverse of 'crude country behaviour.'[22] Its urban source also underscores that it has relevance only in a setting where relations are impersonal, where we encounter people who are neither friend nor foe. 'Neighbourliness' is the spirit of civility, and the slogan 'good fences make good neighbours' is particularly apt, since civility rests on demarcating the private spaces of individuals, rather than overcoming them. Civility is thus at issue precisely in the impersonal yet social relations of citizens. The community to which the civil citizen belongs is clearly a modern one, its relations looser than those of the classical model of the Ancient Greek polis. Civility is the form of care appropriate for public life, distinct from the care of the intimate or private realm. Indeed, the care to which civility refers is best understood in the more muted sense of regard.[23]

It follows from the role of privacy and civility, that though we are connected in virtue of a common political project, those connections nonetheless remain impersonal. Where human diversity, dispute and debate are understood as inherent in a society that seeks the equal flourishing of its members, we must forgo the familial and tribal understandings of interpersonal connections to which some utopians aspire. Comradeship refers to our citizen-roles to the extent that our equality depends on the nurturing of a public good. The egalitarian flourishing state is not neutral, and our citizenship consists of more than rights and duties of resource distribution; it also entails a common commitment to the constituents of human wellbeing.

As comrades we aim for a society that nurtures diverse cultural opportunities and genuine ways of living well. But comradeship remains a political, public relation, distinct from the relations of intimates, friends or family members. For relations of care can be contingent, invasive and arbitrary. Our comradeship has as its purpose, not sharing and caring per se, but the project of furthering equal flourishing. As such, the egalitarian society must be both ambitious and restrained. The latter is best conceived in terms of a strong set of judicial principles that protect individual liberty. In particular, it is important that the equal society has the fair procedures of the rule of law – e.g. certainty, specificity, publicity – to ensure that individuals are not subject to arbitrary power.[24]

In upholding the principle that individuals are entitled to a sphere of unimpeded human activity, it is nonetheless possible for society to encourage good choices to enable human flourishing. Those who criticise perfectionism for violating privacy betray a false view of the person as an abstract, detached chooser, uninfluenced by external factors. On this view, any attempt by political society to shape human choices is tyrannical and paternalistic. My argument suggests that it is utopian indeed – in the sense of dangerously implausible – to demand that our political institutions should have no role whatsoever in influencing our choices, including even non-coercive means. Such institutions, in contrast to the efforts of the market or our family background, are after all subject to at least putative democratic control, standards of transparency, and social monitoring. Moreover, they can be deployed to counter the insidious influence of the market and the potentially unjust influences of family.

Paternalism is a bugbear here, since this model entails a role for the state in shaping the conditions for individuals' decisions, however benign the motives or modest the effects. The political community is seeking to provide direction, in some form, to its adult members, not leaving them utterly unfettered in their decisions. But not doing anything, with the argument that each person is best placed to make his or her own decision, is not so innocent of paternalism. Laissez-faire is paternalistic, too, for it assumes that some people's lesser lot is all they are capable of, that the school dropout could aspire to no more, that high ambitions and lofty ideals are the stuff of only the few. This is not utopian, of course; it is dystopian, in the miserable way so well captured by the novels of Zamyatin, Huxley or Orwell, where a 'natural' hierarchy is given state sanction.

## Improvement and Perfection

A difficulty with understanding egalitarianism as a perfectionist project is the concept of perfection itself. Wellbeing and flourishing are useful terms, for they involve the idea that the project of furthering equality involves attending to how material disadvantage prevents people from living well. Such a position is dubbed 'perfectionist' because perfectionism seeks to improve how people live in light of criteria of genuine value. Perfectionism is 'the view that promotion of human excellence is one of the factors that should be weighed in judging the political and social worth of a society.'[25] We seek the fuller and more equal realisation of access to material goods, good health, high levels of education and cultural pursuits, and these all have objective value. Some sources of value, such as health, will be so basic that they should be universally enjoyed. Others, though of objective value, will be diversely weighted, the weight given to each a matter of individual choice, though the political community will seek to encourage and promote valuable pursuits among which individuals make their choices.

The egalitarian seeks a society where we are self-determining in our enjoyment of wellbeing. But self-determining does not mean the self can wholly determine his or her fate. The problem of 'programming perfection' is rife among parents, who aim to produce the perfect embryo, or ward off all chance of failure to ensure their children reach the apex of success and status. What Sandel calls 'hyperparenting' is one aspect of a general cultural pressure to perform, an anxiety about success that is a far cry from human flourishing.[26] My position counters trends in contemporary culture that hope to extinguish contingency and chance. Flourishing should be understood in a rich sense to permit disappointment and struggle, setbacks and reversals. It involves developing our capacities to confront and cope with the unexpected or uncontrollable, be it ageing or human frailty more generally, an 'openness to the unbidden.'[27] Sensitivity to factors beyond one's control can ground an egalitarian politics that seeks to mitigate disadvantage, not in the luck egalitarian sense of isolating those disadvantages that merit remedy and those that do not. Rather, the realities of human experience involve coping with unexpected turns of events; the significance of choice needs to be detached from its 'supposed opposition to luck.'[28]

I have argued that autonomy is inherent in human flourishing, and autonomy means being self-determining in a context of uncertainty. It also means a respect for the precarious sources of value, such as nature and other species, historic architecture and vulnerable but valuable forms of life, which set constraints on what we might rightly choose. Thus we need a disposition of humility that eschews the idea of total control of one's destiny, mastery over all contingencies. Perfection serves only as a target to which one strives rather than something that is achieved; we might think this is especially true for those with disabilities, but it is true for us all as fragile, mortal beings who begin and end life vulnerable and helpless. In writing this book, I therefore opted for 'flourishing,' recognising though that the term 'perfectionism' is unavoidable, given the modes of expression in contemporary political philosophy. But the word needs to be used in a guarded, self-conscious way, aware of its possible unhelpful connotations.

The inadequacy of the idea of perfection to capture egalitarian flourishing indicates a general problem that touches on all the themes of this concluding chapter. This is the need to reckon with our finitude, a challenge to any progressive politics that seeks human improvement. The idea of a perfect, immortal person appeared in some of the more fantastic understandings of 'communist man' amongst the Russian Bolsheviks. It had its roots in Marx's Promethean idea of human mastery of nature through labour, and his vision of communism as a solution to the riddle of history, devoid of conflict or tension. The denial of death reached its zenith in the preposterous ideas of regeneration that inspired the embalming of Lenin. Such crackpot notions may seem peripheral to a serious inquiry into questions of political philosophy. But notions like these represent the extreme of a more general propensity in our culture. The denial of our finitude is not restricted to radical utopianism but is, in secular form, an underlying conceit of modernity as a whole, and our efforts to defy age, risk, or disappointment. Contemporary consumerism represents a kind of denial of death in which people seek infinite material gratification, oblivious to the mortification of nature (a creed which, of course, has succeeded the failure of the Bolshevik project in Russia).[29]

We are flawed beings, capable of error and conceit. Our efforts to do well can go badly, and our political theories and practices, like the lives we lead, must always be thought of as provisional, subject to criticism, revision and renewal. We should interact with each other, with our social institutions, and with nature, in the knowledge that we need procedures and policies that protect the old as well as promote the new. We must leave the world for others after us and thus we should be cautious our projects do not have outcomes that could be deleterious or disastrous. We are mortal and resources are scarce: such is the stuff of politics, and the obligation to adopt a posture of conservation should temper our aspiration to utopia.[30]

This book has sought to renew the ideal of equality in a beleaguered context, beleaguered as much by the commitments of contemporary egalitarians as the hostility of anti-egalitarians. Material equality has been sidestepped in current preoccupations with culture and identity, and those theories that do address economic disadvantage are mired in odd debates and concerns. The concept of human flourishing is offered as a way of conceptualising what really matters in our project of making humankind more equal. It involves contentment, autonomy, and objective wellbeing. Wellbeing or flourishing does not admit of straightforward measurement or a catchall formula or recipe. Nonetheless it is flourishing, a partly subjective, partly objective criterion, that best captures what disadvantage and advantage amount to. It is ambitious, and as such it can be dubbed utopian.

In our political theories as well as our practical efforts to achieve more equal and greater human flourishing, we must recognise that we aspire to an ideal that will always be just beyond us; hence the importance of tempering our utopian aspirations. But pursue this ideal we must, however much we know that its full realisation is in some way elusive. This paradoxical project is both grounded and heady: in short, it is an egalitarian political philosophy which centres on human flourishing, a utopia for mortals. And it requires, not just a radical redistribution of resources, but the maintenance of a rich cultural environment, and a constant, open and lively inquiry into that ancient question that inaugurated political philosophy: how should we live?

## Notes

1 I am grateful to my mother, Marcia Sypnowich, for this joke.
2 Morris, 'Art and Socialism,' 211.
3 Morris, 'Art Under Plutocracy,', 191.
4 New World Encyclopedia, (2016) 'Utopia.' www.newworldencyclopedia.org/entry/Utopia
5 See Laclau and Mouffe, *Hegemony and Socialist Strategy*, 152.
6 See Berlin, 'Two Concepts of Liberty.'
7 E. Burke, *Reflections on the Revolution in France.*
8 F.A. Hayek, *The Road to Serfdom.*
9 Hobbes, *Leviathan*, 161.
10 Marx and Engels, 'The Communist Manifesto,' 498.
11 Ibid.
12 Karl Marx, 'Afterword,' *Capital*, 299. I discuss these issues in 'G.A. Cohen's Socialism.'
13 F. Engels, 'Socialism: Utopian and Scientific,' 700.
14 Cohen, *Rescuing Justice and Equality.*
15 D. Miller, *Justice for Earthlings*, 248–9.
16 Ibid., 230, 232. See also I. Roebyns, 'Ideal Theory in Theory and Practice,' 343.
17 A. Swift, 'The Value of Philosophy in Non-ideal Circumstances,' 364.
18 D. Estlund, 'Utopophobia: Concession and Aspiration in Democratic Theory,' ch. 14; and 'Human Nature and the Limits (if any) of Political Philosophy.'
19 For a useful collection that surveys the vast literature in this area, see T. Christiano, ed., *Philosophy and Democracy.*
20 T. Christiano, *The Rule of the Many*, 56. See C. Sypnowich, 'Ruling or Overruled? The People, Rights and Democracy.'
21 D. Weinstock, 'Saving Democracy from Deliberation,' 83.
22 E.B. Aresty, *The Best Behavior: The Course of Good Manners – from Antiquity to the Present – as Seen through Courtesy and Etiquette Books*, 10.
23 I explore this in 'The Civility of Law: Between Public and Private.'
24 This is a theme prominent in my *Concept of Socialist Law*; see also D. Dyzenhaus (ed.) *Recrafting the Rule of Law.*
25 J. Kupperman, 'Perfectionism.'
26 Sandel, *The Case Against Perfection*, 52.
27 W.F. May, address to the President's Council on Bioethics, 17 October, 2002, quoted in Ibid., 45.
28 Sher, *Equality for Inegalitarians*, 107–11.
29 I explore these themes in 'Death in Utopia: Marxism and the Mortal Self.'
30 For a provocative argument that calls for reviving the ideals of failed historic struggles, see Žižek, *In Defense of Lost Causes.*

# Bibliography

Ackerman, B. (1989) 'Why Dialogue?,' *Journal of Philosophy*, 86, 1.

Adorno, T. (1982) 'Cultural Criticism and Society,' in *Prisms*, trans. S.W. Nicholsen and S. Weber, Cambridge, MA: MIT Press.

Ahmed, S. (2000) *Transformations: Thinking through Feminism*, London: Routledge.

Alcoff, L. (1988) 'Cultural Feminism versus Poststructuralism: The Identity Crisis in Feminist Theory,' *Signs*, 13, 3.

Alcoff, L. (2006) *Visible Identities: Race, Gender and the Self*, Oxford: Oxford University Press.

Anderson, B. (1996) *Imagined Communities*, London: Verso.

Anderson, E. (1999) 'What Is the Point of Equality?' *Ethics*, 109, 2.

Appiah, K.A. (1992) *In My Father's House: Africa in the Philosophy of Culture*, New York: Oxford University Press.

Appiah, K.A. (1994) 'Identity, Authenticity, Survival: Multicultural Societies and Social Reproduction,' in C. Taylor (ed.) *Multiculturalism*, Princeton: Princeton University Press.

Appiah, K.A. (1996) 'Cosmopolitan Patriots,' in J. Cohen (ed.) *For Love of Country*, Boston: Beacon Press.

Appiah, K.A. (1996) 'Race, Culture, Identity: Misunderstood Connections,' in K.A. Appiah and A. Gutmann, *Color Consciousness*, Princeton: Princeton University Press.

Appiah, K.A. (2005) *The Ethics of Identity*, Princeton: Princeton University Press.

Archard, D. and Macleod, C. (eds) (2002) *The Moral and Political Status of Children*, Oxford: Oxford University Press.

Archibugi, D. (2008) *The Global Commonwealth of Citizens: Toward Cosmopolitan Democracies*, Princeton: Princeton University Press.

Aresty, E.B. (1970) *The Best Behavior: The Course of Good Manners – from Antiquity to the Present – as Seen through Courtesy and Etiquette Books*, New York: Simon and Schuster.

Aristotle (1977) *Politics*, (ed.) E. Barker, Oxford: Oxford University Press.

Aristotle (1980) *Nichomachean Ethics*, trans. D. Ross, Oxford: Oxford University Press.

Armstrong, C. (2006) *Rethinking Equality: The Challenge of Equal Citizenship*, Manchester: Manchester University Press.

Arneil, B. (2006) *Diverse Communities: The Problem with Social Capital*, Cambridge: Cambridge University Press.

Arneson, R. (1997) 'Egalitarianism and the Undeserving Poor,' *Journal of Political Philosophy*, 5, 4.

Arneson, R. (1997) 'Equality and Equal Opportunity for Welfare' in L. Pojman and

R. Westmoreland (eds) *Equality: Selected Readings*, New York: Oxford University Press.

Arneson, R. (2000) 'Perfectionism and Politics,' *Ethics*, 111, 1.

Arneson, R. (2003) 'Liberal Neutrality on the Good: An Autopsy,' in S. Wall and G. Klosko (eds) *Perfectionism and Neutrality: Essays in Liberal Theory*, Lanham, MD: Rowman and Littlefield.

Arneson, R. (2014) 'Neutrality and Political Liberalism,' in R. Merrill and D. Weinstock (eds) *Political Neutrality: A Re-Evaluation*, London: Palgrave Macmillan.

Asante, M.K. (2008) *The Afrocentric Manifesto*, Cambridge: Polity.

Baier, A. (1985) *Postures of the Mind*, Minneapolis: University of Minnesota Press.

Bailey, T. (2014) *Rawls and Religion*, New York: Columbia University Press.

Baker, J., Lynch, K., Cantillon, S., and Walsh, J. (2004) *Equality: From Theory to Action*, Basingstoke, Hampshire: Palgrave Macmillan.

Bakhurst, D. (2011) *The Formation of Reason*, Oxford: Wiley-Blackwell.

Bakhurst, D. and Sypnowich, C. (eds) (1995) *The Social Self*, London: Sage.

Ball, C.A. (1997) 'Moral Foundations for a Discourse on Same-Sex Marriage, Looking Beyond Political Liberalism,' *Georgetown Law Journal*, 85.

Banting, K. and Kymlicka, W. (2010) 'Canadian Multiculturalism: Global Anxieties and Local Debates,' *British Journal of Canadian Studies*, 23, 1.

Barnes, M. (2012) *Care in Everyday Life: An Ethic of Care in Practice*, Oxford: Oxford University Press.

Barry, B. (1995) 'John Rawls and the Search for Stability,' *Ethics*, 105, 4.

Barry, B. (1995) 'Spherical Justice and Global Injustice,' in D. Miller and M. Walzer (eds) *Pluralism, Justice and Equality*, Oxford: Oxford University Press.

Barry, B. (1995) *Justice as Impartiality*, Oxford: Clarendon Press.

Barry, B. (2001) *Culture and Equality*, Cambridge: Polity.

Beauvoir, S. de (1987) *The Second Sex* trans. and ed. H.M. Parshley, Harmondsworth: Penguin.

Beckett, A. (2006) *Citizenship and Vulnerability, Disability and Issues of Social and Political Engagement*, London: Palgrave Macmillan.

Beitz, C. (1979) *Political Theory and International Relations*, Princeton: Princeton University Press.

Benhabib, S. (2002) *The Claims of Culture: Equality and Diversity in the Global Era*, Princeton: Princeton University Press.

Benjamin, J. (1990) *The Bonds of Love*, London: Virago.

Benjamin, W. (1978) 'The Author and Producer,' *Reflections* ed. and introd. P. Demetz, New York: Harcourt Brace Jovanovich.

Berlin, I. (1982) 'Two Concepts of Liberty,' *Four Essays on Liberty*, Oxford: Oxford University Press.

Bevan, R. (2006) *The Destruction of Memory: Architecture at War*, London: Reaktion Books.

Beveridge, W. (2015) *The Pillars of Security*, Abingdon: Routledge.

Bickenbach, J., Felder, F. and Schmitz, B. (eds) (2013) *Disability and the Good Human Life*, Cambridge: Cambridge University Press.

Bissoondath, N. (1994) *Selling Illusions: The Cult of Multiculturalism in Canada*, Toronto: Penguin.

Bloch, E. (1988) *The Utopian Function of Art and Literature*, trans. J. Zipes and F. Mecklenburg, Cambridge, MA: MIT Press.

Bogdanov, A. (1984) *Red Star*, ed. L.R. Graham and R. Stites, trans. C. Rougle, Indianapolis: Indiana University Press.

Bohman, J. and Richardson, H. (2009) 'Liberalism, Deliberative Democracy, and "Reasons That All Can Accept",' *Journal of Political Philosophy*, 17, 3.

Boxill, B. (1978) 'The Morality of Preferential Hiring,' *Philosophy and Public Affairs*, 7, 3.

Boxill, B. (1991) 'Equality, Discrimination and Preferential Treatment,' in P. Singer (ed.) *A Companion to Ethics*, Oxford: Basil Blackwell.

Braidotti, R. (1989) 'The Politics of Ontological Difference,' in T. Brennan (ed.) *Between Feminism and Psychoanalysis*, London: Routledge.

Brake, E. (2010) 'Minimal Marriage: What Political Liberalism Implies for Marriage Law,' *Ethics*, 120, 2.

Brennan, S. and Noggle, R. (eds) (2007) *Taking Responsibility for Children*, Waterloo: Wilfrid Laurier University Press.

Brighouse, H. (1995) 'Neutrality, Publicity and State Funding of the Arts,' *Philosophy and Public Affairs*, 24, 1.

Brighouse, H. (1996) 'Is there a Neutral Justification for Liberalism?' *Pacific Philosophical Quarterly*, 77, 3.

Brighouse, H. (1998) 'Against Nationalism,' in J. Couture, K. Nielsen and M. Seymour (eds) *Rethinking Nationalism*, Canadian Journal of Philosophy Supplementary Vol. 22, Calgary: Calgary University Press.

Brighouse, H. (2002) *School Choice and Social Justice*, Oxford: Oxford University Press.

Brighouse, H. and Swift, A. (2006) 'Parents' Rights and the Value of the Family,' *Ethics* 117, 1.

Brighouse, H. and Swift, A. (2009) 'Legitimate Parental Partiality,' *Philosophy and Public Affairs*, 37, 1.

Brighouse, H. and Swift, A. (2014) *Family Values: The Ethics of Parent-Child Relationships*, Princeton: Princeton University Press.

Broadbent Institute (2014) 'Haves and Have-Nots: Deep and Persistent Wealth Inequality in Canada,' September, www.broadbentinstitute.ca/haves_and_have_nots.

Broadbent Institute (2014) 'The Wealth Gap: Perceptions and Misconceptions in Canada,' December, www.broadbentinstitute.ca/the_wealth_gap.

Brown, W. (1995) *States of Injury: Power and Freedom in Late Modernity*, Princeton: Princeton University Press.

Brownlee, K. and Cureton, A. (eds) (2011) *Disability and Disadvantage*, Oxford: Oxford University Press.

Buchanan, A. (1991) *Secession: The Morality of Political Divorce*, Boulder, CO: Westview Press.

Burke, E. (1999) *Reflections on the Revolution in France*, Oxford: Oxford University Press.

Butler, J. (1990) *Gender Trouble*, New York: Routledge.

Butler, J. (1997) *Excitable Speech: A Politics of the Performative*, London: Routledge.

Callan, E. (1997) *Creating Citizens*, Oxford: Oxford University Press.

Callinicos, A. (2000) *Equality*, Cambridge: Polity.

Cancian, F. (1989) 'Gender and Power: Love and Power in the Public and Private Spheres,' in A.S. Solnick and J.H. Solnick (eds) *Family in Transition: Rethinking Marriage, Sexuality Childrearing and Family Organization*, London: Scott Freeman.

Caney, S. (1995) 'Anti-perfectionism and Rawlsian Liberalism,' *Political Studies*, 43, 2.

Cardwell, R., Carr, B., and Sypnowich, C. (eds) (2015) *Barriefield: 200 Years of Village Life*, Kingston: Quarry Press.

Carens, J. (ed.) (1995) *Is Quebec Nationalism Just? Perspectives from Anglophone Canada*, Montreal-Kingston: McGill-Queen's University Press.

Carens, J. (2000) *Culture, Citizenship and Community: A Contextual Exploration of Justice as Evenhandedness*, Oxford: Oxford University Press.

Carmichael, S. and Hamilton, C.V. (1992) *Black Power: The Politics of Liberation in America*, New York: Vintage.

Casal, P. (2007) 'Why Sufficiency Is Not Enough,' *Ethics* 117, 2.

Casal, P. and Williams, A. (1995) 'Rights, Equality and Procreation,' *Analyse und Kritik*, 17, 1.

Central Intelligence Agency (2011) *World Fact Book*, https://www.cia.gov/library/publications/download/download-2011/.

Chambers, C. (2002) 'All Must Have Prizes: The Liberal Case for Interference in Cultural Practices,' in P. Kelly (ed.) *Multiculturalism Reconsidered: 'Culture and Equality'*, Cambridge: Polity.

Chambers, C. (2008) *Sex, Culture and Justice*, University Park, PA: Pennsylvania State University Press.

Chambers, C. (2009) 'Each Outcome is Another Opportunity: Problems with the Moment of Equal Opportunity,' in *Politics, Philosophy and Economics*, 8, 4.

Chan, J. (2000) 'Legitimacy, Unanimity and Perfectionism,' *Philosophy and Public Affairs*, 29, 1.

Chodorow, N. (1978) *The Reproduction of Mothering*, Berkeley: University of California Press.

Christiano, T. (1996) *The Rule of the Many*, Boulder, CO: Westview Press.

Christiano, T. (ed.) (2003) *Philosophy and Democracy*, Oxford: Oxford University Press.

Christiano, T. (2008) *The Constitution of Equality: Democratic Authority and its Limits*, Oxford: Oxford University Press.

Christiano, T. and Braynen, W. (2009) 'Inequality, Injustice and Levelling Down,' in B. Feltham (ed.) *Justice, Equality and Constructivism: Essays on G.A. Cohen's Rescuing Justice and Equality*, Oxford: Wiley-Blackwell.

Clarke, S. (1999) 'Contractualism, Liberal Neutrality, and Epistemology,' *Political Studies*, 47, 4.

Cockburn, T. (2005) 'Children and the Feminist Ethic of Care,' *Childhood*, 12, 1.

Code, L. (1991) *What Can She Know? Feminist Theory and the Construction of Knowledge*, Ithaca: Cornell University Press.

Cohen, G.A. (1989) 'On the Currency of Egalitarian Justice,' *Ethics*, 99, 4.

Cohen, G.A. (1993) 'Equality of What? On Welfare, Goods and Opportunities,' in M. Nussbaum and A. Sen (eds), *The Quality of Life*, Oxford: Clarendon Press.

Cohen, G.A. (1994) 'Incentives, Inequality and Community,' in S. Darwall (ed.) *Equal Freedom*, Ann Arbor: University of Michigan Press.

Cohen, G.A. (1995) *Self-Ownership, Freedom and Equality*, Cambridge: Cambridge University Press.

Cohen, G.A. (2000) 'The Pareto Argument for Inequality,' in M. Clayton and A. Williams (eds) *The Ideal of Equality*, London: Macmillan.

Cohen, G.A. (2000) *If You're an Egalitarian, How Come You're So Rich?*, Cambridge, MA: Harvard University Press.

Cohen, G.A. (2008) *Rescuing Justice and Equality*, Cambridge, MA: Harvard University Press.

Cohen, G.A. (2009) *Why Not Socialism?*, Princeton: Princeton University Press.

Cohen, G.A. (2013) 'Rescuing Conservatism: A Defence of Existing Value,' in *Finding Oneself in the Other* (ed.) M. Otsuka, Princeton: Princeton University Press.

Cohen, J. (ed.) (1996) *For Love of Country*, Boston: Beacon Press.

Collins, P.H. (2000) *Black Feminist Thought: Knowledge, Consciousness, and the Politics of Empowerment*, New York: Routledge.

Conference Board of Canada (2011) 'World Income Inequality: Is the world becoming more unequal?' www.conferenceboard.ca/hcp/hot-topics/worldinequality.aspx

Conly, S. (2012) *Against Autonomy: Justifying Coercive Paternalism*, Cambridge: Cambridge University Press.

Conly, S. (2013) 'Three Cheers for the Nanny State,' *New York Times*, 24 March.

Coole, D. (1995) 'The Gendered Self,' in D. Bakhurst and C. Sypnowich (eds) *The Social Self*, London: Sage.

Cornell, D. (1993) *Transformations: Recollective Imagination and Sexual Difference*, New York: Routledge.

Cornell, D. (1995) 'What is Ethical Feminism?,' in S. Benhabib, J. Butler, D. Cornell, N. Fraser (eds), *Feminist Contentions: A Philosophical Exchange*, London: Routledge.

Cornell, D. (1998) *At the Heart of Freedom*, Princeton: Princeton University Press.

Couture, J. and Nielsen, K. (2005) 'Cosmopolitanism and the Compatriot Priority Principle,' H. Brighouse, and G. Brock (eds) *The Philosophy of Cosmopolitanism*, Cambridge: Cambridge University Press.

Crisp, R. (2003) 'Equality, Priority, and Compassion,' *Ethics* 113, 4.

Croix, D. de la and Doepke, M. (2007) 'Politics and the Structure of Education Funding,' Centre for Economic Policy Research, 21 September.

Crowder, G. (2014) 'Neutrality and Liberal Pluralism,' in R. Merrill and D. Weinstock (eds) *Political Neutrality: A Re-Evaluation*, London: Palgrave Macmillan.

Cudd, A. (2006) *Analysing Oppression*, Oxford: Oxford University Press.

D'Agostino, F. (1996) *Free Public Reason: Making it Up as We Go*, New York: Oxford University Press.

D'Souza, D. (1991) *Illiberal Education: The Politics of Race and Sex on Campus*, New York: Free Press.

Dahl, R. (1961) *Who Governs? Democracy and Power in an American City*, New Haven: Yale University Press.

Davis, L. (1996) 'Morris, Wilde, and Marx on the Social Preconditions of Individual Development,' *Political Studies* 44, 4.

Delgado, R. and Stefanic, J. (eds) (2012) *Critical Race Theory: An Introduction*, New York: New York University Press.

den Otter, S. (1996) *British Idealism and Social Explanation*, Oxford: Oxford University Press.

Deresiewicz, W. (2014) *Excellent Sheep: The Miseducation of the American Elite and the Way to a Meaningful Life*, New York: Free Press.

Desai, M. (2003) 'Public Goods: A Historical Perspective,' in I. Kaul, P. Conceicao, K. Le Goulven, R.U. Mendoza (eds), *Providing Global Public Goods: Managing Globalization*, New York: Oxford University Press.

Descartes, R. (1968) *The Meditations*, in *Discourse on Method and the Meditations*, trans. F.E. Sutcliffe, Harmondsworth: Penguin.

Deveaux, M. (2000) *Cultural Pluralism and Dilemmas of Difference*, Ithaca: Cornell University Press.

Donaldson, S. and Kymlicka, K. (2011) *Zoopolis: A Political Theory of Animal Rights*, Oxford: Oxford University Press.

Dworkin, D. (1993) *Life's Dominion: An Argument about Abortion, Euthanasia, and Individual Freedom*, New York: Alfred A. Knopf.

Dworkin, R. (1978) 'Liberalism,' in S. Hampshire (ed.) *Public and Private Morality*, Cambridge: Cambridge University Press.

Dworkin, R. (1985) *A Matter of Principle*, Cambridge, MA: Harvard University Press.

Dworkin, R. (1990) 'Foundations of Liberal Equality,' *Tanner Lectures on Human Values*, Vol. 11, G.B. Peterson (ed.) Salt Lake City: University of Utah Press.

Dworkin, R. (2000) *Sovereign Virtue*, Cambridge, MA: Harvard University Press.

Dworkin, R. (2003) 'Equality, Luck and Hierarchy,' *Philosophy and Public Affairs*, 31, 2.

Dyke, V. (1995) 'The Individual, the State and Ethnic Communities in Political Society,' in W. Kymlicka (ed.) *The Rights of Minority Cultures*, Oxford: Oxford University Press.

Dyzenhaus, D. (ed.) (1999) *Recrafting the Rule of Law*, Oxford: Hart Publishing.

Eisenberg, A. (2006) 'The Debate over Sharia Law in Canada,' in B. Arneil, M. Deveaux, R. Dhamoon and A. Eisenberg (eds) *Sexual/Cultural Justice*, London: Routledge.

Eisenberg, A. and Spinner-Halev, J. (eds) (2005) *Minorities within Minorities: Equality, Rights and Diversity*, Cambridge: Cambridge University Press.

Elster, J. (1985) *Making Sense of Marx*, Cambridge: Cambridge University Press.

Engels, F. (1978) 'Socialism: Utopian and Scientific,' in *Marx-Engels Reader*, (ed.) R.C. Tucker, New York: W.W. Norton (MER).

Engels, F. (1978) 'The Origin of the Family, Private Property and the State,' in MER.

Estlund, D. (1996) 'The Survival of Egalitarian Justice in John Rawls's *Political Liberalism*,' *Journal of Political Philosophy*, 4, 1.

Estlund, D. (1998) 'Debate: Liberalism, Equality and Fraternity in Cohen's Critique of Rawls,' *Journal of Political Philosophy*, 6, 1.

Estlund, D. (2008) 'Utopophobia: Concession and Aspiration in Democratic Theory,' *Democratic Authority: A Philosophical Framework*, Princeton: Princeton University Press.

Estlund, D. (2011) 'Human Nature and the Limits (if any) of Political Philosophy,' *Philosophy and Public Affairs*, 39, 3.

Euractive.com (2014) 'It's official: Last EU election had lowest-ever turnout,' 7 August, www.euractiv.com/section/eu-elections-2014/news/it-s-official-last-eu-election-had-lowest-ever-turnout/.

Finnis, J. (1974) 'The Rights and Wrongs of Abortion,' in M. Cohen, T. Nagel and T. Scanlon (eds) *The Rights and Wrongs of Abortion*, Princeton: Princeton University Press.

Firestone, S. (1972) *The Dialectic of Sex*, New York: Bantam Books.

Fishkin, J. (2014) *Bottlenecks: A New Theory of Equal Opportunity*, New York: Oxford University Press.

Foot, P. (1985) 'Morality, Action and Outcome,' in T. Honderich (ed.) *Morality and Objectivity*, London: Routledge.

Ford, R. (2005) *Racial Culture: A Critique*, Princeton: Princeton University Press.

Fording, R.C. and Berry, W.D. (2007) 'The Historical Impact of Welfare Programs on Poverty: Evidence from the American States,' *Policy Studies Journal*, 35, 1.

Foucault, M. (1980) *Power/Knowledge*, ed. C. Gordon, New York: Pantheon.

Foucault, M. (1980) *The History of Sexuality, Vol. 1: An Introduction*, trans. R. Hurley, New York: Vintage.

Fourie, C. (2015) 'To Praise and to Scorn' in C. Fourie, F. Schuppert, I. Wallimann-Helmer (eds) *Social Equality: What it Means to Be Equals*, Oxford: Oxford University Press.

Fourier, C. (1971) *Harmonian Man*, ed. M. Poster, Garden City, NY: Doubleday.

Frank, R. (1999) *Luxury Fever: Money and Happiness in an Era of Excess*, Princeton: Princeton University Press.

Frankfurt, H. (1987) 'Equality as a Moral Ideal,' *Ethics*, 98, 1.

Fraser, N. (1995) 'From Redistribution to Recognition?,' *New Left Review*, 212.

Fraser, N. (1997) *Justice Interruptus*, London: Routledge.

Fraser, N. (1998) 'Social Justice in the Age of Identity Politics: Redistribution, Recognition and Participation,' G.B. Peterson (ed.) *Tanner Lectures on Human Values*, Vol. 19, Salt Lake City: University of Utah Press.

Fraser, N. and Nicholson, L. (1990) 'Social Criticism without Philosophy,' in L. Nicholson, (ed.) *Feminism/Postmodernism*, New York: Routledge.

Freeman, S. (2002) 'Liberalism and the Accommodation of Group Claims,' in P. Kelly (ed.) *Multiculturalism Reconsidered: 'Culture and Equality*,' Cambridge: Polity.

Fricker, M. (2009) *Epistemic Injustice*, Oxford: Oxford University Press.

Friedman, M. (2003) *Autonomy, Gender, Politics*, New York: Oxford University Press.

Friedman, M. and Bolte, A. (2007) 'Ethics and Feminism,' in E.F. Kittay and L. Alcoff (eds) *The Blackwell Guide to Feminist Philosophy*, Oxford: Blackwell.

Gallagher, I. (1996) 'William Guest Goes Shopping,' *Journal of the William Morris Society*, 11, 4.

Galston, W. (1991) *Liberal Purposes: Goods, Virtues and Diversity in the Liberal State*, Cambridge: Cambridge University Press.

Galston, W. (2012) 'Oakeshott's Political Theory: Recapitulation and Criticisms,' in E. Podoksik (ed.) *The Cambridge Companion to Oakeshott*, Cambridge: Cambridge University Press.

Gamble, A. (2012) 'Oakeshott's Ideological Politics: Conservative or Liberal?,' in E. Podoksik (ed.) *The Cambridge Companion to Oakeshott*, Cambridge: Cambridge University Press.

Gathmann, C. and Keller, N. (2014) 'Return to Citizenship? Evidence from Germany's Recent Immigration Reforms,' Institute for the Study of Labour (IZA), Discussion Paper No. 8064.

Gaus, G.F. (2003) 'Liberal Neutrality: A Compelling and Radical Principle,' in S. Wall and G. Klosko (eds) *Perfectionism and Neutrality: Essays in Liberal Theory*, Lanham, MD: Rowman and Littlefield.

Geertz, C. (1973) *The Interpretation of Cultures*, New York: Basic Books.

Gellner, E. (1996) *Nations and Nationalism*, Oxford: Blackwell.

Gilabert, P. (2012) *From Global Poverty to Global Equality*, Oxford: Oxford University Press.

Gilbert, D. (2007) *Stumbling on Happiness*, New York: Knopf.

Gilbert, M.A. (2009) 'Defeating Bigenderism: Changing Gender Assumptions in the Twenty-first Century,' *Hypatia*, 24, 3.

Gill, R. and Koffman, O. (2013) 'I Matter. And So Does She: Girl Power, (Post)feminism and the Girl Effect' in D. Buckingham, S. Braggs, and M.-J. Kehily (eds) *Youth Cultures in the Age of Global Media*, London: Palgrave Macmillan.

Gilligan, C. (1982) *A Different Voice*, Cambridge, MA: Harvard University Press.

Gitlin, T. (1995) *The Twilight of Common Dreams*, New York: Henry Holt.

Glasier, J.B. (1921) *William Morris and the Early Days of the Socialist Movement*, London: Longmans, Green and Co.

Glazer, N. (1997) *We Are All Multiculturalists Now*, Cambridge, MA: Harvard University Press.

Glyn, A. (2006) *Capitalism Unleashed*, Oxford: Oxford University Press.

Goncharov, I. (2005) *Oblomov*, London: Penguin.

Goodin, R. (1989) *No Smoking*, Chicago: University of Chicago Press.

Gooding-Williams, R. (2006) *Look, a Negro! Philosophical Essays on Race, Culture and Politics*, New York: Routledge.

Grant, R.W. and Orr, M. (1996) 'Language, Race and Politics: From "Black" to "African-American,"' *Politics and Society*, 24, 2.

Green, L. (1994) 'Internal Minorities and their Rights,' in *Group Rights*, (ed.) J. Baker, Toronto: University of Toronto Press.

Greenawalt, K. (1991) *Religious Convictions and Political Choice*, Oxford: Oxford University Press.

Griffin, J. (1986) *Wellbeing*, Oxford: Oxford University Press.

Grimshaw, J. (1986) *Philosophy and Feminist Thinking*, Minneapolis: University of Minnesota Press.

Gutmann, A. (1987) *Democratic Education*, Princeton: Princeton University Press.

Gutmann, A. (1996) 'Responding to Racial Injustice,' in K.A. Appiah and A. Gutmann, *Color Conscious*, Princeton: Princeton University Press.

Gwyn, R. (1995) *Nationalism without Walls: The Unbearable Lightness of Being Canadian*, Toronto: McClelland and Stewart.

Haack, S. (2000) *Manifesto of a Passionate Moderate*, Chicago: University of Chicago Press.

Habermas, J. (1981) 'Modernity versus Postmodernity,' *New German Critique*, 22.

Habermas, J. (1987) *The Philosophical Discourses of Modernity*, trans. F. Lawrence, Cambridge, MA: MIT Press.

Habermas, J. (1994) 'Struggles for Recognition in the Democratic Constitutional State,' in A. Gutmann, (ed.) *Multiculturalism*, Princeton: Princeton University Press.

Hacking, I. (1992) 'Making Up People,' in T. Heller, M. Sousa, D. Wellbery (eds) *Reconstructing Individualism: Autonomy, Individuality and the Self in Western Thought*, New York: Routledge.

Haddad, M. (2012) *The Perfect Storm: Economic Stagnation, the rising cost of living, spending cuts, and the impact on UK poverty*, Oxfam, June. http://policy-practice.oxfam.org.uk/publications/the-perfect-storm-economic-stagnation-the-rising-cost-of-living-public-spending-228591

Haksar, V. (1979) *Equality, Liberty and Perfectionism*, Oxford: Oxford University Press.

Hall, S. (1995) 'Negotiating Caribbean Identities,' *New Left Review* 209.

Hanson, M. (2015) 'Music is a Lifesaver,' *The Guardian*, 14 December, www.theguardian.com/education/2015/dec/14/music-school-system-government-orchestra-education.

Haraway, D. (1991) *Symians, Cyborgs and Women*, New York: Routledge.

Harrington, M. (1985) *The New American Poverty*, London: Firethorn.

Harris, L.C. and Narayan, U. (1997) 'Affirmative Action as Equalizing Opportunity: Challenging the Myth of "Preferential Treatment,"' in H. Lafollette (ed.) *Ethics in Practice: An Anthology*, Oxford: Basil Blackwell.

Hart, C. (2014) *High Price: A Neuroscientist's Journey of Self-Discovery that Challenges Everything You Know about Drugs and Society*, New York: Harper.

Hartmann, H. (1971) 'The Unhappy Marriage of Marxism and Feminism: Toward a More Progressive Union,' in L. Sargent (ed.) *Women and Revolution*, Boston: South End Press.

Hartsock, N. (1987) 'The Feminist Standpoint,' in S. Harding (ed.) *Feminism and Methodology*, Bloomington: Indiana University Press.

Hayek, F.A. (2007) *The Road to Serfdom*, Chicago: Chicago University Press.

Hegel, G.W.F. (2008) *Philosophy of Right*, trans. T.M. Knox, rev. S. Houlgate, Oxford: Oxford University Press.

Hekman, S. (1995) 'Subjects and Agents: The Question for Feminism,' in J.K. Gardiner (ed.) *Provoking Agents: Gender and Agency in Theory and Practice*, Chicago: University of Illinois Press.

Heller, A. and Feher, F. (1988) *The Postmodern Political Condition*, Cambridge: Polity.

Heyman, G. (2009) *Addiction: A Disorder of Choice*, Cambridge, MA: Harvard University Press.

Hirose, I. (2015) *Egalitarianism*, Abingdon: Routledge.

Hirschmann, N.J. (2003) *The Subject of Liberty: Toward a Feminist Theory of Freedom*, Princeton: Princeton University Press.

Hobbes, T. (1968) *Leviathan*, (ed.) C.B. Macpherson, Harmondsworth: Penguin.

Hobhouse, L.T. (1964) *Liberalism*, Oxford: Oxford University Press.

Hobsbawm, E. (1995) *Age of Extremes*, London: Abacus.

Honig, B. (1996) 'Difference, Dilemmas and the Politics of Home,' in S. Benhabib (ed.) *Democracy and Difference: Contesting the Boundaries of the Political*, Princeton: Princeton University Press.

hooks, b. (2000) *Feminist Theory: From Margin to Centre*, London: Pluto.

Horowitz, G. (1987) 'The Foucauldian Impasse: No Sex, No Self, No Revolution,' *Political Theory*, 15, 1.

Houston, B. (1987) 'Rescuing Womanly Virtues,' in M. Hanen and K. Nielsen (eds) *Science, Morality and Feminist Theory*, Supplementary Vol. 13, *Canadian Journal of Philosophy*, Calgary: University of Calgary Press.

Hoxby, C.M. (1994) 'Do Private Schools Provide Competition for Public Schools?,' National Bureau for Education Research, Working Paper 4978.

Hurka, T. (1996) *Perfectionism*, Oxford: Oxford University Press.

Hurka, T. (2002) 'Capability, Functioning and Perfectionism,' *Apeiron*, 35, 4.

Hursthouse, R. (1987) *Beginning Lives*, Oxford: Basil Blackwell.

Husak, D. and de Marneffe, P. (2005) *The Legalisation of Drugs: For and Against*, Cambridge: Cambridge University Press.

Huxley, A. (1969) *Brave New World*, New York: Harper and Row.

Irigaray, L. (1985) *This Sex Which Is Not One*, trans. C. Porter with C. Burke, Ithaca: Cornell University Press.

Jackson, B. (2008) *Equality and the British Left: A Study in Progressive Political Thought: 1900–64*, Manchester: Manchester University Press.

Jaggar, A. (1983) *Feminist Politics and Human Nature*, Sussex: Harvester.

Jaggar, A. (2000) 'Feminism in Ethics: Moral Justification,' in M. Fricker and J. Hornsby (eds) *The Cambridge Companion to Feminism in Philosophy*, Cambridge: Cambridge University Press.

Johnson, M.A. (1998) 'The Ebonics Debate,' *Journal of Pedagogy, Pluralism and Practice*, 1, 3. www.lesley.edu/journal-pedagogy-pluralism-practice/mary-ann-johnson/ebonics-debate/.

Jones, C. (1999) *Global Justice*, Oxford: Oxford University Press.

Kahlenberg, R. (1995) 'Class, Not Race,' *New Republic*, April 3.

Kaul, I., Grunberg I. and Stern, M.A. (1999) 'Defining Global Public Goods,' in I. Kaul, I. Grunberg and M.A. Stern (eds) *Global Public Goods: International Cooperation in the 21st Century*, New York: Oxford University Press.

Kay, G. (1979) *The Economic Theory of the Working Class*, London: Macmillan.

Keller, N. (2014) 'Return to Citizenship? Evidence from Germany's Recent Immigration Reforms,' *Institute for the Study of Labour* (IZA), Discussion Paper 8064, March.

Kelly, P. (2002) 'Introduction: Between Culture and Equality,' in P. Kelly, (ed.) *Multiculturalism Reconsidered: 'Culture and Equality,'* Cambridge: Polity.

Kernohan, A. (1998) *Liberalism, Equality and Cultural Oppression*, Cambridge: Cambridge University Press.

Kim, J. (1995) 'Culture,' in T. Honderich (ed.) *Oxford Companion to Philosophy*, Oxford: Oxford University Press.

Kingwell, M. (1993) 'Is it Rational to Be Polite?' *Journal of Philosophy*, 60, 8.

Kittay, E.F. (1990) *Love's Labor: Essays on Women, Equality and Dependency*, London: Routledge.

Kittay, E.F. and Feder, E.K. (eds) (2002) *The Subject of Care: Feminist Perspectives on Dependency*, Lanham, MD: Rowman and Littlefield.

Kittay, E.F. and Meyers, D. (eds) (1987) *Women and Moral Theory*, Savage, MD: Rowman and Littlefield.

Koggel, C. (1998) *Perspectives on Equality*, Lanham, MD: Rowman and Littlefield.

Kohn, H. (1967) *The Idea of Nationalism*, New York: Collier-Macmillan.

Kolakowski, L. (1978) *Main Currents of Marxism, Vol. 3 The Breakdown*, trans. P.S. Falla, Oxford: Oxford University Press.

Kollontai, A. (1992) *Love of Worker Bees*, (ed.) C. Porter, Chicago: Academy Press.

Kostakopoulou, D. (2008) *The Future Governance of Citizenship*, Cambridge: Cambridge University Press.

Kristeva, J. (1986) 'Woman's Time,' in *The Kristeva Reader*, (ed.) T. Moi, New York: Columbia University Press.

Kroeger-Mappes, J. (1994) 'The Ethic of Care vis-à-vis the Ethic of Rights: A Problem for Contemporary Moral Theory,' *Hypatia*, 9, 3.

Kukathas, C. (1992) 'Are There Any Cultural Rights?,' *Political Theory*, 20, 1.

Kupperman, J. (1995) 'Perfectionism,' (ed.) T. Honderich, *Oxford Companion to Philosophy*, Oxford: Oxford University Press.

Kymlicka, W. (1989) *Liberalism, Community and Culture*, Oxford: Clarendon.

Kymlicka, W. (1995) *Multicultural Citizenship*, Oxford: Oxford University Press.

Kymlicka, W. (1998) *Finding Our Way: Rethinking Ethnocultural Relations in Canada*, Toronto: Oxford University Press.

Kymlicka, W. (2001) *Politics in the Vernacular: Nationalism, Multiculturalism and Citizenship*, Oxford: Oxford University Press.

Kymlicka, W. (2002) *Contemporary Political Philosophy*, Oxford: Oxford University Press.

Kymlicka, W. (2006) 'Left-Liberalism Revisited,' in C. Sypnowich (ed.) *The Egalitarian Conscience: Essays in Honour of G.A. Cohen*, Oxford: Oxford University Press.

Laclau, E. (1991) 'God Only Knows,' *Marxism Today*, December.

Laclau, E. (1996) 'Universalism, Particularism and the Question of Identity,' in E.N. Wilmsen and P. McAllister (eds) *The Politics of Difference*, Chicago: University of Chicago Press.

Laclau, E. and Mouffe, C. (1985) *Hegemony and Socialist Strategy: Towards a Radical Democratic Politics*, London: Verso.

Lane, H. (1979) *The Wild Boy of Aveyron*, London: Paladin.

Larmore, C. (1987) *Patterns of Moral Complexity*, Cambridge: Cambridge University Press.

Larmore, C. (2008) *The Autonomy of Morality*, New York: Cambridge University Press.

Laski, H. (1933) *Democracy in Crisis*, London: George, Allen and Unwin.

Lawson, B.E. (1992) 'Moral Discourse and Slavery,' in H. McGary and B.E. Lawson (eds) *Between Slavery and Freedom*, Indianapolis and Bloomington: Indiana University Press.

Lawson, N. (2001) *How to Be a Domestic Goddess*, London: Hyperion.

Layard, R. (2005) *Happiness: Lessons from a New Science*, London: Penguin.

Lecce, S. (2003) 'Contractualism and Liberal Neutrality: A Defence,' *Political Studies*, 51, 3.

Lecce, S. (2005) 'Should Egalitarians be Perfectionists?,' *Politics*, 25, 3.

Lecce, S. (2008) *Against Perfectionism: Defending Liberal Neutrality*, Toronto: University of Toronto Press.

Lemkin, R. (2005) *Axis Rule in Occupied Europe: Occupation, Analysis of Government, Proposals for Redress*, Clark, NJ: Lawbook Exchange.

Leopold, D. (2007) *The Young Karl Marx*, Cambridge: Cambridge University Press.

Levey, G.B. (1997) 'Equality, Autonomy and Cultural Rights,' *Political Theory*, 25, 2.

Levinson, M. (1999) *The Demands of Liberal Education*, Oxford: Oxford University Press.

Levy, J. (2001) *The Multiculturalism of Fear*, Oxford: Oxford University Press.

Lewis, C.S. (1939) 'William Morris,' *Rehabilitations*, Oxford: Oxford University Press.

Lewis, D. (1972) *Louder Voices: Corporate Welfare Bums*, Toronto: James Lorimer.

Lintott, S. (2012) 'The Sublimity of Gestating and Giving Birth: Toward a Feminist Conception of the Sublime,' in S. Lintott and M. Sander-Staudt (eds) *Philosophical Inquiries into Pregnancy, Childbirth and Mothering: Maternal Subjects*, New York: Routledge.

Lister, A. (2010) 'Public Justification and the Limits of State Action,' *Politics, Philosophy and Economics*, 9, 2.

Lister, A. (2013) *Public Reason and Political Community*, London: Bloomsbury.

Lloyd, G. (1984) *The Man of Reason: 'Male' and 'Female' in Western Philosophy*, London: Methuen.

Lou, E. (2016) 'Five Facts on Canada Aboriginal Community Suicide Crisis,' *Reuters*, 12 April, www.reuters.com/article/us-canada-aboriginal-suicides-factboz-idUSKC N0X92FY?mod=related&channelName=worldNews.

Loury, G. (2002) *The Anatomy of Racial Inequality*, Cambridge, MA: Harvard University Press.

Lowry, C. (2009) 'Beyond Equality of What: Sen and Neutrality,' *Les Ateliers de l'Éthique/the Ethics Forum* 4, 2. http://philpapers.org/archive/LOWBEO.pdf.

Lowry, C. (2011) 'Perfectionism for Neutralists,' *Journal of Social Philosophy* 42, 4.

Lukacs, G. (1973) 'Appearance and Essence,' in G. LeRoy and U. Beitz (eds) *Preserve and Create: Essays in Marxist Literary Criticism*, New York: Humanities Press.

Lukes, S. (1995) *The Curious Enlightenment of Professor Caritat*, London: Verso.

Lukes, S. (2004) *Power: A Radical View*, London: Palgrave Macmillan.

Lyotard, J.-F. (1984) *The Postmodern Condition: A Report on Knowledge*, trans. G. Bennington and B. Massimi, foreword by F. Jameson, Minneapolis: University of Minnesota Press.

MacCarthy, F. (1994) *William Morris: A Life for Our Time*, London: Faber and Faber.

Macedo, S. (1990) *Liberal Virtues*, Oxford: Oxford University Press.

Macedo, S. (1997) 'Sexuality and Liberty: Making Room for Nature and Tradition?,' in D. Estlund and M. Nussbaum (eds) *Sex, Preference and the Family: Essays on Law and Nature*, Oxford: Oxford University Press.

Macedo, S. (2015) *Just Married: Same-Sex Couples, Monogamy and the Future of Marriage*, Princeton: Princeton University Press.

MacIntyre, A. (1981) *After Virtue*, London: Duckworth.

MacKinnon, C. (1987) *Feminism Unmodified*, Cambridge, MA: Harvard University Press.

Macleod, C. (2014) 'Neutrality, Public Reason and Deliberative Democracy,' in R. Merrill and D. Weinstock (eds) *Political Neutrality: A Re-Evaluation*, London: Palgrave Macmillan.

Macpherson, C.B. (1962) *Possessive Individualism*, Oxford: Clarendon Press.

Macpherson, C.B. (1973) *Democratic Theory: Essays in Retrieval*, Oxford: Oxford University Press.

Malson, L. and Itard, J. (1972) *Wolf Children and The Wild Boy of Aveyron*, London: New Left Books.

Marcuse, H. (1964) *One Dimensional Man*, Boston: Beacon Press.

Marcuse, H. (1977) *The Aesthetic Dimension*, Boston: Beacon Press.

Marks, E. and de Courtivron, I. (ed. and introd.) (1988) *New French Feminisms*, New York: Schocken Books.

Marshall, T.H. (1963) *Sociology at the Crossroads*, London: Heinemann.

Marx, K. and Engels, F. (1978) *Marx-Engels Reader*, (ed.) R.C. Tucker, New York: W.W. Norton (MER).

Marx K. (1978) 'Critique of the Gotha Programme,' in MER.

Marx, K. (1978) 'Economic and Philosophical Manuscripts,' in MER.

Marx, K. (1978) 'On the Jewish Question,' in MER.

Marx, K. (1978) *Capital* (extracts), in MER.

Marx, K. and Engels, F. (1978) 'Communist Manifesto,' in MER.

Marx, K. and Engels, F. (1978) 'German Ideology,' in MER.

Mason, A. (1997) 'Special Obligations to Compatriots,' *Ethics*, 107, 3.

Mazzini, G. (1880) 'Europe: Its Condition and Prospects,' *Essays: Selected from the Writings, Literary, Political and Religious of Joseph Mazzini*, ed. W. Clark, London: Walter Scott.

McCabe, D. (2000) 'Knowing about the Good: A Problem with Antiperfectionism,' *Ethics* 110, 2.

McGarvey, R. (2016) 'Money alone won't solve the Attawapiskat crisis,' *Waterloo Region Record*, May 2. www.therecord.com/opinion-story/6521747-money-alone-won-t-solve-the-attawapiskat-crisis/.

McGary, H. (1992) 'Forgiveness and Slavery,' in H. McGary and B.E. Lawson (eds) *Between Slavery and Freedom*, Indianapolis and Bloomington: Indiana University Press.

McNay, L. (2000) *Gender and Identity*, Cambridge: Polity Press.

McRoberts, K. (1997) *Misconceiving Canada: The Struggle for National Unity*, Toronto: Oxford University Press.

Medina, J. (2013) *The Epistemology of Resistance*, Oxford: Oxford University Press.

Meltzer, M. (2010) *Girl Power: The Nineties Revolution in Music*, London: Faber and Faber.

Meyers, D.T. (2002) *Gender in the Mirror: Cultural Imagery and Women's Agency*, Oxford: Oxford University Press.

Mill, J.S. (1966) 'On Liberty,' in *John Stuart Mill: A Selection of His Works*, (ed.) J. Robson, Toronto: MacMillan.

Mill, J.S. (1966) 'Principles of Political Economy,' in *John Stuart Mill: A Selection of His Works*, (ed.) J. Robson, Toronto: MacMillan.

Mill, J.S. (1966) 'Utilitarianism,' in *John Stuart Mill: A Selection of His Works*, (ed.) J. Robson, Toronto: MacMillan.

Mill, J.S. (1970) 'The Subjection of Women,' in J.S. Mill and H. Taylor, *Essays on Sex Equality*, (ed.) A. Rossi, Chicago: University of Chicago Press.

Miller, D. (1995) *On Nationality*, Oxford: Clarendon Press.

Miller, D. (1998) 'Equality and Justice,' in A. Mason (ed.) *Ideals of Equality*, Oxford: Basil Blackwell.

Miller, D. (1999) *Principles of Social Justice*, Cambridge, MA: Harvard University Press.

Miller, D. (2007) *National Responsibility and Global Justice*, Oxford: Oxford University Press.

Miller, D. (2013) *Justice for Earthlings*, Cambridge: Cambridge University Press.

Miller, D. (2016) 'Majorities and Minarets: Religious Freedom and Public Space,' *British Journal of Political Science*, 46, 2.

Miller, R. (2005) 'Cosmopolitan Respect and Patriotic Concern,' in H. Brighouse and G. Brock (eds) *The Philosophy of Cosmopolitanism*, Cambridge: Cambridge University Press.

Mills, C. (1997) *The Racial Contract*, Ithaca: Cornell University Press.

Mills, C. (2003) *From Class to Race: Essays in White Marxism and Black Radicalism*, Lanham, MD: Rowman and Littlefield.

Mills, C. (2010) *Radical Theory, Caribbean Reality: Race, Class and Social Domination*, Kingston, Jamaica: University of the West Indies Press.

Minow, M. (1990) *Making all the Difference*, Ithaca: Cornell University Press.

Moore, H. (1994) *A Passion for Difference: Essays in Anthropology and Gender*, Cambridge: Polity.

Moore, M. (2001) *The Ethics of Nationalism*, Oxford: Oxford University Press.

Moore, M. (2015) *A Political Theory of Territory*, New York: Oxford University Press.

Morris, W. (1966) *The Collected Works of William Morris*, 24 volumes, introd. M. Morris, New York: Russell and Russell (CWWM).

Morris, W. (1966) 'Art and Socialism,' CWWM, Vol. XXIII.

Morris, W. (1966) 'Art Under Plutocracy,' CWWM, Vol. XXIII.

Morris, W. (1966) 'Dawn of a New Epoch,' CWWM, Vol. XXIII.

Morris, W. (1966) 'Hopes and Fears for Art,' CWWM, Vol. XXII.

Morris, W. (1966) 'How I Became a Socialist,' CWWM, Vol. XXIII.

Morris, W. (1966) 'How We Live and How We Might Live,' CWWM, Vol. XXIII.

Morris, W. (1966) 'The Aims of Art,' CWWM, Vol. XXIII.

Morris, W. (1966) 'The Socialist Ideal,' CWWM, Vol. XXIII.

Morris, W. (1966) 'True and False Society,' CWWM, Vol. XXIII.

Morris, W. (1973) 'A Dream of John Ball,' W. Morris, *Selected Writings*, (ed.) A. Briggs, Harmondsworth: Penguin.

Morris, W. (1973) 'The Earthly Paradise,' W. Morris, *Selected Writings*, (ed.) A. Briggs, Harmondsworth: Penguin.

Morris, W. (1984) *News from Nowhere*, (ed.) A. Briggs, Harmondsworth: Penguin.

Morris, W. (1994) *The Tables Turned, or Nupkins Awakened*, (ed. and introd.) P.B. Wiens, Athens, OH: Ohio University Press.

Morton, A.L. (1986) 'Morris, Marx and Engels,' *Journal of the William Morris Society*, 7, 1.

Moss, J. (2014) *Reassessing Egalitarianism*, London: Palgrave Macmillan.

Mouffe, C. (1994) 'Political Liberalism, Neutrality and the Political,' *Ratio Juris*, 7, 3.

Mulhall, S. and Swift, A. (1996) *Liberals and Communitarians*, Oxford: Basil Blackwell.

Murphy, L. (1998) 'Institutions and the Demands of Justice,' *Philosophy and Public Affairs*, 27, 4.

Nagel, T. (1986) *The View from Nowhere*, Oxford: Oxford University Press,.

Nagel, T. (1991) *Equality and Partiality*, Oxford: Oxford University Press.

Narayan, U. (1997) *Dislocating Cultures: Identities, Traditions, and Third-World Feminism*, New York: Routledge.

Narayan, U. (2000) 'Undoing the "Package Picture" of Cultures,' *Signs*, 25, 4.

National Trust UK (2015) *Playing Our Part: National Trust Annual Report*, www.nationaltrustannualreport.org.uk/wp-content/uploads/2015/08/playing_our_part.pdf.

Nedelsky, J. (1993) 'Reconceiving Rights as Relationship,' *Review of Constitutional Studies*, 1, 1.

Nersessian, D. (2005) 'Rethinking Cultural Genocide Under International Law,' *Human Rights Dialogue*, Spring.

Nettle, D. (2006) *Happiness: The Science Behind Your Smile*, Oxford: Oxford University Press.

Neuhouser, F. (2013) 'Rousseau's Critique of Economic Inequality.' *Philosophy and Public Affairs*, 41, 3.

*New World Encyclopedia*, (2016) 'Utopia,' 13 January, www.newworldencyclopedia.org/entry/Utopia.

Nicholson, L. (ed.) (1990) *Feminism/Postmodernism*, London: Routledge.

Nietzsche, F. (1968) *The Will to Power*, ed. W. Kaufmann, New York: Vintage.

Noddings, N. (1984) *Caring: A Feminine Approach to Ethics and Moral Education*, Berkeley: University of California Press.

Norman, R. (1998) 'The Social Basis of Equality,' in A. Mason (ed.) *Ideals of Equality*, Oxford: Basil Blackwell.

Nozick, R. (1974) *Anarchy, State and Utopia*, New York: Basic Books.

Nussbaum, M. (1995) 'Human Capabilities, Female Human Beings,' in M. Nussbaum and J. Glover (eds) *Women, Culture and Development*, Oxford: Oxford University Press.

Nussbaum, M. (1999) 'A Plea for Difficulty,' in S.M. Okin (ed.), *Is Multiculturalism Bad for Women?*, Princeton: Princeton University Press.

Nussbaum, M. (1999) *Sex and Social Justice*, Oxford: Oxford University Press.

Nussbaum, M. (1999) *Women and Human Development*, Cambridge: Cambridge University Press.

Nussbaum, M. (2007) *Frontiers of Justice*, Cambridge, MA: Harvard University Press.

Nussbaum, M. (2010) *Creating Capabilities: The Human Development Approach*, Cambridge, MA: Harvard University Press.

Nussbaum, M. (2010) *Not For Profit: Why Democracy Needs the Humanities*, Princeton: Princeton University Press.

Nussbaum, M. (2011) 'Perfectionist Liberalism and Political Liberalism,' *Philosophy and Public Affairs*, 39, 1.

O'Brien, M. (1983) *The Politics of Reproduction*, London: Routledge.

O'Neill, M. (2008) 'What Should Egalitarians Believe?' *Philosophy and Public Affairs*, 36, 2.

O'Neill, M. and Williamson, T. (eds) (2012) *Property-Owning Democracy: Rawls and Beyond*, London: Wiley-Blackwell.

O'Neill, O. (2000) *Bounds of Justice*, Cambridge: Cambridge University Press.

O'Reilly, A. (ed.) (2009) *Maternal Thinking: Philosophy, Politics, Practice*, Toronto: Demeter Press.

Oakeshott, M. (1991) *Rationalism in Politics and Other Essays*, Indianapolis: Liberty Fund.

Offer, A. (2006) *The Challenge of Affluence: Self-Control and Wellbeing in the United States and Britain Since 1950*, Oxford: Oxford University Press.

Okin, S.M. (1993) 'Book Review,' *American Political Science Review*, 87, 4.

Okin, S.M. (1978) *Women in Western Political Thought*, Princeton: Princeton University Press.

Okin, S.M. (1989) *Justice, Gender and the Family*, New York: Basic Books.

Okin, S.M. (1999) 'Is Multiculturalism Bad for Women?,' in S.M. Okin (ed.) *Is Multiculturalism Bad for Women?* Princeton: Princeton University Press.

Organisation for Economic Co-operation and Development (OECD) (2013) 'Sweden is a generous aid donor that has put development at the heart of its foreign policy,' *Sweden – DAC Peer Review of Development Co-operation, 2013*, www.oecd.org/dac/peer-reviews/peer-review-sweden.htm

Otsuka, M. (2006) 'Prerogatives to Depart from Equality,' *Royal Institute of Philosophy Supplements*, 58.

Overall, C. (1987) *Ethics and Human Reproduction*, Winchester, MA: Allen and Unwin.

Padden, C. and Humphries, T. (2005) *Inside Deaf Culture*, Cambridge, MA: Harvard University Press.

Paglia, C. (1990) 'Madonna – Finally, A Real Feminist,' *New York Times*, 14 December.

Parekh, B. (2000) *Rethinking Multiculturalism: Cultural Diversity and Political Theory*, London: Palgrave.

Parekh, B. (2002) 'Barry and the Dangers of Liberalism,' in P. Kelly (ed.) *Multiculturalism Reconsidered: 'Culture and Equality,'* Cambridge: Polity.

Parfit, D. (1986) *Reasons and Persons*, Oxford: Oxford University Press.

Parfit, D. (2000) 'Equality or Priority?' in M. Clayton and A. Williams, *The Ideal of Equality*, London: Macmillan.

Pateman, C. (1988) *The Sexual Contract*, Cambridge: Polity.

Patten, A. (2014) *Equal Recognition: The Moral Foundation of Minority Rights*, Princeton: Princeton University Press.

Patterson, O. (1997) *The Ordeal of Integration: Progress and Resentment in America's 'Racial' Crisis*, Washington: Civitas/Counterpoint.

Phillips A. (2007) *Multiculturalism without Culture*, Princeton: Princeton University Press.

Phillips, A. (1993) *Democracy and Difference*, Cambridge: Polity.

Phillips, A. (1995) *The Politics of Presence*, Oxford: Clarendon Press.

Phillips, A. (1999) *Which Inequalities Matter?* Cambridge: Polity.

Phillips, T. (2005) 'Sleepwalking to Segregation,' Commission for Racial Equality, London.

Pinketty, T. (2014) *Capital in the Twenty-First Century*, Cambridge, MA: Harvard University Press.

Plaisted, C. (1998) *Girl Power Get It! Flaunt It! Use It!*, London: Picadilly Press.

Pogge, T. (1989) *Realising Rawls*, Ithaca: Cornell University Press.

Pogge, T. (1998) 'Human Rights and Human Responsibilities,' in J. Couture, K. Nielsen and M. Seymour (eds) *Rethinking Nationalism*, Canadian Journal of Philosophy Supplementary Vol. 22, Calgary: Calgary University Press.

Pogge, T. (2002) 'Can the Capability Approach be Justified?,' *Philosophical Topics*, 30, 2.

Pogge, T. (2002) *World Poverty and Human Rights*, Cambridge: Polity Press.

Pogge, T. (2013) 'Concluding Reflections,' in G. Brock (ed.) *Cosmopolitanism versus Non-Cosmopolitanism*, Oxford: Oxford University Press.

Pojman, L.P. (1997) 'The Moral Status of Affirmative Action,' in J. Sterba (ed.) *Morality in Practice*, Belmont, CA: Wadsworth.

Quong, J. (2010) *Liberalism without Perfection*, Oxford: Oxford University Press.

Rawls, J. (1971) *A Theory of Justice*, Cambridge, MA: Harvard University Press.

Rawls, J. (1985) 'Justice as Fairness: Political Not Metaphysical,' *Philosophy and Public Affairs*, 14, 3.

Rawls, J. (1993) *Political Liberalism*, New York: Columbia University Press.

Rawls, J. (1999) *The Law of Peoples*, Cambridge, MA: Harvard University Press.

Rawls, J. (2001) *Justice as Fairness: A Restatement*, Cambridge, MA: Harvard University Press.

Raz, J. (1986) *The Morality of Freedom*, Oxford: Clarendon Press.

Raz, J. (1994) *Ethics in the Public Domain: Essays in the Morality of Law and Politics*, Oxford: Oxford University Press.

Readings, B. (1996) *The University in Ruins*, Cambridge, MA: Harvard University Press.

Richards, J.R. (1980) *The Sceptical Feminist*, Harmondsworth: Penguin.

Ripstein, A. (1997) 'Context, Continuity and Fairness,' in R. McKim and J. McMahan (eds), *The Morality of Nationalism*, New York: Oxford University Press.

Robin, R. (1992) *Socialist Realism: An Impossible Aesthetic*, Stanford: Stanford University Press.

Roebyns, I. (2008) 'Ideal Theory in Theory and Practice,' *Social Theory and Practice*, 34, 3.

Roemer, J. (1995) *A Future for Socialism*, Cambridge, MA: Harvard University Press.

Roemer, J. (1996) *Theories of Distributive Justice*, Cambridge, MA: Harvard University Press.

Rorty, R. (1983) 'Postmodernist Bourgeois Liberalism,' *Journal of Philosophy*, 80, 10.

Rorty, R. (1989) *Contingency, Irony and Solidarity*, Cambridge: Cambridge University Press.

Rorty, R. (1998) *Achieving Our Country*, Cambridge, MA: Harvard University Press.

Rothstein, B. and Uslaner, E.M. (2005) 'All for One: Equality, Corruption and Social Trust,' *World Politics*, 58, 1.

Rousseau, J.-J. (1993) 'The Social Contract,' in *The Social Contract and Discourses*, trans. and introd. G.D.H. Cole, and introd., London: Everyman Library.

Rousseau, J.-J. (1979) *Emile*, ed. and trans. A. Bloom, New York: Basic Books.

Ruddick, S. (1980) 'Maternal Thinking,' *Feminist Studies*, 6, 2.

Ruskin, J. (1903–12) *The Works of John Ruskin*, ed. E.T. Cook and A. Wedderburn, London: George Allen.

Ruskin, J. (1968) *Unto this Last, Political Economy of Art, Essays on Political Economy*, London: J.M. Dent.

Samuelson, P. (1955) 'Diagrammatic Exposition of a Theory of Public Expenditure,' *Review of Economics and Statistics*, 37, 4.

Sandel, M. (1982) *Liberalism and the Limits of Justice*, Cambridge: Cambridge University Press.

Sandel, M. (2007) *The Case Against Perfection*, Cambridge, MA: Harvard University Press.

Sandel, M. (2009) *Justice: What's the Right Thing to Do?*, New York: Farrar, Straus and Giroux.

Scanlon, T. (1993) 'Value, Desire and the Quality of Life,' in M. Nussbaum and A. Sen (eds) *The Quality of Life*, Oxford: Clarendon Press.

Scanlon, T. (1995) 'The Significance of Choice,' in S. Darwall (ed.) *Equal Freedom: Selected Tanner Lectures on Human Values*, Ann Arbor: University of Michigan Press.

Scanlon, T. (1999) *What We Owe Each Other*, Cambridge, MA: Harvard University Press.

Scanlon, T. (2003) *The Difficulty of Tolerance*, Cambridge: Cambridge University Press.

Scanlon, T. (2006) 'Justice, Responsibility and the Demands of Equality,' in C. Sypnowich (ed.) *The Egalitarian Conscience: Essays in Honour of G.A. Cohen*, Oxford: Oxford University Press.

Scheffler, S. (1997) 'Liberalism, Nationalism and Egalitarianism,' in R. McKim and J. McMahan (eds) *The Morality of Nationalism*, New York: Oxford University Press.

Scheffler, S. (2003) 'What Is Egalitarianism?' *Philosophy and Public Affairs*, 31, 1.

Scheffler, S. (2005) 'Choice, Circumstance, and the Value of Equality,' *Politics, Philosophy, and Economics*, 4, 1.

Scheffler, S. (2006) 'Is the Basic Structure Basic?' in C. Sypnowich (ed.) *The Egalitarian Conscience: Essays in Honour of G.A. Cohen*, Oxford: Oxford University Press.

Schemmel, C. (2011) 'Why Relational Egalitarians Should Care about Distributions,' *Social Theory and Practice*, 37, 3.

Schlesinger, A. (1992) *The Disuniting of America*, New York: W.W. Norton.

Schwichtenberg, C. (ed.) (1993) *The Madonna Connection: Representational Politics, Subcultural Identities and Cultural Theory*, Boulder, CO: Westview.

Segal, L. (1987) *Is the Future Female? Troubled Thoughts on Contemporary Feminism*, London: Virago.

Segall, S. (2013) *Equality and Opportunity*, Oxford: Oxford University Press.

Selby, T. (2005) *We Who Are Dark: The Philosophical Foundations of Black Solidarity*, Cambridge, MA: Harvard University Press.

Sen, A. (1992) *Inequality Reexamined*, Oxford: Clarendon Press.

Sen, A. (1999) 'Global Justice: Beyond International Equity,' in I. Kaul, I. Grunberg and M.A. Stern (eds) *Global Public Goods: International Cooperation in the 21st Century*, New York: Oxford University Press.

Sen, A. (1999) *Development as Freedom*, Oxford: Oxford University Press.

Sen, A. (2009) *The Idea of Justice*, Cambridge, MA: Harvard University Press.

Serageldin, I. (1999) 'Cultural Heritage as Public Good: Economic Analysis Applied to Historic Cities,' in I. Kaul, I. Grunberg and M.A. Stern (eds) *Global Public Goods: International Cooperation in the 21st Century*, New York: Oxford University Press.

Shachar, A. (2001) *Multicultural Jurisdictions: Cultural Differences and Women's Rights*, Cambridge: Cambridge University Press.

Sher, G. (1997) *Beyond Neutrality: Perfectionism and Politics*, Cambridge: Cambridge University Press.

Sher, G. (2014) *Equality for Inegalitarians*, Cambridge: Cambridge University Press.

Shlapentokh, V. (1988) 'The Stakhanovite Movement: Changing Perceptions over Fifty Years,' *Journal of Contemporary History*, 23, 2.

Simmons, J. (2001) *Justification and Legitimacy*, Cambridge: Cambridge University Press.

Singer, P. (1997) 'The Drowning Child and the Expanding Circle,' *New Internationalist*, 289.

Skinner, Q. (1991) 'The Paradoxes of Political Liberty,' in D. Miller (ed.) *Liberty*, Oxford: Oxford University Press.

Smith, R. (2009) 'The Long Slide to Happiness,' in R. Cigman and A. Davis (eds) *New Philosophies of Learning*, Oxford: Wiley-Blackwell.

Spellman, E. (1990) *Inessential Woman: Problems of Exclusion in Feminist Thought*, London: Women's Press.

Spinner-Halev, J. (1994) *The Boundaries of Citizenship*, Baltimore: Johns Hopkins University Press.

Spinner-Halev, J. (1999) 'Cultural Pluralism and Partial Citizenship,' in C. Joppke and S. Lukes (eds) *Multicultural Questions*, Oxford: Oxford University Press.

Spivak, G. (1988) 'French Feminism in an International Frame,' *In Other Worlds*, New York: Routledge.
Squires, J. (2002) 'Culture, Equality and Diversity,' in P. Kelly, (ed.) *Multiculturalism Reconsidered: 'Culture and Equality,'* Cambridge: Polity.
Standing, G. (2011) *The Precariat: The New Dangerous Class*, London: Bloomsbury.
Stansky, P. (1983) *William Morris*, Oxford: Oxford University Press.
Stiglitz, J. (2012) *The Price of Inequality*, New York: W.W. Norton.
Stone, A. (2004) 'Essentialism and Anti-Essentialism in Feminist Philosophy,' *Journal of Moral Philosophy*, 1, 2.
Suits, B. (2005) *The Grasshopper: Games, Life, and Utopia*, Toronto: Broadview Press.
Sunstein, C. (1991) 'Preferences and Politics,' *Philosophy and Public Affairs*, 20, 3.
Sunstein, C. (2014) *Why Nudge?*, New Haven: Yale University Press.
Swift, A. (1995) 'The Sociology of Complex Equality,' in D. Miller and M. Walzer (eds) *Pluralism, Justice and Equality*, Oxford: Oxford University Press.
Swift, A. (2002) *How Not to Be a Hypocrite: School Choice for the Morally Perplexed Parent*, London: Routledge.
Swift, A. (2005) 'Justice, Luck and the Family: The Intergenerational Transmission of Economic Advantage from a Normative Perspective,' in S. Bowles, H. Gintis, and M. Osborne-Groves (eds) *Unequal Chances: Family Background and Economic Success*, Princeton: Princeton University Press.
Swift, A. (2008) 'The Value of Philosophy in Non-ideal Circumstances,' *Social Theory and Practice*, 34, 3.
Sypnowich, C. (1990) *The Concept of Socialist Law*, Oxford: Clarendon Press.
Sypnowich, C. (1991) 'Rights, Community and the Charter,' *British Journal of Canadian Studies*, 6, 1.
Sypnowich, C. (1992) 'The Future of Socialist Legality,' *New Left Review*, 193.
Sypnowich, C. (1995) 'Death in Utopia: Marxism and the Mortal Self' in D. Bakhurst and C. Sypnowich (eds) *The Social Self*, London: Sage.
Sypnowich, C. (2000) 'The Civility of Law: Between Public and Private,' in M. Passerin d'Entreves and U. Vogel (eds) *Public and Private: Legal, Political and Philosophical Perspectives*, London: Routledge.
Sypnowich, C. (2006) 'Begging,' in C. Sypnowich (ed.) *The Egalitarian Conscience: Essays in Honour of G.A. Cohen*, Oxford: Oxford University Press.
Sypnowich, C. (2007) 'Ruling or Overruled? The People, Rights and Democracy,' *Oxford Journal of Legal Studies*, 27, 4.
Sypnowich, C. (2012) 'G.A. Cohen's Socialism: Scientific but also Utopian,' *Socialist Studies* 8, 1.
Sypnowich, C. (2016) 'Bottlenecks to Flourishing and the "Road Less Travelled" in Political Philosophy,' *Review Journal of Political Philosophy*, 12.
Tamas, G. (1992) 'Socialism, Capitalism and Modernity,' *Journal of Democracy*, 3, 3.
Tamir, Y. (1993) *Liberal Nationalism*, Princeton: Princeton University Press.
Tan, K.C. (2002) *Toleration, Diversity and Global Justice*, Philadelphia: University of Pennsylvania Press.
Tan, K.C. (2004) 'Justice and Personal Pursuits,' *Journal of Philosophy*, 101, 7.
Tan, K.C. (2004) *Cosmopolitanism, Nationalism and Patriotism*, Cambridge: Cambridge University Press.
Tan, K.C. (2004) *Justice without Borders*, Cambridge: Cambridge University Press.
Tan, K.C. (2012) *Justice, Institutions and Luck: The Site, Ground and Scope of Inequality*, Oxford: Oxford University Press.
Tawney, R.H. (1931) *Equality*, London: George Allen and Unwin.

Taylor, C. (1979) 'Atomism,' in A. Kontos (ed.) Essays in Honour of C.B. Macpherson: Powers, Possessions and Freedoms, Toronto: University of Toronto Press.

Taylor, C. (1982) 'Foucault on Freedom and Truth,' Philosophical Papers, vol. 2, Cambridge: Cambridge University Press.

Taylor, C. (1991) 'What's Wrong with Negative Liberty,' in D. Miller (ed.) Liberty, Oxford: Clarendon Press.

Taylor, C. (1994) 'The Politics of Recognition' in A. Gutmann (ed.) Multiculturalism, Princeton: Princeton University Press.

Taylor, C. (2002) 'Why Democracy Needs Patriotism,' in J. Cohen (ed.) For Love of Country, Boston: Beacon Press.

Taylor, P. (2013) Race: A Philosophical Introduction, Cambridge: Polity.

Temkin, L. (2000) 'Equality, Priority and the Levelling Down Objection,' in M. Clayton and A. Williams (eds) The Ideal of Equality, London: Macmillan.

Thaler, R. and Sunstein, C. (2009) Nudge: Improving Decisions about Health, Wealth and Happiness, London: Penguin.

Thernstrom, A. (1987) Whose Votes Count? Affirmative Action and Minority Voting Rights, Cambridge, MA: Harvard University Press.

Thompson, E.P. (1977) William Morris: Romantic to Revolutionary, New York: Pantheon.

Thomson, J.J. (1974) 'A Defence of Abortion,' in M. Cohen, T. Nagel and T. Scanlon (eds) The Rights and Wrongs of Abortion, Princeton: Princeton University Press.

Thomson, J.J. (1976) 'Preferential Hiring,' in M. Cohen, T. Nagel and T. Scanlon (eds) Equality and Preferential Treatment, Princeton: Princeton University Press.

Tickle, L. and Bawden, A. (2015) 'Cuts Could Serve up an End to Free Healthy School Dinners for Infants' The Guardian, 1 September, www.theguardian.com/education/2015/sep/01/cuts-free-healthy-school-dinners-infants-budget-universal.

Tierney, J. (2013) 'The Rational Choices of Crack Addicts,' New York Times, 16 September.

Tully, J. (1995) Strange Multiplicities, Cambridge: Cambridge University Press.

Tully, J. (2002) 'The Illiberal Liberal: Brian Barry's Polemical Attack on Multiculturalism,' in P. Kelly (ed.) Multiculturalism Reconsidered: 'Culture and Equality,' Cambridge: Polity.

Vallier, K. (2011) 'Convergence and Consensus in Public Reason,' Public Affairs Quarterly, 25, 4.

Vallier, K. (2014) Liberal Politics and Public Faith: Beyond Separation, London: Routledge.

Van Parijs, P. (1991) 'Why Surfers Should Be Fed: The Liberal Case for an Unconditional Basic Income,' Philosophy and Public Affairs, 20, 2.

Van Parijs, P. (1995) Real Freedom for All, Oxford: Oxford University Press.

Victor, P.A. (2008) Managing without Growth: Slower by Design, Not Disaster, Cheltenham: Edward Elgar.

Villa, D. (2012) 'The Cold War Critique of Political Rationalism,' in E. Podoksik (ed.) The Cambridge Companion to Oakeshott, Cambridge: Cambridge University Press.

Vonnegut, K. (1998) 'Harrison Bergeron,' in Welcome to the Monkey House, New York: Dial Press.

Vrousalis, N. (2012) 'Jazz Bands, Camping Trips and Decommodification: G.A. Cohen on Community,' Socialist Studies 8.

Waldron, J. (1993) Liberal Rights, Cambridge: Cambridge University Press.

Waldron, J. (1995) 'Money and Complex Equality,' in D. Miller and M. Walzer (eds) Pluralism, Justice and Equality, Oxford: Oxford University Press.

Waldron, J. (1999) 'Minority Cultures and the Cosmopolitan Alternative' in W. Kymlicka (ed.) *The Rights of Minority Cultures*, Oxford: Oxford University Press.

Waldron, J. (2000) 'Cultural Identity and Civic Representation,' in W. Kymlicka and W. Norman (eds) *Citizenship in Diverse Societies*, Oxford: Oxford University Press.

Waldron, J. (2014) 'It's All for Your Own Good,' *New York Review of Books*, 9 October.

Wall, S. (1998) *Liberalism, Perfectionism and Restraint*, Cambridge: Cambridge University Press.

Wall, S. (2013) 'Moral Environmentalism,' in C. Coons and M. Weber (eds) *Paternalism: Theory and Practice*, Cambridge: Cambridge University Press.

Walzer, M. (1983) *Spheres of Justice*, New York: Basic Books.

Walzer, M. (1995) 'Pluralism: A Political Perspective,' in W. Kymlicka (ed.) *The Rights of Minority Cultures*, Oxford: Oxford University Press.

Warnke, G. (2007) *Debating Sex and Gender*, Oxford: Oxford University Press.

Weale, A. (2000) 'Public Interest' in *The Concise Routledge Encyclopedia of Philosophy*, London: Routledge.

Webb, B. and Hutchins, B. (1909) 'Socialism and the National Minimum,' *Fabian Socialist Series*, 6, London: Fabian Society.

Webber, J. (1994) *Reimagining Canada: Language, Culture, Community and the Canadian Constitution*, Montreal-Kingston:: McGill-Queen's Press.

Weinstock, D. (1999) 'Neutralizing Perfection: Hurka on Liberal Neutrality,' *Dialogue: Canadian Philosophical Review*, 38, 1.

Weinstock, D. (2001) 'Saving Democracy from Deliberation,' in R. Beiner and W. Norman (eds) *Canadian Political Philosophy: Contemporary Reflections*, Toronto: Oxford University Press.

Weinstock, D. (2006) 'A Neutral Conception of Reasonableness?' *Episteme*, 3, 3.

Weinzweig, M. (1987) 'Pregnancy Leave, Comparable Worth, and Concepts of Equality,' *Hypatia*, 2, 1.

Weithman, P. (2011) *Why Political Liberalism? On John Rawls's Political Turn*, Oxford: Oxford University Press.

Wellman, C. (2000) 'Relational Facts in Liberal Political Theory: Is there Magic in the Pronoun "My"? *Ethics*, 110, 3.

Wenar, L. (1995) 'Political Liberalism: An Internal Critique,' *Ethics*, 106, 1.

West, C. (1993) *Race Matters*, Boston: Beacon Press.

West, R. (1993) 'Jurisprudence and Gender,' in P. Smith (ed.) *Feminist Jurisprudence*, Oxford: Oxford University Press.

West, R. (1997) *Caring for Justice*, New York: New York University Press.

Whitaker, R. (1995) 'Quebec's Self-Determination and Aboriginal Self-Government: Conflict and Reconciliation?' in J. Carens (ed.) *Is Quebec Nationalism Just? Perspectives from Anglophone Canada*, Montreal-Kingston: McGill-Queen's University Press.

White, S. (1991) *Political Theory and Postmodernism*, Cambridge: Cambridge University Press.

Wiggins, D. (2009) 'Solidarity and the Root of the Ethical,' *Tijdschrift voor Filosofie*, 71.

Wilkins, D. (1996) 'Introduction,' in K.A. Appiah and A. Gutmann, *Color Consciousness*, Princeton: Princeton University Press.

Wilkinson, R. and Pickett, K. (2009) *The Spirit Level: Why More Equal Societies Almost Always Do Better*, London: Allen Lane.

Williams, B. (1973) 'Critique of Utilitarianism,' in J.J.C. Smart and B. Williams, *Utilitarianism For and Against*, Cambridge: Cambridge University Press.

Williams, B. (1993) 'Rawls Rethinks Rawls,' *London Review of Books*, 13 May.

Williams, P. (1991) *The Alchemy of Race and Rights*, Cambridge, MA: Harvard University Press.

Williams, R. (1980) 'Utopia and Science Fiction,' *Problems in Materialism and Culture*, London: Verso.

Wilson, W.J. (1990) *The Truly Disadvantaged: The Inner City, the Underclass, and Public Policy*, Chicago: University of Chicago Press.

Winant, H. (1997) 'Behind Blue Eyes: Whiteness and Contemporary U.S. Racial Politics,' *New Left Review*, 225.

Wolff, J. (1998) 'Fairness, Respect, and the Egalitarian Ethos,' *Philosophy and Public Affairs*, 27, 2.

Wolff, J. (2000) 'Levelling Down,' in K. Dowding, J. Hughes and H. Margetts (eds) *Challenges to Democracy: The PSA Yearbook 2000*, London: Palgrave.

Wolff, J. (2010) 'Fairness, Respect and the Egalitarian Ethos Revisited,' *Journal of Ethics*, 14, 3–4.

Wolff, J. and De-Shalit, A. (2007) *Disadvantage*, New York: Oxford University Press.

Wolf, N. (1993) *Fire with Fire: The New Female Power and How to Use It*, New York: Fawcett Columbine.

Wollstonecraft, M. (1999) *Vindication of the Rights of Woman*, ed. J. Todd, Oxford: Oxford University Press.

Wood, E.M. (1986) *The Retreat from Class*, London: Verso.

Woolf, V. (1989) *A Room of One's Own*, New York: Harcourt Brace.

Wright, E. and Brighouse, H. (2002) 'On Alex Callinicos's *Equality*,' *Historical Materialism* 10, 1.

Wright, M. and Bloemraad, I. (2012) 'Is There a Trade-off between Multiculturalism and Socio-Political Integration? Policy Regimes and Immigrant Incorporation in Comparative Perspective,' *Perspectives on Politics*, 10, 1.

Young, I.M. (1990) *Justice and the Politics of Difference*, Princeton: Princeton University Press.

Young, I.M. (1997) *Intersecting Voices: Dilemmas of Gender, Political Philosophy and Policy*, Princeton: Princeton University Press.

Zamyatin, Y. (1993) *We*, trans. and intro. C. Brown, Harmondsworth: Penguin.

Zaslo, E. (2009) *Feminism, Inc.: Coming of Age in Girl Power Media Culture*, New York: Palgrave Macmillan.

Žižek, S. (2009) *In Defense of Lost Causes*, London: Verso

# Index

# Taylor & Francis eBooks

## Helping you to choose the right eBooks for your Library

Add Routledge titles to your library's digital collection today. Taylor and Francis eBooks contains over 50,000 titles in the Humanities, Social Sciences, Behavioural Sciences, Built Environment and Law.

**Choose from a range of subject packages or create your own!**

**Benefits for you**
» Free MARC records
» COUNTER-compliant usage statistics
» Flexible purchase and pricing options
» All titles DRM-free.

REQUEST YOUR **FREE** INSTITUTIONAL TRIAL TODAY
**Free Trials Available**
We offer free trials to qualifying academic, corporate and government customers.

**Benefits for your user**
» Off-site, anytime access via Athens or referring URL
» Print or copy pages or chapters
» Full content search
» Bookmark, highlight and annotate text
» Access to thousands of pages of quality research at the click of a button.

## eCollections – Choose from over 30 subject eCollections, including:

| | |
|---|---|
| Archaeology | Language Learning |
| Architecture | Law |
| Asian Studies | Literature |
| Business & Management | Media & Communication |
| Classical Studies | Middle East Studies |
| Construction | Music |
| Creative & Media Arts | Philosophy |
| Criminology & Criminal Justice | Planning |
| Economics | Politics |
| Education | Psychology & Mental Health |
| Energy | Religion |
| Engineering | Security |
| English Language & Linguistics | Social Work |
| Environment & Sustainability | Sociology |
| Geography | Sport |
| Health Studies | Theatre & Performance |
| History | Tourism, Hospitality & Events |

For more information, pricing enquiries or to order a free trial, please contact your local sales team:
www.tandfebooks.com/page/sales

Routledge
Taylor & Francis Group | The home of Routledge books | **www.tandfebooks.com**

52931808R00151